T0328816

SOCIAL SECURITY REFORM

As population aging has become increasingly acute in many countries, the debate over how to reform often creaking public pension systems has gathered momentum. In many cases, this debate has become politicized and the focus on some of the underlying economic issues has been lost. This volume hopes to redress some of this imbalance. It begins by examining the rationale behind why public pension systems were introduced originally – out of fear that individuals do not adequately save for retirement. It then systematically examines different aspects of reforming these systems. It covers the fiscal repercussions of reform, the implications of the Baby Boom on asset returns in the years ahead, the political economy of the reform process, and, finally, the risk-sharing implications that are inherent in reform. An important additional goal of this volume is to make these papers accessible to as wide an audience as possible: students, academics, and policy makers.

Robin Brooks is an economist in the Financial Studies Division of the Research Department at the International Monetary Fund (IMF) in Washington, D.C. His research focuses on the growing importance of financial linkages across countries and their implications for risk-reduction strategies in portfolio management. Before joining the IMF, Dr. Brooks was a Research Fellow in the Economic Studies Program at the Brookings Institution, where he studied the effects of population aging on financial markets.

Assaf Razin is the Mario-Henrique Simonsen Professor of Public Economics at Tel Aviv University and the Friedman Professor of International Economics at Cornell University. He is particularly known for his work on human capital growth, the economics of the family, public economics, and international economics. Professor Razin has coauthored numerous books, including *Fiscal Policies and Growth in the World Economy, Labor, Capital, and Finance: International Flows* (Cambridge University Press, 2001), and the forthcoming *The Decline of the Welfare State: Political Economics of Aging, Migration, and Globalization.*

Social Security Reform

FINANCIAL AND POLITICAL ISSUES IN INTERNATIONAL PERSPECTIVE

Edited by

ROBIN BROOKS
International Monetary Fund

ASSAF RAZIN
Tel Aviv University

CAMBRIDGE
UNIVERSITY PRESS

CAMBRIDGE UNIVERSITY PRESS
Cambridge, New York, Melbourne, Madrid, Cape Town, Singapore,
São Paulo, Delhi, Dubai, Tokyo

Cambridge University Press
32 Avenue of the Americas, New York, NY 10013-2473, USA

www.cambridge.org
Information on this title: www.cambridge.org/9780521141864

First published 2005
This digitally printed version 2010

A catalog record for this publication is available from the British Library

Library of Congress Cataloging in Publication data

Social security reform : financial and political issues in international
perspective / edited by Robin Brooks, Assaf Razin.

p.   cm.

Includes bibliographical references and index.

ISBN 0-521-84495-9

1. Social security.   2. Social security – Economic aspects.   3. Pension trusts.
I. Brooks, Robin.   II. Razin, Assaf.

HD7091.S625   2005
368.4′3 – dc22   2004054516

ISBN 978-0-521-84495-6 Hardback
ISBN 978-0-521-14186-4 Paperback

Contents

Preface

As population aging has become increasingly acute in many countries, the debate over how to reform often creaking public pension systems has gathered momentum. In many cases, this debate has become politicized and the focus on some of the underlying economic issues has been lost. This volume hopes to redress some of this imbalance. It begins by examining the rationale behind why public pension systems were introduced originally – out of fear that individuals do not adequately save for retirement. It then systematically examines different aspects of reforming these systems. It covers the fiscal repercussions of reform, the implications of the Baby Boom on asset returns in the years ahead, the political economy of the reform process, and, finally, the risk-sharing implications that are inherent in reform. An important additional goal of this volume, besides highlighting some key economic issues inherent in reforming public pension systems, is to make these papers accessible to as wide an audience as possible: students, academics, and policy makers.

Many of the papers in this volume are previously unpublished and represent new, state-of-the-art research on topics relating to social security reform. Previously unpublished work includes the chapter by Fehr, Jokisch, and Kotlikoff; the chapter by Razin and Sadka; and the chapter by Lucas. We also would like to thank the publishers of those chapters that have been published elsewhere previously. Here, we would like to thank the *Review of Economics and Statistics* for allowing us to reprint the chapters by Abel and by Poterba; the Brookings Institution for allowing us to reprint the chapter by Laibson, Repetto, and Tobacman; the *American Economic Review* for the chapter by Brooks, the chapter by Diamond and Geanakoplos, and the contribution from Boeri, Börsch-Supan, and Tabellini. We also thank the Carnegie Rochester Conference Series on Public Policy for the chapter by Bohn and the chapter by Storesletten, Telmer, and Yaron.

Contributors

Andrew Abel (Wharton, University of Pennsylvania)

Tito Boeri (Bocconi University)

Axel Börsch-Supan (University of Mannheim)

Henning Bohn (University of California, Santa Barbara)

Robin Brooks (IMF)

Peter Diamond (MIT)

Hans Fehr (University of Würzburg)

John Geanakoplos (Yale University)

Sabine Jokisch (University of Würzburg)

Larry Kotlikoff (Boston University)

David Laibson (Harvard University)

Deborah Lucas (Northwestern University)

James Poterba (MIT)

Assaf Razin (Tel Aviv University)

Andrea Repetto (Universidad de Chile)

Efraim Sadka (Tel Aviv University)

Kjetil Storesletten (Stockholm University)

Guido Tabellini (Bocconi University)

Chris Telmer (Carnegie Mellon University)

Jeremy Tobacman (Harvard University)

Amir Yaron (Wharton, University of Pennsylvania)

Introduction

In the coming decades, the population of the industrialized world is forecast to age dramatically. In the European Union, old-age dependency, defined as the ratio of the population aged 60 and older to those between ages 15 and 59, is projected to rise from 35 percent in 2000 to 66 percent in 2050. Within the European Union, aging is expected to be most pronounced in Germany, Italy, and Spain, where this ratio is forecast to rise to 71, 76, and 81 percent, respectively, by 2050. Aging trends are almost as severe in Japan, where old-age dependency is forecast to rise from 36 to 70 percent over the same period. In comparison, projected population trends in the United States look almost benign. The Census Bureau currently forecasts that the old-age dependency ratio will reach 47 percent in 2050, up from 27 percent in 2000.[1]

These projections are raising doubts over the viability of public pension systems in industrial countries. The *Financial Times* of May 11, 2002, writes: "Pensions policy will come under increasing strain everywhere. In mainland Europe, where benefits are generous and pensions are not funded, governments will find it difficult to raise enough taxation to fulfill pension promises. The O.E.C.D. predicts that France, for example, will have to spend 33 percent more as a share of gross domestic product than it does now." The *Economist* of August 24, 2002, looks at another dimension of the financial burden: "On some estimates, by 2050, government debt could be equivalent to almost 100 percent of national income in America, 150 percent in the EU as a whole, and over 250 percent in Germany and France."[2]

Such doubts over the viability of public pension systems are creating momentum for reform. Most recently in the United States, the President's Commission to Strengthen Social Security was charged with investigating ways to restore the fiscal

---

[1] These numbers are taken from Brooks (2003), who reports global trends in youth and old-age dependency in greater detail.

[2] For additional discussion of the effects of population aging and globalization on the welfare state, see Razin and Sadka (2003).

soundness of Social Security and develop a workable system of personal retirement accounts. Since the Commission issued its final report in 2001, its recommendations have been hotly debated on both sides of the political spectrum. This debate has focused on three important issues. First, who will pay for the unfunded liabilities in Social Security? Will it be current generations, in the form of benefit cuts on retirees or tax increases on workers? What if the cost of these liabilities is financed through a rise in government debt, to be paid off by future generations? Second, what are the benefits and risks of different mechanisms for retirement saving – ranging from the government-run, pay-as-you-go model to individual accounts-based systems? With regard to government-run systems, what is the rationale for government involvement in the provision of retirement security in the first place? With regard to personal retirement accounts, are they welfare enhancing, by giving people otherwise unable to the opportunity to invest in private securities, which supposedly pay higher returns than pay-as-you-go systems? Or do they reduce welfare, by exposing individuals to risks they would not otherwise face? And, if they are indeed welfare reducing, are there guarantee or insurance arrangements that could reduce the risks of investing in private securities? Third, how politically viable are different reform proposals? How do they fare in the court of public opinion? And, how compatible are they with institutional constraints – rigid balanced-budget rules such as the Stability and Growth Pact in the European Union come to mind – that make no exceptions for structural changes in public pension systems?

The rate-of-return argument made by the proponents of individual accounts-based systems – that such systems would yield higher returns on contributions than existing pay-as-you-go systems – has already come under scrutiny by, for example, Geanakoplos, Mitchell, and Zeldes (1998). In Chapter 10 of this book, Razin and Sadka, based on Krugman (2002), show that the rate-of-return argument is flawed. They put it like this:

> Imagine an overlapping-generations model with just one young working person and one old retired person each period, with each individual living for two periods. Suppose there is a pay-as-you-go pension system by which the worker contributes one euro to finance the pension benefit of one euro paid to the retiree. Each young person contributes one euro when young and working and receives one euro upon retirement. Evidently, the young person earns a zero return on her contribution to the pay-as-you-go security system. If instead the young person were to invest her one euro in an individual account, she would earn a real market rate of return of, say, 100 percent, allowing her a pension of two euros at retirement. Is this young person better off, taking into account the transition from the pay-as-you-go pension system to the individual accounts-based system? Not if the government wishes to honor the existing "social contract" or political norm to pay a pension benefit of one euro to the old at the time of the transition. In order to meet this liability, the government could issue debt of one euro. The interest to be paid by the government on this debt at a market rate of 100 percent will be one euro in each period, starting from the next period ad infinitum. Hence the young person will be levied a tax of

one euro in the next period when old, to finance this interest payment. Thus, her net-of-tax balance in the individual account will only be one euro, implying a zero net-of-tax return in the individual account; the same return as in the pay-as-you-go system. Now, suppose that the individual invests the one euro in equity markets and gets a better return than the 100 percent that the government pays in interest? If capital markets are efficient, the higher equity return (relative to the government bond rate) reflects nothing other than a risk premium. That is, the equity premium is equal to the risk premium through arbitrage. Therefore, equity investment offers no gain in risk-adjusted terms over government bonds. If capital markets are inefficient, then the government can, as a general policy, issue debt in order to invest in equity markets, irrespective of the issue of replacing social security by individual retirement accounts.

Although it may now be well understood that simple rate-of-return comparisons of different retirement systems can be misleading, many open questions regarding the politics and finance of reforming Social Security remain. This volume reexamines the current debate over Social Security reform from the perspective of the three key issues outlined previously: (i) who will pay for the unfunded liabilities in Social Security?; (ii) what are the benefits and risks of the different mechanisms for retirement saving – ranging from the government-run, pay-as-you-go model to individual accounts-based systems?; and (iii) how politically viable are different reform proposals, both in the court of public opinion and given institutional constraints, such as rigid balanced-budget rules, that may impede reform? The remainder of this introductory chapter describes how this collection of papers addresses these questions.

The first part of the volume addresses who will pay for the unfunded liabilities in Social Security. In Chapter 1, Fehr, Jokisch, and Kotlikoff develop and simulate a new dynamic general equilibrium life-cycle model capable of studying the interdependent demographic transitions in the United States, Japan, and the European Union. The model extends previous studies, such as Attanasio and Violante (2000) and Brooks (2003), by including international trade and investment but also by incorporating immigration, age-specific fertility, life-span extension and uncertainty, and unintended bequests. The simulations show that aging will have a dramatic negative impact on developed world economies. Specifically, the model predicts substantial crowding out of capital as a result of major increases in payroll tax rates that are needed to pay for promised retiree benefits. This crowding out leads to a roughly one-fifth reduction in real wages throughout the developed world as well as significant increases in real interest rates. The deterioration in the macroeconomic climate of the developed world makes the welfare losses experienced by current middle-aged, young, and future generations significantly worse.

The authors find that immigration proves to be a false elixir. Even an immediate and sustained doubling of immigration – an extreme response by most policy maker's standards – does little to mitigate fiscal stresses in developed countries.

This is because of three factors. First, dependency ratios still rise dramatically. Second, most immigrants arrive with little human capital, so that their contribution to effective labor supply is limited. Third, because benefits are provided on a progressive basis and immigrants are disproportionately low-wage workers, immigrants accrue disproportionately greater claims to old-age benefits than do native workers.

Instead, Fehr, Jokisch, and Kotlikoff argue for paying off the accrued liabilities of government pension systems using a consumption tax. Such a policy would impose modest welfare losses on current generations, including today's middle class and high-income elderly. But it would protect today's poor elderly because the real value of pension and health benefits are protected against price changes caused by consumption taxation. It also would preclude what appears to be the most likely policy alternative – highly regressive payroll tax increases and old-age benefit cuts.

In Chapter 2, Bohn uses a very different approach to address the same question. With the population rapidly aging in the United States, he explores if economic and political factors will cause policy makers to renege on obligations to take care of retirees who previously contributed to Social Security. Focusing first on economic factors, he examines the allocational implications of an aging population and of rising medical costs. He concludes that aging actually has positive implications for the viability of Social Security – increasing the savings rate, wages, and the capital-labor ratio – and that an efficient allocation of resources also will likely display a growing gross domestic product (GDP)-share of medical spending. Turning to the political dimension, Bohn uses an intertemporal model of Social Security to explain why working-age voters can rationally expect future benefits in exchange for their current transfers to retirees. He models the intertemporal link as a repeated voting game with trigger strategies. To support Social Security as a sequential equilibrium, it has to be the case for the median-age voter that the present value of future benefits exceeds the value of payroll taxes until retirement. In a partial equilibrium setting, he finds that the net present value of Social Security is positive for the median voter (age 45) for a variety of specifications. He also argues that general equilibrium arguments provide additional support for Social Security, because a vote against Social Security would raise the capital-labor ratio and reduce interest rates, making private saving a less attractive alternative to Social Security. In contrast to Chapter 1, Bohn finds substantial economic and political evidence in favor of the viability of Social Security. Why this difference? Chapter 1 presents a purely economic analysis, devoid of political considerations. Chapter 2 focuses on the political dimension. Of course, in reality, these two dimension will interact and the true answer to the question of who will pay for the unfunded liabilities in Social Security will likely include aspects of both scenarios.

The second part of the volume turns to the second question. It asks what rationale there is for government involvement in the provision of retirement security? What considerations drove the introduction of public pension systems in the first place? In Chapter 3, Laibson, Repetto, and Tobacman explore hyperbolic discounting as a possible reason for undersaving while young. Such behavior typically involves an inconsistency whereby agents at birth determine an optimal consumption path. As they advance through the life-cycle, however, they revise this initial consumption path and consume too much ahead of retirement. For example, Bernheim (1995) examines household survey data and finds that there is a 10 percent gap (as a share of income) between households' targeted saving and actual saving rates. Hall (1998) illustrates hyperbolic discounting in a simple three-period model, where the individual is portrayed as self 1, self 2, and self 3 in the three periods. As Hall explains, there is only one inconsistency in this model: self 1 weights utility in periods 2 and 3 equally, whereas self 2 puts greater weight on period 2 than on period 3, as in hyperbolic discounting. In the model, self 3 has a passive role, consuming simply whatever wealth earlier selves have left to it. Self 2 takes the wealth that self 1 leaves and divides it between consumption in periods 2 and 3. Self 1 considers all available wealth and thinks through the behavior of self 2 in the course of deciding how much to consume in period 1 and how much to leave to self 2. Consequently, consumption in this model declines over time, illustrative of a tendency to spend early in life rather than save. Now suppose that self 1 can commit to future levels of consumption. This would take a mechanism where self 1 can set aside some wealth that is inaccessible to self 2 but is available to self 3 – pretty much the effect of a 401(k) plan. The model with commitment generates lower consumption in period 2 and higher consumption in period 3. The mechanism of commitment, therefore, results in more midlife saving, whereas without commitment, the individual undersaves in middle age. Consistent with this simple example, Laibson, Repetto, and Tobacman show that life-cycle consumption and asset accumulation patterns observed in the data are consistent with such hyperbolic preferences. In addition, they argue that consumers with such preferences are willing to give up some fraction of their annual income to induce government to implement optimal revenue-neutral saving incentives. Such commitment devices could amount to defined-contribution pension schemes with early withdrawal penalties, which would be associated with higher national savings.[3]

Of course, even if in reality agents do not provide adequately for retirement, this still leaves open the question of what kind of mandatory retirement system is optimal.

---

[3] In addition to the realization that individuals may undersave when young, another factor behind the introduction of public pension systems is the notion of intergenerational risk-sharing, a point made by Gordon and Varian (1988), for example. They examine the role of government debt and tax-transfer policies that improve the allocation of risk between generations, based on the notion that markets fail to allocate risk between two generations efficiently whenever the two generations are not both alive prior to the occurrence of a stochastic event. This implies that government policies transferring risk between generations have the potential to create first-order welfare improvements. Gordon and Varian provide a model that gives a non-Keynesian justification for the debt-finance of wars and recessions, as well as an added rationale for social security–type tax-transfer schemes that aid unlucky generations – for example, the Depression generation – at the expense of luckier generations.

The third part of the volume discusses the benefits and risks of different mechanisms for retirement saving – ranging from the government-run, pay-as-you-go model to individual accounts-based systems. In Chapter 4, Diamond and Geanakoplos explore the general equilibrium impact of Social Security portfolio diversification into private securities, either through the trust fund or private accounts. Their analysis depends critically on heterogeneities in saving, production, assets, and taxes. Social Security diversification is likely to change the rate of interest, requiring higher income taxes to pay the higher coupons on government bonds. However, limited diversification is found to only weakly increase interest rates, reduce the expected return on short-term investment (and the equity premium), decrease safe investment, and increase risky investment. More generally, Social Security diversification creates the potential for welfare improvements. But, the effects on aggregate investment, long-term capital values, and the utility of young savers hinge on assumptions about technology. Aggregate investment and long-term asset values can move in opposite directions.

Chapter 5 by Lucas is motivated by the concern that existing public pension systems will be unable to pay benefits to a rapidly aging population without sharp tax increases. Also, it is motivated by the prospect of higher average returns on stocks than on government securities. Both aspects are drawing the attention of policy makers worldwide to the option of investing public pension assets in stocks. On the one hand, including stock market investments in public pension plans could improve risk-sharing within and between generations and could perhaps lead to faster market development in some countries. On the other hand, it also could result in excessive risk-taking, higher transactions costs, and a false sense of increased financial security. This chapter assesses these issues, with an emphasis on the considerations that are of special importance to developing markets. A contrast is drawn between the demographic outlook in East Asia and the major industrialized countries. Some lessons are drawn from the reform experience in Chile and elsewhere in Latin America.

Lucas argues that the allure of using the higher average rates of return on stocks to offset demographic pressures fades when the implications of such an investment strategy are examined more closely. Fundamentally, demographic pressures only can be eased by higher rates of economic growth, which pension policy affects primarily through its influence on savings rates. Switching a fixed amount of investment from government bonds to stocks can be expected to have, at most, a small effect on capital formation and growth.

In Chapter 6, Storesletten, Telmer, and Yaron argue that an important aspect of the current U.S. social security system is the tradeoff between the risk-sharing it provides and the distortions it imparts on private decisions. They focus on this tradeoff as it applies to labor market risk and capital accumulation. Specifically, they compare the current U.S. system to a particular proposal put forth in 1996 by the federal Advisory Council on Social Security (1996). They also examine the merits of abolishing social security altogether. The authors find that, absent general equilibrium effects, the risk-sharing benefits of the current system out-weigh the distortions associated with either the alternative or a system of privately administered pensions. However, once they incorporate equilibrium effects, the interaction among the social security system, private-savings decisions, and the means with which the government finances its nonpension expenditures results in a significant welfare benefit being associated with either reform or abolition. These welfare gains arise despite the fact that they explicitly incorporate the "social security debt:" the social cost of meeting obligations associated with the current system.

The fourth part of the volume investigates the benefits and risks of different mechanisms for retirement saving from yet another angle. It asks to what extent financial markets will be adversely affected when the Baby Boomers retire and how individuals fare under different pension systems in the event of a "market meltdown"? This part of the volume comes against the background of several articles in the popular financial press that have linked the rise in U.S. stock prices in the 1990s to the growing demand for financial assets as the Baby Boomers begin to save for retirement. These accounts often warn that the Baby Boomers may earn returns on their retirement saving far below historical returns because they will have to sell their financial assets to a smaller generation of young investors. This part contains three articles that examine the relationship between asset returns and demographic change.

From the perspective of social security reform, this question is important for two reasons. The building momentum for privatizing Social Security raises the question of how the transition should be financed. From an *ex post* perspective, a better understanding of which generations benefit from the asset market effects of the Baby Boom and which generations lose is key for the current policy debate over who should pay for the transition. From an *ex ante* perspective, some argue that defined-benefit (DB) Social Security may be optimal in terms of intergener-ational insurance because it can offset movements in wages and asset returns that disadvantage large cohorts, by taxing smaller cohorts more heavily. In fact, Bohn (2001) finds that wage and asset return effects may be so large that, even with a DB system the size of Social Security and Medicare, the Baby Boomers are worse off than smaller cohorts around them.

Chapter 7 by Brooks explores the quantitative impact of the Baby Boom on stock and bond returns. It augments a real business cycle model with overlapping generations and a portfolio decision over risky capital and safe bonds. The model has two exogenous sources of uncertainty, technology shocks and population growth, and is used to simulate the asset market effects of recent changes in the U.S. population structure. His results suggest that, although the Boomers will likely earn returns on retirement saving about 100 basis points below current returns, they will nonetheless be better off in terms of lifetime consumption than their parents or children. This is because asset returns move in Boomers' favor during their working lives and because they have relatively few children, which boosts their consumption and ability to save early on. Together, these effects outweigh the impact of poor asset returns in retirement. This result questions the apparent political consensus to exempt pension benefits of those retiring soon, some of the older Baby Boomers among them, from reforms. In addition, because the Boomers in the model are better off even in a specification without DB Social Security, the welfare loss from the crowding out private capital formation by such a system may in practice outweigh the need to offset movements in the capital-labor ratio that disadvantage large cohorts.

Poterba in Chapter 8 provides empirical evidence to support this result. He finds little evidence of a robust empirical relationship between real returns on financial assets and demographic change in Canada, the United Kingdom, and the United States. He attributes this result to two factors. First, the small effective number of observations – demographic change is a very low frequency phenomenon – limits the statistical power of his regressions. Second, he argues that data on wealth accumulation over the life-cycle shows that agents do not dissave dramatically in retirement. As a result, he argues that there will be no "market meltdown" when the Baby Boomers retire.

In contrast, Abel in Chapter 9 argues that the Baby Boom may cause substantial movements in the real price of capital, even if agents have a bequest motive. He develops a rational-expectations, general-equilibrium model with a bequest motive. In this model, the Baby Boom increases stock prices, and stock prices are rationally anticipated to fall when the Baby Boomers retire, even though consumers continue to holds assets throughout retirement. The continued high demand for assets by retired Baby Boomers does not attenuate the fall in the price of capital.

Why do Chapters 7 and 9 come to such different conclusions? Brooks presents a model with four overlapping generations, whereas Abel uses a two-period overlapping generations model. As the number of periods rises, more generations trade in financial assets, which tends to dampen the effects of a given demographic shock on asset returns. This is one reason why Chapter 7 finds more modest asset market effects than Chapter 9. Another reason is that Abel uses a model with convex adjustment costs, which generate an endogenous price of capital, whereas Brooks does not. As a result, the price of capital in Abel's analysis can change over a demographic shift, whereas it is fixed in the analysis by Brooks. Both chapters thus offer very different modeling approaches and the true impact of demographic change on financial markets will likely incorporate aspects of both.

Finally, the fifth part of the volume asks how politically viable different reform proposals are? How do they fare in the court of public opinion? And how compatible are they with institutional constraints – rigid balanced-budget rules such as the Stability and Growth Pact in the European Union come to mind – that make no exceptions for structural changes in public pension systems? In Chapter 10, Razin and Sadka follow up on the premise that aging can tilt the political power balance toward downscaling the welfare state; see, for instance, Razin, Sadka, and Swagel (2002). One of the well-publicized proposals on how to reduce the size of the welfare state is to shift from pay-as-you-go national pensions to individual retirement accounts. They develop a simple political-economy model, with which they analyze how aging can be a driving force behind such reform. They also examine how rigid balanced-budget rules (e.g., the Stability and Growth Pact in the European Union) that do not make exceptions for fundamental structural changes in social security can impede this reform.

In Chapter 11, Boeri, Börsch-Supan, and Tabellini attempt to understand the political-economy feasibility of social security reform by analyzing citizens' opinions on different aspects of the welfare state and its redistributive programs. They focus specifically on the German and Italian public pension systems and report the results of a survey conducted in these countries in the spring of 2000 and the fall of 2001. They describe how informed the citizens of Germany and Italy are and present opinions of these citizens on various reform options. They find that reforms are unsuccessful in two respects: they have made people aware of what they might lose but not of potential gains they may derive.

Robin Brooks (International Monetary Fund) and Assaf Razin (Tel Aviv University, Cornell University, NBER, CEPR and CESifo)
November 3, 2003

REFERENCES

Attanasio, Orazio, and Gianluca Violante. 2000. "The Demographic Transition in Closed and Open Economies: A Tale of Two Regions." Inter-American Development Bank Working Papers 412, Inter-American Development Bank.

Bernheim, B. Douglas. 1995. "Do Households Appreciate Their Financial Vulnerabilities? An Analysis of Actions, Perceptions and Public Policy." *Tax Policy for Economic Growth in the 1990s*. Washington, DC: American Council for Capital Formation, pp. 1–30.

Bohn, Henning. 2001. "Social Security and Demographic Uncertainty: The Risk Sharing Properties of Alternative Policies," in J. Y. Campbell and M. Feldstein, eds., *Risk Aspects of Investment-Based Social Security Reform*. Chicago: University of Chicago Press, pp. 203–41.

Brooks, Robin. 2003. "Population Aging and Global Capital Flows in a Parallel Universe." *IMF Staff Papers*, Vol. 50, No. 2: 200–21.

Geanakoplos, John, Olivia, Mitchell, and Stephen Zeldes. 1998. "Would a Privatized Social Security System Really Pay a Higher Rate of Return?" National Bureau of Economic Research Working Paper, 6713.

Gordon, Roger, and Hal Varian. 1988. "Intergenerational Risk-Sharing." *Journal of Public Economics*, Vol. 37, No. 2 (November): 185–202.

Hall, Robert. 1998. Comment on "Self-Control and Saving for Retirement," by D. Laibson, A. Repetto, and J. Tobacman. Brookings Papers on Economic Activity. Volume 1. The Brookings Institution, Washington, DC.

Krugman, Paul. 2002. "Notes on Social Security." www.wws.princeton.edu/~pkrugman/.

Razin, Assaf, Efraim Sadka, and Philip Swagel. 2002. "The Aging Population and the Size of the Welfare State." *Journal of Political Economy*, Vol. 110, No. 4 (August): 900–18.

Razin, Assaf, and Efraim Sadka. 2003. *The Decline of the Welfare State: Demography and Globalization*, MIT Press (forthcoming).

1 The Developed World's Demographic Transition – The Roles of Capital Flows, Immigration, and Policy

The developed world is about to experience an unprecedented demographic change. In virtually all Organization for Economic Cooperation and Development (OECD) countries, people are getting older – a lot older. And everywhere the reason is the same – a dramatic Baby Boom followed by an equally dramatic Baby Bust, all accompanied by a remarkable increase in life expectancy. These demographic events are slated, over the next four decades, to more than double the dependency ratio – the ratio of retirees to workers. Because the elderly depend on the young to pay their government-guaranteed pension and health care benefits, the extraordinary aging of developed societies augers a fiscal crisis of the first order. Indeed, payroll taxes, which are already extremely high in most developed countries, will, it seems, need to more than double to pay promised benefits. The alternative to such massive tax hikes is, of course, major benefit cuts. Both policies are, of course, anathema to politicians. So whatever fiscal adjustments are eventually made will likely be delayed to the last minute, making those adjustments that much more painful.

This bleak assessment of developed economies' future fiscal prospects ignores two factors that are increasingly raised as possible sources of economic salvation. The first is the macroeconomic impact of aging, specifically the potential for capital deepening. The second is the option to dramatically increase immigration.

Were aging to raise the stock of capital compared to the supply of labor, real wages would increase and, thereby, expand the taxable wage base. This would limit the need for higher payroll taxes. The prospect for such capital deepening arises from the fact that the elderly are the primary owners and, thus, the main suppliers

Research support by the Deutsche Forschungsgemeinschaft (grant: FE 377/4-1), the Universitätsbund Würzburg, the National Institute of Aging, the Smith Richardson Foundation, and Boston University is gratefully acknowledged. We also would like to thank Charles Horioka, Bernd Raffelhüschen, and Reinhold Schnabel for providing data on wealth, population, and health care.

of capital, whereas the young are the main suppliers of labor. All else equal, more oldsters relative to youngsters means a greater supply of capital relative to labor.

Unfortunately, all else will not be equal in either the short or long runs. In particular, if benefits are paid as promised, the requisite tax increases will undermine capital formation as workers' wages, some of which would otherwise be saved, are taken from them and handed over to the elderly to finance immediate consumption.

Thus, the net impact on capital intensity, real wages, and the payroll tax base of aging cannot be determined a priori and must be simulated within a fully articulated and carefully calibrated model. The same is true when it comes to understanding the fiscal implications of increased immigration. Importing additional workers will certainly raise the payroll tax base. But, more immigrants also mean more expenditures on education, public safety, water and sewer systems, and a host of other public goods. More immigrants also mean more government pension and health care spending because immigrants also accrue rights to such benefits. Moreover, most developed countries provide benefits to the elderly on a progressive basis. And, because immigrants are disproportionately low-wage earners, they typically receive more benefits per dollar of tax payments than do native workers. Hence, the precise benefit to the developed world's future fiscal finances and economies from immigration also requires detailed computation rather than simply theoretical contemplation.

Calculations of the type to which we are referring occupy a large and growing literature. Many of these studies are based on the overlapping generation model (OLG) developed by Auerbach and Kotlikoff (1987). Typically, such studies focus on a single, closed economy. Auerbach et al. (1989) is an exception. It models four OECD countries but treats each as a small open economy. This treatment rules out either crowding out or crowding in of capital per worker, as capital flows in or out of small open economies until the return from capital equals the level set from abroad. The one exception to this statement arises in the case of differential changes in corporate tax rates at home and abroad.

More recent contributions have begun to explore the effects of aging within general equilibrium, open-economy models. The French INGENUE (2002) team has developed an OLG model that divides the world into six large regions, three developed and three developing areas, each of which has quite different demographics. They find a small negative impact of aging on the world interest rate. Börsch-Supan et al. (2002) have set up a three-region OLG model, featuring Germany, Europe, and the rest of the OECD, to examine the international ramifications of alternative German pension reforms. They find very little change in capital-labor ratios in their open-economy simulations.

In this paper, we also specify and simulate a large open-economy model. Our model features three developed regions – the United States (U.S.), the European Union (EU), and Japan. For each region, we incorporate a detailed set of fiscal institutions. We also include capital adjustment costs, immigration, age-specific fertility rates, life-span extension, life-span uncertainty, bequests arising from incomplete annuitization, and intracohort heterogeneity. Many of these features have been included in other studies, but this appears to be the first study to include all of these elements in the same framework.

Like other dynamic life-cycle models featuring fertility, our model features monozygotic reproduction. But, to achieve a realistic pattern of births by age, we follow Kotlikoff et al. (2001) in assuming that agents in their child-bearing years give birth each year to fractions of children. By specifying how age-specific fertility rates change through time, we can line up our model's age-specific population counts of children and workers fairly closely with those forecast for the three regions. To do the same with respect to the population of the elderly, we assume that agents die with realistic mortality probabilities starting at age 68.

Agents fully appreciate their longevity uncertainty and maximize, at each point in time, their expected remaining life-time utilities. The inclusion of life-span uncertainty provides three advantages in addition to getting agents to die, on time. First, it permits a more realistic modeling of bequests and inheritances. The standard method for including bequests in dynamic simulation models is to posit that agents derive utility from leaving bequests. Here, we make no such assumption. Instead, we generate bequests by assuming, realistically, that agents fail to annuitize their assets in old age. Hence, when they die, they leave undesired bequests to their children. This treatment of bequests finds support in a recent study by Gokhale et al. (2001), which shows that a model of undesired bequests and earnings inequality can closely replicate the U.S. distribution of wealth, including its Gini coefficient and top tail.

The second advantage involves the age-distributions of bequests and inheritances. With the exception of De Nardi, İmrohoroğlu, and Sargent (1999), previous modeling of bequests in dynamic models have assumed that all agents die at a given age and all agents inherit at a given age. In our model, agents die at different ages, based on realistic mortality probabilities, and their heirs inherit at different ages.

The third advantage of incorporating uninsurable life-span uncertainty is that it leads to a gradual decline in consumption in old age. This is a feature of actual longitudinal age-consumption profiles. The other key feature of actual consumption profiles is the hump that appears during child-rearing years. Our model delivers this hump as well, because agents in our model care about their children's utility when they are young and spend more on consumption when their kids are at home.

A final feature of our framework worth flagging at the outset is the inclusion of capital adjustment costs. As is well known, these costs can drive temporary wedges between the marginal products of capital in different regions and lead the market values of capital assets to temporarily differ from their replacement costs. The inclusion of adjustment costs generates what amounts to regional stock markets and permits us to explore how stock values respond to aging as well as policy responses to aging.

Our paper begins by describing the demographic transition in the three regions and simulating closed-economy baseline transition paths. We then show
how the three closed economies response to increased immigration and pension
privatization. These results provide useful reference points for our subsequent
presentation of the open-economy baseline and policy reforms.

Our baseline simulations keep immigration at current levels, incorporate projected increases over time in life expectancy, and maintain current pay-as-you-go
finance of government retirement and old-age health care benefits. With these
baseline results as a reference point, we consider the macroeconomic and welfare
effects of two alternative policy reforms – a doubling of immigration and the
privatization of government pension systems, in which the payoff of the accrued
liabilities of the existing systems is financed by a special consumption tax.

1.1 Modeling the World Economy

This section discusses the demographic and economic structure of our model.
A more detailed description of population projections, data sources, model assumptions, and calibration is provided in Fehr et al. (2003). To limit notation, we
suppress regional indices to the extent possible.

1.1.1 Demographic Structure

Each region is populated by households who live up to a maximum age of 90.
Consequently, we distinguish up to 91 generations within each period t. The
individual life-cycle of a representative agent is described in Figure 1.1. Between
ages 0 and 20, our agents are children, who earn no money and are supported by
their parents. At age 21, our agents leave their parents and start working. Between
ages 23 and 45, our agents give birth to fractions of children at the beginning of
each period – that is, the first (fraction of) children are born when the parents
are 23 and the last are born when they are age 45. An agent's first-born children
(fractions of children) leave home when the parents are age 43, whereas the last-
born leave their parents when they are age 66. Our agents die between ages 68
and 90. The probability of death is one at age 91. Children always outlive their
parents, meaning that parents always outlive grandparents. To see this, note that
if a parent reaches age 90, his or her oldest children will be 67. These are children
who were born when the parent was age 23.

In each year, new immigrants arrive with their children. After crossing the
border, immigrants automatically become natives in an economic sense – that
is, they have identical wealth endowments (which we assume they bring with
them) to natives in the same age-cohort and earnings class. They also have the
same preferences and fractions of children of different ages as natives in their
age-cohort and earnings class.

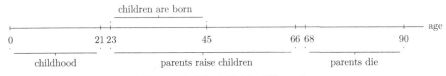

Figure 1.1. The individual life-cycle

The starting points for specifying the current and future demographic structure of each region are the year-2000 existing age-specific population [$\overline{N}(a, 2000)$] and age-specific net-immigration [$\overline{NM}(a, 2000)$] structures. To determine the numbers and ages of children alive in 2000, we used data on birth rates prior to 2000. To determine the evolution over time of population in each region, we applied region- and age-specific mortality [$d(a, i)$] and birth rates to the cohorts alive in 2000 as well as to their children as they reach their ages of fertility and mortality.

In constructing existing as well as future age-population counts, we have to link each initial cohort between the ages of 1 and 68 to those of their parents who are still alive. The reason is that children receive bequests from their parents and the levels and timing of these inheritances depend on the ages of their parents. This linkage is achieved by applying past *relative* fertility rates to each cohort of age 1 to 68 in 2000. If, for example, 15 percent of the parents of newborns in 1980 were 25 years old, then 15 percent of the 20-year-olds in 2000 are assigned to parents age 45. In addition, each cohort is split into three income classes k. Specifically, we assume that 30 percent of each cohort belongs to the lowest income class, 10 percent to the top income class, and the remaining 60 percent to the middle income class. Formally, we denote the final population vector for 2000 as $N(a, 2000, s, k)$ where $a = 1, \ldots, 90$, $s = 23, \ldots, 45$, and $k = 1, 2, 3$. The term s references the age of the parent at the time of birth of agents age a in 2000.

We use the population age structure in 2000 as well as projected future fertility, mortality, and net-immigration rates to compute the population vector $N(a, t, s, k)$ for the years t between 2001 and 2050. After 2050, mortality rates and net immigration rates are kept constant and fertility rates are endogenously adjusted in order to achieve a stable population age structure in the future. In the baseline path, we assume annual net-immigration of 1 million per year in the United States, 450,000 in the EU, and 54,000 in Japan. Figures 1.2 and 1.3 report

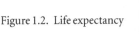

Figure 1.2. Life expectancy

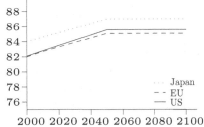

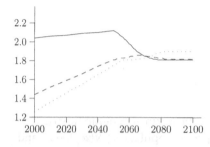

Figure 1.3. Total fertility (births per woman)

our projected life expectancy and the fertility rates in the three regions between 2000 and 2100.

Our exogenous predictions of the current and future mortality and fertility rates follow the medium variant of United Nations Population Division (UNPD) (2003). Although mortality is decreasing in all three regions until 2050, the Japanese have a significantly higher life expectancy than Americans or EU citizens. Because people don't die in the model before age 68, life expectancies at birth are higher than predicted. However, in 2000, the model's life expectancies conditional on reaching age 60 in our model are close to those reported by the UNDP (2003).

Total fertility rates are currently much higher in the United States than in Japan or in Europe. Although the Japanese and European rates are predicted to increase until 2050, the U.S. rates remains roughly constant. The drop in the U.S. fertility rate starting in 2050 reflects our assumption of zero population growth in all three regions after that year. In the United States, the high rate of immigration requires a reduction in the fertility rate after 2050 to achieve zero population growth. Figures 1.4 and 1.5 report the resulting change in the total population and the dependency ratio.

Because of its relatively high fertility and immigration rate, the U.S. population increases from 275 million in 2000 to 505 million in 2100. In Europe, the total population falls over the century from 375 to 340 million. And, in Japan, the population falls from 126 million to 83 million! As one would expect, dependency ratios are increasing in all three regions up to 2050. However, the three regions

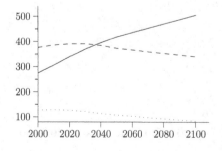

Figure 1.4. Total population (millions)

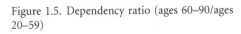

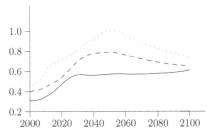

Figure 1.5. Dependency ratio (ages 60–90/ages 20–59)

experience important differences in their population aging. First, the increase in the dependency ratio is much greater in Japan and Europe than in the United States. Second, dependency ratios fall in Europe and Japan after peaking in 2050, whereas they remain roughly stable after 2030 in the United States.

As agents age, their household compositions change as they have more children and as older children reach adulthood. These changes materially alter consumption and saving decisions. Given age a of an agent in income class k in a specific year t, the number of her children is calculated as

$$KID(a, t, k) = \sum_{j=u}^{m} \frac{N(j, t, a - j, k)}{\sum_{s=23}^{45} N(a, t, s, k)} \qquad 23 \le a \le 65, \ k = 1, 2, 3 \quad (1.1)$$

where $u = \max(0; a - 45)$ and $m = \min(20, a - 23)$. Recall that agents younger than 23 have no children and those over 65 have only adult children; that is, $KID(a, t, k) = 0$ for $0 \le a \le 22$ and $66 \le a \le 90$. Agents in between these ages have children. Take, for example, a 30-year-old agent. Such an agent has children who were born in the years $(a - j)$ in the years since he was 23. In year t, these children are between age $0 \le j \le 7$. The KID function (1.1) sums the total number of kids of the respective parent-income class generation and divides it by the total number of parents of age a in year t who belong to income class k. The KID function (1.1) takes into account that the family's age structure will change over time due to changing fertility. Our approach also permits the distribution of births by the age of parents to change over time. This is an improvement compared to Kotlikoff et al. (2001).

1.1.2 Preferences and Household Budget Constraints

As previously mentioned, we do not distinguish between natives and immigrants in the model once the immigrants have joined their domestic earnings- and age-specific cohorts. The model's preference structure is represented by a time-separable, nested CES utility function. Remaining lifetime utility $U(j, t, s, k)$ of a generation of age j at time t whose parents were age s at time of birth and who belongs to income class k takes the form

$$U(j, t, s, k) = V(j, t, s, k) + H(j, t, s, k) \tag{1.2}$$

where $V(j, t, s, k)$ records the agent's utility from her/his own goods and leisure consumption and $H(j, t, s, k)$ denotes the agent's utility from the consumption of her/his children. The two subutility functions are defined as follows:

$$V(j, t, s, k) = \frac{1}{1 - \frac{1}{\gamma}} \sum_{a=j}^{90} \left(\frac{1}{1+\theta}\right)^{a-j}$$

$$\times P(a, i) \left[c(a, i, s, k)^{1-\frac{1}{\rho}} + \alpha \ell(a, i, s, k)^{1-\frac{1}{\rho}} \right]^{\frac{1-\frac{1}{\gamma}}{1-\frac{1}{\rho}}} \tag{1.3}$$

$$H(j, t, s, k) = \frac{1}{1 - \frac{1}{\gamma}} \sum_{a=j}^{90} \left(\frac{1}{1+\theta}\right)^{a-j} P(a, i) KID(a, i, k) c_K(a, i, s, k)^{1-\frac{1}{\gamma}} \tag{1.4}$$

where $c(a, i, s, k)$ and $\ell(a, i, s, k)$ denote consumption and leisure, respectively, and i is defined as $i = t + a - j$. The children's consumption of income class k parents who are age a at period i and whose parents were age s at the time of their birth is defined as $c_K(a, i, s, k)$. Note that the number of children is independent of the grandparents' age at the time of the birth of the parents.

Because life span is uncertain, the utility of consumption in future periods is weighted with the survival probability of reaching age a in year i

$$P(a, i) = \prod_{u=j}^{a} [1 - d(u, u - a + i)] \tag{1.5}$$

which are determined by multiplying the conditional survival probabilities from year t (when the agents age is j) up to year i. Note that d(,) is the annual mortality probability. The parameters θ, ρ, α, and γ represent the "pure" rate of time preference, the intratemporal elasticity of substitution between consumption and leisure at each age a, the leisure preference parameter, and the intertemporal elasticity of substitution between consumption and leisure in different years, respectively.

Given the asset endowment $a(j, t, s, k)$ of the agent in year t, maximization of (1.2) is subject to a lifetime budget constraint defined by the sequence:

$$a(j+1, t+1, s, k) = [a(j, t, s, k) + I(j, t, s, k)](1 + r(t))$$
$$+ w(t)E(a, k)[h(a, t) - \ell(a, t, s, k)]$$
$$- T(j, t, s, k) - c(j, t, s, k)$$
$$- KID(j, t, k)c_K(j, t, s, k) \tag{1.6}$$

where $r(t)$ is the pretax return on savings and $I(j, t, s, k)$ denotes the inheritance the agent receives in year t. When the parents die between age 68 and 90, their remaining assets are split among their children. Consequently, inheritances of agents who are age j in year t and whose parents were age s at their birth are defined as follows:

$$I(j, t, s, k) = \frac{d(j+s)\bar{A}(j+s, t, k)}{\sum_{u=23}^{45} N(j+s-u, t, u, k)}$$ (1.7)

The numerator defines the aggregate assets of income class k parents who die in year t at age $j+s$. The denominator defines these parents' total number of children who are between ages $j+s-45$ and $j+s-23$ in year t. The receipt of inheritances requires us to distinguish members of each cohort according to the ages of their parents at birth. The parents' ages at death determine when the children receive their inheritances. Although the first children of parents (born when their parents were age 23) receive their inheritances between ages 45 and 67, the latest born children (born when their parents were age 45) receive their inheritances earlier in life, between ages 23 and 45.

As in Altig et al. (2001) and Kotlikoff et al. (2001), we assume that technical progress causes the time endowment $h(\cdot)$ of each successive generation to grow at the rate λ; that is,

$$h(a, i) = (1 + \lambda)h(a, i - 1)$$ (1.8)

Gross labor income of the agent in year t is derived as the product of her/his labor supply and her/his wage rate. The latter is the product of the gross wage rate $w(t)$ in period t and the age- and class-specific earnings ability.

$$E(a, k) = \xi(k)e^{4.47+0.033(a-20)-0.00067(a-20)^2}(1+\lambda)^{a-21} \text{ with}$$
$$\xi(1) = 0.2, \quad \xi(2) = 1.0, \quad \xi(3) = 5.0$$ (1.9)

The middle-income class profile is taken from Auerbach and Kotlikoff (1987, 52). The shift parameters $\xi(k)$ are then applied to derive income-class–specific profiles. Moreover, because technological change is an important determinant of secular growth over the life-cycle, we add this growth by multiplying the age-specific longitudinal earnings ability profile by the term involving λ. Hence, the longitudinal age-wage profile is steeper the greater is the rate of technological change.

The net-taxes $T(j, t, s, k)$ of an agent in year t consist of consumption, capital income, and progressive wage taxes as well as social security contributions net of pensions. Because of a contribution ceiling, pension, disability insurance, and health care contribution rates may differ across agents. Each agent's pension benefits depend on her/his preretirement earnings history, whereas health care and disability transfers are provided on a per capita basis to all eligible age groups.

Given individual consumption, leisure, and asset levels of all agents, we can compute the aggregate variables. For example, aggregate assets $A(t+1)$ of agents who live in period t are computed from

$$A(t+1) = \sum_{k=1}^{3} \sum_{a=21}^{90} \underbrace{\sum_{s=23}^{45} a(a+1, t+1, s, k) N(a, t, s, k)}_{\bar{A}(a+1, t+1, k)} \qquad (1.10)$$

Because households die at the beginning of each period, we have to aggregate across all agents who lived in the previous period in order to compute $\bar{A}(a+1, t+1, k)$, which we need for the calculation of bequests; see (1.7). If we aggregate across agents who live in period $t+1$; that is,

$$\mathcal{A}(t+1) = \sum_{k=1}^{3} \sum_{a=21}^{90} \sum_{s=23}^{45} a(a, t+1, s, k) N(a, t+1, s, k) \qquad (1.11)$$

assets of the arriving immigrants of period $t+1$ are included.

Finally, aggregate labor supply of agents in year t, $L(t)$, is computed from the individual labor supplies; that is,

$$L(t) = \sum_{k=1}^{3} \sum_{a=21}^{90} \sum_{s=23}^{45} E(a, k) [h(a, t) - \ell(a, t, s, k)] N(a, t, s, k) \qquad (1.12)$$

1.1.3 The Government Sector

The consolidated government issues new debt $\Delta B(t)$ and collects net-taxes from households in order to finance general government expenditures $G(t)$ as well as interest payments on its debt.

$$\Delta B(t) + \sum_{k=1}^{3} \sum_{a=21}^{90} \sum_{s=23}^{45} T(a, t, s, k) N(a, t, s, k) = G(t) + r(t) B(t) \qquad (1.13)$$

With respect to public debt, we assume that the government maintains an exogenously fixed ratio of debt to output. The progressivity of the wage tax system is modeled as in Auerbach and Kotlikoff (1987). Specifically, marginal wage tax rates rise linearly with the tax base.

$PY(t)$ defines the aggregate payroll tax base, which differs from total labor earnings because of the ceiling on taxable wages. This ceiling is fixed at twice average income in the United States and European Union and at 168 percent of average income in Japan. Aggregate average social security payroll tax rates $\hat{\tau}^p$, $\hat{\tau}^h$, and $\hat{\tau}^d$ are computed each period from the relevant budget constraint for the program and region in question. For the United States, we determine the values of three payroll tax rates for the Social Security pension system, Medicare, and the Social Security disability insurance system; that is,

$$\hat{\tau}^P(t) PY(t) = PB(t) \quad \hat{\tau}^h(t) PY(t) = HB(t) \quad \text{and} \quad \hat{\tau}^d(t) PY(t) = DB(t)$$
$$(1.14)$$

where $PB(t)$, $HB(t)$, and $DB(t)$ are total outlays of the pension, health care, and disability systems, respectively. In the European Union and Japan, disability insurance is part of their respective state pension systems. Hence, we do not calculate separate disability insurance payroll tax rates for those regions.

Because of the contribution ceiling, individual pension and health insurance payroll tax rates can differ from the payroll tax rate. Above the contribution ceiling, marginal social security contributions are zero and average social security contributions fall with the agent's income. To accommodate this nonconvexity of the budget constraint, we assume that the highest earnings class in each region pay pension and, in the European Union and Japan, health insurance payroll taxes up to the relevant ceilings but, at the margin, face no pension and no health care payroll taxes. The other earnings classes are assumed to face the full statutory rate on all earnings. In the United States, the disability payroll tax is modeled in an equivalent manner. However, because there is no ceiling on U.S. Medicare taxes, all earnings groups are assumed to face the health insurance payroll tax at the margin.

If a k-income class agent, whose parents were s years old at his birth, retires in year z at the exogenously set retirement age $\bar{a}(z)$, his pension benefits $\text{Pen}(a, i, s, k)$ in years $i \geq z$ when he is age $a \geq \bar{a}(z)$ depend linearly on his average earnings during his working time $\bar{W}(z, s, k)$:

$$\text{Pen}(a, i, s, k) = \omega_0 + \omega_1 \times \bar{W}(z, s, k) \tag{1.15}$$

The region-specific parameters ω_0, ω_1 were chosen to approximate the replacement rates relative to individual lifetime earnings as reported in Whitehouse (2002, 55).

General government expenditures $G(t)$ consist of government purchases of goods and services, including educational expenditures and health outlays. Over the transition, government purchases of goods and services are held fixed per capita with an adjustment for annual technological change. Age-specific education, health, and disability outlays are also held fixed over the transition with the same adjustment for technological change. The government's budget (1.13) is balanced each year by adjusting the intercept on our linear formula for the average wage tax rate.

1.1.4 The Production Side

The economy is populated by a large number of identical firms, the sum total of which we normalize to unity. Aggregate output (net of depreciation) is produced using Cobb-Douglas production technology; that is,

$$F(K(t), L(t)) = \phi K(t)^\varepsilon L(t)^{1-\varepsilon} \tag{1.16}$$

where $K(t)$ is aggregate capital in period t, ε is capital's share in production, and ϕ is a technology parameter. Because we posit convex capital adjustment cost, the firms' marketable output in year t, $Y(t)$, is given by the difference between gross output and adjustment costs; that is,

$$Y(t) = F(K(t), L(t)) - 0.5 \; \psi \; \Delta K(t)^2/K(t) \qquad (1.17)$$

where $\Delta K(t)$ measures investment in year t. The term ψ is the adjustment cost coefficient. Larger values of ψ imply greater marginal costs of new capital goods for a given rate of investment. The installation technology is linear homogeneous and shows increasing marginal cost of investment (or, symmetrically, disinvestment): faster adjustment requires a greater than proportional rise in adjustment costs.

We abstract from any taxation at the corporate level. Arbitrage between new and existing capital, therefore, implies that the latter has a price per unit of

$$q(t+1) = 1 + \psi \; \Delta K(t)/K(t) \qquad (1.18)$$

Similarly, the arbitrage condition arising from profit maximization requires identical returns to financial and real investments.

$$r(t)q(t) = F_{K(t)} + 0.5 \; \psi \; (\Delta K(t)/K(t))^2 + q(t+1) - q(t) \qquad (1.19)$$

The left side gives the return on a financial investment of amount $q(t)$ while the return on one unit of real capital investment is the net return to capital (which includes the marginal product of capital $F_{K(t)}$ plus the reduction in marginal adjustment costs) and capital gains.

1.1.5 World Equilibrium

Up to now, we've described the model for the representative economy. Because we assume no migration between our three regions, the closed-economy capital market equates national asset holdings from (1.11) to the sum of the market values of the domestic capital stock and the outstanding stock of government debt. In the open-economy case, the aggregate value of world assets equals the market value of the worldwide capital stock plus the value of all outstanding regional government bonds:

$$\sum_{x \in W} A(t, x) = \sum_{x \in W} [q(t, x)K(t, x) + B(t, x)] \quad \text{with } W = \{US, EU, Japan\}$$

$$(1.20)$$

1.1.6 Solving the Model

To solve the model, we first need to specify the preference, technology, and policy parameters. Table 1.1 reports our main parameter values. The preference and technology parameters are mostly taken from Kotlikoff et al. (2001). The reported debt levels in the United States, Europe, and Japan were chosen to match real interest payments reported in European Commission (2003) for 2000, whereas the retirement ages are taken from Bloendal and Scarpetta (1999) for the United States and

Table 1.1. *Parameter values of the model*

	Symbol	US	EU	Japan
Utility function				
time preference rate	θ		0.02	
intertemporal elasticity of substitution	γ		0.25	
intratemporal elasticity of substitution	ρ		0.4	
leisure preference parameter	α		1.5	
Production function				
technology level	ϕ		1.05461	
capital share in production	ε		0.25	
adjustment cost parameter	ψ		10.0	
technical progress	λ		0.01	
Policy parameters				
consumption tax rate (in percent)		11.3	19.5	5.0
capital tax rate (in percent)			20.0	
debt (in percent of national income)	B/Y	40	50	44
age of retirement		63	60	60

the European Union and from Whitehouse (2002) for Japan. The consumption tax rate for the United States is taken from Kotlikoff et al. (2001). For the European Union, the consumption tax rate is the unweighted average of the indirect tax rates in the member states, and the Japanese consumption tax rate is set at the current value of the value added tax (VAT). In addition, we specify the progressive parameters of the wage tax systems in each region in order to generate realistic average and marginal tax rates (reported later), whereas the proportional term is computed endogenously so that the government budget is balanced by the wage tax.

In calibrating our model, we use a Japanese age-specific government health care expenditures profiles for Japan. In the case of the European Union, we use the German profile. For the United States, the Medicare program applies only to households older than 65. We assume uniform Medicare expenditures by age among those over age 65. We make the same uniform age-distribution assumption with respect to the U.S. disability system, which we assume applies to only those under age 65.

We use the German age-specific education profile for all regions in the model and rescale it to get realistic education outlays in 2000 in each region (discussed later). In addition to these parameter values, our model requires an initial distribution of assets by age and income class for each region. These profiles are region-specific.[1]

To run our model as an open world economy, we also need to specify how aggregate world assets are distributed across regions. These world asset shares were chosen to generate realistic current accounts vis à vis the other regions for

---

[1] Data on Japanese asset profiles were provided by Charles Horioka, whereas the European profiles were adjusted from German data provided by Reinhold Schnabel. U.S. data were derived from the 1998 Survey of Consumer Finances.

our initial year. Finally, we have to specify the capital stocks in each region in our initial year 2000 in each region. Here, we take the endogenous initial-year values that arise from a simulation without adjustment costs.

Given the initial world capital stock and asset profiles, our model applies a Gauss-Seidel algorithm to solve for the perfect foresight general equilibrium transition path of the economy. Our algorithm starts with initial guesses for the capital stocks and labor supplies in each region for the remaining years of the transition. Next, we compute from equation (1.18) the path of region-specific market prices of capital. The path for the world interest rate after 2000 is derived from the arbitrage condition (1.19) for the United States. This condition (1.19) is also used to update values of the existing capital stock in 2000 in each region. Next, the wage rates are computed in each region that are equal to the respective marginal products of labor. From the capital market equilibrium condition (1.20), we derive aggregate initial asset holdings in 2000, apply the region-specific saving shares, and update age-specific asset holdings in 2000 in each region. Given these initial assets, the time path of tax rates (which are based on guesses in the first iteration) and factor prices, household decisions on consumption and labor supply are computed and aggregated. Then, we update the path for wage tax rates, the social security payroll tax rate, and debt given the government budget constraints (1.13) and (1.14). Finally, we compute new paths for the capital stocks in each region using the capital market equilibrium condition (1.20) as well as (1.18). The new values for capital and labor are then weighted with the initial guesses of these supplies to form guesses of the time paths of these variables. The algorithm then iterates until the path of capital stock and labor converges. We give our economy 300 years to reach a steady state. Our model, in fact, reaches a steady state to many decimal places prior to year 300. It also converges very tightly around the equilibrium transition path.

1.2 Initial Equilibrium and Baseline Path in the Case of Closed Economies

First, our model is solved by treating every region as a closed economy. Table 1.2 reports the macroeconomic variables in 2000 in the three regions. Note that there is a fairly close accordance between actual and computed national income account measures of private consumption and government purchases. The one exception here is with respect to Japanese government purchases. The official data seem too high given the official reported ratio of tax revenues to national income. In our calibration, we chose to benchmark against the ratio of tax revenues to national income.

The reported shares in education, pensions, and health are very close to actual levels.[2] The same applies to the social security payroll tax rates and the level and progressivity of the income tax in the United States and European Union. By contrast, the average wage tax rate in Japan is obviously too high. Because

[2] See European Commission (2003), Dang et al. (2001, 26), IPSS (2003, 3), and OECD (2002, 178, and 2003).

Table 1.2. *The year 2000 of the baseline path with closed economies**

	Model			Official**		
	US	EU	Japan	US	EU	Japan
National income						
private consumption	77.6	69.5	78.5	77.6	67.8	67.8
government purchases of goods and services	23.0	32.4	22.7	23.0	32.1	33.4
national saving rate	2.8	4.4	4.1	2.8	6.3	5.6
Government indicators						
aggregate education outlays	5.9	5.9	4.4	5.9	6.0	4.3
aggregate pension benefits	5.9	11.4	10.8	5.7	11.6	10.8
aggregate health benefits	2.1	6.3	5.3	2.5	6.2	6.8
aggregate disability benefits	1.3	–	–	0.9	–	–
pension contribution rate (in %)	8.9	16.9	16.6	10.6	–	17.3
health care contribution rate (in %)	2.9	9.5	8.1	2.9	–	8.0
disability insurance contribution rate (in %)	1.9	–	–	1.9	–	–
interest payment on public debt	3.6	4.5	4.0	4.2	4.5	4.0
tax revenues	22.5	30.0	21.0	26.6	32.5	20.7
direct taxes	13.7	16.4	17.0	17.9	16.5	10.5
indirect taxes	8.8	13.6	4.0	8.7	16.0	10.2
wage tax rates (in %)						
average	10.1	13.7	14.2			
marginal	17.1	19.3	20.3			
capital output ratio		3.2	3.2	3.3		
interest rate (in %)	9.0			–		

* in percent of national income if not stated differently
** European Commission (2003)

we have assumed a fairly low consumption tax rate in Japan (see Table 1.1), tax revenues from indirect taxes are too low in Japan.[3] Finally, the model's year 2000 capital-output ratios seem reasonable.

Next, we turn to the baseline paths of the economies, where we assume that current pension systems and other government policies are maintained. The transition paths for the three closed economies are reported in the first parts of Tables 1.3 through 1.5.

The tables demonstrate that the three regions face quite different future dynamics. At first glance, it might seem strange that the effective labor supply in all three regions is rising steadily although the economies are aging. This is mainly because of the assumed labor-augmenting technical progress. It more than offsets the future reduction in the labor force reported earlier (see Figure 1.4) in the European Union and Japan and substantially augments project growth in

[3] In future research, we plan to improve this calibration.

Table 1.3. Simulation results for the U.S. (closed economy)

	Year	National income	Capital stock	Effective labor supply	Before-tax wage	Capital price	Interest rate	OASHDI cost rate	Average wage tax
Base case	2000	1.00	1.00	1.00	1.00	1.000	0.090	0.137	0.101
	2005	1.10	1.00	1.13	0.97	1.048	0.092	0.137	0.106
	2010	1.20	1.02	1.27	0.95	1.086	0.093	0.149	0.109
	2020	1.42	1.10	1.55	0.92	1.109	0.091	0.192	0.125
	2030	1.64	1.17	1.85	0.89	1.078	0.105	0.234	0.141
	2050	2.18	1.34	2.59	0.85	1.125	0.118	0.239	0.159
	2075	3.13	1.75	3.83	0.82	1.160	0.126	0.246	0.160
	2100	4.32	2.45	5.26	0.83	1.167	0.122	0.258	0.155
Doubling immigration	2000	1.01	1.00	1.00	1.00	1.012	0.090	0.137	0.099
	2005	1.13	1.01	1.16	0.97	1.063	0.092	0.137	0.104
	2010	1.25	1.04	1.33	0.94	1.105	0.094	0.145	0.108
	2020	1.53	1.14	1.69	0.91	1.136	0.093	0.183	0.125
	2030	1.84	1.25	2.10	0.88	1.114	0.107	0.218	0.140
	2050	2.61	1.55	3.12	0.84	1.163	0.117	0.225	0.157
	2075	3.96	2.18	4.87	0.82	1.186	0.126	0.237	0.156
	2100	5.65	3.21	6.86	0.83	1.184	0.119	0.254	0.148
Privatizing pensions	2000	1.01	1.00	1.01	1.00	1.051	0.090	0.048	0.098
	2005	1.11	1.03	1.14	0.98	1.104	0.087	0.048	0.101
	2010	1.22	1.08	1.28	0.96	1.143	0.086	0.049	0.102
	2020	1.46	1.23	1.56	0.95	1.171	0.081	0.058	0.112
	2030	1.72	1.39	1.85	0.93	1.153	0.087	0.068	0.120
	2050	2.34	1.84	2.56	0.92	1.186	0.087	0.068	0.124
	2075	3.41	2.68	3.74	0.92	1.194	0.088	0.070	0.117
	2100	4.75	3.99	5.10	0.94	1.189	0.081	0.072	0.108

Table 1.4. *Simulation results for the EU (closed economy)*

	Year	National income	Capital stock	Effective labor supply	Before-tax wage	Capital price	Interest rate	Social security cost rate	Average wage tax
Base case	2000	1.00	1.00	1.00	1.00	1.000	0.090	0.264	0.137
	2005	1.06	0.98	1.09	0.97	1.035	0.096	0.273	0.140
	2010	1.12	0.97	1.18	0.95	1.066	0.096	0.288	0.143
	2020	1.22	0.99	1.32	0.93	1.095	0.094	0.331	0.156
	2030	1.27	0.99	1.39	0.92	1.044	0.097	0.407	0.185
	2050	1.38	0.89	1.61	0.86	1.009	0.130	0.455	0.231
	2075	1.62	0.84	2.02	0.80	1.087	0.153	0.430	0.262
	2100	2.04	0.96	2.62	0.78	1.159	0.156	0.412	0.268
Doubling immigration	2000	1.00	1.00	1.00	1.00	1.002	0.090	0.264	0.137
	2005	1.07	0.98	1.10	0.97	1.039	0.097	0.272	0.139
	2010	1.14	0.97	1.20	0.95	1.073	0.097	0.284	0.142
	2020	1.26	1.00	1.37	0.92	1.107	0.095	0.324	0.155
	2030	1.34	1.01	1.48	0.91	1.060	0.100	0.391	0.184
	2050	1.54	0.97	1.80	0.86	1.047	0.128	0.431	0.226
	2075	1.91	0.98	2.39	0.80	1.117	0.150	0.409	0.253
	2100	2.48	1.19	3.18	0.78	1.180	0.150	0.398	0.253
Privatizing pensions	2000	1.02	1.00	1.02	0.99	1.090	0.090	0.092	0.132
	2005	1.09	1.02	1.11	0.97	1.135	0.087	0.093	0.131
	2010	1.16	1.07	1.19	0.97	1.174	0.084	0.094	0.129
	2020	1.29	1.20	1.32	0.97	1.215	0.075	0.098	0.129
	2030	1.38	1.36	1.39	0.99	1.187	0.069	0.106	0.141
	2050	1.56	1.63	1.55	1.01	1.157	0.069	0.114	0.149
	2075	1.89	2.00	1.87	1.01	1.163	0.070	0.109	0.148
	2100	2.42	2.53	2.39	1.01	1.180	0.069	0.106	0.142

Table 1.5. *Simulation results for Japan (closed economy)*

	Year	National income	Capital stock	Effective labor supply	Before-tax wage	Capital price	Interest rate	Social security cost rate	Average wage tax
Base case	2000	1.00	1.00	1.00	1.00	1.000	0.090	0.247	0.142
	2005	1.04	0.99	1.06	0.98	1.031	0.085	0.273	0.146
	2010	1.07	0.98	1.10	0.97	1.026	0.081	0.313	0.155
	2020	1.11	0.95	1.17	0.95	1.012	0.092	0.363	0.167
	2030	1.12	0.92	1.20	0.93	1.004	0.093	0.403	0.182
	2050	1.12	0.82	1.24	0.90	0.959	0.108	0.481	0.214
	2075	1.19	0.69	1.43	0.83	1.041	0.136	0.431	0.231
	2100	1.42	0.75	1.76	0.81	1.116	0.138	0.402	0.236
Doubling immigration	2000	1.00	1.00	1.00	1.00	1.000	0.090	0.247	0.142
	2005	1.04	0.99	1.06	0.98	1.031	0.085	0.272	0.146
	2010	1.07	0.98	1.11	0.97	1.028	0.081	0.312	0.154
	2020	1.13	0.95	1.19	0.95	1.016	0.093	0.359	0.166
	2030	1.15	0.93	1.23	0.93	1.010	0.095	0.397	0.181
	2050	1.17	0.84	1.31	0.90	0.976	0.108	0.468	0.211
	2075	1.29	0.74	1.55	0.83	1.056	0.135	0.419	0.228
	2100	1.57	0.84	1.94	0.81	1.129	0.135	0.394	0.230
Privatizing pensions	2000	1.01	1.00	1.02	1.00	1.087	0.090	0.079	0.135
	2005	1.06	1.03	1.07	1.00	1.125	0.076	0.084	0.138
	2010	1.09	1.07	1.10	1.00	1.128	0.071	0.089	0.142
	2020	1.16	1.16	1.17	1.00	1.141	0.073	0.100	0.142
	2030	1.22	1.28	1.20	1.02	1.152	0.064	0.105	0.145
	2050	1.26	1.49	1.19	1.06	1.085	0.058	0.118	0.157
	2075	1.38	1.61	1.31	1.06	1.097	0.063	0.108	0.154
	2100	1.67	1.87	1.62	1.04	1.125	0.065	0.101	0.153

the actual number of workers in the United States. Consequently, whereas the Japanese labor supply only increases by 76 percent over the next 100 years, the European effective labor supply more than doubles, and the U.S. effective labor supply increases by more than a factor of 5.

The transition paths of capital stocks also differ dramatically across the regions. The capital stock rises steadily in the United States and more than doubles in the long run, but it falls in the European Union and Japan. The key finding here is that capital per unit of human capital declines in all three regions; that is, the general equilibrium dynamic transition path entails a long-run capital shortage. The reason for this crowding out of capital is the reduction in saving associated with the rise over time in taxes, particularly payroll taxes. Over the course of the century, the capital shortages lower real wages per unit of human capital by 17 percent in the United States, by 22 percent in the European Union, and by 19 percent in Japan. This decline in real wages implies even higher payroll and wage tax rates (used to finance general government expenditures) than demographic changes, by themselves, would suggest.

The crowding out of capital also portends dramatic long-run increases in real interest rates in all three regions. This increase is greatest in Europe, where interest rates rise over the century from 9.0 to 15.6 percent. In Japan, rates rise from 9.0 to 12.2 percent. In addition to these increases in interest rates, there are major long-run increases in the market values of capital in all three regions. In the United States, stock values rise over the century by 16.7 percent. The corresponding European and Japanese long-term capital gains are 15.8 and 11.2 percent, respectively. However, in contrast to the steady increase over time in interest rates, share valuations don't rise continuously over the transition.

Social security payroll tax rates and wage tax rates are reported in the right columns. As one would expect from the population dynamics described previously (see Figure 1.5), the largest increase in payroll tax rates in the medium run occurs in Japan, where they double from 24.7 to 48.1 percent in the next 50 years. Although the EU payroll tax rates are currently higher than in Japan, their future increase is somewhat less pronounced, and they peak at 45.5 percent. After 2050, contribution rates fall again slightly in both regions. Because of its less severe population aging, social security payroll tax rates rise much less in the United States, from 13.7 percent in 2000 to 23.4 percent in 2030 and further to 25.8 percent in the long run.

The picture is very similar in the case of wage tax rates. Because of the generous public good expenditures per capita in the European Union, the average wage tax rate has to increase steadily over the whole transition in order to balance the budget. Although the current level is 13.7 percent, it almost doubles in the long run, reaching 26.8 percent. In Japan, the wage tax rate rises from 14.2 to 23.6 percent. In the United States, public expenditures per capita are lower than in Japan or the European Union. Hence, the U.S. wage tax rate, which equals

10.1 percent in 2000, peaks at 16.0 percent in 2075 and falls to 15.5 percent by the end of the century.

To summarize, our closed-economy, baseline policy simulations show very severe deterioration in macroeconomic and fiscal conditions in all three regions. In the long run, the combined values of payroll and average wage tax rates exceed 40 percent in the United States and 60 percent in Japan and the European Union.

1.3 Macroeconomic and Welfare Effects of Policy Reforms in the Closed Economies

In this section, we consider two policy reforms. The first involves doubling immigration in every region. The second involves privatizing the pension system. We highlight the consequences of these policy reforms for the transition paths of each region's macroeconomic variables and levels of welfare.

1.3.1 Doubling Immigration

First, we consider a doubling of immigration in each region starting in 2001 and continuing through 2050. This means that every year over the next half century, the United States experiences immigration of 2 million people, the European Union of 900,000 people, and Japan of 108,000 people.

As Tables 1.3 through 1.5 indicate, doubling immigration has nonnegligible effects on macroeconomic variables and tax rates in all three regions. The increase in the effective labor supply occurs gradually. Because immigrants arrive with assets, the capital stock effects are quantitatively quite similar and, consequently, factor prices are almost constant. In the medium and long runs, capital prices increase, whereas payroll and wage tax rates fall significantly in all three regions.

However, the quantitative impact of immigration policy is quite different in the three regions. In the United States, the effective labor supply in 2030 is $[(210-185)/185]$ 13.5 percent larger, whereas in 2100 it is $[(686-526)/526]$ – 30 percent larger than in the baseline path. Payroll and wage taxes, by contrast, fall during the same years from 37.5 and 41.3 percent in the baseline path to 35.8 and 40.2 percent, respectively.

In Europe, immigration is lower than in the United States. Consequently, doubling immigration in Europe has a smaller effect on the macroeconomy. In 2030 and 2100, effective labor supply only increases by 6.5 and 21 percent, respectively. However, Europe benefits more from immigration due to its more severe population aging. Payroll and wage taxes fall in 2030 from 59.2 percentage points to 57.5 percentage points and in 2100 from 68 percentage points to 65 percentage points.

In Japan, immigration is very modest. Doubling immigration increases the effective labor supply in 2030 only by 2.5 percent and in 2100 only by about 10 percent. Therefore, the impact on payroll and wage taxes is also modest. In the years 2030 and 2100, they fall from 68.5 to 67.8 percentage points and from 63.8 to 62.4 percentage points, respectively. Note, however, that the long-run reduction of both taxes combined is 1.4 percentage points in Japan, whereas it is more modest in the United States, where they are reduced by 1.1 percentage points.

The welfare effects of the immigration policy are reported in Table 1.6. The numbers show the change in welfare measured as a percentage of remaining lifetime resources. In all three regions, the existing elderly experience small welfare gains from immigration because of the rise in capital prices. Younger and future generations are better off because of the fall in wage and payroll tax rates. Note that the welfare gains for cohorts born in 2030 are strongest in Europe, smaller in Japan, and lowest in the United States. In Europe, the very distortive tax rates are reduced in the long run by 3 percentage points. In Japan, the long-run reduction is only 1.4 percentage points. In the United States, the long-run reduction is even lower and, in addition, the distortions of the baseline system are much smaller compared to Europe and Japan. This explains the welfare differences among the three regions. Of course, in all three regions, rich households benefit from the reform less because their income is above the contribution ceiling.

1.3.2 Privatizing Pensions

Our pension privatization reform eliminates existing public pension systems at the margin, while still paying successive retirees all those benefits they accrued under the existing system. This reform is modeled in the following way: pension benefits of initial retirees are paid in full, and benefits for new retirees are phased out linearly over a 45-year period starting in 2000. Furthermore, the contribution rate to the pension system is eliminated, and transitional benefits are financed by a new consumption tax.

In the United States, this additional consumption tax rate is initially 7.9 percent. It rises to a maximum value of 8.7 percent in 2020 and gradually declines thereafter. After 2071, the added tax is zero. The U.S. payroll tax rate declines immediately by 8.9 percentage points. Over the transition, the payroll tax rate rises by 2.4 percentage points because expenses for health care and disability insurance grow. In the European Union, the added consumption tax rate has an initial value of 16.9 percent. It then rises to a maximum value of 18 percent in 2012 and then declines. The additional tax is zero after 2074. Because of this reform, the payroll tax is reduced by 17.2 percentage points in 2000 and rises to a maximum of 11.4 percent in 2050. In Japan, the consumption tax rate is initially 14.2 percent. It then rises to a maximum of 18.3 percent in 2014 before declining. As in the European Union, the targeted consumption tax is zero after 2074. The payroll

Table 1.6. *Welfare effects of doubling immigration (closed-economy case)*

(Open-economy case)

Birth year	US Income class			EU Income class			Japan Income class		
	1	2	3	1	2	3	1	2	3
1910	0.30	0.26	0.23	0.09	0.05	0.02	0.01	0.00	0.00
1920	0.33	0.26	0.17	0.08	0.05	0.05	0.03	0.02	0.01
1930	0.39	0.32	0.21	0.11	0.09	0.08	0.06	0.04	0.02
1940	0.43	0.38	0.29	0.19	0.15	0.09	0.09	0.07	0.05
1950	0.28	0.31	0.29	0.18	0.17	0.14	0.07	0.08	0.07
1960	−0.11	0.08	0.20	0.03	0.10	0.13	−0.01	0.04	0.06
1970	0.05	0.15	0.16	0.12	0.17	0.13	0.06	0.09	0.06
1980	0.41	0.34	0.16	0.34	0.31	0.16	0.22	0.20	0.06
1990	0.56	0.46	0.13	1.23	0.97	0.17	0.58	0.48	0.08
2000	0.98	0.80	0.24	2.53	2.06	0.32	1.18	0.98	0.13
2010	1.18	0.96	0.30	4.23	3.59	0.56	1.98	1.70	0.20
2020	1.17	0.94	0.30	5.33	4.61	0.74	2.66	2.34	0.28
2030	1.54	1.18	0.45	6.06	5.20	0.94	3.03	2.63	0.35

tax, however, is 16.8 percentage points lower in 2000, and the maximum value reached is 11.8 percent in 2050.

Of course, because part of the tax burden is shifted from payroll taxes toward consumption taxes, the burden on younger households falls and that on the elderly rises. The intergenerational redistribution associated with the consumption tax depresses aggregate consumption, which permits an increase in national saving and capital formation. The long-run consequences of this reform are dramatic in all three regions. Relative to the base-case simulations, the year 2100 capital stock increases by 62.9 percent in the United States, by 163.5 percent in the European Union, and by 149.3 percent in Japan. The higher capital stocks increase gross wages, which rise until 2100 by [(94−83)/83] 13 percent in the United States, by [(101−78)/78] 29 percent in Europe, and by [(104−81)/81] 28 percent in Japan. The combination of higher gross wages and reduced payroll and wage taxes boosts net wages, especially in Europe and Japan. They almost triple from 0.25 [0.78(1−0.68)] to 0.75 [1.01(1−0.25)] in Europe and from 0.30 [0.81(1−0.64)] to 0.78 [1.04(1−0.25)] in Japan. The reductions in labor supplies in the three regions, reported in Tables 1.3 through 1.5, are a direct consequence of the positive income effects experienced by younger generations. Finally, capital accumulation drives up capital valuations in all economies and leads to lower 2100 interest rates.

However, the advantageous macroeconomic effects of privatization come at a cost, which is shown in Table 1.7. The privatization reform implies a strong redistribution from older generations in all three economies toward younger and future generations. Again, the intergenerational and intragenerational redistribution is less severe in the United States compared to the European Union and Japan. The elderly are hurt because a large part of the financing burden of the pension system is shifted toward them via the consumption tax. However, welfare losses for the elderly in the highest income class are quite small. This is because our policy reform leads to an enormous increase in the initial capital prices. Elderly people in the highest income class gain the most from this higher valuation so that their overall welfare losses are quite modest compared to middle-income and poor elderly. Younger and future generations benefit enormously from such a policy. In Europe and Japan, which face larger long-run financing problems, long-run welfare almost doubles compared with the baseline path.

1.4 Initial Equilibrium and Baseline Path in the Case of Open Economies

Next, we turn to the case of open economies. The calibration of the simulation model is the same as for closed economies. However, we now have to give each region an initial share of total world assets. These shares, taken from the closed-economy case, are 35 percent for the United States, 48.4 percent for the European Union, and 16.4 percent for Japan. Because in the open-economy model the interest rate path is quite different, the macroeconomic structure even in the year 2000

Table 1.7. *Welfare effects of privatizing pensions (closed-economy case)*

(Open-economy case)

Birth year	US Income class			EU Income class			Japan Income class		
	1	2	3	1	2	3	1	2	3
1910	−3.86	−2.13	−0.59	−7.10	−2.90	−0.58	−5.70	−1.88	−0.28
1920	−4.12	−2.26	−0.65	−9.47	−5.55	−2.28	−9.22	−5.09	−1.61
1930	−4.71	−2.80	−0.94	−10.16	−6.30	−2.92	−10.32	−5.77	−1.85
1940	−6.60	−3.99	−1.49	−10.89	−6.76	−2.89	−11.50	−7.38	−3.31
1950	−6.28	−3.83	−1.72	−8.45	−6.01	−3.35	−8.98	−6.05	−3.28
1960	−3.11	−2.03	−1.67	−2.37	−2.13	−3.27	−1.46	−1.04	−3.11
1970	1.09	0.93	−1.04	4.02	2.62	−2.46	5.02	3.81	−2.41
1980	4.40	3.28	−0.18	11.56	8.58	−0.42	12.06	9.32	−0.81
1990	9.60	6.88	0.91	23.61	17.10	1.78	24.00	18.05	1.10
2000	15.95	11.35	2.48	42.58	30.60	4.82	40.65	29.67	3.54
2010	21.58	15.21	4.04	64.76	46.52	8.35	60.22	43.60	6.22
2020	26.01	18.19	5.33	82.65	58.96	11.37	76.79	55.32	8.51
2030	29.37	20.43	6.31	94.50	66.88	13.62	85.03	60.62	9.95

Table 1.8. *The year 2000 of the baseline path with open economies**

	US	EU	Japan
National income			
private consumption	77.4	69.4	78.7
government purchases of goods and services	22.8	32.9	22.4
current account	0.2	−1.2	3.1
national saving rate	3.1	4.1	4.1
Government indicators			
aggregate education outlays	5.9	6.0	4.4
aggregate pension benefits	5.9	11.4	10.8
aggregate health benefits	2.1	6.4	5.2
aggregate disability benefits	1.3	–	–
pension contribution rate (in %)	8.8	16.9	16.5
health care contribution rate (in %)	2.8	9.6	8.0
disability insurance contribution rate (in %)	1.9	–	–
interest payment on public debt	3.6	4.5	4.0
Tax revenues	22.3	30.3	20.9
wage tax	7.3	10.5	10.5
capital tax	6.3	6.3	6.5
consumption tax	8.7	13.5	3.9
Wage tax rates (in %)			
average	10.0	14.2	14.1
marginal	17.0	19.7	20.2
capital output ratio	3.2	3.2	3.3
interest rate (in %)	9.0		

* in percent of national income

will change. Table 1.8, however, shows that the differences compared to Table 1.2 are fairly small.

The macroeconomic structures of the open economies are almost the same as those of the closed economies. However, some differences are worth mentioning. National income is now lower in the European Union and slightly higher in the United States and Japan. Consequently, wage taxes are now higher in the European Union and slightly lower in United States and Japan compared to the closed-economy case. In Japan, the current account shows a 3.1 percent surplus in 2000. The EU current account is in deficit, but its size – 1.2 percent of national income – is smaller than that of Japan. The U.S. current account, in contrast, shows a small 2000 surplus. In considering these values, bear in mind that our model does not include trade with China, Southeast Asia, and the rest of the world outside of our three regions.

Next, we compare the macroeconomic variables during the transition in the open and closed economy. In the closed-economy baseline, interest rates increased the most in the European Union and the least in the United States (see Tables 1.3 through 1.5). Consequently, in the open economy, capital will predominantly flow from the U.S. economy toward the European Union. The baseline path of the open economy, therefore, shows for the United States (Table 1.9) less and for the European Union (Table 1.10) more capital accumulation than in the respective closed-economy cases. Japan experiences initial capital outflows, which change to inflows in the long run (see Table 1.11). Because of these capital flows, the United States and Japan experience short-run current-account surpluses, whereas the European Union faces current-account deficits. In the United States and Japan, the wage tax rate increases are reduced slightly during the transition, whereas they increase slightly in the European Union (compared to the closed economy).

The initial current-account deficit in the European Union turns into a temporary surplus in the medium run. The more dramatic aging process in the European Union and Japan will reverse the capital flows in the medium run so that the United States will experience capital inflows. The high net foreign debt, however, prevents the current account from returning to surplus again.

Finally, the world interest rate rises until 2075 and then falls slightly thereafter. The level is somewhere in the middle of the closed-economy levels for the United States and the European Union.

1.5 Macroeconomic and Welfare Effects of Policy Reforms in the Open Economies

Now we consider again the consequences of doubling immigration and privatizing the retirement system.

1.5.1 Doubling of Immigration

The economic adjustment after a doubling of immigration is very similar to the case of the closed economies. However, because of capital flows, additional immigration now has a different impact on the world interest rate. Whereas the reduction in interest rates is weaker in Europe, it is stronger in the United States and Japan compared to the closed-economy case. As a consequence, capital income taxes fall less in Europe, progressive wage taxes increase less compared to the closed economy. Comparing Tables 1.6 and 1.12 reveals that in Europe, future agents in the top (low and middle) income class are better (worse) off than before. Exactly the opposite happens in the United States and Japan (see Table 1.13).

Interestingly, initially the elderly in the European Union and Japan benefit more from the doubling of immigration in the open economy than in a closed economy. The opposite happens in the United States. The reason is the region-specific capital price reaction after the policy reform. Whereas in the United States capital prices increase by 12 percent on impact, they increase in Europe only by 3 percent and in Japan they even fall slightly. In the closed economy, the domestic elderly benefit only from the increase in their domestic asset prices.

Table 1.9. *Simulation results for the US (open economy)*

	Year	National income	Capital stock	Effective labor supply	Current account	Before-tax wage	Capital price	Interest rate	OASHDI cost rate	Average wage tax
Base case	2000	1.00	1.00	1.00	0.002	1.00	1.000	0.090	0.135	0.100
	2005	1.10	1.00	1.13	0.002	0.97	1.046	0.093	0.137	0.103
	2010	1.20	1.02	1.27	0.003	0.95	1.081	0.093	0.148	0.107
	2020	1.42	1.11	1.55	−0.005	0.92	1.114	0.093	0.191	0.121
	2030	1.65	1.19	1.85	−0.003	0.90	1.086	0.100	0.231	0.138
	2050	2.18	1.33	2.58	0.024	0.85	1.082	0.122	0.238	0.156
	2075	3.00	1.60	3.72	0.020	0.81	1.131	0.136	0.255	0.146
	2100	4.06	2.14	5.06	0.015	0.81	1.150	0.134	0.274	0.133
Doubling immigration	2000	1.01	1.00	1.00	0.002	1.00	1.012	0.090	0.136	0.098
	2005	1.13	1.01	1.16	0.001	0.97	1.063	0.093	0.136	0.102
	2010	1.25	1.04	1.32	0.002	0.94	1.102	0.094	0.144	0.106
	2020	1.53	1.15	1.68	−0.005	0.91	1.142	0.094	0.182	0.122
	2030	1.86	1.28	2.09	−0.001	0.88	1.118	0.103	0.215	0.138
	2050	2.61	1.54	3.11	0.021	0.84	1.124	0.121	0.224	0.154
	2075	3.83	2.01	4.75	0.019	0.81	1.160	0.135	0.244	0.143
	2100	5.35	2.85	6.62	0.014	0.81	1.168	0.130	0.267	0.128
Privatizing pensions	2000	1.01	1.00	1.01	−0.016	1.00	1.077	0.090	0.047	0.093
	2005	1.12	1.04	1.14	−0.018	0.98	1.132	0.085	0.047	0.097
	2010	1.23	1.11	1.28	−0.019	0.97	1.172	0.083	0.048	0.099
	2020	1.48	1.32	1.56	−0.031	0.96	1.213	0.077	0.056	0.109
	2030	1.77	1.57	1.86	−0.033	0.96	1.200	0.076	0.065	0.119
	2050	2.46	2.19	2.60	−0.008	0.96	1.187	0.076	0.064	0.126
	2075	3.58	3.18	3.76	−0.002	0.96	1.179	0.078	0.066	0.118
	2100	4.93	4.56	5.11	0.002	0.97	1.167	0.075	0.070	0.108

Table 1.10. *Simulation results for the EU (open economy)*

	Year	National income	Capital stock	Effective labor supply	Current account	Before-tax wage	Capital price	Interest rate	Social Security cost rate	Average wage tax
Base Case	2000	1.00	1.00	1.00	−0.012	1.00	1.000	0.090	0.265	0.142
	2005	1.07	0.98	1.10	−0.011	0.97	1.038	0.093	0.274	0.145
	2010	1.13	0.98	1.19	−0.006	0.95	1.063	0.093	0.288	0.150
	2020	1.24	0.99	1.33	0.006	0.93	1.074	0.093	0.332	0.165
	2030	1.28	0.98	1.40	−0.001	0.92	1.028	0.100	0.410	0.194
	2050	1.41	0.92	1.63	−0.022	0.87	1.039	0.122	0.451	0.241
	2075	1.72	0.95	2.10	−0.024	0.82	1.119	0.136	0.412	0.279
	2100	2.23	1.18	2.76	−0.019	0.81	1.172	0.134	0.387	0.290
Doubling immigration	2000	1.00	1.00	1.00	−0.012	1.00	1.003	0.090	0.266	0.140
	2005	1.07	0.98	1.11	−0.011	0.97	1.041	0.093	0.273	0.144
	2010	1.15	0.98	1.21	−0.006	0.95	1.069	0.094	0.285	0.149
	2020	1.28	1.00	1.39	0.005	0.92	1.085	0.094	0.325	0.164
	2030	1.35	1.01	1.49	−0.003	0.91	1.047	0.103	0.395	0.193
	2050	1.57	1.00	1.83	−0.020	0.86	1.073	0.121	0.428	0.236
	2075	2.02	1.10	2.48	−0.024	0.82	1.146	0.135	0.394	0.269
	2100	2.70	1.45	3.33	−0.019	0.81	1.192	0.130	0.378	0.274
Privatizing pensions	2000	1.02	1.00	1.02	−0.003	0.99	1.075	0.090	0.093	0.138
	2005	1.09	1.02	1.12	0.000	0.97	1.118	0.085	0.094	0.138
	2010	1.16	1.06	1.20	0.007	0.97	1.146	0.083	0.095	0.137
	2020	1.28	1.16	1.33	0.021	0.96	1.165	0.077	0.100	0.138
	2030	1.35	1.26	1.39	0.020	0.97	1.134	0.076	0.110	0.148
	2050	1.52	1.43	1.55	0.009	0.98	1.126	0.076	0.119	0.154
	2075	1.81	1.70	1.86	0.003	0.97	1.152	0.078	0.115	0.152
	2100	2.33	2.19	2.40	−0.002	0.97	1.183	0.075	0.111	0.148

Table 1.11. *Simulation results for Japan (open economy)*

	Year	National income	Capital stock	Effective labor supply	Current account	Before-tax wage	Capital price	Interest rate	Social security cost rate	Average wage tax
Base Case	2000	1.00	1.00	1.00	0.031	1.00	1.000	0.090	0.245	0.141
	2005	1.03	0.96	1.05	0.029	0.98	1.028	0.093	0.274	0.142
	2010	1.05	0.94	1.08	0.011	0.97	1.047	0.093	0.318	0.147
	2020	1.09	0.91	1.15	−0.004	0.94	1.064	0.093	0.369	0.160
	2030	1.09	0.86	1.18	0.015	0.92	1.017	0.100	0.412	0.177
	2050	1.05	0.73	1.19	−0.019	0.88	1.016	0.122	0.504	0.202
	2075	1.19	0.67	1.43	−0.008	0.83	1.116	0.136	0.430	0.226
	2100	1.43	0.77	1.76	−0.006	0.81	1.186	0.134	0.398	0.235
Doubling immigration	2000	1.00	1.00	1.00	0.031	1.00	0.999	0.090	0.245	0.141
	2005	1.03	0.96	1.06	0.031	0.98	1.025	0.093	0.274	0.141
	2010	1.05	0.94	1.09	0.013	0.96	1.045	0.094	0.318	0.146
	2020	1.10	0.90	1.17	−0.002	0.94	1.064	0.094	0.365	0.159
	2030	1.11	0.86	1.21	0.014	0.92	1.023	0.103	0.406	0.176
	2050	1.11	0.75	1.26	−0.021	0.88	1.041	0.121	0.488	0.200
	2075	1.29	0.73	1.56	−0.010	0.83	1.135	0.135	0.418	0.223
	2100	1.60	0.87	1.96	−0.008	0.82	1.204	0.130	0.388	0.229
Privatizing pensions	2000	1.01	1.00	1.02	0.042	1.00	1.071	0.090	0.079	0.135
	2005	1.04	1.00	1.07	0.040	0.99	1.106	0.085	0.084	0.134
	2010	1.07	1.01	1.09	0.027	0.99	1.130	0.083	0.090	0.135
	2020	1.13	1.06	1.15	0.019	0.98	1.156	0.077	0.103	0.138
	2030	1.16	1.10	1.18	0.038	0.99	1.126	0.076	0.110	0.141
	2050	1.16	1.13	1.16	0.001	1.00	1.117	0.076	0.127	0.144
	2075	1.28	1.22	1.29	0.000	0.99	1.156	0.078	0.116	0.145
	2100	1.57	1.48	1.60	−0.005	0.99	1.206	0.075	0.106	0.148

Table 1.12. *Welfare effects of doubling immigration*

(Open-economy case)

Birth year	US Income class			EU Income class			Japan Income class		
	1	2	3	1	2	3	1	2	3
1910	0.15	0.12	0.10	0.20	0.11	0.04	0.22	0.09	0.02
1920	0.18	0.14	0.08	0.12	0.09	0.08	0.16	0.11	0.09
1930	0.23	0.19	0.11	0.16	0.12	0.11	0.24	0.17	0.10
1940	0.27	0.23	0.17	0.25	0.20	0.13	0.27	0.22	0.17
1950	0.14	0.19	0.18	0.24	0.23	0.18	0.23	0.22	0.19
1960	−0.21	−0.02	0.10	0.07	0.15	0.17	0.06	0.14	0.17
1970	0.01	0.09	0.11	0.16	0.21	0.16	0.07	0.14	0.15
1980	0.38	0.31	0.13	0.54	0.45	0.15	0.20	0.21	0.11
1990	0.53	0.43	0.10	1.30	1.04	0.20	0.52	0.45	0.12
2000	0.97	0.78	0.22	2.64	2.17	0.35	1.08	0.89	0.13
2010	1.18	0.93	0.27	4.44	3.83	0.63	1.93	1.64	0.16
2020	1.17	0.90	0.22	5.42	4.74	0.86	2.94	2.57	0.21
2030	1.58	1.16	0.34	5.85	5.06	1.10	3.40	2.95	0.30

Table 1.13. *Welfare effects of privatizing pensions*

(Open-economy case)

Birth year	US Income class			EU Income class			Japan Income class		
	1	2	3	1	2	3	1	2	3
1910	-3.36	-1.65	-0.20	-7.58	-3.22	-0.69	-6.12	-2.08	-0.32
1920	-3.75	-1.95	-0.45	-9.72	-5.76	-2.46	-9.37	-5.18	-1.66
1930	-4.57	-2.69	-0.85	-10.32	-6.42	-3.05	-10.35	-5.72	-1.80
1940	-6.71	-4.11	-1.53	-10.91	-6.76	-2.93	-11.39	-7.18	-3.07
1950	-6.60	-4.15	-1.97	-8.50	-5.99	-3.30	-8.24	-5.54	-2.97
1960	-3.38	-2.39	-2.05	-2.40	-2.02	-3.10	-0.74	-0.57	-2.76
1970	1.08	0.70	-1.41	4.19	2.92	-2.19	5.82	4.30	-2.07
1980	4.52	3.16	-0.47	11.89	9.02	-0.12	12.96	9.79	-0.58
1990	10.36	7.07	0.67	23.87	17.63	2.14	25.18	18.74	1.18
2000	17.56	11.95	2.29	42.93	31.52	5.47	40.65	29.61	3.24
2010	23.88	16.07	3.78	65.26	48.07	9.42	60.00	43.65	5.71
2020	28.96	19.32	4.96	81.46	59.69	12.84	77.22	56.39	8.12
2030	32.95	21.87	5.86	90.44	65.78	15.39	83.51	60.58	9.73

In the open economy, however, the region-specific asset shares are identical across all households. Consequently, European and Japanese elderly benefit from the strong increase of U.S. assets in the same way as native U.S. savers and vice versa.

1.5.2 Privatizing Pensions

Next, we simulate the privatization of the existing pension systems in an open economy. Not surprisingly, the consequences are again very similar to those in the closed economy.

In the United States, the consumption tax increases slightly less in the open than in the closed economy, whereas in Europe the consumption tax increases slightly more in the open economy. The reason is that privatization has a stronger positive effect on wages in the open U.S. economy compared to the closed U.S. economy, whereas the opposite applies in the European Union and Japan. Finally, the drop in the interest rate because of privatization is greater in the open than in the closed U.S. economy. In Europe and Japan, exactly the opposite happens.

The main thing to note, however, is the huge long-run welfare gains experienced by future low- and middle-income agents from the simulated privatization reform. In the European Union, for example, future low-income agents experience a 90.44 percent welfare gain. In Japan and the United States, the comparable figures are 83.51 and 32.95 percent, respectively.

The open-economy welfare effects are quite similar to the closed-economy effects, but some differences should also be mentioned. In the United States, the elderly lose more in the closed compared to the open economy whereas the opposite happens in Europe and Japan. This is because of the previously mentioned changes in consumption tax rates. By contrast, the long-run intragenerational redistribution favors the European top income class in the open economy more than in the closed economy. The opposite happens in the United States. Again, this is because of the long-run interest rate, which decreases less (more) in the open-economy European Union (United States) and consequently progressive wage taxes are lower (higher).

1.6 Conclusion

In this paper, we presented a new dynamic simulation model to analyze the general equilibrium impact of aging in the world's three major industrialized regions. Our simulation results show that aging will greatly damage the U.S., EU, and Japanese economies by crowding out those regions' capital stocks. This capital shortage lowers real wages by 19 percent and raises real interest rates by more than 400 basis points.

However, aging is not identical in all three areas considered. It is most profound in Japan and Europe and less dramatic in the United States. Consequently, the macroeconomic impacts of aging under baseline policy are quite different in the three regions. These differences in the aging process cause capital to flow from the United States to the European Union and Japan in our baseline path. Stated differently, the U.S. capital shortage is exacerbated by the need to supply capital to Japan and the European Union.

Although a doubling of immigration has some beneficial macroeconomic effects, they are extremely small. By contrast, one can expect a significant long-run welfare improvement from eliminating current pension systems and financing accrued pension rights with an earmarked consumption tax. Although the welfare losses of initial elderly and middle-aged are modest, the welfare gains for younger and future low- and middle-income generations are extraordinarily large.

REFERENCES

Altig, D., A. J. Auerbach, L. J. Kotlikoff, K. A. Smetters, and J. Walliser. 2001. "Simulating Fundamental Tax Reform in the United States." *American Economic Review* 91: 574–95.

Auerbach, A. J., L. J. Kotlikoff, R. P. Hagemann, and G. Nicoletti. 1989. "The Economic Dynamics of an Aging Population: The Case of Four OECD Countries." *OECD Economic Studies* 12: 97–130.

Auerbach, A. J., and L. J. Kotlikoff. 1987. *Dynamic Fiscal Policy*, Cambridge.

Bloendal, S., and S. Scarpetta. 1999. "The Retirement Decision in OECD Countries." OECD Economics Department Working Paper 202, Paris.

Börsch-Supan, A., A. Ludwig, and J. Winter. 2002. "Aging and International Capital Flows," in A. J. Auerbach and H. Herrmann (Eds.), *Aging, Financial Markets, and Monetary Policy*, pp. 55–83.

Dang, T. T., P. Antolin, and H. Oxley. 2001. *Fiscal Implications of Aging: Projections of Age-Related Spending*. Economics Department Working Paper No. 305, OECD, Paris.

De Nardi, M., S. İmrohorolu, and T. J. Sargent. 1999. "Projected U.S. Demographics and Social Security." *Review of Economic Dynamics*, Vol. 2(3): 575–615.

European Commission. 2003. Statistical Annex to European Economy No. 4, Brussels.

Fehr, H., G. Halder, S. Jokisch, and L. J. Kotlikoff. 2003. "A Simulation Model for the Demographic Transition in the OECD." Discussion Paper, University of Wuerzburg.

Gokhale, J., L. J. Kotlikoff, J. Senfton, and M. Weale. 2001. "Simulating the Transmission of Wealth Inequality via Bequests." *Journal of Public Economics* 79: 93–128.

INGENUE. 2002. "Macroeconomic Consequences of Pension Reforms in Europe: An Investigation with the INGENUE World Model." Discussion Paper, Paris.

Institute of Population and Social Security Research (IPSS). 2003. "The Cost of Social Security in Japan." Statistical Report No. 13, Tokyo.

Kotlikoff, L. J., K. A. Smetters, and J. Walliser. 2001. "Finding a Way Out of America's Demographic Dilemma." NBER Working Paper No. 8258, Cambridge.

OECD. 2002. *Education at a Glance*, Paris.

OECD. 2003. *Health Data*, 4th ed., Paris.

United Nations Population Division (UNPD). (2003). *World Population Prospects: The 2002 Revision*, New York.

Whitehouse, E. 2002. "Pension Systems in 15 Countries Compared: The Value of Entitlements." Discussion Paper 02/04, Centre for Pensions and Superannuation, Sydney.

2 Will Social Security and Medicare Remain Viable as the U.S. Population Is Aging? An Update

This is an updated and shortened version of my 1998 Carnegie-Rochester conference paper (Bohn 1999). At the time, the paper was received with great skepticism. Although most of the conference audience seemed convinced that social security reform was imminent, the paper's voting analysis suggested that a majority will rationally support the existing pay-as-you-go programs. Five years later, no reforms have occurred. The political debate is dominated instead by proposals for new Medicare drug benefits, suggesting that voter preferences favor expanded pay-as-you-go programs over cost-reducing reforms. This update reexamines the viability of social security on the basis of current, much different fiscal and economic projections. The results are similar, even strengthened because of lower interest rates and deflated stock market expectations.

2.1 Introduction

The U.S. social security system – broadly defined to include Medicare – faces tremendous financial problems as the population is aging. According to Social Security Administration (SSA) projections, the ratio of workers to retirees will fall from 3.9 in 2003 to 2.4 in 2035 (Figure 2.1). The cost of retirement benefits (OASI) will rise from 3.8 percent of GDP in 2003 to 5.5 percent by 2035 (Figure 2.2). Medicare costs are projected to grow even faster, from 2.5 to 5 percent of GDP by 2035. Although long- run projections are always uncertain, the underlying demographics are firmly in place: the growth rate of the labor force has declined sharply (Figure 2.3) and life expectancy is rising (Figure 2.4).

Not surprisingly, these alarming projections have created doubts about the system's viability. According to opinion polls, many young Americans do not expect to receive any social security benefits when they are old. Economists have

Department of Economics, University of California at Santa Barbara, Santa Barbara, CA 93106; Research Fellow, CESifo, Munich. Phone: (805)-893-4532. E-mail: bohn@econ.ucsb.edu.

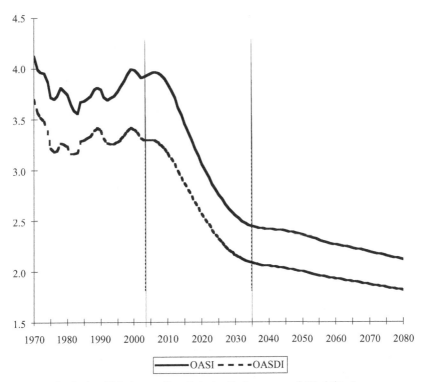

Figure 2.1. The Ratio of Workers to Beneficiaries: Retirement and Disability Insurance
Notes: The chart illustrates the rapid decline in the worker-retiree ratio between now and 2035 under the Social Security Administration (2003), Intermediate Projection. The OASDI series is lower than the OASI series because it includes the disabled. See Section 2.2 for more explanation.

voiced similar concerns. Some have concluded that continuing social security is simply infeasible (e.g., President's Commission to Strengthen Social Security, 2001); others are mainly thinking about alternative versions of radical reforms, apparently taking the existing system's demise for granted.

Although the social security debate sometimes focuses narrowly on retirement, this paper examines retirement and retiree medical insurance together. This is because OASI and Medicare share the same payroll tax, have common beneficiaries, and raise similar public-choice issues. To anticipate, I find that despite the rising cost, social security remains viable, economically and politically. To the extent caveats are required, the most likely source of trouble is Medicare and not retirement insurance.[1]

---

[1] I should emphasize that the paper is not about the normative desirability of marginal, system-saving adjustments versus more fundamental social security reforms, nor primarily about forecasting the future of social security. Whereas a negative answer to the viability question should strongly affect expectations and may create momentum for reform, a positive answer does not rule out that voters might prefer some

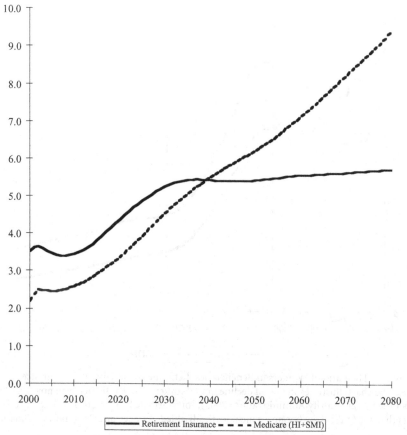

Figure 2.2. Retirement (OASI) and Medicare Cost in Percent of GDP
Note: From Social Security Administration (2003), Intermediate Projection.

   The biggest challenge in modeling social security is perhaps the lack of consensus about the basic nature of the system. Does the government have an obligation – moral or otherwise – to take care of retirees who previously contributed to social security? If so, does this "entitlement" include an open-ended promise to cover all "necessary" medical expenses even when health care costs are rising sharply? Or is social security just a transfer program that Congress could repeal at any time?

   Such interpretational questions are especially relevant for social security be-cause the existing laws do not provide a coherent plan for the future. Instead, the law specifies fixed benefits and fixed tax rates, which are almost surely incon-sistent in the long run and must be modified periodically to adapt to changing

other alternative to the status quo. The challenge for reformers is to convince voters without using the cheap argument that reforms are inevitable.

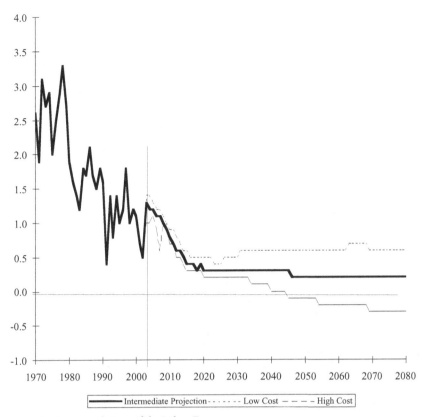

Figure 2.3. The Growth Rate of the Labor Force
Note: Historical data and alternative projections from Social Security Administration (2003).

circumstances. The question to what extent benefits and taxes can be adjusted within the system is, therefore, important for the system's overall viability.

When discussing changes, the interpretation of promised benefits is a key issue. To those who believe that social security represents an irrevocable obligation, the question of viability is about economic feasibility, about honoring a moral commitment, and not about politics. To discuss the politics of terminating social security might even be viewed as immoral, no less outrageous than a debate about defaulting on Treasury bills. To those who consider social security a transfer program without meaningful intertemporal dimension, questions about viability are entirely about politics, about the odds that social security retains majority support; and any comment about moral obligations might be viewed as unscientific or politically naive.[2]

---

[2] Politicians seem to pick the best of both views, telling workers that payroll taxes entitle them to retirement benefits, but denying that the promised benefits should appear as liabilities in the budget (see Bohn 1992, 1997).

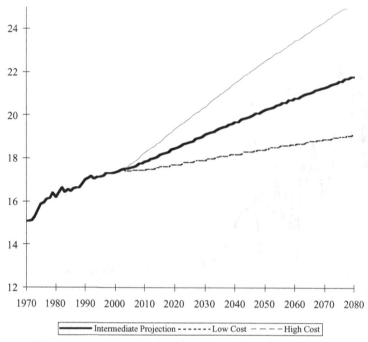

Figure 2.4. Life Expectancy at Age 65
Note: Average of male and female life expectancy, historical data, and alternative projections from Social Security Administration (2003).

All sides apparently agree that Congress is legally sovereign and has the ability to modify social security at will. Hence, majority support is a necessary condition for the existence of social security. From this perspective, the politics of social security should be a legitimate topic, even if one views social security as a moral commitment.[3] By contrast, if one views social security as discretionary, an economic analysis of voter behavior cannot ignore that rational voters have to form expectations about the likely voting behavior of others. This creates a potential for multiple equilibria and for public debate – perhaps revolving around moral obligations – to serve as an equilibrium selection mechanism. From this perspective, social security can be given an intertemporal dimension without assuming a moral commitment.

Thus, the viability question is ultimately political. Is social security likely to maintain majority support as the population ages? To obtain robust answers, I will

---

[3] Note that Congressional sovereignty cannot be used to dismiss the moral commitment view of social security because a sovereign Congress also could default on government bonds. Because entitlements are paid out automatically, while it takes an act of Congress to raise the statutory debt ceiling, it would actually take a stronger political consensus among House, Senate, and President to end social security than to default on the national debt. Pursuing the analogy with debt, it is worth knowing under what conditions a government might default on bonds, even if one views the idea of defaulting on government bonds as outrageous. The same argument applies to social security.

examine several different political-economy models. Purely economic concerns play a role in this context as voters weigh the cost and benefits of social security: How expensive would it be to continue the current system? Is it even feasible? To put the politics in context, I first examine the allocational implications of an aging population and of rising medical cost. The main points are (a) that aging has basically favorable implications – increasing the savings rate, wages, and the capital-labor ratio; and (b) that an efficient allocation will likely display a growing GDP-share of medical spending.

Thereafter, I examine the politics of social security. Two key issues are altruism and the intertemporal dimension of the social security system. Altruism is almost too powerful to be interesting: social security is obviously viable if the young are eager to make transfers to the old. But, if social security were based on pure altruism, why should high-income workers receive higher transfers in retirement than low-income workers? The linkage between benefits and prior contributions suggests that intertemporal arguments play a role. Hence, I will focus on intertemporal models of social security and, to make it challenging, abstract from operational altruism.[4]

In any intertemporal model of social security, the main task is to explain why working-age voters can rationally expect future benefits in exchange for their current transfers to retirees. Following Cooley and Soarez (1996, 1999), I interpret the intertemporal linkage as a repeated voting game with trigger strategies. To support social security as a sequential equilibrium, one has to show that for the median-age voter, the present value of future benefits exceeds the value of payroll taxes until retirement. In a partial equilibrium setting, I find that the net present value (NPV) of social security is positive for the median voter (about age 45) for a variety of specifications. General equilibrium arguments provide additional support for social security because a vote against social security would raise the capital-labor ratio and reduce interest rates, making private savings a less attractive alternative to social security. Overall, Cooley and Soarez's (1999) approach provides substantial evidence in favor of viability, contrary to their own (1996) conclusions.

Throughout the political-economy analysis, the criterion for viability is that social security finds majority support at all times against the alternative of ending social security. To limit the scope of the paper, I do not explicitly examine more elaborate transition paths or reforms that replace social security with some other government-sponsored retirement system. I show, however, that social security gains substantial voter support if partial payments to current retirees would be continued after a no vote. Because the reform plans in the current policy debate

---

[4] It is important to distinguish between operational altruism supporting transfers on the margin and "latent" altruism that might become operational if social security ever lost majority support. Although I doubt that the current benefit structure can be justified by altruism, the existence of general welfare and supplemental social security (SSI) suggests latent altruism. This is important for the politics of social security because the young gain less from abolishing social security if most retirees would still be entitled to SSI benefits (presumably motivated by altruism toward the poor).

largely protect current retirees, the paper suggests that their political prospects are either doubtful or really because of other features (e.g., implicit capital-income tax reform via tax-favored retirement accounts).

The paper is organized as follows. Section 2.2 reviews the demographic and financial trends. Section 2.3 examines efficiency issues with particular emphasis on Medicare. Section 2.4 considers intertemporal models of social security without operational altruism. Section 2.5 briefly comments on other considerations. Section 2.6 concludes.

2.2 The Demographic Problem

The aging of the U.S. population is driven by two main forces: declining birth rates and increasing life expectancy. Both of these demographic changes increase the ratio of social security beneficiaries to workers. Their economic effects are somewhat different. At a fixed life expectancy, declining fertility would reduce the number of workers per retiree but not the expected time each person spends in retirement. Rising life expectancy increases the length of retirement and, therefore, the per-capita cost. The per-capita costs increases are especially severe for Medicare because medical costs, are increasing with age.

Although the demographic projections until about 2030–40 are relatively clear – the 20-year ahead labor force has already been born – there is considerable uncertainty about further-ahead projections. As is common in the literature, I focus on the Social Security Administration's (SSA) Intermediate Projection as the baseline forecast and use its alternative projections as a suggestive measure of uncertainty.

Figures 2.3 through 2.5 show the SSA's three alternative projections for the growth rate of the labor force, the life expectancy at age 65 (averaged male and female), and the ratio of retirees to contributors. In all cases, the population growth rate is expected to stabilize once the Baby Boom has passed through but at different levels depending on the projection. Life expectancy, in contrast, is rising persistently but slowly. Combining the two trends, the ratio of retirees to contributors will increase sharply between 2010 and 2035 as the Baby Boom retires. The path beyond 2035 is more uncertain, but the growth seems to slow down considerably, except in the most pessimistic alternative.

The financial implications are best examined separately for the different components of the social security system. Figure 2.6 shows the projected rise in the cost of retirement benefits as share of GDP. Because the cost rises when revenues/GDP are constant or slightly declining, the OASI program faces a funding shortfall around 2018. In the baseline projection, the funding gap grows quickly until about 2035, then stabilizes at 1.5 to 2 percent of GDP.[5] The alternative projections

---

[5] Until about 2040, the projected OASDI cash-flow shortfall could be covered from the social security trust fund. But, because the trust fund holds Treasury securities, its value is questionable (see later). The

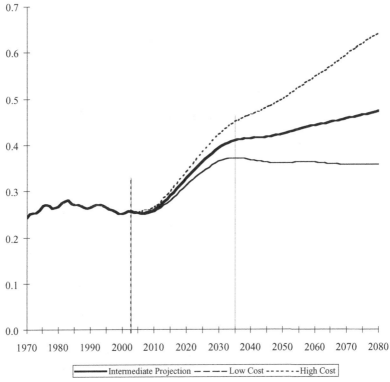

Figure 2.5. The Ratio of Beneficiaries to Workers: Historical and Projected
Note: Historical data and alternative projections from Social Security Administration (2003).

show similar paths until 2040 and then diverge, as uncertainty increases with the forecast horizon. Except in the most pessimistic case, cost/GDP stops rising after about 2035, consistent with the demographic trends.

In terms of economic feasibility, a 1.5 to 2 percent funding gap is serious but far from insurmountable, especially with more than a quarter century advance warning. (It's not uncommon for Congress to debate fiscal changes impacting 2 percent of GDP.) Beyond 2035, cost increases are largely due to slow growth in life expectancy. This suggests that a one-time adjustment covering the 1.5 percent funding gap of 2035 plus an indexation of retirement age to life expectancy should be sufficient to stabilize the OASI cost rate permanently.

The projections for Medicare look much more troubling in comparison. Figure 2.7 shows the projected outlays and revenues of the hospital insurance fund

disability component (DI) of OASDI is excluded for most of my analysis because DI covers the working-age population and is, therefore, not an intergenerational program. DI financing is also unbalanced because projected outlays of about 2.5 percent of payroll by 2030 well exceed the program's fixed 1.8 percent of payroll revenue base.

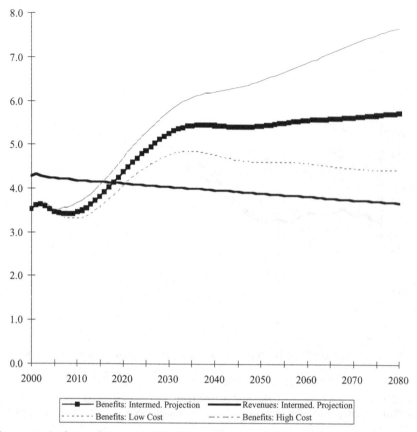

Figure 2.6. Outlays and Revenue of the Retirement Insurance Fund (OASI) in Percent of GDP
Notes: Projections from Social Security Administration (2003). Trust-fund transactions and taxes on benefits are excluded.

(HI, a.k.a. Medicare Part A). Revenues are insufficient even in the most optimistic scenario. In the intermediate case, the HI benefit cost as a fraction of GDP will almost double by 2035, and total Medicare cost (Parts A&B, as shown in Figure 2.2) will exceed the cost of retirement insurance. More ominously, the ratio of Medicare cost to GDP shows no sign of stabilizing; by 2080, HI cost is projected to exceed HI revenues by a 3:1 ratio. Because OASI and Medicare are subject to similar demographic pressures, the relative growth of Medicare must be attributed to increased per-capita medical spending. These projections suggest that studies of intergenerational redistribution should pay at least as much attention to Medicare as to retirement insurance.

These trends raise a number of questions. First, what are the economic consequences if the growing cost of social security is financed through rising taxes on the young? Second, is it politically viable to continue social security? If voters

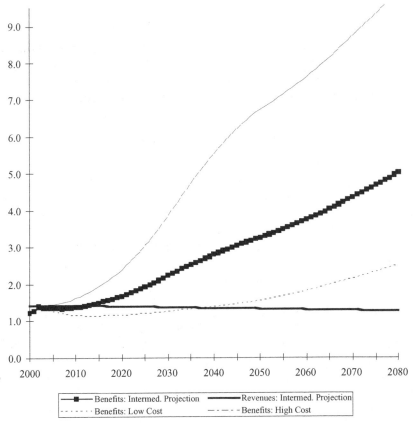

Figure 2.7. Outlays and Revenue of the Hospital Insurance Fund (HI) in Percent of GDP
Notes: Projections from Social Security Administration (2003). Trust-fund transactions and taxes on benefits are excluded.

care about cost-benefit tradeoffs, the answer will depend on the economic consequences, but it is ultimately a question about politics.

2.3 Efficient Responses to Demographic Change

This section examines some basic economic questions about demographic change: What are the macroeconomic effects of lower population growth and higher life expectancy? How are they modified in the presence of social security? And how should we interpret the rising GDP share of Medicare? The answers may surprise those who see demographic change as a huge problem: lower population growth and rising life expectancy will raise wages and reduce interest rates even if rising taxes crowd out capital. A growing GDP share of medical spending is an efficient response to these demographic changes. And, after one generation, welfare is unambiguously improved.

2.3.1 Demographic Change without Government

For the basic analysis, consider a standard Diamond (1965) two-period OG model. Generation t consists of N_t members who consume and work (earning w_t) in period t and retire in period $t + 1$. Individuals survive into retirement with probability μ_{t+1}, which is also the aggregate, deterministic fraction of survivors. Individuals have utility

$$U_t = u(c_t^1) + \rho \cdot \mu_{t+1} \cdot u(c_{t+1}^2) \tag{2.1}$$

where c_t^1 and c_{t+1}^2 are the first- and second-period consumption and ρ is a discount factor; μ is increasing, concave, and (to obtain a steady state) homothetic.

With stochastic survival, the availability of annuities is important for savings decisions. If fair annuities are available, a market interest rate r_{t+1} translates into a survival-contingent gross return of $(1 + r_{i+1})/\mu_{t+1}$ on individual assets a_t. Because private annuity markets are empirically highly imperfect, I model survival-contingent returns more generally as $(1 + r_{t+1})/\mu_{t+1}^{1-\lambda}$, where $\lambda \geq 0$ is the "charge" on annuities ($\lambda = 0$ means fair annuities, $\lambda = 1$ means no annuities).

The budget equations are then $c_t^1 = w_t - a_t$ and $c_{t+1}^2 = (1 + r_{t+1})/\mu_{t+1}^{1-\lambda} \cdot a_t$. Combined with the first-order condition $u'(c_t^1) = \rho\mu_{t+1}u'(c_{t+1}^2) \cdot (1 + r_{t+1})/\mu_{t+1}^{1-\lambda} = u'(c_{t+1}^2) \cdot \rho(1 + r_{t+1})\mu_{t+1}^{\lambda}$, they imply a savings function $a_t = s(1 + r_{t+1}, \mu_{t+1})w_t$. The savings rate s is unambiguously increasing in μ_{t+1}; that is, individuals save more when the life expectancy rises.

To close the model, suppose output is produced with a Cobb-Douglas technology with capital share α, full depreciation between generational periods, and an exogenous productivity index γ_t that grows at rate g:

$$Y_t = K_t^\alpha (N_t\gamma_t)^{1-\alpha}, \text{ where } \gamma_t = \gamma_{t-1}(1 + g) \text{ and } N_t = N_{t-1}(1 + n_t) \tag{2.2}$$

Then, the capital-labor ratio $k_t \equiv K_t/(N_t\gamma_t)$ determines the interest rate $r_t = \alpha k_t^{\alpha-1}$, the wage $w_t = (1 - \alpha)k_t^\alpha \gamma_t$, and all other relevant variables; its dynamics are characterized by

$$k_t = \frac{a_{t-1}}{(1 + n_t)\gamma_t} = \frac{1 - \alpha}{(1 + n_t)(1 + g)} s(\alpha k_t^\alpha, \mu_t)k_{t-1}^\alpha \tag{2.3}$$

As in Diamond (1965), one must assume a positive or "not too negative" interest elasticity of savings to ensure uniqueness, dynamic stability, and monotone convergence.

How then does demographic change affect welfare? Equation (2.3) shows that any reduction in the population growth and any increase in the survival rate will raise the capital-labor ratio and, hence, raise wages and lower interest rates. Although higher wages are clearly a plus, lower interest rates are negative for savers. A decline in n_t is definitely welfare-reducing for generation $t - 1$ because it reduces r_t without changing w_{t-1}: this is the U.S. Baby Boomers' problem. A rise in μ_t will also reduce c_t^2, but assuming people like to live, their utility should nonetheless rise. For all subsequent generations $t + i$ ($i \geq 0$), a lower n_t and/or a higher μ_t are unambiguously positive: one can show that their utility increases, provided the economy is dynamically efficient and the model displays monotone convergence ($0 < dk_{t+1}/dk_t < 1$). It also is true that a permanent reduction in population growth and/or a permanent increase in μ_t will increase utility in steady state. Overall, one must conclude that (a) the demographic changes observed in the United States are basically good news for future generations; and (b), lower population growth reduces the welfare of the "last" cohort prior to the decline – the Baby Boomers.

2.3.2 Government Debt and Social Security

How does government activity modify these conclusions? From a positive perspective, social security and government debt are likely to dampen the macroeconomic effects of demographic change because the existing national debt and social security obligations will impose a lighter (heavier) per-capita burden on larger (smaller) cohorts. From a normative perspective, a defined-benefits social security system, therefore, provides valuable insurance against demographic changes.

To examine the positive role of government, suppose there is a social security system with payroll tax θ_t and benefit rate b_t, and a fiscal authority that imposes net taxes τ_t^1 on the young and τ_t^2 on the old (both expressed as wage-shares). Real government spending is ignored to avoid being sidetracked into public-finance issues. Government debt must nonetheless be included because social security, debt, and direct transfers are close substitutes for purposes of intergenerational redistribution (Auerbach et al. 1991). For the United States, the regular budget is also important because the social security trust fund holds Treasury securities. If they are – as planned – redeemed between 2015 and 2040, who pays?

To answer this question, let D_t denote gross Treasury debt and let TR_t denote the trust fund, both at the start of period t. Initial debt is financed by taxes and new debt, and social security benefits and trust-fund accumulations are financed by payroll taxes, as captured by the budget equations

$$D_t = \tau_t^1 w_t N_t + \tau_t^2 w_t \mu_t N_{t-1} + \frac{D_{t+1}}{1 + r_{t+1}} \tag{2.4}$$

and

$$b_t w_t \mu_t N_{t-1} + \left(\frac{TR_{t+1}}{1 + r_{t+1}} - TR_t \right) = \theta_t w_t N_t \tag{2.5}$$

Individual consumption values $c_t^1 = (1 - \theta_t - \tau_t^1)w_t - a_t$ and $c_{t+1}^2 = (b_{t+1} - \tau_{t+1}^2)w_{t+1} + \frac{1 + r_{t+1}}{\mu_{t+1}^{1-\lambda}} \cdot a_t$ depend on taxes and social security only through the total tax rate $\theta_t + \tau_t^1$ and the net benefit rate $b_{t+1} - \tau_{t+1}^2$. Hence, individual behavior depends only on the unified government budget equation

$$\frac{D_{t+1} - TR_{t+1}}{1 + r_{t+1}} + \left(\theta_t + \tau_t^1 \right) w_t N_t = (D_t - TR_t) + \left(b_t - \tau_t^2 \right) w_t \mu_t N_{t-1} \tag{2.6}$$

and not on its components. The net, or publicly held, debt $D_t - TR_t$ is the only relevant measure of public liabilities. Capital market equilibrium requires $K_{t+1} + (D_{t+1} - TR_{t+1})/(1 + r_{t+1}) = a_t N_t$; that is, also involves net debt. According to Equations 2.4–2.6, trust fund redemptions must either be financed by taxes on the old τ_t^2 or by taxes on the young τ_t^1, or they impose a burden on future generations by increasing $D_{t+1} - TR_{t+1}$.

For our purposes, the most relevant transfer to the old is the general funds subsidy to Supplemental Medical Insurance (SMI, a.k.a. Medicare Part B). Hence, let $\tau_t^2 = -m_t^{SMI} < 0$ be the Medicare subsidy as a share of wages and abstract from other taxes on the old. (Debt and social security would be irrelevant if the government could simply tax its creditors, the old; see Bohn 1992.) Let the benefits financed through payroll taxes, $b_t = \beta_t + m_t^{HI}$, be the sum of retirement benefits β_t and HI m_t^{HI}.

In the OG model, the macroeconomic effects of alternative policies depend critically on their impact on savings and capital accumulation. The case of log-utility, $u(c) = \ln(c)$, is most instructive here because it yields easily interpretable formulas. Specifically, one finds

$$k_{t+1} = \frac{1 - d_{t-1}^+}{(1 + n_t)(1 + g)} \cdot \frac{\rho\mu_t}{1 + \rho\mu_t + (1 - \alpha)/\alpha . d_t^{++}} \cdot (1 - \alpha)k_t^\alpha \qquad (2.7)$$

where $d_t^+ \equiv \frac{D_t - TR_t}{Y_t(1-\alpha)} + \frac{\mu_t}{1+n_t}(b_t - \tau_t^2)$ and $d_t^{++} \equiv d_t^+ + (b_t - \tau_t^2)\frac{\mu_t^{1-\lambda}}{1+n_t}(1 - \mu_t^\lambda)$.[6] Equation (2.7) provides answers about the impact of alternative policies. If d_t^+ and d_t^{++} are held constant, lower population growth and higher survival rates will raise the capital-labor ratio, reduce interest rates, and raise wages, as in the model without government.

At a constant debt-GDP ratio, holding d_t^+ constant is equivalent to keeping tax rates constant. Social security is, however, a defined-benefits system. With constant benefits, d_t^+ and d_t^{++} will increase as μ_t rises and/or n_t falls. This implies a crowding-out effect that raises interest rates and reduces wages. But, unless the fixed benefits are huge, the net effect of the demographic changes is still to reduce interest rates and to raise wages, just somewhat less than without a defined-benefits social security system.[7] One may conclude that *a defined-benefit social security system dampens the macroeconomic effects of demographic change*, without

---

[6] The variable d_t^+ is a sum of debt, social security claims, and transfers that can be interpreted as the old cohort's generational account (Auerbach et al., 1991) scaled by wages, and d_t^{++} is an adjusted version that accounts for imperfect annuity markets. With perfect annuity markets, all transfers are equivalent and d_t^+ is the only relevant policy variable ($\lambda = 0 \Rightarrow 1 - \mu_t^\lambda = 0 \Rightarrow d_t^{++} = d_t^+$). With imperfect annuities, social security benefits contingent on survival are more valuable than other transfers ($\lambda > 0 \Rightarrow 1 - \mu_t^\lambda > 0 \Rightarrow d_t^{++} > d_t^+$).

[7] This is consistent with the calibration results in Bohn (2001). Additional support is provided by simulation evidence in larger-scale models, notably De Nardi et al. (1999). De Nardi et al. simulate alternative policies in a 69-period OG model over the period 1975–2060 and show that interest rates decline in every scenario.

realistically overturning them. Hence, one should not be overly concerned about the economic viability of U.S. social security as a defined-benefits system.

One caveat concerns distortionary taxation. At fixed benefits, tax rates would rise as μ_t rises and n_t falls, perhaps triggering increased tax-avoidance. Feasibility may become an issue as one approaches the peak of the Laffer curve. This is a valid concern in theory but a remote possibility for the United States because the total U.S. tax burden is well below that of many other countries (Hansson and Stuart 2002). Hence, I do not attempt to model the Laffer curve nor tax distortions. Another caveat relates to growth in Medicare spending, which increases d_t^+ and, therefore, reduces the capital labor-ratio, depresses wages, and raises interest rates; because Medicare growth has these effects, it is examined more closely in the next section.

2.3.3 The Rising Cost of Medical Care

Medical costs are worth modeling separately because they are the fastest growing component of social security and because health insurance raises separate efficiency issues. Does Medicare create viability problems?

For the analysis, I reinterpret old-age consumption in the two-period OG model as a CES-composite of health care consumption h_{t+1} and "regular" consumption c_{t+1}^*

$$c_{t+1}^2 = \left[(c_{t+1}^*)^\varepsilon + \eta_{t+1}^{1-\varepsilon} \cdot h_{t+1}^\varepsilon \right]^{1/\varepsilon} \tag{2.8}$$

where $1/(1-\varepsilon)$ is the elasticity of substitution and η_{t+1} parameterizes the weight of medical care in utility. Empirically, medical needs are strongly correlated with age, suggesting that η_{t+1} will increase over time as life expectancy rises. Working-age medical costs are omitted because they do not affect social security (ignoring disability).

Retiree medical care is funded by three sources: payroll taxes covering HI, general taxes subsidizing Medicare SMI (about 75 percent of SMI cost), and payments by the retirees themselves. Let p_t be the exogenous relative price of medical services, let h_t^{HI} and h_t^{SMI} be the real medical services provided by HI and SMI, and let $h_t^* = h_t - (h_t^{HI} + h_t^{SMI})$ be privately funded medical services. Medicare costs as share of the wage are then $m_t^{HI} = p_t h_t^{HI}/w_t$ and $m_t^{SMI} = p_t h_t^{SMI}/w_t$; and the individual budget constraints are

$$c_t^1 = \left(1 - \theta_t - \tau_t^1\right) w_t - a_t \text{ as before, and} \tag{2.9}$$

$$c_{t+1}^* + p_{t+1} h_{t+1}^* = \beta w_{t+1} + (1 + r_{t+1})/\mu_{t+1} \cdot a_t \tag{2.10}$$

To simplify, I assume log-utility over c_t^1 and c_{t+1}^2, and – as an efficiency benchmark – perfect annuities. Then, the first-order conditions for h_{t+1}^* and a_t are

$$h_{t+1}/c_{t+1}^* = \eta_{t+1} \cdot p_{t+1}^{-1/(1-\varepsilon)} \text{ and } 1/c_t^1 = \rho(c_{t+1}^*)^{\varepsilon-1}/(c_{t+1}^2)^\varepsilon (1 + r_{t+1}) \tag{2.11}$$

which simplifies to

$$c^*_{t+1} = \frac{\rho(1 + r_{t+1})}{1 + \eta^*_{t+1}} c^1_t \qquad (2.12)$$

where $\eta^*_{t+1} = \eta_{t+1} \cdot p^{-\varepsilon/1-\varepsilon}_{t+1}$ is a composite of demand (η) and price (p). This composite also determines the share of medical services in total spending, $p_t h_t / c^*_t = \eta^*_t$.

It is a nontrivial exercise to translate the policy debate about the "cost explosion" in Medicare into a preference-technology framework. Although it seems undisputed that demand (η) is rising rapidly as a result of new treatment options, the role of price changes is more obscure. Some argue that rising relative prices (p) combined with a low elasticity of substitution contribute to the observed growth in medical spending (Cutler 1997). But, it is difficult to believe that rapid technical progress would not lead to declining relative prices if one properly adjusted for quality improvements. In any case, it seems clear that the composite η^*_t is rising, as is the share of medical services in total spending.

The latter is the main point: *In response to rising life-expectancy and improvements in medical technology, a growing share of medical spending within overall consumption is efficient.* Thus, projections like Figure 2.7 that show unending growth in medical spending are not per se evidence of inefficiency. Like increases in μ_t in the previous section, increases in η^*_t will increase individual savings, the capital-labor ratio, and wages, and reduce interest rates. Again, such "unbalanced" growth does not prove inefficiency; to the contrary, it would be inefficient to keep the economy on a balanced growth path.

One must recognize, however, that Medicare spending growth beyond the efficient amount, or a wasteful use of Medicare revenue, is problematic. Indeed, much of the Medicare policy debate seems to be about moral hazard – the incentives of insured patients to overuse medical services (see Cutler 1997). As discussed in Bohn (1999), a failure to address moral hazard could threaten the system's economic feasibility. Perhaps worse, moral hazard creates a political economy dilemma: To convince voters that future benefits are secure, social security is likely to *require* some "rigidity" in the name of precommitment. Voters may interpret "unfair" cost controls as a breach of an intergenerational commitment – as a signal that social security cannot be trusted. Discretionary interventions to resolve moral hazard may, therefore, destroy the system's political viability. A failure to intervene, by contrast, results in wasteful spending and adversely affects voters cost-benefit calculations.

2.4 The Political Economy of Social Security

From the perspective of voting theory, the existence of social security is a mystery. Because retirees are a minority, standard median voter arguments imply that workers should not let themselves be taxed for the benefit of the retirees. To rationalize social security in a democracy, the key task is to explain why a substantial fraction of workers vote in favor of social security.

The literature has provided several explanations. The most prominent ones are based on intertemporal considerations and altruism. Intertemporal models build on the fact that individual social security benefits are linked to past contributions. Hence, workers may be induced to vote in favor if they expect future benefits that outweigh the payroll tax. This argument is consistent with the political rhetoric surrounding social security, but it is logically tricky. If there is a sequence of votes, each about whether or not to pay a transfer to current retirees, it is not obvious why current voters should care about past voting outcomes. By the same logic, current workers should not expect future voters to compensate them for their current support of social security. The centerpiece of virtually all intertemporal models of social security is, therefore, an expectational linkage between current and future voting outcomes.

I examine models of this kind, with the focus on pure age-dependent voting. This is not to deny other considerations but rather to document that intertemporal arguments alone can provide majority support for social security.

Whereas early intertemporal models such as Browning (1975) and Boadway and Wildasin (1989a,b) simply assume static expectations, recent models have used an explicitly game-theoretic reasoning that imposes sequential rationality – notably, Cooley and Soarez (1996, 1999). The task is to show that an equilibrium with social security is a sequential equilibrium in an infinitely repeated voting game. The critical support mechanism is provided by trigger strategies. The failure of any cohort to adhere to the proposed equilibrium triggers a negative change in voters' expectations about future benefits that destroys social security. Because survival and collapse are discrete alternatives, trigger-strategy models provide a natural definition of what is meant by social security being viable.[8]

Because the U.S. social security system is a defined-benefit system, I assume throughout this section that a collapse would be triggered by a failure to pay promised benefits to old. The main steps in determining the viability of the system are then:

(a) to sort voters by age, to determine the age of the median voter; and
(b) to determine if the median-age voter would keep social security under the working assumption that the system is viable in the future.

---

[8] There is a long literature on intertemporal models. Aaron (1966) first suggested that median-aged voters compare their contributions to the present value of future benefits, treating past contributions as sunk. Hu (1982) recognized the revoting problem. Sjoblom (1985) presents a first model of social security as a dynamic game. Note that one can give the early static-expectations models (in which voters believe the current system will remain in place for their lifetimes) a modern game-theoretic interpretation because a static majority for social security at all times means that the system is supported by the simple trigger strategy of voting in favor as long as all prior votes have gone in favor. Kotlikoff et al.'s (1988) generational contracting explanation for social security is differently motivated but represents a similar approach. Kotlikoff et al. assume that cohorts pass on a "generational contract" obliging each generation to receive benefits from their successor. The assumption that nonpayment by the young invalidates the "contract" is essentially a trigger mechanism.

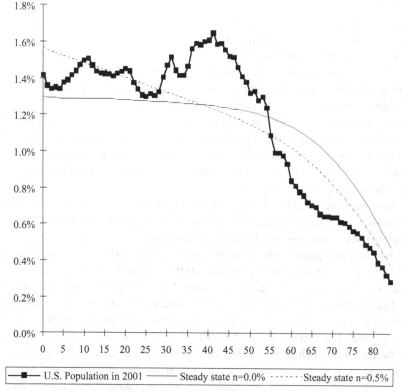

Figure 2.8. The U.S. Age Distribution
Notes: Actual distribution from the Statistical Abstract of the United States, 2002. Steady states from SSA Period Life Table for 1999 and own calculations, assuming unchanged mortality.

If these two conditions are satisfied now and in the future, there is sequential equilibrium with a majority for social security.

2.4.1 How Old Is the Median Voter?

Without altruism, voters decide about social security by comparing the present value of benefits to the present value of their own current and future contributions. Retirees are obviously in favor. Workers will be increasingly in favor as they approach retirement age. To obtain a majority for social security, benefits must be high enough for the median-age voter that they outweigh the remaining contributions. To determine the relevant present values, the first question is: How old is the U.S. median voter?

Figure 2.8 shows the U.S. age distribution for 2001 and the steady-state age distributions for 0.0 and 0.5 percent population growth. The comparison highlights the Baby Boom phenomenon. As of 2001, the median age of the U.S.

Table 2.1. *How old is the U.S. median voter?*

Age groups	Voting-age population (2001)	Percent of age group that is:		
		Registered Nov. 2000	Voting Nov. 2000	Registered Nov. 1998
18–20	**12.3%**	40.5%	28.4%	32.1%
21–24	**15.6%**	49.3%	35.4%	35.0%
25–34	**39.6%**	54.7%	43.7%	52.4%
35–44	**45.0%**	63.8%	55.0%	62.4%
45–64	**64.5%**	71.2%	64.1%	71.1%
65+	**35.3%**	76.1%	67.6%	75.4%
Voters 65+	16.6%	19.8%	20.5%	20.4%
Voters 45+	47.0%	53.6%	56.1%	55.4%
Median Voter	**43**	**46**	**47**	**47**

Notes: From Statistical Abstract of the United States (2002) and own calculations. To compute the age of the median voter, voter participation is assumed constant within each age bracket. Several elections are listed because voter participation varies: Nov. 2000 refers to the most recent presidential election (registration and voting data). Nov. 1998 refers to the Congressional election (registration only; voting data not available).

voting-age population was 43 years. This estimate might be too low, however, because voter registration and actual voter participation are positively correlated with age. Table 2.1 shows the raw population shares of different age groups and the shares of voters that were (a) registered to vote, and (b) actually voted in recent elections. If one assumes that voting participation within age groups is constant, the median age of actual voters is around 46–47. These numbers should be interpreted cautiously, however, because the young might start to vote more in the future if social security becomes more burdensome.

Table 2.2 illustrates how the age of the median voter will rise over time as the U.S. population ages and the Baby Boom passes through retirement. Two estimates are provided for each year, one based on population size and one corrected for age-dependent participation rates. The raw median is more conservative because it does not rely on the empirical correlation of age and voter participation. But, the corrected number is more accurate if voter participation remains unchanged.

As the Baby Boomers age, the median age rises from 43 to 48. Age 48 is also the median of the 0 percent growth steady-state distribution in Figure 2.8. If U.S. population growth is near zero in the long run, as projected by the SSA beyond 2030, this limiting distribution provides a conservative estimate of the post–Baby Boom median age (conservative because life expectancy is likely to increase). At historical participation rates, the age of the median voter will rise from 46 to 52 by 2030 and stabilize at this age.

Table 2.2. *How old are likely median voters in the future?*

Year	Equal participation		Participation as in Nov. 2000	
	Median voter	Share 65+	Median voter	Share 65+
2003	44	16.7%	47	19.8%
2010	46	17.4%	49	20.6%
2020	47	21.7%	51	25.3%
2030	48	26.3%	52	30.5%
2040	48	26.8%	52	31.1%
2050	48	26.6%	52	30.9%
Zero Growth	48	24.8%		

Note: Statistical Abstract of the United States, 2002; SSA Period Life Table for 1999; and own calculations, using Social Security Administration (2003) intermediate assumptions about increasing survival rates.

2.4.2 Voting Decisions

This section examines how voters' net present value of social security depends on age and on various modeling assumptions. In contrast to Cooley and Soarez (1999), I assume voters take interest rates and wages as given. This partial equilibrium analysis is instructive because it allows a more detailed modeling of the life-cycle than a more parsimonious general equilibrium model. As explained later, endogenous factor prices can only strengthen voter support for social security, so the fixed-rate assumption is conservative. A partial equilibrium analysis also provides a useful perspective on how voters should evaluate social security in an open economy.

The setting is a "many-period" OG model with stochastic survival. Cohort t enters the workforce at time t and consists of N_t members. Age is indexed by $i = 1, \ldots, I_{max}$, with upper bound I_{max}. The unconditional survival probability to age i is $\mu_{t,i}$. Over time, the size of cohorts grows at a time-varying rate $n_t = N_t/N_{t-1} - 1$. One may interpret this setting as a time-disaggregated version of the OG model of Section 2.3. The retirement age $I_{ret} < I_{max}$ is assumed exogenous. To focus on intertemporal issues, I abstract from within-cohort heterogeneity. All workers of the same cohort earn the same wage and all retirees of the same cohort obtain the same benefits.[9]

The net present value of social security is computed by discounting sequences of benefits $b_{t,i}^*$ and taxes $\theta_{t,i}^*$, to be specified later. Let $P_{t,j}^i$ be the set of discount factors for j-period-ahead survival-contingent claims at time t and age i. Then,

---

[9] Homogeneity is a conservative assumption. Given the skewness of the income distribution and given a benefit formula biased toward lower incomes, voter support for social security is likely strengthened by heterogeneity (see Section 2.5). The ramifications of variable family structure – differences in benefits for single, married, and widowed participants – are left for future research.

the present value of benefits at retirement is

$$NPV^*_{t,I_{ret}} = \sum_{j=0}^{I_{max}-I_{ret}} P^{I_{ret}}_{t,j} b^*_{t+j} w_{t+j} > 0 \qquad (2.13)$$

For individuals of age $i < I_{ret}$, the net present value of benefits is

$$NPV^*_{t,i} = - \left[\sum_{j=0}^{I_{ret}-i-1} P^I_{t,j} \theta^*_{t+j} e_{i+j} w_{t+j} \right] + P^i_{t,I_{ret}-i} \cdot NPV^*_{t+I_{ret}-i, I_{ret}}. \qquad (2.14)$$

where e_{i+j} are the relative earnings of an age-$(i+j)$ worker. Because the years after median age are empirically years with relatively high earnings, age-earnings variations are a likely negative for social security and, therefore, deserve to be modeled.

Going backward a year, benefits are discounted and a year of contributions is deducted. Hence, the net present value series for ages $i < I_{ret}$ satisfy the backwards recursion

$$NPV^*_{t,i} = P^i_{t,1} \cdot NPV^*_{t+1,i+1} - \theta^*_t e_i w_t \qquad (2.15)$$

The recursion implies that if $NPV^*_{t+1,i+1} < 0$ for any age i, then $NPV^*_{t,i} < 0$ at all younger ages. Hence, there is either a unique age i^* at which a worker becomes net beneficiary ($NPV^*_{t-1,i^*-1} < 0$ and $NPV^*_{t,i} > 0$) or $NPV^*_{t,1} > 0$, which means that even workers entering the labor force anticipate net benefits. (If the latter were true for all cohorts, social security would be beneficial in the Pareto sense, an unlikely scenario for the United States.)

Overall, social security imposes payroll taxes for OASI, DI, and HI at rates θ^{OASI}_t, θ^{DI}_t, θ^{HI}_t (including the employer share). These taxes pay for retirement benefits $\beta_{t,i}$ and HI benefits $m^{HI}_{t,i}$ to individuals of age $i \geq I_{ret}$, and for disability benefits to ages $i < I_{ret}$. If voters view the entire system as a unit, they will weigh the sum of taxes against the sum of benefits. If not, each component must prove its own viability.[10] Because the latter is a more stringent requirement, I will examine OASI and HI separately. I exclude disability insurance from most calculations (except for robustness checks) because taxes and benefits involve the same working-age cohorts. I similarly exclude SMI because it is financed from general revenues.

Social security benefits vary over time and over age groups. Retirement benefits are indexed to aggregate wages until age 60 and inflation-indexed thereafter. If real wages are growing, the replacement rate in terms of current wages is declining over time, $\beta_{t,i} = \beta_{t+I_{ret}-i, I_{ret}} \cdot w_{t+I_{ret}} / w_{t+i}$. From 2003 to 2027, the regular retirement age is scheduled to increase from 65 to 67. I capture this by varying I_{ret} over time,

---

[10] Game-theoretically, the issue is whether or not a failure to pay one type of benefits would trigger a shift in expectations about all categories of future benefits in the sense of Cooley and Soarez (1996, 1999). In Kotlikoff et al.'s (1988) contracting context, the equivalent question is if there is one comprehensive social contract or separate social contracts for OASI and for Medicare.

which leaves replacement rate at retirement, $\beta_{t+I_{ret}, I_{ret}}$, roughly constant. The value of medical benefits is, in contrast, rising with age and increasing over time.

It is not obvious how individuals value survivors benefits. To be conservative, I exclude survivor benefits from the benchmark calculations – also consistent with the assumed absence of altruism – and weigh the total OASI contributions against the "OAI" benefits paid to workers and their families during the worker's lifetime.[11]

Also to be conservative, I will not rely on trust fund sales to sustain promised benefits in excess of payroll taxes. The benchmark assumption, to determine if the existing defined-benefit system is viable, is that future payroll taxes will be increased to match the projected cost whenever the cost rate exceeds the current contribution rate.[12] Throughout, taxes on benefits are treated as benefit reductions and not as revenues; this is economically appropriate but differs from SSA accounting.

For discounting taxes and benefits, I follow the SSA Intermediate Projection and assume a 3 percent real interest rate. The discount rate is important because a too-low discount rate would overstate the NPV of future benefits. The SSA value is above observed market yields on inflation-indexed Treasury bonds (below 2.7 percent at all maturities as of April 2003) and, therefore, yields conservative NPV estimates. Higher discount rates are considered in the sensitivity analysis.

With these assumptions, what are the critical ages i^* for the various U.S. transfer programs? And how are they likely to change as the U.S. population ages?

Table 2.3 provides answers for a set of benchmark calculations. The economic and demographic assumptions are taken from the SSA Intermediate Projection. To be conservative, I further assume a zero value of survivor benefits, average lifetime earning (i.e., above median), retirement at the normal retirement age (except in the final row), and no correction for incomplete annuities. Table 2.3 shows that the critical ages i^* for OASI and HI are rising over time as the Baby Boom generation retires, but they remain well below the corresponding median ages shown in Table 2.2. Even if one added the cost of disability insurance to retirement insurance and assumed a zero value of benefits, the critical ages remain below the median age, as shown under OASDI. Because all columns show values below the median age, the NPVs are also positive if one treated old-age retirement, HI, and/or DI as a unit.[13]

---

[11] This is perhaps overly conservative, not only because most people have some level of concern for their closest relatives but also because spouses vote and because the relevant decision unit may well be the family. Moreover, federal law requires spousal consent for married workers to choose single-life annuities (Diamond 1998), so that even in a model of selfish workers, survivor benefits should not be excluded when one compares the return on social security with the return on annuitized private savings.

[12] The specific assumptions about taxes are inessential, provided social security pays all promised benefits. Then workers will face rising taxes, either explicitly through higher payroll taxes or indirectly through higher general taxes (e.g., to redeem trust fund securities). In the sensitivity analysis later, I also examine voter support for social security with constant tax rates and proportionally reduced benefits.

[13] Even if SMI were included and one arbitrarily assumed that the entire SMI cost falls on workers through general taxes subsidizing SMI (and a zero value of DI and survivors insurance), the critical age for the

Table 2.3. *At what age are voters starting to benefit from social security?*

| Year | Benchmark values | | |
	OASI	HI	OASDI
2003	38	25	41
2010	39	26	42
2020	41	29	44
2030	42	30	45
2040	42	31	45
2050	42	32	45
2030 Age 65	*41*	*30*	*44*

Notes: The table entries are the critical ages i^* at which the NPVs of projected taxes and benefits turn positive, all based on SSA intermediate projections. Whenever costs exceed revenues under current law, payroll taxes are assumed to rise as necessary to cover PAYG cost. Normal retirement age is assumed, except in the last row, which shows age 65 (early) retirement in 2030.
OASI: Weighs retirement benefits against OASI taxes, assuming a zero value of survivor benefits.
HI: Weighs hospital insurance benefits against HI taxes, excluding the disability component.
OASDI: Weighs retirement benefits against OASDI taxes, assuming a zero value of survivor and disability benefits.

Table 2.4 provides critical age values for the SSA's High Cost and Low Cost projections and for a scenario with fixed tax rates and pro-rated benefits. Interestingly, the High Cost scenario yields more near-term voter support for social security and Medicare than the Intermediate or (even less) the Low Cost scenario. Intuitively, rising benefits increase the ratio future benefits to current payments, provided the system remains viable – then everyone likes to be in the first generation that receives new benefits. This logic applies to and largely explains the variation in critical ages across the High, Intermediate, and Low Cost scenarios; the variations over time as the Baby Boom passes through; and the very low critical ages for HI (because health care costs are expected to rise). After 2030, when the Baby Boom effect has largely vanished, the High, Low, and Intermediate Cost scenarios yield similar critical ages for OASI and a more narrow range of i^* -values for HI.

Because expansion helps, the Fixed-Tax-Rates calculations serve as an instructive "worst-case" scenario: for OASI, the critical ages are slightly higher than with defined benefits, but they remain below the median age, suggesting that the "expansionist" logic is not a major factor, except perhaps before 2030 and in the High Cost scenario. For HI, holding tax rates fixed is more important because

entire HI+SMI system would not exceed age 37. For close cases, note that the viability condition is still satisfied when i^* equals the median age because i^* is determined by the NPV at the start of the year.

Table 2.4. *Alternative projections*

Year	Low cost		High cost		Fixed tax rates	
	OASI	HI	OASI	HI	OASI	HI
2003	41	43	34	*	42	43
2010	42	42	35	*	43	44
2020	42	37	38	23	43	44
2030	43	31	39	28	43	44
2040	42	29	40	31	42	44
2050	42	29	41	33	42	44
2030 Age 65	42	31	39	28	42	44

Notes: Entries are critical ages i^* at which NPVs turn positive, as in Table 2.3, except for the following changes:
Low cost = based on SSA low cost projection
High cost = based on SSA high cost projection
Fixed tax rates = SSA intermediate projection, but whenever benefit costs exceed revenues under current law, benefits are reduced proportionally to keep payroll taxes frozen at 2003 levels
Stars (*) denote cases where the NPV is positive for all age groups, due to high projected growth in benefits.

fixed rates would require severe cuts in benefits (e.g., 46 percent reduction by 2030, 75 percent by 2030) that raise the i^*-values significantly. In all cases, the critical values nonetheless remain below the respective median values in Table 2.2.

Table 2.5 examines the sensitivity of critical age values to specification issues. To save space, this is done only for 2030, the peak of the Baby Boom retirement. To start, note that the calculations are robust against a substantial number of changes. Social security looks better if workers value the survivors component (line 1) or if one includes an explicit surcharge of $\lambda = 0.25$ on private annuities (line 2). It looks worse, if Medicare is inefficient (line 3), if one considers a high-income worker (line 4) or if voters are males with lower survival rates than females (line 5). In the case of high-income workers, the increase in i^* for HI is large but i^* remains far below the median age of 48. With this exception, all these changes are minor in comparison to the next two.

The first critical issue is whether or not a vote against social security really ends all payments to the old. By abstracting from altruism, this is implicitly assumed. But, if a substantial fraction of the old would be destitute without social security, a small amount of latent altruism (not operational when social security operates) would be sufficient for voters to maintain some welfare support. This would significantly reduce the benefits of voting against social security.[14]

[14] The history of Cooley and Soarez's (1996) paper highlights the relevance of this issue: in a draft circulated at the Carnegie-Rochester conference, they argued that social security is not viable assuming all costs are avoided by a no vote. In the published version, they assert that the old simply cannot be cut off at all,

Table 2.5. *Sensitivity analysis*

Scenarios and assumptions	Critical ages i^* for	
	OASI	HI
Benchmark values for 2030	42	30
A. Changes with relatively minor impact		
1 Voters value OASI Survivor Insurance	37	N/A
2 Imperfect annuities: 25% surcharge over the actuarially fair level	40	23
3 Inefficient Medicare: 80% value/cost	N/A	37
4 High income: Reduced replacement rate at 160% of average wage	45	43
5 Lower survival: Male life table	44	35
B. Latent Altruism: i^* declines		
6 Unavoidable welfare cost 20%	37	*
7 Unavoidable welfare cost 40%	29	*
C. Higher Discount rates: i^* increases		
8 Real rate r = 5%	49$^?$	44
9 Real rate r = 6%	51$^?$	47
10 r = 5% & Welfare cost = 20%	46	43
11 r = 6% & Welfare cost = 40%	45	42
12 r = 5% & Annuity surcharge = 50%	46	39
13 r = 6% & Annuity surcharge = 100%	45	36

Notes: Entries are critical ages i^* at which NPVs turn positive, as in Table 2.3, but with modified assumptions as noted, all for votes taken in the year 2030. Stars (*) denotes cases where the NPV is positive for all age groups. A question mark ($^?$) indicates that a majority for the program is questionable because the value exceeds 48, the median age in 2030, but remains below 52, the median age of registered voters in 2030 based on the Nov. 2000 registration pattern.

Lines 6–7 show how the critical ages decline if just 20–40 percent of social security costs are unavoidable. Under current law, retirees without income are entitled to Supplemental Social Security (SSI) and Medicaid benefits. SSI benefits to individuals amount to about 20 percent of average wages – that is, about half of the OASI replacement rate for average earners. If one views SSI as revealing voter preferences toward poverty, it suggests that terminating social security would avoid only about half the cost, even less than I assume in lines 6–7. If so, OASI has positive NPV for voters age 29 and older, and HI has positive NPV for everyone, suggesting an overwhelming majority support for social security.

The second critical issue is the discount rate. For discount rates in the 5–6 percent range – for example, motivated by stock returns, naively disregarding risk – the critical age rises toward the median (lines 8–10). But, even then, majority support for social security remains solid if one uses somewhat less conservative assumptions along other dimensions of the model – for example, a small unavoidable

and find – not surprisingly – that social security is viable. The existence of general welfare raises some deeper issues, however, notably about the need for forced savings to avoid moral hazard.

welfare cost (lines 11–12) or imperfect annuities (lines 13–14).[15] It is nonetheless clear that the support for social security is weakened if individuals become convinced that private savings will deliver huge real returns. Excessive optimism about the stock market is, therefore, a problem for social security, and this may explain the popularity of social security reform during the 1990s stock market boom.

Overall, the results strongly suggest that social security is viable. The NPV of social security is positive for a majority of the voting population even under quite adverse assumptions and positive for an overwhelming majority under reasonable assumptions. Compared to the results with 1997 SSA projections reported in Bohn (1999), the critical age values here are equal or lower than the corresponding values previously reported. A major reason for the lower values is the decline in real interest rates (3.7 percent in Bohn 1999 versus 3 percent here), but it is not the only one because much has changed. Most important, the conclusions about viability remain unchanged and appear robust, not contingent on a particular vintage of SSA projections.

2.4.3 General Equilibrium Considerations

General equilibrium issues are examined in more detail in Bohn (1999) and in Cooley and Soarez (1996, 1999). Endogenous interest rates do change the calculus for voting decisions. Namely, if social security crowds out capital and raises interest rates, a termination of social security will increase capital accumulation, thereby reducing interest rates. Voters who understand this linkage will realize that a successful no vote would reduce the return on their own retirement savings. They are *more* likely to support social security than voters who employ partial equilibrium reasoning. The partial equilibrium estimates of voter support for social security are, therefore, conservative. General equilibrium considerations can only strengthen voter support for social security.[16]

2.4.4 What Could Go Wrong?

Although this analysis presents a strong case for the viability of social security, it would be unbalanced if I did not discuss some important caveats. This section focuses on multiple equilibria and uncertain medical cost, the two issues that I consider most troubling for the United States.

---

[15] As motivation, note that private annuities are typically fixed-income products. A real return on private savings in the 5–6 percent range presumably requires significant stock market investments. Hence, the higher return one assumes, the less plausible it is to assume annunitization. Risk-adjustment is beyond the scope of this deterministic model.

[16] The capital accumulation effect is also a common argument for why "privatizing" social security would be good for the U.S. economy. Advocates of privatization do not seem to realize that for savers, lower interest rates are an argument against privatization. General equilibrium arguments also provide endogenous upper bounds on the size of social security; this is discussed in Bohn (1999) and omitted here.

The first concern is that a repeated voting game with trigger strategies has a huge number of sequential equilibria supported by different expectations. Intertemporal, trigger-type models of social security assume that voters agree on how to form expectations about future votes. Some variations in voting strategies could probably be accommodated (presumably anything that keeps the median voter in place). But, the widespread skepticism about U.S. social security among the young suggests that a major shift in expectations cannot be ruled out.

To think about changing expectations, one might imagine an evolutionary process in which some fraction of each new cohort is born with "mutant" expectations. The most interesting mutation would be the belief that future voters will abolish social security just when oneself reaches old age. If only a small fraction of voters hold such beliefs and vote against social security, social security will retain its majority and the skeptics will be proven wrong. In this sense, the equilibrium with social security is evolutionary stable. But, if a large fraction suddenly starts to hold skeptical beliefs, they would be proven right. Note, however, that the popular skepticism about social security seems concentrated in the under-30 age group. These cohorts are irrelevant in the median voter context, provided they have learned about the stability of the system by the time they reach their 40s.[17]

The second significant concern is about uncertainty, notably about uncertain Medicare cost in a setting where voters view Medicare as an unconditional promise to subsidize all medically justified care regardless of cost. The political viability of such a system requires that future median voters receive a higher expected utility with than without Medicare in all states of nature, and this requirement may be violated if doubts develop about the system's ability to pay off in the highest cost state. (See Bohn 1999 for more analysis.) Thus, Medicare is arguably the most problematic part of the overall social security system.

2.5 Additional Considerations: Income Inequality and Altruism

The previous section focused on purely intertemporal considerations. This section briefly comments on two other issues, intracohort income inequality and altruism, that are also likely to influence voting decisions on social security. (Additional issues are discussed in Bohn 1999.)

Within-cohort heterogeneity is important because social security promises a replacement rate that declines with income. This is illustrated in Figure 2.9. Figure 2.9(a) shows that retirement benefits under current law are a concave function of average lifetime wages. Figure 2.9(b) shows the implied negative relationship between income and replacement rates. Income-independent Medicare

---

[17] Another stabilizing factor is the built-in inertia of the U.S. political system. To change an entitlement program, one needs a majority in the House, the Senate, and approval by the president; they often represent different parties. Hence, a repeal of social security may, in effect, require a supermajority; see Hansson and Stuart (1989) for the implications.

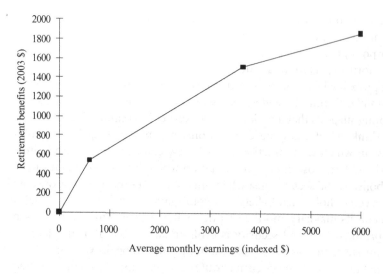

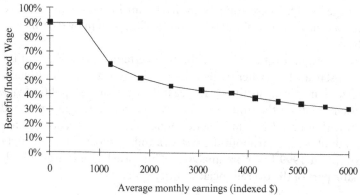

Figure 2.9(a). Monthly Retirement Benefits as Function of Lifetime Wages. B. Replacement Rate
Notes: From Social Security Administration (2003) and own calculations.

benefits are an even better deal for low-income workers. Conditional on viability
in the future, low-income workers will, therefore, vote for social security at a much
younger age than predicted in Tables 2.3–2.5, whereas high-income earners will
not be supportive until a higher age. (For the latter, Table 2.5, line 4, provides an
upper bound.) Given a skewed income distribution, more than 50 percent of a
cohort has below-average incomes. Hence, income inequality is likely to increase
the voter support for social security.

Altruism is important because, in the presence of an altruistically motivated
welfare system, social security cannot be terminated without increasing the cost
of welfare. As noted in the intertemporal model earlier, this reduces workers'
incentives to vote against social security. More strikingly, Tabellini (1990) has
shown that altruism alone may suffice to rationalize social security, without any

intertemporal arguments. Tabellini considers an OG model with heterogeneous within-cohort incomes and mutual altruism between parents and children. In his model, a coalition of all the old plus the low-income young can provide a majority for social security. The young poor vote in favor because their wage-proportional tax is small and they have altruistic feelings toward their parents.

In summary, intertemporal arguments, income inequality, and altruism provide a multitude of mutually reinforcing reasons for voters to support social security. Although Section 2.4 has shown that intertemporal arguments alone are sufficient to obtain majority support, this is not to deny the relevance of other factors.

2.6 Conclusion

Despite all the concerns about social security, my economic and voting analysis concludes that the system is almost certainly viable. The U.S. median voter is currently about 43–46 and will be about 48–52 at the peak of Baby Boom retirement. Under a variety of assumptions and cost-benefit projections, the net present value of social security is reliably positive for the critical age range. The system's viability is further reinforced by altruism, imperfect private annuity markets, within-cohort redistribution, and other considerations, but such additional considerations are not even necessary.

The most serious caveats to this conclusion are about self-confirming skepticism within the population and about Medicare's potential inability to handle moral hazard problems effectively. Because retirees are a minority, a majority for social security requires the support of a significant fraction of working-age voters. As long as middle-aged voters believe that for a few more years of contributions, they earn retirement and medical benefits for the rest of their lives, their support can probably be taken for granted. This might change, however, if a substantial fraction of the over-45 age group started to believe that social security is doomed.

Given these concerns and the alarming projected cost increases, it is remarkable that the current political debate is about adding drug benefits to Medicare, not about cost-cutting. This suggests that neither politicians nor most voters are overly concerned about the system's viability, and this is consistent with my cost-benefit analysis.

REFERENCES

Aaron, H. J. 1966. "The Social Insurance Paradox." *Canadian Journal of Economics and Political Science* 32, 371–6.

Auerbach, A., J. Gokhale, and L. Kotlikoff. 1991. "Generational Accounts: A Meaningful Alternative to Deficit Accounting, in: Bradford, David (ed.), *Tax Policy and the Economy* 5, Cambridge, MA: MIT Press, 55–111.

Boadway, R., and D. Widasin. 1989a. "A Median Voter Model of Social Security." *International Economic Review* 30: 307–28.

1989b. "Voting Models of Social Security Determination," in: B. A. Gustafsson and N. Anders Klevmarken (eds.). *The Political Economy of Social Security*. Amsterdam: North-Holland: 29–50.

Bohn, H. 1992. "Budget Deficits and Government Accounting." *Carnegie-Rochester Conference Series on Public Policy* 37: 1–84.

1997. "Social Security Reform and Financial Markets," in: Steven Sass and Robert Triest (eds.), *Social Security Reform*. Boston: Federal Reserve Bank of Boston.

1999. "Will Social Security and Medicare Remain Viable as the U.S. Population Is Aging?" *Carnegie-Rochester Conference Series on Public Policy* 50, 1–53.

2001. "Social Security and Demographic Uncertainty: The Risk-Sharing Properties of Alternative Policies," in: John Campbell and Martin Feldstein (eds.), *Risk Aspects of Investment Based Social Security Reform*. Chicago: University of Chicago Press, 203–41.

Browning, E. K. 1975. "Why the Social Insurance Budget Is Too Large in a Democratic Society." *Economic Inquiry* 13: 373–88.

Cooley, T., and J. Soarez. 1996. "Will Social Security Survive the Baby Boom?" *Carnegie-Rochester Conference Series on Public Policy* 45: 89–121.

1999. "A Positive Theory of Social Security Based on Reputation." *Journal of Political Economy* 107, 135–60.

Cukierman, A., and A. Meltzer. 1989. "A Political Theory of Government Debt and Deficits in a Neo-Ricardian Framework." *American Economic Review* 79: 713–32.

Cutler, D. 1997. "Public Policy for Health Care," in: A. Auerbach (ed.), *Fiscal Policy: Lesson from Economic Research*. Cambridge, MA: MIT Press.

Diamond, P. 1965. "National Debt in a Neoclassical Growth Model." *American Economic Review* 55: 1126–50.

1998. "Economics of Social Security Reform – An Overview," mimeo, MIT.

De Nardi, M., S. Imrohoroglu, and T. Sargent. 1999. "Projected U.S. Demographics and Social Security." *Review of Economic Dynamics* 2, 575–615.

Hansson, A., and C. Stuart. 2003. "Peaking of Fiscal Sizes of Government." *European Journal of Political Economy*.

Hansson, I., and C. Stuart. 1989. "Social Security as Trade Among Living Generations." *American Economic Review* 79, 1182–95.

Hu, S. C. 1982. "Social Security, Majority-Voting Equilibrium, and Dynamic Efficiency." *International Economic Review* 23: 269–87.

Kotlikoff, L., T. Persson, and L. Svensson. 1988. "Social Contracts as Assets: A Possible Solution to the Time-Consistency Problem." *American Economic Review* 78, 662–77.

President's Commission to Strengthen Social Security. 2001. Final Report. Online at http://www.csss.gov/reports/.

Social Security Administration. 2003. Annual Report of the Board of Trustees of the Federal Old-Age and Survivors Insurance and Disability Fund. Washington, DC: U.S. Government Printing Office.

Sjoblom, K. 1985. "Voting for Social Security." *Public Choice* 45: 225–40.

Tabellini, G. 1990. "A Positive Theory of Social Security." NBER Working Paper No. 3272.

U.S. Census Bureau. 2002. *Statistical Abstract of the United States*. Washington, DC.

3 Self-Control and Saving for Retirement

Consumers face two challenges: making good decisions and sticking to them. Economists have adopted optimistic assumptions on both counts. The consumers in mainstream economic models are assumed both to be exceptionally good decision makers and to be able to carry out their plans. These economic assumptions are dubious, particularly in regard to saving for retirement.

First, economists overestimate sophistication in decision making. In fact, numerous studies have documented the very low level of financial sophistication of the typical American consumer.[1] In a 1996 poll of nonretired Americans over the age of 26, the Employee Benefit Research Institute (EBRI) found that only 32 percent had "tried to figure out how much money [they would] need to have saved by the time [they retired] so that [they could] live comfortably in retirement."[2]

Second, economists assume that intentions and actions are aligned. But, examples of a systematic gap between intentions and actions abound. Consider the two-pack-a-day cigarette smoker who decided to quit years ago but, despite ongoing attempts, still has not kicked the habit. Consider the employee who perpetually arrives late at work, resolving day after day to get up a little earlier in the future. In New Year's resolutions, one commits to eat more healthily, exercise more regularly, and watch television less frequently, but many of these promises

[1] See, for example, Bernheim (1994, 1995); Farkas and Johnson (1997).
[2] 1996 Retirement Confidence Survey, cosponsored by the Employee Benefit Research Institute, Matthew Greenwald and Associates, and the American Savings Education Council; cited by Farkas and Johnson (1997, p. 34).

We thank George Akerlof, Christopher Carroll, Eric Engen, William Gale, Robert Hall, and James Poterba for extremely helpful conversations and advice. We are also grateful for the valuable input of Robert Barro, Steve Bergantino, Olivier Blanchard, John Campbell, Daniel Dulitzky, Benjamin Friedman, Drew Fudenberg, Ken Judd, John Shea, Jonathan Skinner, David Wise, and Richard Zeckhauser; participants of seminars at Harvard University, Stanford University, and the University of Maryland; and the Brookings Panel meeting. Laibson acknowledges financial support from the National Science Foundation, the MacArthur Foundation, and a National Bureau of Economic Research Aging Fellowship; and Repetto, from an Alfred P. Sloan Graduate Fellowship.

fail. Such failures consistently arise in problems involving delayed gratification. The consumer resolves, plans, and desires to avoid an activity associated with instantaneous gratification but subsequently succumbs to the temptation. Few people claim to have the opposite type of problem: smoking too few cigarettes, getting to work too early, or watching too little television.[3] Indeed, such problems are so unusual that many of them do not even seem intuitively plausible. People have a systematic tendency to err – as judged by their own standards – in the direction of instantaneous gratification.

The gap between intentions and actions is also evident in life-cycle saving, and this is the focus of our paper. Three types of evidence document the troubling temptation of immediate gratification.[4] First, popular and professional financial advice highlights the value of using external commitments to prevent overconsumption.[5] From the *New York Times*, for example: "Use whatever means possible to remove a set amount of money from your bank account each month before you have a chance to spend it."[6] Or, from American Express: "If you wait until the end of the month to put money into your investments, you'll probably encounter months in which there's nothing left over. To keep this from happening, pay yourself first by having money set aside from each paycheck into a savings account or 401(k) plan."[7] Financial planners routinely advise their clients to cut up credit cards; to leave them at home or in a safe deposit box; to use excess withholding as a forced saving device; and to use Christmas clubs, vacation clubs, and other low-interest, low-liquidity goal clubs to regulate saving flows.[8] And, in 1995, American consumers deposited their holiday savings in roughly 10 million Christmas club accounts.[9] Their use of such commitment devices implies that consumers have and are aware of problems of self-control.

Self-reports about preferred consumption paths provide a second type of evidence for the gap between intentions and actions. Consumers report a preference for flat or rising real consumption paths, even when the real interest rate is zero and the budget constraint is made explicit – that is, higher future consumption

---

[3] The eating disorder anorexia nervosa may represent one of the few counter-examples to this claim. However, it is not clear that it should be conceptualized as a reversal of the delay of gratification problem. Anorexia nervosa is associated with both short-term disutility (hunger, malaise) and long-term disutility (malnutrition, death). Hence, rather than yielding too much long-term felicity at the expense of short-term felicity, the disorder leads to lower utility flows at all times. "Workaholics" may provide a better, although still imperfect, example of behavior that is characterized by too much investment.

[4] This evidence is reviewed in Laibson (1998).

[5] Such advice may be directed primarily at people who have a problem saving, and so may not be generalizable.

[6] Deborah M. Rankin, "How to Get Ready for Retirement: Save, Save, Save," *New York Times*, March 13, 1993, p. 33 ("Your Money" column).

[7] American Express Financial Advisors (1996, p. 14).

[8] For interesting evidence on the relatively widespread use of intentional overwithholding, even in the absence of penalties for underwithholding, see Shapiro and Slemrod (1995).

[9] Simmons Market Research Bureau (1996).

implies lower current consumption.[10] But, they actually implement downward-sloping consumption paths when they are not effectively liquidity constrained.[11] Moreover, in the late 1990s, the typical Baby Boomer household was saving well below the rate required to finance a standard of living in retirement comparable to that it currently enjoys.[12]

Survey data contrasting actual and normative saving rates provide the third type of evidence for the gap between intentions and actions. A 1997 survey by Public Agenda finds that 76 percent of respondents believe that they should be saving more for retirement.[13] Of those who feel that they are at a point in their lives when they "should be seriously saving already," only 6 percent report being "ahead" in their saving, whereas 55 percent report being "behind."[14] The report concludes: "The gaps between people's attitudes, intentions, and behavior are troubling and threaten increased insecurity and dissatisfaction for people when they retire. Americans are simply not doing what logic – and their own reasoning – suggests that they *should* be doing."[15] These findings echo a 1993 Luntz Webber–Merrill Lynch survey of Baby Boomers (i.e., consumers between the ages of 29 and 47).[16] Respondents were asked, "What percentage of your annual household income do you think you should save for retirement? ('Target saving')"; and then, "What percentage of your annual household income are you now saving for retirement? ('Actual saving')." The median reported gap between target and actual saving is 10 percent and the mean gap is 11.1 percent; 77.2 percent of respondents believe that they are saving too little for retirement and 70.7 percent believe that the shortfall represents at least 5 percent of income. Only 4.7 percent of respondents report that they are saving above their target rate.

Standard economic theories allow consumers to make mistakes but imply that those mistakes will not be systematic: they will tend not to lie in the same direction. By contrast, the evidence reviewed herein indicates that most consumers view themselves as saving too little. Such systematic, self-acknowledged error contradicts the standard economic model of the maximizing consumer.[17] This paper

---

[10] Barsky and others (1997). See Loewenstein and Sicherman (1991) for related evidence.

[11] Gourinchas and Parker (1997).

[12] Bernheim (1995). Bernheim points out that this calculation assumes a best-case scenario: he assumes that all savings are available for retirement, and that mortality rates, tax rates, social security benefits, medicare benefits, and health care costs do not change during the next 50 years. For a critique of his calculations, see William G. Gale, "Will the Baby Boom Be Ready for Retirement?," *Brookings Review*, Summer 1997, pp. 4–9.

[13] Farkas and Johnson (1997, p. 9).

[14] Farkas and Johnson (1997, p. 33).

[15] Farkas and Johnson (1997, p. 27).

[16] Analyzed in Bernheim (1995), from which the following numbers are taken.

[17] There is an alternative interpretation of this evidence. Consumers may report that they are behind in their saving because they would like to have more savings, ceteris paribus (i.e., they would like to have more savings, holding current consumption constant). However, this interpretation would not explain why consumers prefer rising consumption paths – holding the net present value of the consumption stream constant – but actually implement downward-sloping consumption paths.

explores an alternative model, from the psychology literature, that can make sense of the apparent conflicts between attitudes, intentions, and behavior in the domain of saving.

Research on both animal and human behavior has led psychologists to conclude that short-run discount rates are much higher than long-run rates. Such preferences are formally modeled with discount functions that are generalized hyperbolas: events τ periods away are discounted with factor $(1 + \alpha\tau)^{-\gamma/\alpha}$, with $\alpha, \gamma > 0$. This discount structure sets up a conflict between today's preferences and those that will be held in the future, implying that preferences are dynamically inconsistent. For example, from today's perspective, the discount rate between two far-off periods, t and $t + 1$, is a long-term low discount rate; however, from the time t perspective, it is a short-term high discount rate. This type of "change" in preference is reflected in many common experiences. For example, today one may desire to start an aggressive saving plan next month (i.e., to act patiently next month), but when next month rolls around, one will want to postpone any sacrifice by another month.

Hence, hyperbolic consumers will report a gap between what they feel they should save and what they actually do save. Normative saving rates will lie above actual saving rates because short-run preferences for instantaneous gratification will undermine a consumer's effort to implement long-run optimal plans. However, the hyperbolic consumer is not doomed to be an underachiever. Commitment devices such as pensions and illiquid assets can help the hyperbolic consumer commit to the patient, welfare-enhancing course of action. The availability of illiquid assets is thus a critical determinant of national saving rates as well as of consumer welfare. But, too much illiquidity can be problematic. Consumers face substantial uninsurable labor income risk and need liquid assets to smooth their consumption. Hyperbolic agents seek financial instruments that strike the right balance between commitment and flexibility.

The hyperbolic model helps us to analyze the problem of undersaving in the United States. It enables economists to assess the likely magnitude of undersaving and to identify the types of financial instruments that will alleviate the problem. For example, one goal of this paper is to evaluate tax-deferred defined contribution (DC) pension plans. We ask whether these instruments increase national saving and consumer welfare and whether they are more effective in an economy populated by consumers with problems of self-control.

To answer such questions, we develop and calibrate a numerical simulation model. We build our framework on three organizing principles. The first two echo the approach of Eric Engen, William Gale, and John Scholz, who also use a simulation model to evaluate the efficacy of tax-deferred DC pension plans.[18] First, our model adopts the standard technological assumptions of mainstream

---

[18] Engen, Gale, and Scholz (1994).

consumption models, such as those originally developed by Christopher Carroll and Angus Deaton.[19] These authors assume a realistic income process and incomplete markets: consumers cannot borrow against uncertain future labor income. Second, we include two illiquid retirement assets in a consumer's portfolio: an illiquid defined-benefit pension plan and a partially illiquid DC plan. The third assumption – the fundamental innovation in our paper – is that consumers have hyperbolic discount functions. We show that the hyperbolic assumption has important implications for both positive and normative conclusions about saving behavior. Our analysis complements the large and active empirical literature on the efficacy of tax-deferred saving instruments such as Individual Retirement Accounts (IRAs) and 401(k) plans.[20] We do not come down firmly on one side or the other but, instead, find that one's conclusions about the efficacy of these instruments depend critically on poorly identified features of consumer preferences.

Because we are the first to simulate the behavior of a hyperbolic consumer facing a realistic life-cycle decision problem, we evaluate the empirical validity of the hyperbolic model before turning to the efficacy of tax-deferred DC pension plans. We first describe the hyperbolic discount function and motivate our use of it. Then we present our simulation model. Next, we describe our calibration decisions; compare our choices with those of Engen, Gale, and Scholz; and discuss some of the theoretical problems that constrain our calibration choices. We then show that the calibrated one asset (i.e., no DC pension plan) hyperbolic economy is nearly indistinguishable from the equivalent exponential economy. However, we do identify two phenomena that differ between the calibrated one-asset hyperbolic and exponential economies: hyperbolic consumers are more likely to face binding liquidity constraints and they are expected to exhibit the missing precautionary saving effects documented by Karen Dynan.[21]

When we introduce a second asset, a DC pension modeled after a 401(k), we find that hyperbolic consumers show a greater responsiveness than exponential consumers, reflected in both larger saving effects and larger welfare effects. Our results are sensitive to the calibration of the coefficient of relative risk aversion: higher values significantly reduce the DC plan effects in both exponential and hyperbolic economies. We discuss the robustness of our findings and conclude with directions for future research.

3.1 Hyperbolic Discount Functions

There is a systematic conflict between actors' long- and short-term preferences. When two alternative rewards are far away in time, decision makers will generally act relatively patiently: for example, I prefer to take a 30-minute work break

---

[19] See Carroll (1992) and Deaton (1991).
[20] For reviews of this literature, see Hubbard and Skinner (1996); Poterba, Venti, and Wise (1995); Engen, Gale, and Scholz (1996).
[21] Dynan (1993).

in 101 days, rather than a 15-minute break in 100 days. But when both rewards are brought forward in time, decision makers reverse their preferences, becoming more impatient: I prefer to take a 15-minute break right now rather than a 30-minute break tomorrow. Evidence of such reversals has been found in experiments using a wide range of real rewards, including money, durable goods, fruit juice, sweets, video rentals, relief from noxious noise, and access to video games.[22]

A number of authors have used multiple-self frameworks to model this gap between short- and long-term preferences.[23] They highlight the conflict between the long-run desire to be patient and the short-run desire for instantaneous gratification. This conflict can be captured in a particularly parsimonious fashion by allowing discount functions to decline at a steeper rate in the short run than in the long run. The data support this intuition. When researchers use subject choices to estimate the shape of the discount function, the estimates consistently approximate generalized hyperbolas: events τ periods away are discounted with factor $(1 + \alpha\tau)^{-\gamma/\alpha}$, with α, $\gamma > 0$.[24] This observation was first made by Shin-Ho Chung and Richard Herrnstein in relation to animal behavior.[25] Their conclusions were later shown to apply to human subjects as well.[26]

Figure 3.1 graphs the standard exponential discount function (assuming the discount factor $\delta = 0.951$), the generalized hyperbolic discount function (assuming $\alpha = 25 \times 10^4$, $\gamma = 10^4$), and the quasi-hyperbolic discount function – an analytically convenient approximation of the generalized hyperbola. The quasi-hyperbolic function is a discrete time function with values $\{1, \beta\delta, \beta\delta^2, \beta\delta^3, \ldots\}$; Figure 3.1 plots the case of $\beta = 0.85$ and $\delta = 0.964$.[27] The discrete points of the quasi-hyperbolic function have been joined in Figure 3.1. When $0 < \beta < 1$, the quasi-hyperbolic discount structure mimics the qualitative properties of the

[22] See, for example, Solnick and others (1980); Navarick (1982); Millar and Navarick (1984); King and Logue (1987); Kirby and Herrnstein (1995); Kirby and Marakovic (1995, 1996); Kirby (1997); Read and others (1998). For a partisan review of this literature, see Ainslie (1992); for a critique, see Mulligan (1997).

[23] See, for example, Thaler and Shefrin (1981); Schelling (1984); Loewenstein and Prelec (1992); Hoch and Loewenstein (1991); Akerlof (1991); Ainslie (1992); Laibson (1994, 1996, 1997a); O'Donoghue and Rabin (1997a, 1997b).

[24] See Loewenstein and Prelec (1992) for an axiomatic derivation of this discount function.

[25] Chung and Herrnstein (1967) claim that the appropriate discount function is an exact hyperbola: events τ periods away are given a weight that is directly proportional to $1/\tau$. This discount function describes well-defined preferences as long as time-dated goods are evaluated strictly before the good is actually consumed. The exact hyperbola generates the same discount rates as the generalized hyperbola when $\alpha = \gamma \to \infty$.

[26] See Ainslie (1992) for a survey.

[27] This discount function was first analyzed by Phelps and Pollak (1968). However, their application is one of imperfect intergenerational altruism, and the discount factors apply to nonoverlapping generations of a dynasty. Following Laibson (1997a), we apply this discount function to an intrapersonal problem and assume that the horizon is finite. Phelps and Pollak assume an infinite horizon, which admits a continuum of equilibria; see Laibson (1994).

Value of discount function

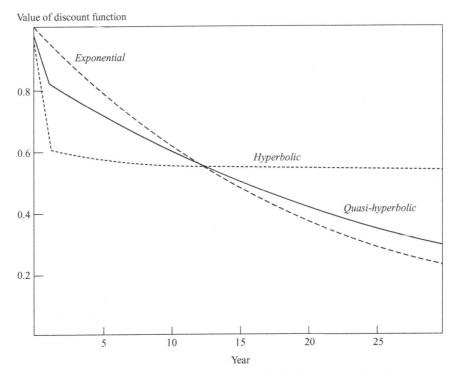

Figure 3.1. Exponential, Hyperbolic, and Quasi-Hyperbolic Discount Functions[a]
[a] Figure plots three discount functions: exponential: δ^τ, with $\delta = 0.951$ and τ representing the year; hyperbolic: $(1 + \alpha\tau)^{-\gamma/\alpha}$, with $\alpha = 25 \times 10^4$ and $\gamma = 10^4$; and quasi-hyperbolic: $\{1, \beta\delta, \beta\delta^2, \beta\delta^3 \ldots\}$, with $\beta = 0.85$ and $\delta = 0.964$.

hyperbolic discount function, while maintaining most of the analytical tractability of the exponential discount function. We return to this point later.

Hyperbolic discount functions imply discount rates that decline as the discounted event is moved farther away in time. Events in the near future are discounted at a higher implicit discount rate than events in the distant future. Given a discount function, $f(\tau)$, the instantaneous discount rate τ periods in the future is defined as

$$-\frac{f'(\tau)}{f(\tau)}$$

Hence, an exponential discount function, δ^τ, is characterized by a constant discount rate, $\ln(1/\delta)$, while the generalized hyperbolic discount function is characterized by an instantaneous discount rate that falls as τ rises:

$$\frac{\gamma}{1 + \alpha\tau}$$

Psychologists and economists believe that such declining discount rates, even if unanticipated, are important in generating problems of self-regulation.[28]

These problems arise because hyperbolic discount functions induce dynamically inconsistent preferences. From the perspective of period 0, the relevant discount rate for tradeoffs in period t is $\gamma/(1 + \alpha t)$. However, from the perspective of period t, the relevant discount rate for tradeoffs at period t is $\gamma/(1 + \alpha \cdot 0)$, which is greater than $\gamma/(1 + \alpha t)$. Hence, an individual's preferences at period 0 differ from the same individual's preferences at period t. Self 0 prefers patient tradeoffs at period t, but self t disagrees. In this sense, the hyperbolic consumer is involved in a decision that sets up an intrapersonal strategic struggle. Early selves would like to commit later selves to honor the preferences of those early selves; however, later selves do their best to maximize their own interests. Economists have modeled this situation as an intrapersonal game played among the consumer's temporally situated selves.

Hyperbolic discount functions recently have been used to explain a wide range of anomalous economic choices, including procrastination, deadlines, drug addiction, retirement timing, and undersaving.[29] But, despite the new developments in this literature, hyperbolic models are still much cruder than their exponential analogs. Intrapersonal games involve much greater analytic complexity than analogous nonstrategic intertemporal maximization, and this has hindered the development of rich and, hence, realistic hyperbolic analysis. This paper partly closes the gap by introducing a hyperbolic model whose richness matches contemporary exponential models of consumption over the life-cycle. Our approach represents a behavioral alternative that can be calibrated, and its quantitative empirical predictions can be compared directly with those of the leading exponential consumption models. The model also can generate quantitative forecasts and welfare analysis for policy proposals.

3.2 The Model

In the remainder of this paper, we develop and evaluate a simulation model of the behavior of hyperbolic consumers. Simulations are a critical tool for forecasting the long-term effects of newly implemented policies and for evaluating the short- and long-term effects of untested policy proposals. Our simulation approach has a major shortcoming that we wish to flag in advance: we adopt the standard economic assumption of unlimited sophistication in problem solving. The consumers in our model solve perfectly a complex backward induction problem when making choices about consumption and asset allocation.

---

[28] See Ainslie (1975, 1986, 1992); Prelec (1989); Loewenstein and Prelec (1992); O'Donoghue and Rabin (1997a, 1997b).

[29] See, for example, Akerlof (1991); Barro (1997); Diamond and Köszegi (1998); Laibson (1994, 1996, 1997a); O'Donoghue and Rabin (1997a, 1997b).

We chose this approach for two reasons. First, the assumption of perfect rationality is the natural benchmark for an economist. We make this assumption not because it necessarily aptly describes consumer behavior but, rather, because it represents the starting point for all economic analysis. Second, even if one wanted to weaken assumptions about consumer sophistication, it is not clear how to do so in a parsimonious and realistic fashion. Although economists and psychologists have a great deal of evidence that consumers are not perfectly rational, they do not necessarily know what alternative to rationality should be adopted. There are no well-developed bounded rationality models applicable to the problem of life-cycle saving.[30]

We are sympathetic to one alternative, first proposed by Robert Strotz and more recently studied by George Akerlof and Edward O'Donoghue and Matthew Rabin.[31] These authors suggest that decision makers with dynamically inconsistent preferences make current choices under the false belief that later selves will act in the interests of the current self. This modeling approach assumes that consumers do not foresee that they will hit the snooze button on their alarm clocks, despite the fact that they have consistently done so in the past. O'Donoghue and Rabin call such consumers naifs. The naif assumption strikes us as extreme and perhaps no more believable than the assumption of perfect sophistication. Both naifs and sophisticates are assumed to solve perfectly a backward induction problem: the naifs with rosy beliefs about the good behavior of future selves ("I will not procrastinate on the next project") and the sophisticates with correct beliefs ("I always procrastinate"). Neither approach seems precisely correct to us, but we focus on the sophisticate model.[32]

3.2.1 An Individual's Consumption Problem

Taking our cue from the contemporary consumption literature, we explicitly model the rich array of constraints and stochastic income events that consumers face. Such rich models are not analytically tractable and, therefore, they require numerical analysis. Our simulation framework follows most closely the work of Engen, Gale, and Scholz; we highlight the assumptions that distinguish our analysis from theirs. We divide the presentation of the model into seven domains: demographics, income, bequests, asset allocation, taxes, preferences, and equilibrium.

---

[30] We are keenly interested in the recent developments in the reinforcement learning literature; for example, Erev and Roth (1998); Camerer and Ho (1997). However, such reinforcement models are difficult to apply to the analysis of saving decisions because it is not clear why, or even if, saving decisions are rewarding in the short run. Perhaps the lack of short- and medium-run reinforcement provides an explanation for undersaving.

[31] Strotz (1956); Akerlof (1991); O'Donoghue and Rabin (1997a, 1997b).

[32] Had we chosen the naif model, we would probably have found smaller effects of DC plans for hyperbolic consumers. Naifs do not value the commitment properties of DC plans because they think that future selves will act in the interest of the current self.

3.2.1.1 Demographics

The economy is populated by consumers who face a time-varying, exogenous hazard rate of survival s_t, where t indexes age. Consumers live for a maximum of $T+N$ periods, where T and N are exogenous variables that represent the maximum lengths of preretirement life and retirement, respectively. If a consumer is alive at age $20 \leq t \leq T$, that consumer is in the workforce. If a consumer is alive at age $T < t \leq T + N$, that consumer is retired. We assume that economic life begins at 20 and do not model consumption decisions before this age.

We divide our population into three educational categories: consumers without a high school diploma, high school graduates, and college graduates. We take education to be exogenous and assign a different preretirement life (T), retirement duration (N), labor income process, and bequest process to each category.

3.2.1.2 Labor Income

Labor effort is supplied inelastically. Let Y_t represent labor income when $20 \leq t \leq T$, and defined-benefit pension income when $T < t \leq T + N$. Let $y_t \equiv \ln(Y_t)$. We refer to y_t as labor income, regardless of whether it is a preretirement wage payment or a postretirement defined-benefit pension payment. During working life,

$$y_t = f^W(t) + u_t^W \tag{3.1}$$

where $f^W(t)$ is a cubic polynomial in age, $u_t^W = \alpha u_{t-1}^W + \epsilon_t^W$, and ϵ_t^W is normally distributed, $N(0, \sigma_W^2)$. During retirement,

$$y_t = f^R(t) + u_t^R \tag{3.2}$$

where $f^R(t)$ is linear in age and u_t^R is distributed $N(0, \sigma_R^2)$. The elements of the income process – $f^W(\cdot)$, α, σ_W, $f^R(\cdot)$, and σ_R – vary across educational categories.

Except for the stochastic component of retirement income, our labor income process replicates that used by Glenn Hubbard, Jonathan Skinner, and Stephen Zeldes, and Engen, Gale, and Scholz.[33] We choose not to use the integrated labor income process adopted by Carroll because we cannot take advantage of his technique of eliminating a state variable.[34] We are prevented from doing so by the fact that our problem is not scalable, because we consider simulations with investment-capped tax-deferred assets – for example, IRAs or 401(k)s – and fixed tax brackets.

3.2.1.3 Bequests

Consumers receive bequests throughout their lives. We would have liked to make bequests a state variable but, to keep the model computationally tractable (the model already has three state variables: labor income, liquid assets, and assets in a DC pension plan), we instead assume that bequests at time t are independent

---

[33] Hubbard, Skinner, and Zeldes (1995); Engen, Gale, and Scholz (1994).
[34] Carroll (1992).

of the history of bequests. We believe that this assumption creates relatively little distortion in our results because for the typical real-world consumer, the timing and magnitudes of bequests are difficult to predict far in advance, and the number of bequests received over a lifetime should be modeled as a stochastic variable. In an ideal model, the probability of bequest realizations would be negatively autocorrelated.

We assume that the hazard rate of receiving a bequest depends solely on the age of the consumer and not on the prior history of bequests:

$$p(t) = \text{Prob}(q < h(t) \mid q \sim N(0, \sigma^2)) \tag{3.3}$$

where $h(\cdot)$ is a cubic polynomial. This is a standard probit formulation. Conditional on receiving a bequest, the natural logarithm of the value of the bequest, $\ln(B_t) \equiv b(t)$, is given by

$$b(t) = g(t) + \eta_t \tag{3.4}$$

where $g(t)$ is a cubic polynomial in age, and η_t is distributed $N(0, \sigma_B^2)$. The polynomials $h(\cdot)$ and $g(\cdot)$ vary across educational categories.

Our bequest process contrasts with that of Engen, Gale, and Scholz, who assume deterministic and homogeneous bequests. In their model, all 45-year-olds receive identical bequests, regardless of educational level, and consumers at all other ages receive no bequests.

3.2.1.4 Assets and the Dynamic Budget Constraint

We have discussed the income flows associated with defined-benefit pensions; those flows appear in Y_t. We now consider DC pensions and regular liquid assets. We focus on the special case in which the DC pension is a stylized version of an IRA or a 401(k).

Let X_t represent liquid asset holdings at age t. Let Z_t represent the DC plan. The dynamic budget constraint is given by

$$X_{t+1} + Z_{t+1} = R(X_t + Z_t + Y_t + M_t - C_t - T_t + B_{t+1}) \tag{3.5}$$

where R is the gross pretax interest rate, $1 + r$; B_{t+1} is bequests, received on January 1 of year $t + 1$; Y_t is labor income, received on December 31 of year t; M_t is the employer-matching contribution to the DC plan, received on December 31 of year t; C_t is consumption, chosen on December 31 of year t; and T_t is taxes, including penalties for preretirement withdrawals from the DC plan, chosen on December 31 of year t.

Let I_t represent the employee contribution to the DC plan. Thus, the dynamic budget constraint can be expressed

$$X_{t+1} + Z_{t+1} = R[X_t + (Z_t + I_t + M_t) + Y_t - I_t - C_t - T_t + B_{t+1}] \tag{3.6}$$

where $Z_{t+1} = R(Z_t + I_t + M_t)$.

Our assumptions about the DC plan, including the matching provisions, are motivated by existing 401(k) regulations and are summarized as follows:

- $I_t \leq \$10,000$.
- If $I_t \leq 0$, then $M_t = 0$.
- If $I_t > 0$, then $M_t = \min\{\phi I_t, \phi \psi Y_t\}$.
- If $I_t < 0$ and $t < 60$, then the consumer pays a tax penalty of ωI_t.
- If $I_t < 0$, then the consumer declares additional taxable income of I_t.
- $I_t \leq 0$ if $t > T$.

In words, these rules imply that the employee contribution must be less than or equal to \$10,000; if the employee contribution is negative, matching does not occur; if the employee contribution is positive, matching is equal to ϕ times the employee contribution, capping out at $\phi \psi Y_t$; if the employee withdraws money from the 401(k) before age 60, then the employee pays a tax penalty of 100ω percent of the withdrawal; withdrawals from the 401(k) count as taxable income; and no further contributions to the 401(k) are allowed after retirement.[35]

We assume that employers offset their match payments with a reduction in pre-retirement labor income payments. This reduction applies to all workers, whether or not they contribute to the DC plan. Specifically, we reduce all preretirement labor income payments by a fixed percentage, Λ, such that match payments plus labor income payments in the new steady state with the DC plan are equal to labor income payments in the original steady state with no DC plan. We perform this calculation separately for each educational group. Note that the size of the adjustment depends on the saving decisions of consumers, so that we have to calculate a different adjustment factor for each simulation. Finding Λ requires numerically solving a fixed point problem: Λ has to be adjusted to offset the level of realized match payments, and the equilibrium level of realized match payments depends on the value of Λ.

Following Engen, Gale, and Scholz, we assume that in all periods, both the X assets and the Z assets are bounded below by zero:

$$X_t \geq 0$$
$$Z_t \geq 0$$

These assumptions do not preclude borrowing against X collateral to invest in a DC plan because the collateral and the debt are both in the X account. However, we rule out borrowing that uses the Z asset as collateral. Although many 401(k) plans do have facilities for this type of borrowing, they are generally highly restrictive, as discussed later.

---

[35] The assumption about the employee contribution cap may be too generous, as many workers are constrained by limits set by the firm below the IRS limit of approximately \$10,000.

3.2.1.5 Taxes

Consumers face a progressive tax structure. Taxable income is

$$Y_t - I_t + \left(\frac{r}{R}\right) X_t$$

which captures the tax-deductible nature of contributions to the DC plan. Recall that R and r are the gross and net interest rates, respectively.

3.2.1.6 Preferences

The total utility of self t is given by

$$U_t = u(C_t) + \beta \sum_{i=1}^{T+N-t} \delta^i \left(\prod_{j=1}^{i} s_{t+j}\right) u\left(C_{t+i}\right)$$

where $u(\cdot)$ is an isoelastic utility function with coefficient of relative risk aversion ρ. Recall that s_t is the probability of surviving to age t conditional on being alive at age $t - 1$. These preferences imply no bequest motive and, hence, realized bequests are purely accidental.[36]

To develop an intuition for the parameters β and δ, consider the special case in which s_t is equal to unity for all t. Self t's preferences reduce to

$$U_t = u(C_t) + \beta \sum_{i=1}^{T+N-t} \delta^i u(C_{t+i})$$

The discount function is the quasi-hyperbolic function described earlier. Note that the discount factor between adjacent periods n and $n + 1$ represents the weight placed on utils at time $n + 1$ relative to the weight placed on utils at time n. From the perspective of self t, the discount factor between periods t and $t + 1$ is $\beta\delta$, but the discount factor that applies between any two later periods is δ. Because we take β to be less than one, this implies a short-term discount rate greater than the long-term discount rate.

Later selves will not validate these preferences. Continuing to assume 100 percent survival, the total utility of self $t + 1$ is given by

$$U_{t+1} = u(C_{t+1}) + \beta \sum_{i=1}^{T+N-(t+1)} \delta^i u(C_{t+1+i})$$

From the perspective of self $t + 1$, $\beta\delta$ is the relevant discount factor between periods $t + 1$ and $t + 2$. Hence, selves t and $t + 1$ disagree about the desired level of patience at time $t + 1$.

---

[36] In our model, bequest receipts are exogenously specified. We assume that the difference between exogenous bequest receipts and endogenous accidental bequests reflects estate taxes. Note that consumers would leave no accidental bequests if a sufficiently fair annuity market existed.

When the survival hazard rates are included, this discount structure is only slightly altered. From the perspective of self t, the discount factor at time $t+1$ is δs_{t+1}; from self $t+2$'s perspective, it is $\beta\delta s_{t+2}$.

3.2.1.7 Equilibrium

The dynamic inconsistency in preferences implies that the consumption problem cannot be treated as a straightforward dynamic optimization problem. Late selves will not implement the policies that are optimal from the perspective of early selves. Following the work of Strotz, we model consumption choices as an intra-personal game.[37] Selves $\{20, 21, \ldots, T+N-1, T+N\}$ are the players. Taking the strategies of other selves as given, self t picks a strategy for time t that is optimal from its own perspective. This strategy is a mapping from the state variables, $\{t, X, Z, Y\}$, to $\{C, X, Z\}$. An equilibrium is a fixed point in the strategy space, such that all strategies are optimal given the strategies of the other players. We restrict our focus to Markov equilibria and solve for the equilibrium strategies using a numerically implemented backward induction algorithm.

Our choice of the quasi-hyperbolic discount function simplifies the induction algorithm. Let $V_{t,\,t+1}$ represent the time $t+1$ continuation payoff function of self t. Thus, the objective function of self t is

$$u(C_t) + \beta\delta s_{t+1} E_t[V_{t,t+1}(X_{t+1},\ Z_{t+1},\ Y_{t+1})] \qquad (3.7)$$

Self t chooses C_t to maximize this expression. The time t continuation payoff function of self $t-1$ can be calculated as

$$V_{t-1,t}(X_t,\ Z_t,\ Y_t) = u(C_t) + \delta s_{t+1} E_t[V_{t,t+1}(X_{t+1},\ Z_{t+1},\ Y_{t+1})] \qquad (3.8)$$

where C_t is the consumption chosen by self t. The induction continues in this way. The dynamic inconsistency in preferences is evident from the fact that a β term appears in Equation 3.7, reflecting the discount factor of self t between periods t and $t+1$, but does not appear in Equation 3.8 because self $t-1$ does not use the β factor to discount between periods t and $t+1$.

Equations 3.7 and 3.8 jointly define a functional equation that is not a contraction mapping. Hence, the standard dynamic programming results do not apply to this problem. Specifically, V does not inherit concavity from u, the objective function is not single peaked, and the policy functions are, in general, discontinuous and nonmonotonic.[38] We adopt a numerically efficient solution algorithm, based on local grid searches, which iterates our functional equation in the presence of these nonstandard properties. We document some of the nonstandard properties later.

---

[37] Strotz (1956).
[38] See Laibson (1997b).

3.3 Calibration

In this section, we discuss our calibration decisions, except for the choice of preference parameters. Most of this analysis is standard, and those who desire instantaneous gratification may jump to the discussion of preference parameter calibration without loss of continuity.

3.3.0.1 Demographics

In our model, consumers live for a maximum of 90 years (T + N), although they do not enter the workforce or make economically meaningful decisions until age 20. The conditional hazard rates of survival are taken from the life tables of the U.S. National Center for Health Statistics, which report the probability of living to age $t + 1$, conditional on having lived to age t.[39] This one-year survival probability is close to 1 through age 70, drops to 96.3 percent by age 80, and to 67.6 percent by age 89.

Following Engen, Gale, and Scholz, we use survival rates for a single individual, even though the consumers in our model are, in fact, abstractions of multiperson households. Conceptually, our model assumes that households are of fixed size, and that all members of the household die when the head dies. We chose not to model the mortality of both spouses to avoid an additional state variable.[40]

We calculate educational group population weights from the Michigan Panel Study of Income Dynamics (PSID), and replicate the assumption of Engen, Gale, and Scholz that these weights are approximately 0.25 for high school dropouts, 0.50 for high school graduates, and 0.25 for college graduates.

3.3.0.2 Labor and Pension Income

We define income as pretax nonasset income. We include labor income and transfers such as aid to families with dependent children, supplemental security income, workers' compensation, and unemployment insurance. Our definition is, therefore, broader than that of Engen and Gale, who use only labor earnings, or that of Hubbard, Skinner, and Zeldes, who add only unemployment insurance payments to labor income.[41]

The sample of households is taken from the PSID. We use the family files for the interview years between 1980 and 1992. We exclude all households where the

---

[39] U.S. National Center for Health Statistics (1994).

[40] Our approach engenders two subtle biases in opposite directions. On the one hand, it may yield too much simulated retirement saving because the model implicitly rules out insurance effects that arise when spouses have independent mortality outcomes; an n-person marriage creates a partial annuity that becomes perfect as n goes to infinity. On the other hand, our mortality assumption may imply too little simulated retirement saving because widows and widowers have expenses that fell by less than 50 percent when their spouses died.

[41] Engen and Gale (1993); Hubbard, Skinner, and Zeldes (1994, 1995).

head is younger than 20 years of age, that report annual income of less than $1,000 (in 1990 dollars, deflated by the Consumer Price Index for urban consumers), or that have any crucial variable missing.[42] To calculate preretirement income, we follow the approach of Bernheim, Skinner, and Steven Weinberg, who define a year as preretirement if any household member works 1,500 hours or more in that or any subsequent year.[43] A household is retired if no member works more than 500 hours in the current year or in any year in the future.[44]

We estimate the regression equation

$$y_{it} = \alpha_1 (FS)_{it} + (1, \text{ age, age}^2, \text{ age}^3)\alpha_2 + \alpha_3 (TE)_{it}$$
$$+ (\text{cohort dummies})\alpha_4 + \xi_{it} \tag{3.9}$$

by weighted least squares, using the PSID population weights. We estimate the equation twice, once for households in the labor force and once for retired households. Log income of individual i at time t is determined by a family size effect $(FS)_{it}$, a polynomial in age, a time effect $(TE)_{it}$, and a cohort effect. We specify the polynomial as a cubic for the preretirement regression and linear for the postretirement regression. Following Pierre-Olivier Gourinchas and Jonathan Parker, and to circumvent the problem that age, time, and birth year are perfectly correlated, we assume that the time effect is related to the business cycle and can be proxied by the unemployment rate.[45] We use the unemployment rate in the household's state of residence, taken from the World Wide Web page of the Bureau of Labor Statistics. Our cohort effects control for birth year, to account for permanent differences in productivity that affect cohorts in different ways.[46] We use five-year age cohorts, the oldest born in the period 1910–14 and the youngest born in 1970–74. Table 3.1 reports the income regressions for each educational group.

We calculate f^W and f^R – the polynomials in the model of the previous section – by setting the cohort, family size, and unemployment effects equal to the sample means. This allows us to recover the age-specific effect for a household that has a constant size, experiences no business cycle effects, and has a constant cohort effect over the life-cycle.[47] Figure 3.2 plots the exponentiated values of f^W and f^R for the three educational categories.

To study the stochastic component of preretirement nonasset household income, we exploit the panel dimension of the PSID. We model the unexplained part of measured nonasset income (ξ_{it}) as the sum of an individual fixed effect, a first-order autoregressive process (y_{it}^W), and a purely transitory shock (v_{it}), which

---

[42] We believe that reported income of less than $1,000 is likely to reflect a coding or reporting error. Recall that by our definition, income includes all government transfers.

[43] Bernheim, Skinner, and Weinberg (1997).

[44] Household-years that meet neither of these conditions are dropped from the regression analysis.

[45] Gourinchas and Parker (1997).

[46] See Attanasio and Weber (1993) for a discussion of cohort effects.

[47] Our model precludes variation in household size over the life-cycle. If we were to include family size effects, the simulations would generate lower saving among young households.

Table 3.1. *Estimated age-income profiles from regressions*[a]

Independent variable	High school dropouts	High school graduates	College graduates
Labor force households[b]			
Age	0.059	0.058	0.224
	(0.033)	(0.018)	(0.026)
Age^2/100	−0.034	−0.017	−0.388
	(0.079)	(0.044)	(0.061)
Age^3/10,000	−0.030	−0.055	0.211
	(0.061)	(0.034)	(0.045)
Other effects[c]	8.557	8.835	6.776
Retired households[d]			
Age	−0.007	−0.008	−0.034
	(0.003)	(0.004)	(0.009)
Other effects[c]	9.673	10.158	12.399

[a] Dependent variable is the natural log of nonasset household income. Panel spans 1980–92. Standard errors are in parentheses.

[b] A household is in the labor force if any member works 1,500 hours in the current year or in any future year.

[c] Includes a constant plus the effects of cohort dummies, family size, and the unemployment rate in the household's state of residence, evaluated with each regressor set equal to its sample mean.

[d] A household is retired if no member works more than 500 hours in the current year or in any future year.

Source: Authors' calculations based on data from the Michigan Panel Study of Income Dynamics (PSID), 1980–92.

represents measurement error:

$$\xi_{it} = \vartheta_i + u_{it}^W + v_{it} = \vartheta_i + \alpha u_{i,t-1}^W + \epsilon_{it}^W + v_{it}$$

The individual fixed effect is included to account for permanent differences in income that are not completely captured by the educational categories, such as differences in human capital and earning ability. It is necessary to include the individual effect in this equation to correctly estimate the persistence of income shocks. However, we set it equal to zero in our actual simulations. This latter decision is dictated by computational considerations because our problem is not scalable and would have to be solved for every value of the fixed effect.

Let σ_v^2 be the variance of the transitory shock v, and let σ_W^2 be the variance of ϵ^W. Also, let $Cov_k \equiv E(\Delta\xi_t \Delta\xi_{t-k})$ represent the theoretical autocovariances of $\Delta\xi$. Then

$$Cov_0 = 2\sigma_W^2/(1+\alpha) + 2\sigma_v^2$$
$$Cov_1 = -\sigma_W^2(1-\alpha)/(1+\alpha) - \sigma_v^2$$
$$\vdots$$
$$Cov_d = -\sigma_W^2\alpha^{d-1}(1-\alpha)/(1+\alpha)$$

Income (thousands of 1990 dollars)

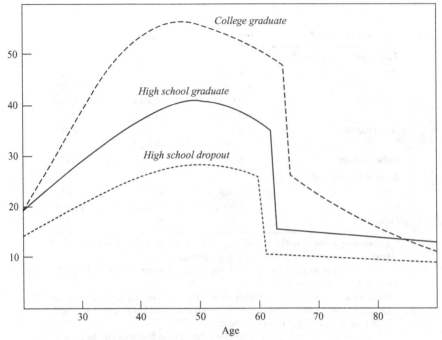

Figure 3.2. Estimated Age-Income Profiles[a]
[a] Figure plots estimated nonasset household income, by age and educational group. Values are calculated from a regression of the natural log of income on a cubic polynomial in age, cohort dummies, family size, and the unemployment rate in the household's state of residence. Figure plots age effects, with other regressors set equal to their means. See Table 3.1 for details.
Source: See Table 3.1.

We estimate the parameters σ^2_W, σ^2_ν, and α using weighted generalized method of moments (GMM), minimizing the distance between the theoretical and empirical first 12 autocovariances. The estimated parameters are presented in Table 3.2. Because we include an individual fixed effect (and possibly also because of the different definition of income), these estimated processes are much less persistent than those estimated by Hubbard, Skinner, and Zeldes, and a little less persistent than that used by Engen, Gale, and Scholz.[48] To calibrate the stochastic component of postretirement income, we set $\sigma^2_R = 0.05$, a value somewhat lower than that of σ^2_W. Most authors do not assume any stochastic component in pension income. We do so for technical reasons: income uncertainty reduces behavioral pathologies – such as nonmonotonicities and discontinuities in the consumption function – in dynamic games.[49]

---

[48] Hubbard, Skinner, and Zeldes (1994); Engen, Gale, and Scholz (1994).
[49] See Laibson (1997b).

Table 3.2. *Estimated age-income process parameters for households in the labor force*[a]

Parameter	High school dropouts	High school graduates	College graduates
α	0.511	0.688	0.686
	(0.013)	(0.004)	(0.009)
Variance of ϵ	0.073	0.052	0.059
	(0.012)	(0.005)	(0.005)
Variance of υ	0.043	0.024	0.013
	(0.008)	(0.003)	(0.007)

[a] A household is in the labor force if any member works 1,500 hours in the current year or in any future year. Characteristics are from the following panel regression model:

$$y_{it} = \alpha_1(FS)_{it} + (1,\ age,\ age^2,\ age^3)\alpha_2 + \alpha_3(TE)_{it} + (\text{cohort dummies})\alpha_4 + \zeta_{it}$$

$$\xi_{it} = \zeta_i + U_{it} + \upsilon_{it} = \zeta_i + \alpha U_{i,t-1} + \upsilon_{i,t}$$

where y_{it} is the natural log of nonasset income of household i in year t, $(FS)_{it}$ is a family-size effect, $(TE)_{it}$ is a time effect given by the unemployment rate in the household's home state, and ζ_{it} is a disturbance term. The coefficient α and the variances of ϵ and υ are estimated using the GMM. Standard errors are in parentheses.
Source: Authors' calculations based on data from the PSID, 1980–92.

To calculate the typical retirement age by educational group, we look at PSID households that experienced the transition to retirement during the sample period. We record the age of each household head in the last year when any member of the household worked more than 500 hours. We then calculate the mean of these retirement ages within each educational group. Finally, we assume that each of the simulated households retires at the mean age for its respective educational group. For households whose head did not graduate from high school, the simulated retirement age is 61; for those with high school graduate and college graduate heads, the mean ages are 63 and 65, respectively.

Given our income estimates, the implicit mean replacement rates at retirement are 41 percent for the low-education group, 45 percent for high school graduates, and 55 percent for college graduates (or relative to the average of the highest three years' earnings while in the labor force: 38, 38, and 47 percent, respectively). The replacement rates at retirement are, therefore, higher for the college-educated group, contrary to the calibration of Engen, Gale, and Scholz. However, as real retirement income falls faster for this group, the ratio of average retirement income to the average of the highest three years' earnings is smaller for highly educated households: 31 percent compared with 41 percent for the other educational categories.

3.3.0.3 Bequests
To estimate the age distribution of inheritances, we use data from the 1984 PSID. In that year, respondents were asked whether they had received a bequest during the past five years. However, the PSID does not contain information on the source of

Table 3.3. *Estimated age-bequest profiles from regressions*

Independent variable	Dependent variable	
	Probability of bequest[a]	Log size of bequest[b]
Age	−0.056	0.379
	(0.058)	(0.195)
Age^2/100	0.176	−0.673
	(0.124)	(0.415)
Age^3/10,000	−0.134	0.393
	(0.084)	(0.280)
Dummy variables		
High school dropout	−0.698	2.217
	(0.091)	(2.893)
High school graduate	−0375	2.737
	(0.071)	(2.875)
College graduate		2.939
		(2.872)
Constant	−0.845	
	(0.852)	
Summary statistic		
Variance of error term		0.09

[a] Coefficients from a probit model. Dependent variable is equal to 1 if the household received at least one bequest during 1980–84, and to zero otherwise. Spousal bequests are excluded. Standard errors are in parentheses.
[b] Dependent variable is the natural log of bequests received by the household during 1980–84. Panel is restricted to observations in which a positive bequest occurs. Households whose head is older than 80 years and spousal bequests are excluded. Standard errors are in parentheses.
Source: Authors' calculations based on data from the PSID, 1984.

bequests. To correct for intrahousehold bequests, we set to zero the inheritances received by households for which the marital status of the head changed from married to widowed over the previous seven years.[50]

We run a probit regression to estimate age-dependent probabilities of receiving a bequest. The independent variables are a third-degree polynomial in age, a constant, and two educational dummy variables. We assume that the age polynomial is the same for each of the three educational groups but allow for different means. We do not estimate a separate regression for each group because there are very few observations for some groups at certain ages. The regression results are reported in Table 3.3, and the probabilities of receiving a bequest are plotted in Figure 3.3. Our estimation procedure yields the expected hump-shaped pattern of bequests, but the peak probabilities occur at age 67, suggesting that the parents

---

[50] Note that this method eliminates spousal bequests irrespective of whether the decedent was formerly the head of the household. The correction eliminates 60 of the 462 reported bequests.

Probability

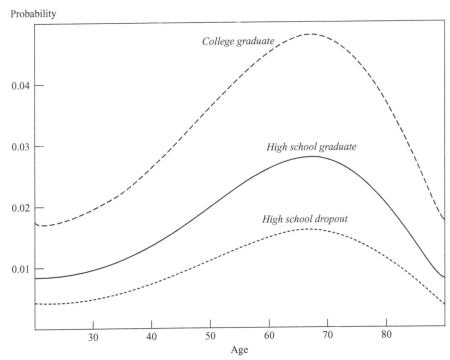

Figure 3.3. Estimated Probability of Receiving a Bequest, by Age[a]
[a] Figure plots the probability of receiving a bequest, by age and educational group. Values are calculated from a probit regression on a cubic polynomial in age and educational dummies; see Table 3.3 for details.
Source: See Table 3.3.

of these recipients die in their 90s. This puzzle is mitigated by the fact that, in general, bequests are not received until both parents have died.

We also estimate the age profile of bequest magnitudes (conditional on having received a bequest). To do so, we restrict the sample to households with positive bequests. We estimate a regression for the natural logarithm of bequests on education dummies and a third-degree polynomial in age. Figure 3.4 plots the exponentiation of this polynomial, and Table 3.3 also reports the associated regression results, including the estimated variance of the disturbance term that is used to calibrate σ_B^2. The bequest magnitudes show a sharp rise late in life, which is driven by the actual reported bequests of the elderly and is not due to an endpoint polynomial effect.[51]

---

[51] We restrict our bequest magnitude regression to households whose head is aged 80 or younger, and then extrapolate the curve out through age 90. When we ran the regression for the complete population, the rapid rise in the bequest magnitude function late in life was even more dramatic. There is a small number of very old households that report receiving very large bequests.

Bequest (thousands of 1990 dollars)

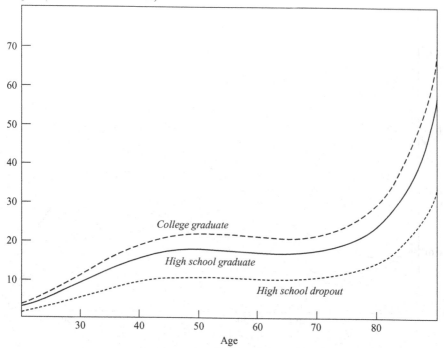

Figure 3.4. Estimated Age-Bequest Profiles[a]

[a] Figure plots, by age and educational group, the magnitude of bequests received, conditional on receiving a positive bequest. Values are calculated from a regression of the natural log of bequests on a cubic polynomial in age and educational dummies; see Table 3.3 for details. *Source:* See Table 3.3.

3.3.0.4 Taxes

We assume a progressive tax structure with marginal tax rates of 15 percent for income up to $41,200; 28 percent for income between $41,200 and $99,600; and 31 percent for income above $99,600. We also allow for a standard deduction of $6,900 and a personal exemption of $2,650. Contributions to the DC pension are tax-deductible, and withdrawals are taxed at the relevant marginal tax rate. This structure mimics the 1997 federal tax rates for married couples filing jointly, except that we excluded the 36 and 39.6 percent tax brackets because almost none of our simulated consumers receives enough income to qualify for these higher brackets.[52]

3.3.0.5 Assets and the Dynamic Budget Constraint

We set the value of the pretax real interest rate equal to 5 percent, consistent with Engen, Gale, and Scholz. Furthermore, we assume that employers match

---

[52] The 36 percent bracket starts at an income level of $151,750.

50 percent of DC plan contributions up to the first 6 percent of pay (i.e., $\phi = 0.5$, $\psi = 0.06$). This is, by far, the most common matching arrangement for 401(k) plans and is reported by 21 percent of the firms in a survey of such plans conducted by Hewitt Associates.[53] We also consider the no-match case (i.e., $\phi = 0$).

3.4 Preference Parameters

In this section, we describe our choice of preference parameters.

3.4.1 Coefficient of Relative Risk Aversion

We adopt a utility function with a constant coefficient of relative risk aversion. In the benchmark calibration, we set the coefficient of relative risk aversion, ρ, equal to 1 (log utility). To support this choice, we offer four observations. First, estimation procedures that do not require linearization or aggregation of the Euler equation have yielded estimated values below one for the coefficient of relative risk aversion. Gourinchas and Parker, for example, report a point estimate of 0.5.[54]

Second, estimation procedures that are based on first-order linearization of the Euler equation and focus on consumers with high levels of liquid wealth – effectively controlling for second-order terms – have yielded values near 1 for the coefficient of relative risk aversion. For example, Zeldes runs separate analyses for consumers who are liquidity constrained and those who are not.[55] Assuming that the second-order terms in the Euler equation are small for the unconstrained consumers, one can calculate estimates of the coefficient of relative risk aversion for those consumers: Zeldes's point estimates imply values that lie between 0.7 and 2.3. John Shea also splits his sample into constrained and unconstrained consumers, and his point estimates from the high-wealth consumers imply values that lie between 0.2 and 0.4.[56] Neither author's results are estimated with high precision, however.[57]

Third, estimation procedures that are based on linearization of the Euler equation but do not control for second-order terms yield highly mixed results.[58] Fourth,

[53] Hewitt Associates (1997).

[54] Gourinchas and Parker (1997). Hansen and Singleton (1982) use a GMM framework to estimate ρ with aggregate data. They report point estimates between 0.6 and 1, but we are skeptical of the representative agent methodology that they use.

[55] Zeldes (1989).

[56] Shea (1995).

[57] We are skeptical of the analyses of Zeldes and Shea because they identify variation in the interest rate by using marginal tax rates. This technique implicitly assumes that the aftertax rate of return falls with income – a hypothesis that our accountants do not accept.

[58] Hall's (1988) results imply that the measured elasticity of intertemporal substitution is probably between 0 and 0.2. This finding is supported by Campbell and Mankiw (1989). But it is contradicted by Mankiw, Rotemberg, and Summers (1985), who find that the measured elasticity of intertemporal substitution is greater than unity, and by Beaudry and van Wincoop (1996), who find that it is equal to unity. Note that in a world of complete markets, the measured elasticity of intertemporal substitution is equal to the inverse of the coefficient of relative risk aversion.

such estimation procedures, which rely on variation in the aftertax interest rate to measure the elasticity of intertemporal substitution, do not identify the value of the coefficient of relative risk aversion. This point has recently been established by Carroll, who shows that the response of liquidity-constrained consumers – for example, buffer stock consumers – to changes in the interest rate will be muted, implying that the measured elasticity of intertemporal substitution will be less than the inverse of the coefficient of relative risk aversion.[59] We have confirmed Carroll's finding and quantify the effect in a life-cycle context. With ρ equal to 1, the measured elasticity of intertemporal substitution in our hyperbolic model is 0.22, which is consistent with the available empirical evidence. We return to this result later, in describing the properties of our simulated model.

The coefficient of relative risk aversion governs risk aversion, prudence, and the willingness of consumers to substitute consumption intertemporally. If ρ is relatively large, household saving decisions will be relatively insensitive to the introduction of a tax-deferred saving instrument that raises the aftertax rate of return. Also, a higher ρ generates more precautionary savings for the same level of income uncertainty, increasing the opportunities for asset shifting. Hence, the choice of this parameter has important implications for the efficacy of a DC plan.

We also consider the case when ρ is equal to 3, both to demonstrate that our results are highly sensitive to the choice of ρ and so that our results can be compared with those of Engen, Gale, and Scholz.

3.4.2 Time Preference Parameter β

We simulate herein hyperbolic economies and exponential economies. In doing so, we assume that an economy is either populated exclusively by hyperbolic consumers, with β equal to 0.85, or exclusively by exponential consumers, with β equal to 1.

For the hyperbolic simulations, we would have preferred to have set β much lower – approximately equal to 0.6 – as Laibson has done in previous work on undersaving.[60] Most of the experimental evidence suggests that the one-year discount rate is at least 40 percent.[61] However, a value of 0.6 generates pathologies in discrete time simulations: strongly nonmonotonic and noncontinuous consumption functions. Such effects are commonplace in dynamic games such as the intrapersonal game that we consider.[62] In our simulations, these pathologies vanish as β approaches unity. Specifically, we find that strong pathologies only arise for values of β below 0.8, which motivates our decision to adopt a value of 0.85.

It has recently been numerically shown that such pathologies are sensitive to the amount of stochastic variation in the income process: increasing the income

[59] Carroll (1997b).
[60] Laibson (1996).
[61] See Ainslie (1992) for a review.
[62] See Laibson (1997b) for an analysis of these effects.

variation drives out the pathologies.[63] However, we choose not to pursue this "fix" because in our model, the income processes are exogenously calibrated.

It also can be shown that the discontinuities vanish if the model is implemented in continuous time.[64] Hence, the discrete time framework that we use implicitly limits the range of the parameter space that can be used to generate sensible results. Nevertheless, it is possible to get some idea of how the model would perform if the value of β were below 0.85. Specifically, one can rerun the simulations for values of β in the neighborhood of 0.85 – say, 0.8 – and use the local change in results to estimate the effect of much lower values. We pursue this extrapolation exercise and find that the hyperbolic effects increase approximately linearly in the gap between β and 1.

3.4.3 Time Preference Parameter δ

Having fixed all of the other parameters, we are left with three free parameters in the hyperbolic economy – $\delta_{\text{hyperbolic}}^{\text{NHS}}, \delta_{\text{hyperbolic}}^{\text{HS}}, \delta_{\text{hyperbolic}}^{\text{COLL}}$ – and three free parameters in the exponential economy – $\delta_{\text{exponential}}^{\text{NHS}}, \delta_{\text{exponential}}^{\text{HS}}, \delta_{\text{exponential}}^{\text{COLL}}$. The superscripts NHS, HS, and COLL represent the three educational categories: did not graduate from high school, high school graduate, and college graduate, respectively. We pick values of δ so that our simulations replicate actual levels of preretirement wealth holding, according to data taken from the Federal Reserve's Survey of Consumer Finances (SCF) for 1983. Specifically, we pick δ such that the simulated median ratio of wealth to income for individuals between the ages of 50 and 59 matches the actual median in the data.

Although IRAs and 401(k)s were introduced in the 1970s – in 1974 and 1978, respectively – their use was not initially widespread. Eligibility for IRAs was made universal in 1982, and only 13.3 percent of households with at least one employed member were eligible for 401(k)s in 1984.[65] Therefore, we take the 1983 data as an approximation of a no DC plan steady state. We simulate a no DC plan economy and search for the values of δ that match the 1983 accumulation levels. We then use the same values of δ for the DC plan simulations. We choose to calibrate consumer preferences by matching the characteristics of a no DC plan steady state because the U.S. economy is still in transition from the no DC plan steady state to the DC plan steady state.

In the 1983 SCF, the median ratio of net wealth to income is 1.83 for households whose head did not graduate from high school, 2.66 for households whose head's highest educational attainment is a high school diploma, and 3.59 for households whose head has a college degree.[66] The discount rates $(1 - \delta)$ that replicate these

---

[63] See Laibson (1997b).

[64] At least in theory, the nonmonotonicities may persist.

[65] See Poterba, Venti, and Wise (1995). They consider the population of households whose head is aged between 25 and 65, where at least one employed member of the household is not self-employed.

[66] Our definition of net worth includes liquid assets and illiquid assets; for more details, see later.

Table 3.4. *Calibrated long-term discount rates[a]*

Education	Exponential consumers		Hyperbolic consumers	
	CRRA = 1[b]	CRRA = 3[b]	CRRA = 1[b]	CRRA = 3[b]
High school dropouts	0.0490	0.0870	0.0360	0.0745
High school graduates	0.0385	0.0590	0.0275	0.0485
College graduates	0.0305	0.0395	0.0205	0.0295

[a] Table reports the long-term discount rates $(1-\delta)$ generated by the authors' calibration exercise. Rates exclude mortality effects.

[b] CRRA denotes coefficient of relative risk aversion in this and following tables and figures, as applicable.

Source: Authors' calculations.

wealth-to-income ratios are reported in Table 3.4. Four properties stand out. First, these discount rates fall with educational attainment. Because the shape of the labor income profile is roughly similar across educational groups, a relatively low discount rate is needed to replicate the relatively high wealth-to-income ratio of the highly educated. Second, the discount rates rise with the coefficient of relative risk aversion. Because precautionary saving rises with the coefficient of relative risk aversion, an increase in the discount rate is needed to offset an increase in the coefficient of relative risk aversion. Third, the discount rates for hyperbolic consumers are lower than those for exponential consumers. Because hyperbolic consumers have two sources of discounting, β and δ, the hyperbolic δ's must be higher than the exponential δ's. Recall that the hyperbolic and exponential discount functions are calibrated to generate the same amount of preretirement wealth accumulation. In this manner, we "equalize" the underlying willingness to save of the exponential and the hyperbolic consumers before we introduce the DC plan. Fourth, all of the calibrated long-term discount rates are sensible, falling between 0.02 and 0.09. Note, however, that they do not include mortality effects, which add roughly another 0.01, generating net discount rates.

Our calibration of preference parameters can be compared with that of Engen, Gale, and Scholz. These authors do not adopt different discount factors for households with different levels of educational atttainment, but we compare our high school calibration to their aggregate calibration (recall that the high school group represents half of U.S. households). For exponential consumers with ρ equal to 3, we adopt a high school discount rate of 0.059, significantly larger than Engen, Gale, and Scholz's discount rate of 0.04. This difference makes the DC plan more effective in our simulations because households with relatively high discount rates have lower levels of accumulation and are less likely to hit the DC plan contribution caps, strengthening the substitution effect.

3.5 The Calibrated Economy without a Defined Contribution Plan

In this section, we analyze the properties of our calibrated economies without a DC plan, and all discussion pertains to these economies unless otherwise noted. Our

Thousands of 1990 dollars

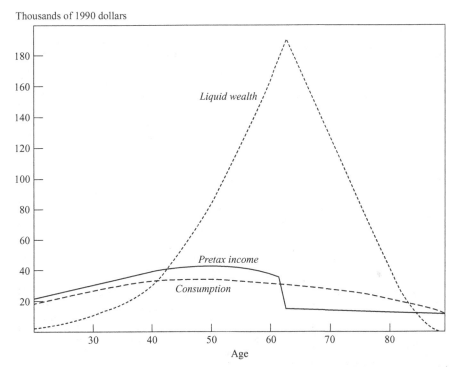

Figure 3.5. Simulated Average Liquid Asset, Income, and Consumption Paths, Exponential Households[a]
[a] Figure plots average values for households with high school graduate head. The coefficient of relative risk aversion is equal to 1.
Source: Authors' simulations.

first finding is that the hyperbolic and exponential economies are observationally very similar. Figure 3.5 plots the average levels of consumption, pretax income, and asset accumulation of exponential, log utility consumers in the high school graduate group. The corresponding graphs for the other educational groups are qualitatively similar. Figure 3.6 plots the path of a single exponential consumer. These figures are similar to their hyperbolic analogs, Figures 3.7 and 3.8; at first glance, it is hard to differentiate between them. The only discernible contrast is that hyperbolic consumers hold less buffer stock wealth early in life than do exponential consumers. Figure 3.9 plots the consumption functions of an exponential consumer and a hyperbolic one. The rough similarity of these functions further underscores the difficulty of distinguishing exponential from hyperbolic consumers.[67]

---

[67] The hyperbolic consumption function is nonmonotonic, but this pathology vanishes as one increases the fineness of the partition of the state space and increases the number of states in the discrete approximation of the stochastic income process.

Thousands of 1990 dollars

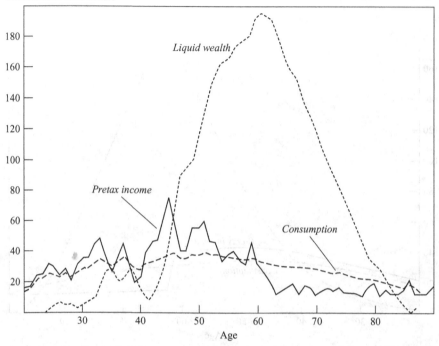

Figure 3.6. Simulated Liquid Asset, Income, and Consumption Paths of One Exponential Household[a]

[a] Figure plots values for a household with high school graduate head. The coefficient of relative risk aversion is equal to 1.

Source: Author's simulations.

Our calibrated exponential and hyperbolic economies replicate empirical life-cycle patterns documented by other authors.[68] Consumption closely tracks income, rising early in life and then falling, as "hump" saving accelerates in the two decades before retirement (see Figures 3.5 and 3.7). Comovement between consumption and income is also apparent at higher frequencies (see Figures 3.6 and 3.8). These basic empirical regularities are consistent with both the exponential and the hyperbolic versions of the buffer stock model.

The exponential and hyperbolic models also imply similar levels of sensitivity to interest rate changes. Table 3.5 reports the measured elasticity of intertemporal substitution for both models. Conceptually, the measured elasticity of intertemporal substitution is the derivative

$$\frac{d(\Delta \ln C_{it})}{dR}$$

---

[68] See Carroll (1992, 1997a); Gourinchas and Parker (1997); Hubbard, Skinner, and Zeldes (1994).

Table 3.5. *Average elasticities of intertemporal substitution*[a]

| | Exponential consumers | | Hyperbolic consumers | |
Education	CRRA = 1	CRRA = 3	CRRA = 1	CRRA = 3
High school dropouts	0.18	0.12	0.15	0.12
High school graduates	0.25	0.16	0.20	0.15
College graduates	0.40	0.18	0.31	0.16
Weighted average[b]	0.27	0.16	0.22	0.15

[a] Conceptually, the elasticity of intertemporal substitution is measured as the derivative

$$\frac{d(\Delta ln\, C_{it})}{dR}$$

where C_{it} is consumption of individual i at age t, and $R = 1 + r$ is the gross interest rate. Table reports the observed average value of this derivative over the life-cycle of simulated individuals in three educational groups (weighting with survivorship probabilities), in the neighborhood of $R = 1.05$.
[b] Uses population weights.
Source: Authors' simulations.

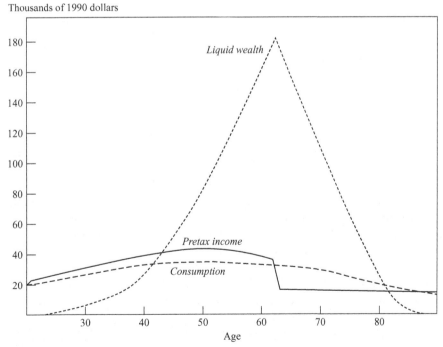

Thousands of 1990 dollars

Figure 3.7. Simulated Average Liquid Asset, Income, and Consumption Paths, Hyperbolic Households[a]
[a] Figure plots average values for households with high school graduate heads.
Source: Authors' simulations.

Thousands of 1990 dollars

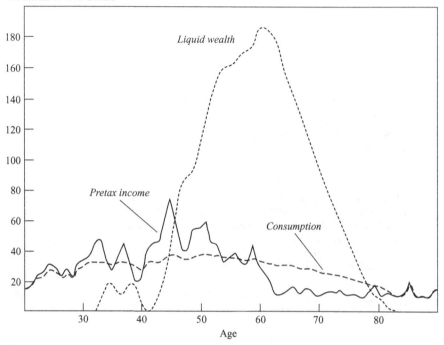

Figure 3.8. Simulated Liquid Asset, Income, and Consumption Paths of One Hyperbolic Household[a]
[a] Figure plots values for a household with high school graduate head.
Source: Authors' simulations.

The table reports the average value of this derivative over the life-cycle (weighted with survivorship probabilities) in the neighborhood of R equal to 1.05. Our numbers are equivalent to running an ordinary least squares regression of $\Delta \ln C_{it}$ on a constant and the deterministic interest rate.[69]

When ρ is equal to 1, the measured elasticities of intertemporal substitution are 0.27 for the exponential model and 0.22 for the hyperbolic model. When ρ is equal to 3, they fall to 0.16 for the exponential model and 0.15 for the hyperbolic model. These values are well below the inverse of the coefficients of relative risk aversion because, at least early in life, our households make choices in a buffer stock framework, implying that the slope of the consumption path is initially determined partly by the slope of the income path, rather than exclusively by the interest rate.[70] As education increases – corresponding to fall in the calibrated discount rates – the measured elasticity of intertemporal substitution rises. Patient households are less likely to be constrained by their income paths. Finally,

---

[69] We obtain almost identical numbers when we replace individual consumption growth, $\Delta \ln C_{it}$, with the growth rate of average consumption within a cohort, $\Delta \ln(\sum C_{it})$.
[70] See Carroll (1997b).

Consumption (thousands of 1990 dollars)

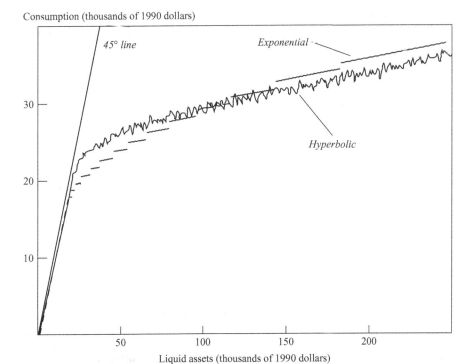

Figure 3.9. Consumption Functions of Exponential and Hyperbolic Households[a]
[a] Figure plots consumption functions for exponential and hyperbolic households with median income among households whose heads are aged 20 and are high school graduates.
[b] Includes liquid savings and current disposable income.

although the measured hyperbolic elasticity of intertemporal substitution is close to the measured exponential elasticity of intertemporal substitution, the former is slightly smaller. This systematic gap reflects the fact that hyperbolic agents are much more likely to hit binding liquidity constraints.

In the body of this section, we discuss two features of our simulations that distinguish the hyperbolic model from its exponential precursors: binding liquidity constraints and missing precautionary saving effects. Before discussing these phenomena, we introduce an analytic tool that provides the intuition for our analysis.

3.5.1 The Generalized Euler Equation

We present an heuristic derivation of a marginal condition that characterizes the equilibrium path of the hyperbolic economy.[71] The heuristic derivation is

---

[71] See Laibson (1996) for an earlier incarnation of this heuristic argument, and Laibson (1997b) for numerical confirmation that the Euler equation does, in fact, characterize the equilibrium path. See Harris and Laibson (1998) for an analytic approach.

based on a classical perturbation argument. The marginal benefit of postponing
$\Delta > 0$ units of consumption generates a stream of utility perturbations from the
perspective of self t. At time t,

$$\Delta u'(C_t)$$

utils are lost. Self t expects to gain

$$E_t\left[\beta\delta\left(\frac{\partial C_{t+1}}{\partial X_{t+1}}\right)R\Delta u'(C_{t+1})\right]$$

utils at time $t+1$, assuming that the hazard rate of survival is unity, to reduce
notation. Note that $\frac{\partial C_{t+j}}{\partial X_{t+j}}$ is the marginal consumption rate at period $t+j$. Self t
excepts to gain

$$E_t\left[\beta\delta^2\left(\frac{\partial C_{t+2}}{\partial X_{t+2}}\right)\left(1-\frac{\partial C_{t+1}}{\partial X_{t+1}}\right)R^2\Delta'(C_{t+2})\right]$$

utils at time $t+2$; and so on. The net effect sums to

$$-\Delta u'(C_t)+E_t\left\{\beta\sum_{i=1}^{T+N-t}\delta^i\left(\frac{\partial C_{t+i}}{\partial X_{t+i}}\right)\left[\prod_{j=1}^{i-1}\left(1-\frac{\partial C_{t+j}}{\partial X_{t+j}}\right)\right]R^i\Delta u'(C_{t+i})\right\}$$

$$(3.10)$$

Setting this expression less than or equal to zero and dividing by Δ yields an
Euler equation:

$$u'(C_t)\geq E_t\left\{\beta\sum_{i=1}^{T+N-t}\delta^i\left(\frac{\partial C_{t+i}}{\partial X_{t+i}}\right)\left[\prod_{j=1}^{i-1}\left(1-\frac{\partial C_{t+j}}{\partial X_{t+j}}\right)\right]R^iu'(C_{t+i})\right\}\quad(3.11)$$

One could repeat this argument for $\Delta < 0$ (assuming that the agent is never
perfectly liquidity constrained), which would enable one to substitute an equality
for the inequality in Equation 3.11. Consider the analogous Euler equation for
period $t+1$:

$$u'(C_{t+1})=$$

$$E_{t+1}\left\{\beta\sum_{i=1}^{T+N-(t+1)}\left(\delta^i\frac{\partial C_{t+1+i}}{\partial X_{t+1+i}}\right)\left[\prod_{j=1}^{i-1}\left(1-\frac{\partial C_{t+1+j}}{\partial X_{t+1+j}}\right)\right]R^iu'(C_{t+1+i})\right\}$$

$$(3.12)$$

Application of the law of iterated expectations and substitution of Equation 3.12
in Equation 3.11 yields

$$u'(C_t)=E_t\left\{\left[\left(\frac{\partial C_{t+1}(X_{t+1})}{\partial X_{t+1}}\right)\beta\delta+\left(1-\frac{\partial C_{t+1}(X_{t+1})}{\partial X_{t+1}}\right)\delta\right]Ru'(C_{t+1})\right\}$$

$$(3.13)$$

which Laibson refers to elsewhere as the generalized Euler equation.[72] Note that Equation 3.13 is identical to a standard Euler equation, except that the term in square brackets replaces the constant discount factor of the classical equation. The discounting term in the generalized Euler equation

$$\left[\left(\frac{\partial C_{t+1}(X_{t+1})}{\partial X_{t+1}} \right) \beta \delta + \left(1 - \frac{\partial C_{t+1}(X_{t+1})}{\partial X_{t+1}} \right) \delta \right] \tag{3.14}$$

is stochastic and varies linearly with next periods' marginal propensity to consume. When β is equal to 1, this bracketed term is equal to δ – the standard exponential discounting case. When β is less than 1, this bracketed term is a weighted average of the one-period discount factor, $\beta \delta$, and the discount factor that applies in all future periods, δ. The respective weights are tomorrow's marginal propensity to consume

$$\left(\frac{\partial C_{t+1}(X_{t+1})}{\partial X_{t+1}} \right) \quad \text{and} \quad \left(1 - \frac{\partial C_{t+1}(X_{t+1})}{\partial X_{t+1}} \right)$$

To interpret Equation 3.13 and the time-varying stochastic discount factor, it is helpful to consider the polar cases of marginal propensities to consume equal to one and to zero. First, consider a consumer who is certain to be liquidity constrained next period; that is, $C_{t+1} = X_{t+1}$, implying a marginal propensity to consume of unity. In this scenario, any savings set aside at time t will be spent in period $t + 1$, implying that self t effectively faces a two-period game. The Euler equation that characterizes self t's equilibrium action can be expressed as

$$u'(C_t) \geq E_t[R \beta \delta u'(C_{t+1})] \tag{3.15}$$

where the hazard rate of survival, s_t, has again been set to unity, to simplify notation. Equation 3.15 holds with equality when savings are positive at time t. This equation can be derived directly with a simple perturbation argument. Self t can use a marginal dollar to generate $u'(C_t)$ utils at time t or $E_t[R u'(C_{t+1})]$ expected utils at time $t + 1$. The utils at time $t + 1$ must be discounted, yielding the final equation. Note that Equation 3.15 implies a great deal of impatience. The one-period discount factor is $\beta \delta$, implying a discount rate of roughly 20 percent, given our calibration values.

Now consider the case of a zero marginal propensity to consume. The generalized Euler equation reduces to

$$u'(C_t) \geq E_t[R \delta u'(C_{t+1})]$$

which is identical to the classical Euler equation for a model with a discount factor of δ. The intuition behind this case is less straightforward and is best understood by considering the general properties of the intrapersonal strategic conflict that arises with hyperbolic preferences.

[72] Laibson (1996).

From the perspective of self t, marginal utility in period $t+1$ is too low relative to marginal utility during subsequent periods: self $t+1$ "underweights" the future by factor β. Self t would like to transfer resources to those future periods after $t+1$. When the marginal propensity to consume of self $t+1$ falls (holding all else equal), such transfers can be made more efficiently. Hence, a low marginal propensity to consume in period $t+1$ is associated with less consumption at time t. As the marginal propensity to consume in period $t+1$ goes to zero, this transfer effect perfectly offsets the effect of β less than 1, recovering the classical Euler equation.

For intermediate values of the marginal propensity to consume, the relevant endogenous discount factor is a weighted average of $\beta\delta$ and δ, where the relevant weights are

$$\left(\frac{\partial C_{t+1}(X_{t+1})}{\partial X_{t+1}}\right) \quad \text{and} \quad \left(1 - \frac{\partial C_{t+1}(X_{t+1})}{\partial X_{t+1}}\right)$$

Consumers will exhibit a great deal of endogenous heterogeneity in implicit patience levels over the life-cycle. For consumers in our high school graduate group with coefficient of relative risk aversion equal to 1, endogenous discount factors vary from $\beta\delta$ equal to 0.8266 (0.85×0.9725) to δ equal to 0.9725. The range of variation would be even more dramatic if we had adopted a lower value for β.

This wide range of discount factors implies that hyperbolic agents occasionally behave very impatiently – and, in doing so, are likely to meet binding liquidity constraints – whereas at other times they demonstrate a willingness to accumulate large stocks of wealth. In this framework, low levels of cash on hand are self-reinforcing: they imply a higher expected marginal propensity to consume (because consumption functions in buffer stock models are concave), which, in turn, lowers the endogenous discount factor.[73] Hence, hyperbolic consumers with low levels of cash on hand tend to act like consumers with extremely high discount rates, increasing the likelihood that their liquidity constraints will turn out to be binding.

An alternative way to see these effects is to compare the consumption functions of exponential and hyperbolic agents. As can be seen from Figure 3.9, hyperbolic agents are relatively more impatient at low levels of wealth holding – in this region, the hyperbolic consumption function lies above the exponential function – and conversely, more patient at high levels of wealth holding. In summary, at low levels of wealth, hyperbolic consumers act like exponential consumers with low levels of patience. At high levels of wealth, hyperbolic consumers act like exponential consumers with high levels of patience.

---

[73] For a proof that consumption functions are concave when consumers have exponential discount functions, see Carroll and Kimball (1996). Their proof does not carry over to the hyperbolic case. Nevertheless, in hyperbolic models, consumption functions are approximately concave; see Figure 3.9.

3.5.2 Binding Liquidity Constraints

Although we choose our calibration values so that exponential and hyperbolic consumers accumulate the same median level of preretirement assets, our results show that the hyperbolic consumers are much more likely to find themselves close to or at binding liquidity constraints. Figures 3.10 through 3.12 graph the percentage of exponential and hyperbolic households that are effectively liquidity-constrained: that is, for households whose head did not graduate from high school, asset holdings of less than $250; for households whose head has a high school diploma only, asset holdings of less than $400; and for households whose head graduated from college, asset holdings of less than $500.[74] We show results for coefficient of relative risk aversion equal to 1 and equal to 3. In all cases, the hyperbolic percentages lie well above the exponential percentages. Consider the first panel of Figure 3.11, which plots the results for households in the high school graduate group with a coefficient of relative risk aversion equal to 1. At age 35, 40 percent of the hyperbolic consumers have less than $400 in wealth, compared with only 21 percent of exponential consumers.

It is useful to compare these results with the percentages of liquidity-constrained consumers reported in the Survey of Consumer Finances. This exercise is not straightforward, however, as the SCF data are not directly comparable with the output from our simulations. Our timing assumption, Equation 3.5, implies that a consumer who always sets annual consumption equal to annual aftertax income (and never receives a bequest) will never have any positive asset holdings.

In the real world, by contrast, income is received at discrete intervals and consumption is implemented continuously. If workers are paid once a month, a consumer who spends all of his aftertax income will have average wealth holding of two weeks of income. If this consumer saves part of his income for a major expenditure (e.g., a vacation or Christmas gifts), his average holdings will be even greater. We adjust the SCF data to remove such intrayear savings. In Tables 3.6 through 3.8, we report the percentage of households that are liquidity constrained – that is, households that hold assets valued below n weeks of aftertax income, where $n = 1, 2, 3, 4$.

Another question that arises when comparing our results with the SCF data is whether a constrained consumer is one with low net worth or one with low liquid assets. Our definition of net worth includes liquid assets – checking accounts, savings accounts, money market accounts, call accounts, certificates of deposit, bonds, stocks, mutual funds, and cash, less credit card debt – and illiquid assets – IRAs, DC pension plans, life insurance, trusts, annuities, vehicles, home equity,

---

[74] Our cutoff of $250 for households whose heads did not graduate from high school reflects the fact that in our simulations, households are constrained to lie on an asset grid. Because the grid for this educational group takes values {$0, $500, $1,000, . . . ,}, we think of all consumers at 0 as having less than $250 dollars in assets. The analogous grids for households in the high school graduate and college graduate groups increase in increments of $800 and $1,000, respectively.

Percent of households

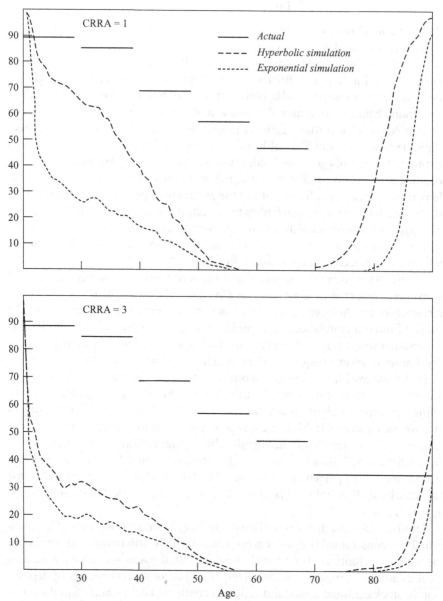

Figure 3.10. Share of High School Dropouts Who Are Liquidity Constrained, by Age[a]
[a] Figure plots percent of households with high school dropout heads that are liquidity constrained (less than $250 in liquid assets) in the actual data and in the simulated hyperbolic and exponential economies.
Source: Authors' simulations and the SCF, 1983.

Percent of households

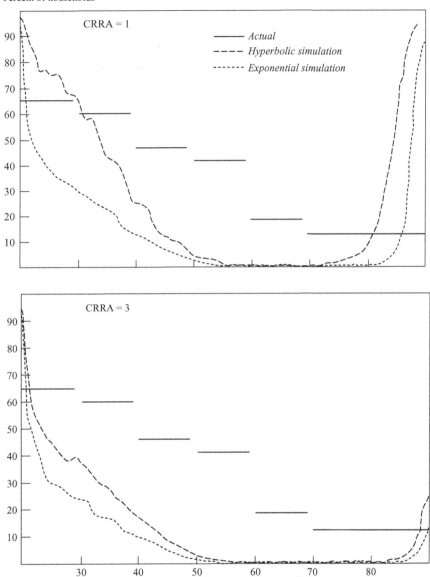

Figure 3.11. Share of High School Graduates Who Are Liquidity Constrained, by Age[a]
[a] Figure plots percent of households with high school graduate heads that are liquidity constrained (less than $400 in liquid assets) in the actual data and in the simulated hyperbolic and exponential economies.
Source: Authors' simulations and SCF, 1983.

Percent of households

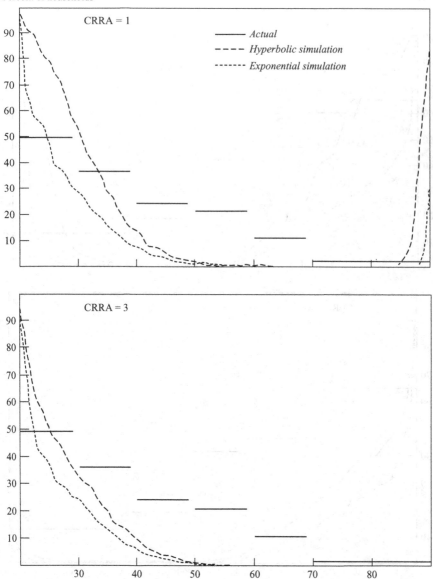

Figure 3.12. Share of College Graduates Who Are Liquidity Constrained, by Age[a]
[a] Figure plots percent of households with college graduate heads that are liquidity constrained (less than $500 in liquid assets) in the actual data and in the simulated hyperbolic and exponential economies.
Source: Authors' simulations and SCF, 1983.

Table 3.6. *Share of high school dropouts who are liquidity constrained[a]*
share, except as indicated

Constraint criterion	Age group					
	20 to 29	30 to 39	40 to 49	50 to 59	60 to 69	70 and over
Net worth limit[b]						
1 week of income +$250	0.29	0.20	0.14	0.16	0.08	0.12
2 weeks of income +$250	0.35	0.22	0.16	0.17	0.09	0.14
3 weeks of income +$250	0.43	0.23	0.18	0.18	0.09	0.15
4 weeks of income +$250	0.48	0.23	0.19	0.19	0.10	0.15
Liquid asset limit[c]						
1 week of income +$250	0.84	0.71	0.60	0.52	0.44	0.30
2 weeks of income +$250	0.89	0.85	0.69	0.57	0.47	0.35
3 weeks of income +$250	0.89	0.89	0.73	0.61	0.48	0.37
4 weeks of income +$250	0.89	0.90	0.77	0.66	0.50	0.39
Addendum						
Median nonasset income[d]	14,522	16,711	17,611	15,324	12,579	7,538

[a] Each table entry gives the share of individuals in a given age group who have net worth or liquid assets less than or equal to the given limit.

[b] Criteria apply to the individual's entire net worth; that is, liquid assets listed in note c below plus IRAs, DC pension plans, life insurance, trusts, annuities, vehicles, home equity, real estate, business equity, jewelry, furniture, antiques, and home durables, less education loans.

[c] Liquid assets include cash, checking accounts, savings accounts, money market accounts, call accounts, certificates of deposit, bonds, stocks, and mutual funds, less credit card debt.

[d] 1990 dollars.

Source: Authors' calculations based on data from the Survey of Consumer Finances, 1983.

real estate, business equity, jewelry, furniture, antiques, and home durables, less education loans. Few of these illiquid assets can be used to generate immediate liquidity without incurring substantial transaction costs. Indeed, many have commitment properties, which would make them appealing to hyperbolic consumers who do not want easy access to their money. We believe that a consumer may face an economically meaningful liquidity constraint even if he or she has many of the illiquid assets listed previously.

Figures 3.10 through 3.12 also plot the percentage of liquidity-constrained consumers from the SCF (using the liquid asset data from the sixth row of Tables 3.6 through 3.8). In each case, the percentage of liquidity constrained consumers tends to lie above both simulation lines, but the hyperbolic line is closer to the actual data than the exponential line. When ρ is equal to 1, the hyperbolic line generally lies slightly below the actual data. When ρ is equal to 3, both the hyperbolic and exponential lines fall well below the actual data, although the hyperbolic line is closer.

These results are only suggestive, however, because the simulated percentages of liquidity-constrained consumers are downward biased (for both exponential and hyperbolic cases). Our benchmark simulations assume that there is only one asset and that it is liquid. Because illiquid and liquid assets are partial substitutes, our

Table 3.7. *Share of high school graduates who are liquidity constrained[a]*
share, except as indicated

Constraint criterion	Age group					
	20 to 29	30 to 39	40 to 49	50 to 59	60 to 69	70 and over
Net worth limit[b]						
1 week of income +$400	0.18	0.10	0.04	0.04	0.02	0.01
2 weeks of income +$400	0.21	0.11	0.05	0.04	0.02	0.01
3 weeks of income +$400	0.22	0.13	0.05	0.04	0.02	0.02
4 weeks of income +$400	0.25	0.14	0.07	0.06	0.02	0.02
Liquid asset limit[c]						
1 week of income +$400	0.61	0.55	0.42	0.37	0.15	0.11
2 weeks of income +$400	0.65	0.60	0.46	0.41	0.18	0.12
3 weeks of income +$400	0.69	0.64	0.49	0.44	0.23	0.15
4 weeks of income +$400	0.73	0.68	0.53	0.47	0.24	0.17
Addendum						
Median nonasset income[d]	18,869	25,159	31,449	30,191	18,869	10,454

[a] Each table entry gives the share of individuals in a given age group who have net worth or liquid assets less than or equal to the given limit.
[b] Criteria apply to an individual's entire net worth, as defined in Table 3.6, note b.
[c] For definition of liquid assets, see Table 3.6, note c.
[d] 1990 dollars.
Source: Authors' calculations based on data from the SCF, 1983.

Table 3.8. *Share of college graduates who are liquidity constrained[a]*
share, except as indicated

Constraint criterion	Age group					
	20 to 29	30 to 39	40 to 49	50 to 59	60 to 69	70 and over
Net worth limit[b]						
1 week of income +$500	0.08	0.04	0.01	0.01	0.02	0.00
2 weeks of income +$500	0.11	0.05	0.01	0.03	0.02	0.01
3 weeks of income +$500	0.11	0.06	0.01	0.04	0.03	0.01
4 weeks of income +$500	0.13	0.07	0.01	0.04	0.06	0.01
Liquid asset limit[c]						
1 week of income +$500	0.44	0.31	0.22	0.20	0.11	0.00
2 weeks of income +$500	0.49	0.36	0.24	0.21	0.11	0.02
3 weeks of income +$500	0.52	0.42	0.28	0.24	0.12	0.02
4 weeks of income +$500	0.58	0.45	0.32	0.25	0.14	0.03
Addendum						
Median nonasset income[d]	22,517	37,738	49,060	41,512	24,092	15,395

[a] Each table entry gives the share of individuals in a given age group who have net worth or liquid assets less than or equal to the given limit.
[b] Criteria apply to an individual's entire net worth, as defined in Table 3.6, note b.
[c] For definition of liquid assets, see Table 3.6, note c.
[d] 1990 dollars.
Source: Authors' calculations based on data from the SCF, 1983.

simulations bias upward the accumulation of liquid assets for both hyperbolic and exponential consumers. Future work should evaluate the simulated percentage of liquidity-constrained consumers in an economy with both liquid assets and illiquid assets such as real estate and durables.

3.5.3 Precautionary Saving

Since Robert Hall's original work in the late 1970s, it has become standard practice to work with Taylor expansions of the Euler equation.[75] The current consensus calls for second-order terms to be included in the approximation. We undertake such analysis on the data generated by the exponential and the hyperbolic simulations. Specifically, we estimate the second-order equation

$$\left(\frac{C_{t+1} - C_t}{C_t}\right) = \frac{1}{\rho}\left(1 - \frac{1}{R\delta}\right) + \frac{\rho+1}{2}E_t\left[\left(\frac{C_{t+1} - C_t}{C_t}\right)^2\right] + \epsilon_{t+1} \quad (3.16)$$

Dynan derives this equation from the classical Euler equation ($\beta = 1$), by expanding C_{t+1} around C_t.[76] She finds that the estimates of ρ – imputed from the coefficient on the conditional variance term – are negative and, hence, anomalously low. We show that the direction of the bias in Dynan's findings is predicted by the generalized Euler equation. We then estimate Dynan's equation with our simulated data.

A second-order Taylor expansion of the generalized Euler equation yields

$$E_t\left(\frac{C_{t+1} - C_t}{C_t}\right) = \frac{1}{\rho}\left(1 - \frac{1}{R\delta}\right) + \frac{1}{\rho}\frac{1}{R\delta}(\beta - 1)E_t\left(\frac{\partial C_{t+1}(X_{t+1})}{\partial X_{t+1}}\right)$$
$$+ O(2) + \epsilon_{t+1} \quad (3.17)$$

where $\frac{\partial C_{t+1}(X_{t+1})}{\partial X_{t+1}}$ has been expanded around zero, and $O(2)$ has been substituted for second-order terms (including the one in Equation 3.16). The first-order expression $\frac{1}{\rho}\frac{1}{R\delta}(\beta - 1)E_t(\frac{\partial C_{t+1}(X_{t+1})}{\partial X_{t+1}})$, which appears in Equation 3.17, vanishes in the exponential case ($\beta = 1$). In the hyperbolic case, this new first-order term is easy to interpret. Recall that when the marginal propensity to consume is expected to be high next period, the discount factor in the generalized Euler equation falls, pulling down the expected slope of the consumption path.

Estimates of ρ inferred from regression analysis of Equation 3.16 will be affected by omitted variable bias when β is less than 1. Assuming that first-order omitted variables dominate second-order omitted variables, the direction of this bias is given by the covariation of

$$\frac{\rho+1}{2}E_t\left[\left(\frac{C_{t+1} - C_t}{C_t}\right)^2\right] \quad \text{and} \quad \frac{1}{\rho}\frac{1}{R\delta}(\beta - 1)E_t\left(\frac{\partial C_{t+1}(X_{t+1})}{\partial X_{t+1}}\right)$$

---

[75] Hall (1978).
[76] Dynan (1993).

To sign this covariation, note that the conditional variability of consumption growth is high when the buffer stock of assets is low, and low assets imply a high marginal propensity to consume (see Figure 3.10). Finally, recall that $(\beta - 1)$ is less than zero, implying that the covariation between

$$\frac{\rho + 1}{2} E_t \left[\left(\frac{C_{t+1} - C_t}{C_t} \right)^2 \right] \quad \text{and} \quad \frac{1}{\rho} \frac{1}{R\delta} (\beta - 1) E_t \left(\frac{\partial C_{t+1}(X_{t+1})}{\partial X_{t+1}} \right)$$

is negative. Omitted variable bias implies that estimates of Equation 3.16 will yield low or even negative estimates of $\frac{\rho+1}{2}$, as Dynan finds using data from the Consumer Expenditure Survey of the Bureau of Labor Statistics.

We confirm these intuitions with our simulated data through regression analysis of Equation 3.16. We operationalize this regression by using instrumental variables to estimate

$$\left(\frac{C_{t+1} - C_t}{C_t} \right) = \alpha_0 + \alpha_1 \left(\frac{C_{t+1} - C_t}{C_t} \right)^2 + \epsilon_{t+1} \qquad (3.18)$$

To instrument for $(\frac{C_{t+1}-C_t}{C_t})$, we follow Dynan and use educational dummies and gross savings at time t.[77] Table 3.9 reports the resulting inferred values of ρ using data from the exponential and the hyperbolic simulations, for both ρ equal to 1 and ρ equal to 3.

The findings reported in Table 3.9 confirm that the anomaly reported by Dynan is predicted by the hyperbolic model. First, in every case, the imputed value of ρ is lower in the regression using hyperbolic simulated data than in the regression using analogous exponential data. Moreover, in every case, the exponential data yield an imputed value of ρ above the true value, presumably a bias generated by the second-order approximation in the derivation of the linearized Euler equation; whereas in three of the four cases, the hyperbolic data yield an imputed value below the true value.[78] Hence, hyperbolic discounting explains – at least qualitatively – Dynan's results.[79] However, our imputed values for ρ do not line up neatly with hers, as most of her point estimates fall between $-1/2$ and -1.

---

[77] Dynan also uses education, occupation, and number of earners in the household, but she omits education and occupation for some of her estimates.

[78] See Carroll (1997b) for more evidence on the inadequacies of the linearized Euler equation; our results support his. Carroll also finds that estimating the linearized Euler equation on simulated exponential data yields regression coefficients that imply too high a value for ρ.

[79] Carroll (1992, 1997a) proposes an alternative explanation, based on heterogeneous discount rates. Consumers with high discount rates will have high levels of consumption variability (and those with low discount rates will have low levels of variability). Omitting the heterogeneous discount rates from the regression will bias α_1 downward.

Table 3.9. *Missing precautionary savings: Bias in regression estimates of the CRRA[a]*

| Sample | Parameter | Simulated data produced with CRRA = 1 | | Simulated data produced with CRRA = 3 | |
		Exponential consumers	Hyperbolic consumers	Exponential consumers	Hyperbolic consumers
All consumers	α_0	−0.009	−0.006	−0.010	−0.009
	α_1	1.926	1.284	2.098	1.761
	Imputed CRRA[b]	2.852	1.568	3.196	2.522
All consumers with positive wealth	α_0	−0.008	−0.002	−0.009	−0.007
	α_1	1.629	−2.917	2.067	0.843
	Imputed CRRA[b]	2.258	−6.834	3.134	0.686

[a] Table reports estimated coefficients from the following regression (Equation 3.18) when it is run on the panel of data produced by simulation described in a given column head:

$$\left(\frac{C_{t+1} - C_t}{C_t}\right) = \alpha_0 + \alpha_1 \left(\frac{C_{t+1} - C_t}{C_t}\right)^2 + \epsilon_{t+1}$$

where C_t indicates individual consumption to time t. Authors instrument for $(\frac{C_{t+1}-C_t}{C_t})$ with resources saved at time t and educational dummies.

[b] Estimated as $2\alpha_1 - 1$, using estimated value of α_1.

Source: Authors' regressions using panel data produced by simulations.

3.6 The Economy with a Defined Contribution Plan

In this section, we analyze the properties of our exponential and hyperbolic economies with a second asset: a DC pension plan. We first consider a perfect commitment technology in the one-asset economy.

3.6.1 Perfect Commitment

Hyperbolic households would like to save more than they do. If they could costlessly and perfectly commit later selves, they would lock in the contingent policy rules of an exponential household with a discount rate taken from the appropriate cell in Table 3.4. For example, a hyperbolic household in the high school graduate group, with coefficient of relative risk aversion equal to 1, would choose to implement policies associated with an exponential household with a discount rate of 0.0275.

The contrasts between the perfect-commitment case and the no-commitment case are striking. Average wealth accumulated peaks at $298,000 with commitment, 62 percent higher than the peak of $184,000 with no commitment. Perfect commitment also generates large welfare gains. From the perspective of the 19-year-old self, the ability to perfectly commit all future selves is as valuable as receiving a one-time tax-free windfall equal to 36 percent of consumption at age 20.[80] The welfare gains evaluated from the perspective of later selves are substantially larger, as later selves benefit the most from the higher rates of accumulation early in life.

For households with coefficient of relative risk aversion equal to 3, the impact of perfect commitment is smaller: peak accumulation rises by only 15 percent and the welfare effect is equivalent to only 2 percent of consumption at age 20. This contrast between the different values of the coefficient of relative risk aversion is reflected in all the results presented later. Commitment – even if perfect – is not valuable to households with a relatively high coefficient of relative risk aversion, implying that they also will not value the cruder commitment properties in DC plans.

3.6.2 Institutional Features of 401(k) Plans

Although perfect-commitment devices are not available in practice, partial-commitment devices are common. Consumers can use illiquid assets, particularly DC pension plans, to constrain future choice sets; 401(k) plans provide an interesting case in point. However, they do not provide a clean case study of commitment because their appeal is enhanced by the tax break on capital income that they offer. In the rest of this section, we evaluate the efficacy of 401(k) plans for exponential and hyperbolic consumers.

A wide range of mechanisms induces employees to contribute to 401(k) plans and to resist withdrawing their accumulating balances. First, tax deferral and employer matching give employees strong incentives to contribute. In a 1997 survey conducted by Hewitt Associates, 81 percent of plans reported that the employer contribution was contingent on the employee contribution, and 21 percent of all plans reported matching contributions from employers of 50 percent up to 6 percent of income.[81] This was, by far, the most common employer arrangement among the plans surveyed.

Second, the standard plan compels participants to set up an automatic deposit system. In many cases, it is difficult or impossible to change the preset deposit levels on short notice. Even if a participant can make a change quickly, the results are unlikely to show up in cash holdings until the next pay cycle, which may be a month or two away. Because most of the steep drop in hyperbolic discount functions comes at horizons of approximately one week, a one-month delay in implementation is more than enough to convince a hyperbolic consumer not to break into a nest egg.[82]

Third, 401(k) assets are partially protected from splurges because withdrawals from the accounts can be freely made only if the account holder is over 59$\frac{1}{2}$ years

---

[80] We assume that the windfall is received in the consumer's 20th year and is expressed as a percentage of consumption at age 20. Note that this is the first year in which consumption choices are made – that is, the first year of economic life.

[81] Hewitt Associates (1997).

[82] See Laibson (1997a).

old. For younger consumers, withdrawals are only allowed in cases of financial hardship or when a worker separates from a firm, and even then generate a 10 percent penalty. In most other cases, the withdrawal penalty is 100 percent. Fourth, for consumers who will be limit contributors in the future, withdrawals cannot be paid back into the account, implying that such consumers are penalized by the loss of future tax deferrals, as well as the original 10 percent withdrawal penalty.

However, the recent trend toward the establishment of 401(k) loan provisions has undermined the effectiveness of these plans as a commitment device. Almost all (90 percent) of the plans surveyed by Hewitt Associates have begun to allow participants to use their 401(k) balance as collateral for a loan.[83] Such loan provisions are generally highly restrictive and costly. For example, loans must be less than 50 percent of the vested account balance (employer contributions are often not counted as collateral) and less than $50,000 in value, and they must be paid back in 5 years (10 years for home loans). Ninety-seven percent of plans restrict the number and type of loans, and 46 percent of plans only allow one outstanding loan.[84] And, the typical plan charges an interest rate 1 percentage point over the prime rate.[85] According to EBRI data, 33 percent of participants have loans against their plan, with an average balance of $2,500.[86]

We do not model all of the institutional features of 401(k) plans. Computational limitations on the feasible number of state variables dictated some simplification. Most imortant, our model neglects the automatic-deposit feature of 401(k)s and also the loan provisions. These choices mimic those of Engen, Gale, and Scholz.

3.6.3 Conceptual Framework for the 401(k) Simulations

Our analysis is an exercise in comparative statics. We compare an economy that has never had and will never have DC plans with one in which DC plans have always been and will always be available. Because we do not evaluate the transition path between steady states, our analysis does not have direct implications for the short-run impact of saving policies.[87] Rather, the analysis is useful for highlighting the long-run differences between exponential and hyperbolic models.

Because it is not entirely clear what the institutional properties of a DC plan system would actually be, we consider a range of arrangements. First, we vary the early-withdrawal penalty rate between 0.10 and 0.50; and, we consider even more values in the robustness checks described later. If plan sponsors enforce the financial-distress rules strictly, denying almost all applications, a penalty rate of

---

[83] Hewitt Associates (1997). In 1991, the corresponding number was 67 percent.

[84] Hewitt Associates (1997).

[85] Hewitt Associates (1995).

[86] This fact was brought to our attention by Eric Engen and William Gale.

[87] Many authors have shown that the short-run effects of changes in tax policy often go in the opposite direction to the long-run impacts; see, for example, Engen, Gale, and Scholz (1994).

Thousands of 1990 dollars

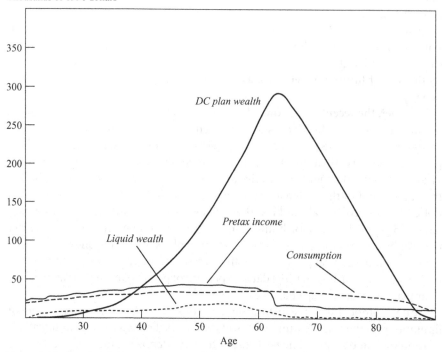

Figure 3.13. Simulated Asset, Income, and Consumption Paths of Exponential Households, Defined Contribution Plan Available[a]
[a] Figure plots life-cycle average consumption, pretax labor income, liquid wealth, and wealth in the DC plan for households with high school graduate heads. The DC plan has a 10 percent early-withdrawal penalty and no employer match. The coefficient of relative risk aversion is equal to 1.
Source: Authors' simulations.

1.00 may be the correct modeling assumption. If their enforcement is weak and they sign off on almost all applications, no matter what their intrinsic merit, a penalty rate of 0.10 would be appropriate. Second, we vary the employer-matching rate between 0 and 0.50, assuming that employers match up to 6 percent of income. We explore these variations both to gain insight into existing heterogeneity among DC plans and to evaluate the long-run effects of potential changes to existing rules and practice.

We begin our analysis with representative examples of our simulations, postponing a summary of our various cases until after we introduce an aggregation framework. Figure 3.13 represents the life-cycle choices of exponential households in the high school graduate group with coefficient of relative risk aversion equal to 1, who have access to a DC plan with a 0 percent match and a 10 percent penalty for early withdrawal. The figure plots average liquid wealth (X), average DC plan wealth (Z), average labor income (Y), and average consumption (C) over

Thousands of 1990 dollars

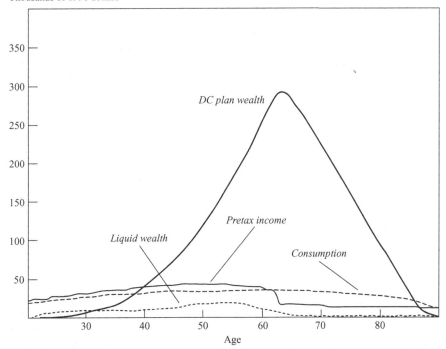

Figure 3.14. Simulated Asset, Income, and Consumption Paths of Hyperbolic Households, Defined Contribution Plan Available[a]

[a] Figure plots life-cycle average consumption, pretax labor income, liquid wealth, and wealth in the DC plan for households with high school graduate heads. The DC plan has a 10 percent early-withdrawal penalty and no employer match. The coefficient of relative risk aversion is equal to 1.

Source: Authors' simulations.

the life cycle. Figure 3.14 represents these life-cycle choices for the corresponding hyperbolic households.

Four properties stand out in Figures 3.13 and 3.14. First, most accumulation occurs in DC plan wealth. Second, total accumulation is dramatically larger than in the economy without DC plans (compare with Figures 3.5 and 3.7); we quantify this difference herein. Third, hyperbolic consumers hold lower levels of liquid assets and higher levels of illiquid assets than exponential consumers. Fourth, growth in DC plan holdings slows after age 60 (when the early-withdrawal penalty drops to zero), and DC plan holdings start to fall at retirement. Similar patterns are apparent in the other cases that we consider.

All of the magnitudes plotted in Figures 3.13 and 3.14 are based on per capita definitions. Linking these per capita magnitudes to national aggregates requires weighting with survival rates and cohort sizes. Aggregation is achieved through a simple overlapping-generations model.

3.6.4 Aggregation

We rule out general equilibrium effects by assuming an open economy with a fixed world interest rate. We assume that the economy is composed of overlapping generations. Intercohort population grows at 1 percent per year; that is, the cohort born in year t is 1 percent larger than the cohort born in year $t - 1$. Intercohort per capita magnitudes grow at 2 percent per year; that is, the outcome variables, such as pretax income at age 35 and taxes paid at age 35, of the cohort born in year t are 2 percent larger than the same outcome variables of the cohort born in year $t - 1$. The latter assumption is slightly distortionary because it implies that tax brackets are cohort specific.

We also assume that the government adjusts expenditures to maintain a balanced budget and carries no debt in steady state. This assumption engenders a bias against finding that DC plans increase net national saving when the coefficient of relative risk aversion is equal to 1, and for finding that they do so when the coefficient of relative risk aversion is equal to 3. This bias arises because when the coefficient of relative risk aversion is equal to 1, all of the economies with DC plans have higher aggregate government tax receipts than the corresponding economies without DC plans, and when the coefficient of relative risk aversion is equal to 3, they have lower receipts (see Tables 3.11 and 3.14). To compensate for this revenue effect, we simply assume that the government runs a balanced budget. Note, however, that we only undertake steady-state analysis. Any negative effects on government saving that occur during the transition are not captured in our steady-state simulations. These transition effects will reduce government saving, offsetting or adding to, respectively, the biases described herein.

Our balanced-budget assumption also engenders a bias against finding that DC plans are particularly effective in hyperbolic economies. This is because introducing the DC plan causes revenue to rise by a greater amount, or fall by a smaller amount, in the hyperbolic economies than in the exponential economies (see Tables 3.11 and 3.14). This bias occurs with both values of the coefficient of relative risk aversion.

We summarize our steady-state analysis with three statistics: the aggregate saving rate, the ratio of government tax revenue to labor income, and the percentage of DC plan wealth accumulation that represents additional saving relative to the economy without a DC plan. Formally, we define aggregate income as

$$(GNP)_t = Y_t + M_t + \frac{r}{R}(X_t + Z_t)$$

where Y_t represents aggregate labor income receipts excluding matching payments, M_t represents aggregate employer matching payments, X_t represents the aggregate stock of the liquid asset, Z_t represents the aggregate stock of the DC plan, r represents the interest rate, and R is equal to $1 + r$. Note that Y_t includes defined benefit pension plans, private and public, because we assume these are funded out of wages on a pay-as-you-go basis.

Saving is the residual between income and consumption, both private and public:

$$S_t = (GNP)_t - C_t - G_t$$

where C_t represents aggregate private consumption and G_t represents aggregate government consumption. The balanced-budget assumption implies that

$$G_t = T_t + E_t - B_{t+1}$$

where T_t represents taxes paid at time t, E_t represents the value of estates left at time t, and B_{t+1} represents the value of bequests received at the start of period $t + 1$. The difference, $E_t - B_{t+1}$, represents bequest taxes (not included in T_t), which turn out to be positive in our simulations.[88]

The aggregate saving rate is given by

$$\frac{S_t}{(GNP)_t}$$

The ratio of government receipts to total labor income is given by

$$\frac{G_t}{Y_t + M_t}$$

Note that the denominator of this ratio is the same in the hyperbolic and exponential economies – Y falls to offset the average match. Finally, the percentage of DC plan wealth accumulation that represents new national saving relative to the no DC plan economy is given by

$$\frac{X_t + Z_t - \tilde{X}_t}{Z_t}$$

where $\tilde{X}_t$ represents the amount of aggregate liquid assets accumulated in the economy without a DC plan.

3.6.5 Results for Coefficient of Relative Risk Aversion Equal to 1

Table 3.10 reports saving rates in the no DC plan and DC plan overlapping-generations economies with coefficient of relative risk aversion equal to 1. Saving rates are reported for each educational group and for the whole economy. We first consider the results for the exponential households.

The exponential economy without a DC plan has a steady-state aggregate saving rate of 4.14 percent. The corresponding rates for the DC plan exponential economies are very different. Consider the case of 50 percent employer matching. With a 10 percent withdrawal penalty, the saving rate rises to 7.63 percent; with a

---

[88] The estate-tax rate implied by our analysis varies between 50 and 75 percent. This is high but not as high as it looks because it includes income taxes on 401(k) assets, which are payable on the death of the consumer.

Table 3.10. *Aggregate saving rates in selected simulated economies, CRRA = 1[a] percent*

Education	DC plan availability	Employer match	Early withdrawal penalty	Exponential consumers		Hyperbolic consumers	
				Saving rate	Percent increase with DC plan	Saving rate	Percent increase with DC plan
High school dropouts	No	...	...	2.70	...	2.30	...
	Yes	50 percent	10 percent	4.92	82.2	4.97	116.1
		50 percent	50 percent	5.41	100.4	6.54	184.3
	Yes	None	10 percent	4.02	48.9	4.26	85.2
			50 percent	3.93	45.6	4.70	104.3
High school graduates	No	...	...	3.93	...	3.62	...
	Yes	50 percent	10 percent	7.46	89.8	7.58	109.4
		50 percent	50 percent	8.44	114.8	9.09	151.1
	Yes	None	10 percent	6.35	61.6	6.96	92.3
			50 percent	6.71	70.7	8.19	126.2
College graduates	No	...	...	5.28	...	5.10	...
	Yes	50 percent	10 percent	9.20	74.2	9.44	85.1
		50 percent	50 percent	9.65	82.8	10.50	105.9
	Yes	None	10 percent	8.34	58.0	8.60	68.6
			50 percent	8.28	56.8	9.09	78.2
All groups[b]	No	...	...	4.14	...	3.91	...
	Yes	50 percent	10 percent	7.63	84.3	7.79	99.2
		50 percent	50 percent	8.35	101.7	9.15	134.0
	Yes	None	10 percent	6.65	60.6	7.08	81.1
			50 percent	6.80	64.3	7.93	102.8

[a] Aggregate saving is defined as aggregate income (labor income, employers' matching contributions, and asset income) less aggregate consumption and government spending. Saving divided by income gives the saving rate.

[b] Assumes that the population comprises 25 percent households with high school dropout heads, 50 percent with high school graduate heads, and 25 percent with college graduate heads.

Source: Authors' simulations.

50 percent penalty, it rises to 8.35 percent. These represent increases of 84.3 and 101.7 percent, respectively. With no matching, the percentage increases are smaller, although still quite large. With a 10 percent penalty, the aggregate saving rate increases by 60.6 percent; with a 50 percent penalty, it increases by 64.3 percent.

One would intuitively expect DC plans to have a bigger impact on hyperbolic economies because hyperbolic households value commitment. Table 3.10 confirms this conjecture. With 50 percent employer matching and a 10 percent withdrawal penalty, the aggregate saving rate increases by 99.2 percent; with a 50 percent penalty, it increases by 134.0 percent. With no matching and a 10 percent penalty, the aggregate saving rate increases by 81.1 percent; with a 50 percent penalty, it increases by 102.8 percent. These results are even larger than the saving increases recorded by the exponential households. DC plans generally double the net saving rates in hyperbolic economies relative to exponential economies.

Three additional features stand out in the simulation results. First, the college graduate group generally realizes the smallest DC plan effects in percentage terms. Because these households have the highest income levels and are the most patient, they are most likely to hit the contribution caps, thereby mitigating the substitution effect. However, the DC plan effects do not fall monotonically with education. In many cases, they are stronger for the high school graduate group than for the households whose head did not graduate from high school, probably reflecting the fact that the DC plan generates more tax relief for the high school graduate group.

Second, hyperbolic consumers respond relatively well to higher penalties for early withdrawal. In the case of 50 percent employer matching, when the penalty rises from 10 to 50 percent, the hyperbolic saving rate rises from 7.79 to 9.15 percent (a 17.5 percent increase), whereas the exponential saving rate only rises from 7.63 to 8.35 percent (a 9.4 percent increase). Likewise, in the no-matching case, when the penalty rises from 10 to 50 percent, the hyperbolic saving rate rises from 7.08 to 7.93 percent (a 12.0 percent increase), whereas the exponential saving rate rises from 6.65 to 6.80 percent (a 2.3 percent increase).

Third, hyperbolic consumers are relatively less sensitive to the elimination of employer matching. In the case of a 10 percent withdrawal penalty, removing the match reduces the hyperbolic saving rate from 7.79 to 7.08 percent (a 9.1 percent decrease), whereas the exponential saving rate falls from 7.63 to 6.65 percent (a 12.8 percent decrease). Likewise, in the case of a 50 percent penalty, removing the match reduces the hyperbolic saving rate from 9.15 to 7.93 percent (a 13.3 percent decrease), whereas the exponential saving rate falls from 8.35 to 6.80 percent (an 18.6 percent decrease). In the no-match condition, exponential consumers have relatively weak incentives to invest. They gain only the tax deferral and pay the price of lost liquidity. By contrast,

Table 3.11. *Government revenue as a share of labor income in selected simulated economics, CRRA = 1[a] percent*

Education	DC plan availability	Employer match	Early withdrawal penalty	Government revenue	
				Exponential consumers	Hyperbolic consumers
High school dropouts	No	...	...	9.82	9.58
	Yes	50 percent	10 percent	10.69	10.58
			50 percent	10.63	11.02
	Yes	None	10 percent	10.01	10.10
			50 percent	10.00	10.26
High school graduates	No	...	...	12.65	12.39
	Yes	50 percent	10 percent	13.50	13.45
			50 percent	13.87	14.08
	Yes	none	10 percent	12.86	13.08
			50 percent	13.10	13.60
College graduates	No	...	...	16.23	15.99
	Yes	50 percent	10 percent	16.68	16.71
			50 percent	16.94	17.39
	Yes	None	10 percent	16.10	16.16
			50 percent	16.14	16.52
All groups[b]	No	...	...	13.34	13.11
	Yes	50 percent	10 percent	14.07	14.04
			50 percent	14.33	14.65
	Yes	None	10 percent	13.45	13.59
			50 percent	13.58	14.02

[a] Government revenue is defined as tax payments (including penalties for early withdrawals from DC plans) plus total estates left, less bequests received by the population. Labor income includes matching payments.
[b] For composition of this population, see Table 3.10, note b.
Source: Authors' simulations.

hyperbolic consumers both gain the tax deferral and partially benefit from the lost liquidity.

Turning to the government sector, Table 3.11 reports government revenue as a percentage of labor income. Our balanced-budget assumption implies that government revenue equals government consumption, generating a cost or benefit of the DC plan regime that is not captured in the higher saving rate. In all of our simulations with coefficient of relative risk aversion equal to 1, the DC plan economy is associated with higher government revenues, and these effects are strongest for the hyperbolic consumers. If some of this increased revenue were channeled into saving instead of government consumption, national saving would

Table 3.12. *Share of defined contribution saving that represents new savings,*
$CRRA = 1^a$ *percent*

Education	Employer match	Early withdrawal penalty	Share of DC savings that represents new savings	
			Exponential consumers	Hyperbolic consumers
High school dropouts	50 percent	10 percent	53.1	59.6
		50 percent	60.8	70.8
	None	10 percent	40.7	51.5
		50 percent	41.1	56.8
High school graduates	50 percent	10 percent	55.3	58.5
		50 percent	63.6	66.9
	None	10 percent	45.4	53.5
		50 percent	54.8	62.3
College graduates	50 percent	10 percent	51.0	53.3
		50 percent	55.5	59.6
	None	10 percent	44.9	47.8
		50 percent	46.6	51.7
All groups[b]	50 percent	10 percent	53.9	56.4
		50 percent	60.1	64.5
	None	10 percent	45.5	51.0
		50 percent	49.9	57.6

[a] Percent new savings is calculated as $(X + Z - \tilde{X})/Z \times 100$, where X and Z represent, respectively, liquid and DC plan assets in the economy with a DC plan, and $\tilde{X}$ represents liquid assets in the economy without a DC plan.
[b] For composition of this population, see Table 3.10, note b.
Source: Authors' simulations.

rise even higher in the DC plan regime. These increases in revenue are substantial, representing approximately 1 percent of labor income.

In Table 3.12, we report the percentage of DC plan accumulation that represents new savings:

$$\frac{X_t + Z_t - \tilde{X}_t}{Z_t}$$

Note that total new savings is equal to the stock of DC plan wealth multiplied by the ratio reported in Table 3.12:

$$Z_t \left(\frac{X_t + Z_t - \tilde{X}_t}{Z_t} \right)$$

This table demonstrates that, in general, values of $(X_t + Z_t - \tilde{X}_t)/Z_t$ are higher for hyperbolic than for exponential consumers. Hence, hyperbolic consumers save more than exponential consumers both because hyperbolic consumers invest

Table 3.13. *Welfare impact of defined contribution plans, CRRA = 1[a] percent of current consumption*

Early withdrawal penalty	Employer match	Age	High school dropouts		High school graduates		College graduates	
			Exponential consumers	Hyperbolic consumers	Exponential consumers	Hyperbolic consumers	Exponential consumers	Hyperbolic consumers
10 percent	50 percent	20	8	39	22	70	59	135
		40	77	123	148	201	216	275
		60	234	288	345	345	377	410
		80	123	127	199	226	266	300
10 percent	None	20	9	27	28	71	70	142
		40	34	81	104	180	187	242
		60	154	215	250	327	300	328
		80	92	99	153	192	224	254
50 percent	50 percent	20	1	32	10	70	40	124
		40	104	192	204	279	228	309
		60	305	463	477	590	447	544
		80	151	203	258	344	302	369
50 percent	None	20	8	24	19	63	66	137
		40	29	89	134	245	179	257
		60	151	281	272	485	315	407
		80	91	125	156	265	232	297

[a] Welfare impact gives the cash equivalent value to each consumer of moving from an economy without a DC plan to one with a DC plan, with the cash value expressed as a percentage of the current annual consumption of the consumer in the economy without a DC plan. There are three steps to calculating this measure. First, calculate the average welfare of households of age t – from the perspective of self t – in the economies with and without a DC plan. Second, record consumption of each household at age t. Third, find λ_t such that giving each t-year-old household in the economy without a DC plan a one-time unexpected after-tax wealth drop of $\lambda_t C_{it}$ raises average welfare in that economy to the level of average welfare in the economy with a DC plan. Table reports values of $100\lambda_t$.

Source: Authors' simulations.

relatively heavily in DC plan accounts and because their DC-plan investments exhibit a uniformly higher percentage of new savings.

Finally, our welfare measure is constructed in three steps. We first calculate the average welfare of households of age t for the economies with and without DC plans. Note that average welfare is calculated from the perspective of self t. Next, we record the consumption (C_{it}) of each household at age t. We then find λ_t, such that giving each t-year-old household in the no-DC-plan economy a one-time unexpected after-tax wealth windfall of $\lambda_t C_{it}$ raises average welfare in that economy to the same level as average welfare in the DC-plan economy. Thus, our welfare measure is $100\lambda_t$. It is defined for each self $\{20, 21, 22, \ldots, T + N\}$ but, in the interest of brevity, we only report it for selves 20, 40, 60, 80.

We report the welfare results in Table 3.13. These effects are quite large. For example, 20-year-old hyperbolic high school graduate households in the no-DC-plan economy need to receive a wealth transfer equal to 70 percent of consumption at age 20 to make them as well off as the average corresponding household in the DC-plan economy with 50 percent employer matching and a 10 percent withdrawal penalty. This effect compares favorably with that for similarly situated exponential households, who experience a welfare effect of 22 percent of consumption. Note that the welfare gains for exponential households arise from the reduction in the taxation of capital income. The hyperbolic consumers benefit both from this tax reduction and from the commitment properties of the DC plan.

Three patterns stand out in Table 3.13. First, welfare effects are uniformly higher for the hyperbolic households, reflecting the value of commitment. Second, the absolute magnitudes of the welfare effects grow until retirement because early accumulation disproportionately benefits the later selves who spend those accumulated assets. Third, welfare effects increase monotonically with education, reflecting the fact that more patient consumers can better exploit tax policies that favor accumulation.

3.6.6 Coefficient of Relative Risk Aversion Equal to 3

We have shown that perfect commitment is much more valuable to hyperbolic consumers with coefficient of relative risk aversion equal to 1 than to those with coefficient of relative risk aversion equal to 3. The results reported later confirm that the gap between DC-plan effects for exponential and hyperbolic consumers shrinks as the coefficient of relative risk aversion increases.

Tables 3.14 through 3.17 are analogous to Tables 3.10 through 3.13 for a coefficient of relative risk aversion equal to 3. Most of the qualitative results in Tables 3.14 through 3.17 mirror those in the earlier tables. In particular, hyperbolic households uniformly respond more favorably to DC plans than do exponential households. This is true by almost all measures, including the national saving rate, government revenue, and consumer welfare.

Table 3.14. Aggregate saving rates in selected simulated economies, CRRA = 3[a] percent

Education	DC plan availability	Employer match	Early withdrawal penalty	Exponential consumers		Hyperbolic consumers	
				Saving rate	Percent increase with DC plan	Saving rate	Percent increase with DC plan
High school dropouts	No	...	...	2.61	...	2.75	...
	Yes	50 percent	10 percent	3.49	33.7	3.76	36.7
		50 percent	50 percent	3.43	31.4	3.73	35.6
	Yes	None	10 percent	3.10	18.8	3.41	24.0
		None	50 percent	3.03	16.1	3.31	20.4
High school graduates	No	...	...	4.10	...	3.96	...
	Yes	50 percent	10 percent	5.49	33.9	5.41	36.6
		50 percent	50 percent	5.42	32.2	5.46	37.9
	Yes	None	10 percent	5.17	26.1	5.16	30.3
		None	50 percent	5.02	22.4	5.06	27.8
College graduates	No	...	...	5.45	...	5.37	...
	Yes	50 percent	10 percent	7.47	37.1	7.36	37.1
		50 percent	50 percent	7.44	36.5	7.47	39.1
	Yes	None	10 percent	6.82	25.1	6.74	25.5
		None	50 percent	6.81	25.0	6.74	25.5
All groups[b]	No	...	...	4.31	...	4.24	...
	Yes	50 percent	10 percent	5.84	35.5	5.80	36.8
		50 percent	50 percent	5.78	34.1	5.86	38.2
	Yes	None	10 percent	5.40	25.3	5.41	27.6
		None	50 percent	5.31	23.2	5.35	26.2

[a] For definition of aggregate saving, see Table 3.10, note a.
[b] For composition of this population, see Table 3.10, note b.
Source: Authors' simulations.

Table 3.15. *Government revenue as a share of labor income in selected simulated economies, CRRA = 3[a] percent*

Education	DC plan availability	Employer match	Early withdrawal penalty	Government revenue Exponential consumers	Hyperbolic consumers
High school dropouts	No	...	...	9.84	9.97
	Yes	50 percent	10 percent	10.20	10.32
			50 percent	9.90	10.10
	Yes	None	10 percent	9.68	9.87
			50 percent	9.67	9.82
High school graduates	No	...	...	13.00	12.89
	Yes	50 percent	10 percent	12.90	12.83
			50 percent	12.78	12.81
	Yes	none	10 percent	12.54	12.55
			50 percent	12.55	12.54
College graduates	No	...	...	16.70	16.59
	Yes	50 percent	10 percent	15.88	15.75
			50 percent	15.96	15.91
	Yes	None	10 percent	15.47	15.40
			50 percent	15.63	15.51
All groups[b]	No	...	...	13.69	13.62
	Yes	50 percent	10 percent	13.43	13.36
			50 percent	13.33	13.37
	Yes	None	10 percent	13.03	13.04
			50 percent	13.08	13.07

[a] For definition of government revenue, see Table 3.11, note a.
[b] For composition of this population, see Table 3.10, note b.
Source: Authors' simulations.

However, the gaps between the exponential and the hyperbolic effects are much smaller in Tables 3.14 through 3.17 than in Tables 3.10 through 3.13. For example, when the coefficient of relative risk aversion is equal to 3, DC plans cause the aggregate saving rate in the exponential economy to rise by between 23.2 and 35.5 percent, depending on the institutional assumptions. Likewise, they cause the aggregate saving rate in the hyperbolic economy to rise by between 26.2 and 38.2 percent. By contrast, when the coefficient of relative risk aversion is equal to 1, DC plans cause the aggregate saving rate in the exponential economy to rise by between 60.6 and 101.7 percent, whereas they cause the aggregate saving rate in the hyperbolic economy to rise by between 81.1 and 134.0 percent.

The choice of the coefficient of relative risk aversion suggests a framework for comparing our results with those of Engen, Gale, and Scholz. These authors

Table 3.16. *Share of defined contribution savings that represents new savings,*
CRRA = 3ᵃ percent

Education	Employer match	Early withdrawal penalty	Percent of DC savings that represents new savings	
			Exponential consumers	Hyperbolic consumers
High school dropouts	50 percent	10 percent	31.1	32.3
		50 percent	33.7	34.6
	None	10 percent	21.8	24.3
		50 percent	21.2	23.3
High school graduates	50 percent	10 percent	30.7	32.0
		50 percent	32.9	35.2
	None	10 percent	26.2	28.0
		50 percent	26.3	29.0
College graduates	50 percent	10 percent	32.6	32.1
		50 percent	34.8	35.2
	None	10 percent	25.6	25.3
		50 percent	27.7	27.0
All groupsᵇ	50 percent	10 percent	31.6	32.1
		50 percent	33.9	35.1
	None	10 percent	25.6	26.5
		50 percent	26.5	27.6

ᵃ For calculation of present new savings, see Table 3.12, note a.
ᵇ For composition of this population, see Table 3.10, note b.
Source: Authors' simulations.

assume a coefficient of relative risk aversion equal to 3 and report that DC plans generate increases in the steady-state saving rate of between 9.1 and 17.2 percent, not far from the range we report herein for exponential discounters.[89] Our work complements theirs, confirming their results and showing how they depend on the coefficient of relative risk aversion.[90]

In summary, when the coefficient of relative risk aversion is close to 3, DC plans are predicted to have limited impact, whether or not preferences are hyperbolic. By contrast, when the coefficient of relative risk aversion is close to unity, such plans will have substantial impact, and their impact will be even greater if discount functions are hyperbolic. Unfortunately, we do not have much insight into

[89] Engen, Gale, and Scholz's (1994) analysis is steady state, in the sense that is performed at a 70-year horizon from the inception of the policy. All consumers alive at this date have had access to 401(k)s throughout their lives.

[90] There are other differences between our model and that of Engen, Gale, and Scholz, but we believe that the coefficient of relative risk aversion assumption is by far the most important. In their model, earnings shocks are more persistent, the contribution cap is lower, the bequest process is perfectly predictable, and the median calibrated discount rate is lower.

Table 3.17. *Welfare impact of defined contribution plans, CRRA = 3[a] percent of current consumption*

Early withdrawal penalty	Employer match	Age	High school dropouts		High school graduates		College graduates	
			Exponential consumers	Hyperbolic consumers	Exponential consumers	Hyperbolic consumers	Exponential consumers	Hyperbolic consumers
10 percent	50 percent	20	<0	1	<0	5	<0	<0
		40	24	44	62	79	112	130
		60	87	106	130	138	193	192
		80	49	71	84	96	119	124
10 percent	None	20	1	1	4	8	8	13
		40	11	23	44	62	97	110
		60	55	71	105	115	144	144
		80	35	55	72	84	93	99
50 percent	50 percent	20	<0	<0	<0	0	<0	<0
		40	22	43	61	83	106	123
		60	109	130	158	173	222	227
		80	58	81	98	113	132	141
50 percent	None	20	0	1	4	7	7	12
		40	10	19	38	54	92	105
		60	52	72	101	123	159	163
		80	34	55	70	89	98	108

[a] Welfare impact gives cash equivalent value to each consumer of moving from an economy without a DC plan to one with a DC plan, with the cash value expressed as a percentage of the current annual consumption of the consumer in the economy without a DC plan. For details of calculation, see Table 3.13, note a.

Source: Authors' simulations.

the value of the coefficient of relative risk aversion. Our preferred model, with coefficient of relative risk aversion equal to 1 and an implied measured elasticity of intertemporal substitution of 0.22, is supported by the available empirical evidence. However, it is also possible to make a case for a coefficient of relative risk aversion equal to 3 with an implied elasticity of intertemporal substitution of 0.15. We hope that future research will be able to pin down these parameters.

3.7 Robustness and Extensions

In this section, we consider several extensions to our benchmark model.

3.7.1 Varying the Value of β

We have discussed our reasons for setting β equal to 0.85. Although the available experimental evidence supports a much lower calibration, such low values generate pathologies in discrete time models. We now demonstrate how our results would likely change if we were to choose lower values of β.

We report simulation results for the exponential case, β equal to 1; our benchmark hyperbolic case, β equal to 0.85; and a new case for comparison, β equal to 0.80. We choose to explore this last case because it is close to our hyperbolic benchmark and does not exhibit the pathologies discussed previously. For β equal to 0.80, we follow the steps described earlier for calibrating the preference parameters. Specifically, we solve for long-run discount factors – $\delta_{\beta\,=\,0.80}^{\mathrm{NHS}}$, $\delta_{\beta\,=\,0.80}^{\mathrm{HS}}$, $\delta_{\beta\,=\,0.80}^{\mathrm{COLL}}$ – so that these simulations replicate the actual level of preretirement wealth holdings.

In Tables 3.18 and 3.19, we report analysis for a DC plan with a 10 percent withdrawal penalty and no employer matching. To a first approximation, the DC plan effects are approximately linear in the magnitude of $(1 - \beta)$. More precisely, the saving rate effects are slightly concave in $(1 - \beta)$, whereas the welfare effects are generally strongly convex in $(1 - \beta)$. For example, introducing the DC plan raises the aggregate saving rate by 60.6 percent in the exponential case, 81.1 percent in our benchmark hyperbolic case, and 86.2 percent in the new comparison case. It generates a welfare gain for 20-year-old high school graduate households equivalent to 28 percent of consumption in the exponential case, 71 percent of consumption in our benchmark hyperbolic case, and 99 percent of consumption in the new comparison case.

If these results apply globally, the hyperbolic effects – the gap between the hyperbolic and the exponential DC plan simulations – will rise significantly as β falls. The available experimental evidence suggests that 0.60 is an appropriate calibration value for β. If the hyperbolic effects rise linearly with $(1 - \beta)$, the true hyperbolic effect is two to three times as large as the effects reported earlier, where our maintained hypothesis was β equal to 0.85.

Table 3.18. *Aggregate saving rate, government revenue, and new savings for selected values of β^a percent*

Item	Value of β		
	1	0.85	0.8
Aggregate saving rate[b]			
No DC plan	4.1	3.9	3.9
With DC plan[c]	6.7	7.1	7.3
Percent difference[d]	60.6	81.1	86.2
Government revenue[e]			
No DC plan	13.3	13.1	13.1
With DC plan[c]	13.5	13.6	13.7
Percent difference[d]	0.8	3.7	4.6
New savings in DC plan[f]	45.5	51.0	52.0

[a] All simulations assume a population comprising the three educational groups in proportions specified in Table 3.10, note b.

[b] Saving as percentage of income; see Table 3.10, note a.

[c] Assumes a 10 percent penalty for early withdrawal and no employer matching contribution.

[d] Percent increase in moving from an economy without a DC plan to an economy with a DC plan.

[e] Percent of labor income; see Table 3.11, note a.

[f] Percent of DC plan savings that represents new savings; see Table 3.12, note a.

Source: Authors' simulations.

3.7.2 Varying the Early Withdrawal Penalty

In the simulations reported earlier, we consider withdrawal penalties of 10 percent and 50 percent. In Table 3.20, we also evaluate a wider range of penalty values – 10, 30, 50, and 70 percent – for a representative case, with no employer matching for high school graduate households and coefficient of relative risk aversion equal to 1. These simulations indicate that penalties in the neighborhood of 50 percent are optimal if the goal is to raise steady-state national saving. Such a penalty creates a strong incentive to avoid early withdrawals from the DC plan, but it is not so high as to discourage contributions in the first place.

3.7.3 Modeling a World with Both Exponential and Hyperbolic Consumers

All of our simulations are based on the premise that an economy is either completely exponential or completely hyperbolic. However, it also is reasonable to assume that the economy comprises a mixed population of exponential and hyperbolic consumers, where the latter are relatively more impatient than the former.

Table 3.19. *Welfare impact of defined contribution plans for*
selected values of β[a] percent of current consumption

Education	Age	Value of β		
		1	0.85	0.8
High school dropouts	20	9	27	41
	40	34	81	95
	60	154	215	220
	80	92	99	118
High school graduates	20	28	71	99
	40	104	180	202
	60	250	327	334
	80	153	192	240
College graduates	20	70	142	183
	40	187	242	264
	60	300	328	349
	80	224	254	277

[a] Welfare impact gives cash-equivalent value to each consumer of moving from an economy without a DC plan to one with a DC plan, with the cash value expressed as a percentage of the current annual consumption of the consumer in the economy without a DC plan. For details of calculation, see Table 3.13, note a. Table assumes a DC plan with a 10 percent penalty for early withdrawal and no employer-matching contribution.

Source: Authors' simulations.

To simulate this case, we assume that each educational group is evenly divided between exponential and hyperbolic consumers.[91] Furthermore, we assume that within each educational group, exponential and hyperbolic households have the same long-term discount factors: δ^{NHS}, δ^{HS}, δ^{COLL}. For all consumers, we set the coefficient of relative risk aversion equal to 1. For the exponential consumers, we set β equal to 1, and for the hyperbolic consumers we set β equal to 0.85. We then follow the steps described earlier for calibrating the preference parameters. We solve for the long-run discount factors, so that the mixed population replicates the actual median level of preretirement wealth holdings. In this way, we obtain long-run discount rates for the three educational groups of 0.0427, 0.0335, and 0.0257, respectively. As expected, these discount rates lie close to the midpoints of the discount rates for exponential and hyperbolic consumers reported in our original calibration exercise (see Table 3.4). Figure 3.15 plots the resulting simulations for exponential and hyperbolic consumers in the high school graduate group in the

[91] If education is an endogenous outcome, it might make sense to assume that households in the college graduate group are disproportionately exponential: it may be easier to invest in education if self-control is not a problem.

Table 3.20. *Aggregate effects of varying the early withdrawal penalty, high school graduates*[a]
percent

Item	Early withdrawal penalty	Exponential consumers		Hyperbolic consumers	
		Level	Percent increase with DC plan	Level	Percent increase with DC plan
Aggregrate saving rate[b]					
No DC plan	. . .	3.9	. . .	3.6	. . .
With DC plan	10 percent	6.4	61.6	7.0	92.3
	30 percent	6.3	59.3	7.5	106.6
	50 percent	6.7	70.7	8.2	126.2
	70 percent	6.2	58.8	7.6	111.0
Government revenue[d]					
No DC plan	. . .	12.7	. . .	12.4	. . .
With DC plan	10 percent	12.9	1.7	13.1	5.6
	30 percent	12.9	1.6	13.3	7.7
	50 percent	13.1	3.6	13.7	10.2
	70 percent	12.8	1.5	13.4	7.8
New savings[b]					
With DC plan[c]	10 percent	45.4	. . .	53.5	. . .
	30 percent	46.8	. . .	57.7	. . .
	50 percent	54.8	. . .	62.3	. . .
	70 percent	47.3	. . .	59.1	. . .

[a] Percent increase in a given rate as a result of moving from an economy without a DC plan to an economy with a DC plan.
[b] Saving as percentage of income; see Table 3.10, note a.
[c] Assumes no employer matching contribution.
[d] Percent of labor income; see Table 3.11, note a.
[e] Percent of DC plan savings that represents new savings; see Table 3.12, note a.
Source: Authors' simulations.

economy without a DC plan. The exponential consumers save far more than the corresponding hyperbolic consumers.

Figure 3.16 plots the percentage of liquidity-constrained high school graduates in our hybrid simulation for an economy with no DC plan. This graph is comparable to the upper panel of Figure 3.11, which plots the percentage of liquidity-constrained consumers in the nonhybrid simulations. Note that the percentage of liquidity-constrained hyperbolic consumers in Figure 3.16 is greater than in Figure 3.11 because the hyperbolic consumers in the hybrid simulation are more impatient than those in the nonhybrid simulation. Similarly, the percentage of liquidity-constrained exponential consumers in Figure 3.16 is less than in Figure 3.11 because the exponential consumers in the hybrid simulation are less impatient than those in the nonhybrid simulation.

Using our calibrated hybrid populations, we then evaluate the impact of DC plans. Table 3.21 reports the results of this simulation. In our hybrid economy,

Thousands of 1990 dollars

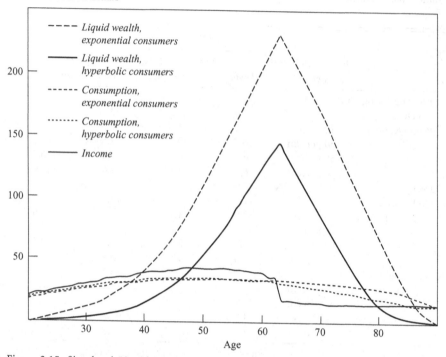

Figure 3.15. Simulated Liquid Asset, Income, and Consumption Paths in a Hybrid World without a Defined Contribution Plan[a]

[a] Figure plots average consumption, pretax labor income, and liquid wealth for households with high school graduate heads. The population comprises 50 percent exponential and 50 percent hyperbolic households, and the model is calibrated under the assumption that both types of households have the same long-term discount factor (δ).

Source: Authors' simulations.

exponential consumers experience an increase of 58.0 percent in the steady-state saving rate, whereas hyperbolic consumers experience an increase of 86.3 percent, yielding an aggregate increase of 68.0 percent. The corresponding increases in the nonhybrid simulations are 60.6 percent for exponential consumers and 81.1 percent for hyperbolic consumers. As expected, the percentage change in the hybrid simulations is lower for the exponential consumers and higher for the hyperbolic consumers than in the nonhybrid simulations. The reason for this is that in the hybrid simulation, the exponential consumers are more patient and the hyperbolic consumers are more impatient than in the nonhybrid simulation, leading to more asset shifting by the former and less by the latter.

The hybrid economy suggests a general point about hyperbolic discounting. If hyperbolic discounters are relatively more impatient than exponential discounters (which is true in the hybrid simulation but not in the nonhybrid simulations), DC plans will have a larger percentage impact on hyperbolic households than on

Percent of households

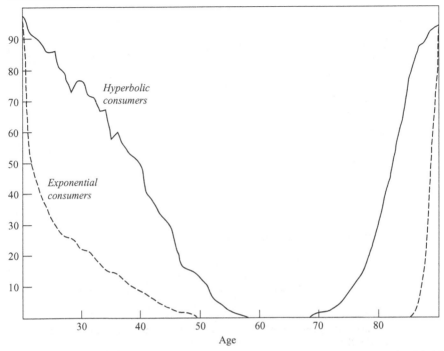

Figure 3.16. Share of High School Graduates Who Are Liquidity Constrained, Hybrid Economy[a]
[a] Figure plots simulated percent of households in the high school group who are liquidity constrained (less than $400 in liquid assets) in the economy in which half of consumers are exponential and half are hyperbolic. The coefficient of relative risk aversion is equal to 1, and exponential and hyperbolic consumers have the same long-term discount factor (δ).
Source: Authors' simulations.

exponential households, for two distinct reasons.[92] First, hyperbolic households value commitment; and, second, hyperbolic households are relatively impatient and are, therefore, less likely to have accumulated assets that they can simply shift into the DC plan.

3.8 Conclusion

In this paper, we start by showing that life-cycle consumption and asset accumulation patterns are consistent with a hyperbolic model. At first glance, the life-cycle choices of hyperbolic and exponential consumers are indistinguishable. However,

[92] In the nonhybrid simulations, the calibration guarantees that the exponential and hyperbolic consumers accumulate the same amount of preretirement savings if they do not have access to the DC plan. In the nonhybrid simulations, the effects of $\beta_{hyperbolic} < \beta_{exponential}$ are offset by setting $\delta_{hyperbolic} > \delta_{exponential}$.

Table 3.21. *Aggregate impact of defined contribution plans for a*
population comprising exponential and hyperbolic consumers[a] percent

Item	Exponential consumers	Hyperbolic consumers	Aggregate population
Aggregrate saving rate[b]			
No DC plan	5.4	2.9	4.2
With DC plan[c]	8.5	5.5	7.0
Percent difference[d]	58.0	86.3	68.0
Government revenue[e]			
No DC plan	14.3	12.4	13.4
With DC plan[c]	15.5	12.7	13.6
Percent difference[d]	8.4	2.6	1.9
New savings in DC plan[f]	44.3	51.9	47.2

[a] Table shows the aggregate impact of DC plans under the assumption that the population comprises 50 percent exponential households and 50 percent hyperbolic households. Long-term discount rates are calibrated such that the preretirement median ratio of wealth to income in the simulated no-DC-plan economy matches the ratio in the data. The underlying long-term discount rates are the same for all consumers within an educational category. For the share of each educational group in the population, see Table 3.10, note a.

[b] Saving as a percentage of income; see Table 3.10, note a.

[c] Assumes a 10 percent penalty for early withdrawal and no employer matching contribution.

[d] Percent increase in moving from an economy without a DC plan to an economy with a DC plan.

[e] Percent of labor income; see Table 3.11, note a.

[f] Percent of DC plan savings that represents new savings; see Table 3.12, note a.

Source: Authors' simulations.

hyperbolic consumers exhibit some special regularities that enable researchers to distinguish them from their exponential counterparts: they are much more likely to encounter liquidity constraints, and they exhibit the anomalous precautionary saving effects documented by Dynan.[93] These hyperbolic phenomena are implied by the generalized Euler equation.

We then consider another distinction between hyperbolic and exponential behavior. We show that hyperbolic consumers will react much more favorably to defined contribution pension plans than equivalent exponential consumers. Our benchmark simulations for an exponential economy – with coefficient of relative risk aversion equal to 1 and a measured elasticity of intertemporal substitution of 0.27 – show that DC plans with early-withdrawal penalties of between 10 and 50 percent raise the steady-state net national saving rate by 61 to 102 percent. By contrast, in a hyperbolic economy (with coefficient of relative risk aversion equal

[93] Dynan (1993).

to 1 and a measured elasticity of intertemporal substitution of 0.22), such plans raise the steady-state net national saving rate by 81 to 134 percent. These results are sensitive to the calibration of the coefficient of relative risk aversion. Higher values of the coefficient of relative risk aversion significantly reduce the effects of DC plans in both exponential and hyperbolic economies.

This work should be extended in several directions. First, the magnitudes of the effects that we find need to be examined for hyperbolic discounters with values of β below those that we consider. We choose relatively high values for this parameter to avoid pathologies. The hyperbolic effects would be much stronger for lower values of β, and most experimental evidence suggests that a value of 0.6 would best match consumer preferences. For reasons that we discussed earlier, simulations with low values for β need to be implemented in continuous time.[94]

Second, the dynamic process that takes an economy from a steady state without a DC plan to a steady state with a DC plan should be evaluated. As Engen, Gale, and Scholz, and others have pointed out, the short-run effects of a tax incentive often take the opposite sign to the long-run effects.[95]

Third, the set of commitment devices available to hyperbolic consumers in the model should be enriched. We compare a world with no endogenous commitment devices to a world with one endogenous commitment device: a DC pension plan. In the real world, there are a wide range of commitment devices and the introduction of DC plans may simply lead hyperbolic consumers to switch from a preexisting commitment device to this new one.

Fourth, if the economy does not, in fact, contain good alternative commitment devices, something may be wrong with the hyperbolic model. If consumers have hyperbolic discount functions and are sophisticated, they should want banks or other financial institutions to sell commitment devices. One sees many instruments with commitment properties but very few that are sold explicitly for this purpose. Perhaps illiquid assets span the commitment space. If they do not, why have banks not filled the gaps? Are consumers too myopic (or too embarrassed) to seek out explicit commitment devices?

Fifth, the other behavioral facets of DC plans should be formally analyzed. To the extent that such plans do raise national saving, they may do so for reasons not modeled in this paper. For example, DC plans simplify the investment process, helping consumers with bounded rationality make good investments; and they make interpersonal comparisons of saving more transparent, perhaps shaming consumers into saving more. Although we do not model automatic deductions in this paper, we believe that this popular feature of DC plans plays a particularly important role in encouraging accumulation. As Public Agenda reports, "Americans overwhelmingly (77 percent) prefer to save for retirement through automatic

---

[94] This requires an alternative approximation to the hyperbolic discount function. The quasi-hyperbolic discount function does not have a direct analog in continuous time.

[95] Engen, Gale, and Scholz (1994).

deductions from their paychecks, with only a fifth (19 percent) preferring to make a savings decision each time they get paid."[96] It is not known why automatic deductions are attractive. Perhaps they serve as a commitment device. Perhaps they simplify decision making for consumers with bounded rationality. Defined contribution plans use a rich array of psychologically appealing features to induce saving.[97] Economists should do more to understand these effects.

REFERENCES

Ainslie, George W. 1975. "Specious Reward: A Behavioral Theory of Impulsiveness and Impulse Control." *Psychological Bulletin* 82(4): 463–96.

———. 1986. "Beyond Microeconomics: Conflict among Interests in a Multiple Self as a Determinant of Value." In Jon Elster (ed.), *The Multiple Self.* Cambridge University Press.

———. 1992. *Picoeconomics.* Cambridge University Press.

Akerlof, George A. 1991. "Procrastination and Obedience." *American Economic Review, Papers and Proceedings* 81(2): 1–19.

American Express Financial Advisors. 1996. "A Commonsense Guide to Personal Money Management." Minneapolis: American Express Financial Corporation.

Andrews, Emily S. 1992. "The Growth and Distribution of 401(k) Plans." In John A. Turner and Daniel J. Beller (eds.), *Trends in Pensions 1992.* Department of Labor, Pension and Welfare Benefits Administration.

Attanasio, Orazio P., and Guglielmo Weber. 1993. "Consumption Growth, the Interest Rate, and Aggregation." *Review of Economic Studies* 60(3): 631–49.

Auerbach, Alan J., and Laurence J. Kotlikoff. 1987. *Dynamic Fiscal Policy.* Cambridge University Press.

Banks, James, Richard Blundell, and Sarah Tanner. 1995. "Consumption Growth, Saving, and Retirement in the U.K." *Ricerche Economiche* 49(3): 255–75.

Barro, Robert J. 1997. "Myopia and Inconsistency in the Neoclassical Growth Model." Unpublished paper. Harvard University (September).

Barsky, Robert B., and others. 1997. "Preference Parameters and Behavioral Heterogeneity: An Experimental Approach in the Health and Retirement Study." *Quarterly Journal of Economics* 112(2): 537–79.

Beaudry, Paul, and Eric van Wincoop. 1996. "The Intertemporal Elasticity of Substitution: An Exploration Using a U.S. Panel of State Data." *Economica* 63(251): 495–512.

Bernheim, B. Douglas. 1994. "Personal Saving, Information, and Economic Literacy: New Directions for Public Policy." In *Tax Policy for Economic Growth in the 1990s.* Washington, DC: American Council for Capital Formation.

———. 1995. "Do Households Appreciate Their Financial Vulnerabilities? An Analysis of Actions, Perceptions, and Public Policy." In *Tax Policy for Economic Growth in the 1990s.* Washington, DC: American Council for Capital Formation.

Bernheim, B. Douglas, Jonathan Skinner, and Steven Weinberg. 1997. "What Accounts for the Variation in Retirement Wealth Among U.S. Households?" Working Paper 6227. Cambridge, MA: National Bureau of Economic Research (October).

Camerer, Colin, and Teck-Hua Ho. 1997. "Experience-Weighted Attraction Learning in Normal-Form Games." Working Paper 1003. California Institute of Technology (December).

---

[96] Farkas and Johnson (1997, p. 28).

[97] See Laibson (1998) for a review of the psychological effects induced by DC plans.

Campbell, John Y., and N. Gregory Mankiw. 1989. "Consumption, Income, and Interest Rates: Reinterpreting the Time Series Evidence." In Olivier Jean Blanchard and Stanley Fischer (eds.), *NBER Macroeconomics Annual 1989*. MIT Press.

Carroll, Christopher D. 1992. "The Buffer-Stock Theory of Saving: Some Macroeconomic Evidence." *BPEA, 2: 1992*, 61–156.

1997a. "Buffer-Stock Saving and the Life-Cycle/Permanent Income Hypothesis." *Quarterly Journal of Economics* 112(1): 1–55.

1997b. "Death to the Log-Linearized Consumption Euler Equation! (And Very Poor Health to the Second-Order Approximation)." Working Paper 6298. Cambridge, MA: National Bureau of Economic Research (December).

Carroll, Christopher D., and Miles S. Kimball. 1996. "On the Concavity of the Consumption Function." *Econometrica* 64(4): 981–92.

Chung, Shin-Ho, and Richard J. Herrnstein. 1967. "Choice and Delay of Reinforcement." *Journal of the Experimental Analysis of Animal Behavior* 10(1): 67–74.

Deaton, Angus. 1991. "Saving and Liquidity Constraints." *Econometrica* 59(5): 1221–48.

Diamond, Peter, and Botond Köszegi. 1998. "Hyperbolic Discounting and Retirement." Unpublished paper. Massachusetts Institute of Technology (March).

Dynan, Karen E. 1993. "How Prudent Are Consumers?" *Journal of Political Economy* 101(6): 1104–13.

Engen, Eric M. 1994. "Precautionary Saving and the Structure of Taxation." Unpublished paper. Federal Reserve Board, Division of Research and Statistics, Fiscal Analysis Section (June).

Engen, Eric M., and William G. Gale. 1993. "IRAs and Saving in a Stochastic Life-Cycle Model." Unpublished paper. University of California, Los Angeles (April).

Engen, Eric M., William G. Gale, and John Karl Scholz. 1994. "Do Saving Incentives Work?" *BPEA* 1:1994, 85–180.

1996. "The Illusory Effects of Saving Incentives on Saving." *Journal of Economic Perspectives* 10(4): 113–38.

Erev, Ido, and Alvin E. Roth. 1998. "Predicting How People Play Games: Reinforcement Learning in Experimental Games with Unique, Mixed Strategy Equilibria." *American Economic Review* (forthcoming).

Farkas, Steve, and Jean Johnson. 1997. *Miles to Go: A Status Report on Americans' Plans for Retirement*. New York: Public Agenda.

Feldstein, Martin S. 1978. "The Welfare Cost of Capital Income Taxation." *Journal of Political Economy* 86(2, pt. 2): S29–S51.

Gentry, William M., and Joseph Milano. 1998. "Taxes and Investment in Annuities." Working Paper 6525. Cambridge, MA: National Bureau of Economic Research (April).

Gourinchas, Pierre-Olivier, and Jonathan A. Parker. 1997. "Consumption Over the Life-Cycle." Unpublished paper. Massachusetts Institute of Technology (January).

Hall, Robert E. 1978. "Stochastic Implications of the Life-Cycle–Permanent Income Hypothesis: Theory and Evidence." *Journal of Political Economy* 86(6): 971–87.

1988. "Intertemporal Substitution in Consumption." *Journal of Political Economy* 96(2): 339–57.

Hansen, Lars Peter, and Kenneth J. Singleton. 1982. "Generalized Instrumental Variables Estimation of Non-Linear Rational Expectations Models." *Econometrica* 50(5): 1269–85.

Harris, Christopher, and David I. Laibson. 1998. "Buffer Stock Models, Euler Equations, and Hyperbolic Discounting." Unpublished paper. Harvard University (January).

Hewitt Associates. 1995. *Trends and Experience in 401(k) Plans*. Lincolnshire, IL.

1997. *Survey Findings: 401(k) Trends and Experience*. Lincolnshire, IL.

Hoch, Stephen J., and George Loewenstein. 1991. "Time-Inconsistent Preferences and Consumer Self-Control." *Journal of Consumer Research* 17(4): 492–507.

Hubbard, R. Glenn, and Jonathan Skinner. 1996. "Assessing the Effectiveness of Saving Incentives." *Journal of Economic Perspectives* 10(4): 73–90.

Hubbard, R. Glenn, Jonathan Skinner, and Stephen P. Zeldes. 1994. "The Importance of Precautionary Motives in Explaining Individual and Aggregate Saving." *Carnegie-Rochester Conference Series on Public Policy* 40: 59–125.

——— 1995. "Precautionary Saving and Social Insurance." *Journal of Political Economy* 103(2): 360–99.

Jappelli, Tullio. 1990. "Who Is Credit Constrained in the U.S. Economy?" *Quarterly Journal of Economics* 105(1): 219–34.

King, George R., and Alexandra W. Logue. 1987. "Choice in a Self-Control Paradigm with Human Subjects: Effects of Changeover Delay Duration." *Learning and Motivation* 18(4): 421–38.

Kirby, Kris N. 1997. "Bidding on the Future: Evidence Against Normative Discounting of Delayed Rewards." *Journal of Experimental Psychology* 126(1): 54–70.

Kirby, Kris N., and R. J. Herrnstein. 1995. "Preference Reversals Due to Myopic Discounting of Delayed Reward." *Psychological Science* 6(2): 83–89.

Kirby, Kris N., and Nino N. Marakovic. 1995. "Modeling Myopic Decisions: Evidence for Hyperbolic Delay-Discounting within Subjects and Amounts." *Organizational Behavior and Human Decision Processes* 64(1): 22–30.

——— 1996. "Delay-Discounting Probabilistic Rewards: Rates Decrease as Amounts Increase." *Psychonomic Bulletin and Review* 3(1): 100–04.

Laibson, David I. 1994. "Self-Control and Saving." Ph.D. dissertation. Massachusetts Institute of Technology (May).

——— 1996. "Hyperbolic Discount Functions, Undersaving, and Savings Policy." Working Paper 5635. Cambridge, MA: National Bureau of Economic Research.

——— 1997a. "Golden Eggs and Hyperbolic Discounting." *Quarterly Journal of Economics* 112(2): 443–77.

——— 1997b. "Hyperbolic Discount Functions and Time Preference Heterogeneity." Unpublished paper. Harvard University (March).

——— 1998. "Comment." In David A. Wise (ed.), *Studies in the Economics of Aging*. University of Chicago Press.

Loewenstein, George F., and Dražen Prelec. 1992. "Anomalies in Intertemporal Choice: Evidence and an Interpretation." *Quarterly Journal of Economics* 107(2): 573–97.

Loewenstein, George F., and Nachum Sicherman. 1991. "Do Workers Prefer Increasing Wage Profiles?" *Journal of Labor Economics* 9(1): 67–84.

Mankiw, N. Gregory, Julio J. Rotemberg, and Lawrence H. Summers. 1985. "Intertemporal Substitution in Macroeconomics." *Quarterly Journal of Economics* 100(1): 225–51.

Millar, Andrew, and Douglas J. Navarick. 1984. "Self-Control and Choice in Humans: Effects of Video Game Playing as a Positive Reinforcer." *Learning and Motivation* 15(2): 203–18.

Mulligan, Casey B. 1997. "A Logical Economist's Argument Against Hyperbolic Discounting." Unpublished paper. University of Chicago (February).

Navarick, Douglas J. 1982. "Negative Reinforcement and Choice in Humans." *Learning and Motivation* 13(3): 361–77.

O'Donoghue, Edward, and Matthew Rabin. 1997a. "Doing It Now or Later." Unpublished paper. Northwestern University (October).

1997b. "Incentives for Procrastinators." Unpublished paper. Northwestern University (February).

Papke, Leslie E. 1997. "Are 401(k) Plans Replacing Other Employer-Provided Pensions? Evidence from Panel Data." Unpublished paper. Michigan State University (October).

Phelps, Edmund S., and Robert A. Pollak. 1968. "On Second-Best National Saving and Game-Equilibrium Growth." *Review of Economic Studies* 35(2): 185–99.

Poterba, James M., Steven F. Venti, and David A. Wise. 1995. "Do 401(k) Contributions Crowd Out Other Personal Saving?" *Journal of Public Economics* 58(1): 1–32.

1996. "How Retirement Saving Programs Increase Saving." *Journal of Economic Perspectives* 10(4): 91–112.

Prelec, Dražen. 1989. "Decreasing Impatience: Definition and Consequences." Unpublished paper. Harvard Business School (August).

Read, Daniel, and others. 1998. "Mixing Virtue and Vice: The Combined Effects of the Immediacy Effect and the Desire for Diversity." Unpublished paper. Leeds University Business School (June).

Sabelhaus, John. 1997. "Public Policy and Saving in the United States and Canada." *Canadian Journal of Economics* 30(2): 253–75.

Schelling, Thomas C. 1984. "Self-Command in Practice, in Policy, and in a Theory of Rational Choice." *American Economic Review, Papers and Proceedings* 74(2): 1–11.

Shapiro, Matthew D., and Joel Slemrod. 1995. "Consumer Response to the Timing of Income: Evidence from a Change in Tax Withholding." *American Economic Review* 85(1): 274–83.

Shea, John. 1995. "Union Contracts and the Life-Cycle/Permanent-Income Hypothesis." *American Economic Review* 85(1): 186–200.

Simmons Market Research Bureau. 1996. *The 1996 Study of Media and Markets.* New York.

Solnick, Jay V., and others. 1980. "An Experimental Analysis of Impulsivity and Impulse Control in Humans." *Learning and Motivation* 11(1): 61–77.

Strotz, Robert H. 1956. "Myopia and Inconsistency in Dynamic Utility Maximization." *Review of Economic Studies* 23(1): 165–80.

Thaler, Richard H., and Hersch M. Shefrin. 1981. "An Economic Theory of Self-Control." *Journal of Political Economy* 89(2): 392–406.

U.S. National Center for Health Statistics. 1994. *Vital Statistics of the United States, 1994.* Department of Health and Human Services.

Zeldes, Stephen P. 1989. "Consumption and Liquidity Constraints: An Empirical Investigation." *Journal of Political Economy* 97(2): 305–46.

4 Social Security Investment in Equities

Policy discussions of social security portfolio diversification into equities have concentrated on the consequences for retirement benefits and the budget viability of the system, ignoring general equilibrium repercussions (and sometimes even claiming there would be none). In contrast, we analyze the general equilibrium ramifications for prices, for utility levels, and for investment. We show that these ramifications can be substantial and paradoxical when part of the population does not adjust its private savings portfolio in response to a change in its social security portfolio. We also show how critically they depend on heterogeneity in saving, in production, in assets, and in taxes.[1]

Among the elderly, Social Security income is distributed very differently than private pension and asset income.[2] For the bottom quintile of the income distribution, 81 percent of income comes from social security, whereas only 6 percent is from pensions plus income from assets. For the top quintile, 23 percent comes from social security, whereas 46 percent is from pensions and assets – dramatically

[1] For policy discussions, see, for example, Advisory Council on Social Security (1997). For examples of claims that make sense in a representative agent model but are not adequate once heterogeneity is recognized, see Financial Economists' Roundtable (1998) and Greenspan (1997). For a discussion of privatization in general, see Diamond (1999). For another analysis of portfolio diversification where general equilibrium effects matter, see Abel (2001). Our paper differs from that of Abel in that we attribute the lack of portfolio diversification of some workers to a lack of savings, whereas Abel focuses on a fixed cost of portfolio diversification. This difference implies a different response to social security portfolio diversification, with Abel finding an income effect lowering investment from consumers who stop paying the fixed cost and stop investing in the stock market because of the change in social security portfolio. Moreover, Abel assumes an aggregate production function, leaving no role for direct choice about the riskiness of aggregate production.
[2] See Mitchell and Moore (1997), Social Security Administration (1996).

The authors are grateful to Saku Aura, Tom Davidoff, and Marek Pycia for research assistance; to Bill Brainard, Alicia Munnell, Jim Poterba, Antonio Rangel, the editor, and anonymous referees for comments; and to the National Science Foundation for research support under grant SBR-9618698. The research reported herein was also supported by a grant from the U.S. Social Security Administration (SSA) funded as part of the Retirement Research Consortium. The opinions and conclusions are solely those of the authors and should not be construed as representing the opinions or policy of SSA or any agency of the Federal Government.

different percentages. Similarly, there are great differences in saving and investing among current workers. Among all those who were paying social security taxes in 1995, fully 59 percent held no stock, either directly or through pension plans. Even among those between 45 and 54 years of age, 50 percent held no stock, directly or indirectly.[3] These differences have important implications for diversification proposals.

We represent this heterogeneity in saving behavior by supposing that there are two types of representative agents, one of which does no saving (except through social security) and the other of which saves and selects a portfolio (and, for simplicity, is assumed not to be covered by social security). We refer to the two types of agents as workers and savers.

Our analysis includes heterogeneity in production. We suppose that there are two short-term technologies, which produce safe and risky output.[4] We also assume there are two long-term real assets, called safe land and risky land, which produce safe and risky output in perpetuity. Distinguishing between safe and risky output allows portfolio diversification to increase production in one technology sector and reduce it in the other, thereby changing the riskiness of aggregate output. Including long-term real assets allows changes in the equilibrium prices of land to redistribute wealth between generations. Wealth redistribution is interesting for its own sake but also because of its effect on investment.

Social security diversification is likely to change the rate of interest, requiring higher taxes to pay the higher coupons on government bonds. But, the increased income tax burden may fall on households in different proportions than the increased interest income from holding government bonds. This, in turn, will have feedback effects on the equilibrium interest rate.

Our analysis integrates all these different effects, showing the impact of a small portfolio diversification on equilibrium, given assumptions on utility and technology. To keep the analysis simple, social security is modeled as an unfunded pay-as-you-go system together with a defined contribution system.[5] Social security diversification occurs when the asset mix in the defined contribution system is suddenly shifted from bonds toward equities, and then maintained at the higher equity level forever after. Many proposed reforms of the U.S. social security system roughly fit this model. For example, if workers were suddenly given discretionary accounts, some of them with little or no outside saving would choose to invest part of their accounts in equities, and then our analysis would apply.[6] The differences between defined benefit and defined contribution systems

---

[3] Quoted in Geanakoplos, Mitchell, and Zeldes (1999). See Kennickell, Starr-McCluer, and Sunden (1997) and Ameriks and Zeldes (in progress).

[4] With two types of production, the aggregate uncertainty in production varies with the mix of the two types. This is a simple way to allow aggregate uncertainty to be endogenous.

[5] Equivalently, we could think of it as a partially funded defined benefits system that adjusts benefits in response to asset returns in the same way.

[6] Because we suppose that all workers have the same utility, it makes no difference whether social security accounts are personal or are managed by a trust fund, provided that they choose the same asset mix and benefits are adjusted in this way.

as distributors of rate-of-return risk have been explored in OLG models with a single representative agent per generation.[7] This paper is meant to complement those studies.

The paper begins in Sections 4.2–4.4 by laying out the model. Five assumptions are spelled out. We suppose that the demands by savers for consumption when young, and for safe and risky consumption when old, are normal; that increases in government bond interest payments raise the payments on government bonds held by social security more than they raise workers' income taxes (and thus raise savers' taxes more than they raise savers' income on the government bonds they hold); that the level of risky investment does not affect the relative outputs across states (short-term risky production is along a ray in state space); that the output from both short-term and long-term risky production is independently and identically distributed each period; and that workers' wages are not stochastic.

Under these five assumptions, (a little) diversification can generate a Pareto gain and necessarily raises a suitable social welfare function.[8] In a weak sense, it increases risky investment, decreases safe investment, raises interest rates, lowers expected returns on short-term risky securities, and reduces the equity premium. Aggregate investment might rise or fall, aggregate land prices might go up or down, and welfare of old and young savers might go up or down. The possibility that the direction of change of some variables depends on technology has not appeared in the social security reform debate.

To isolate each possibility and illuminate its cause, we build our general model gradually. In the first model (Section 4.5), we suppose that risky and safe production each consist of a single linear activity, so that technology determines the rates of return on both safe and risky assets. Diversification cannot change equilibrium prices and, thus, has no effect on the utility of savers. By contrast, diversification does change the level and riskiness of social security benefits, raising the expected utility of workers if they prefer some stocks to an all-bond portfolio.[9] This effect persists in all of the models considered. Moreover, diversification in this model raises risky investment, lowers safe investment, leaves aggregate investment unchanged, and so raises expected output.

---

[7] See, for example, Bohn (1997, 1998, 1999) and Diamond (1997). We are not aware of other equilibrium studies considering portfolio diversification.

[8] Diversification from a point of zero exposure to equities raises the sum total of weighted utility in the economy if household utilities are weighted so that the expected marginal utility of a dollar for sure is the same for every saver and every retired worker. Because workers do not save, their marginal rates of substitution across time are not proportional to interest rates, and it is impossible to require marginal utilities for young workers to match up as well, for all time periods. But, even if they do not match up in the welfare function, the welfare function must be increased by diversification.

[9] This conclusion does not rely on an assumption that workers are more risk tolerant than savers. Presumably they are not. The welfare gains come from the superior risk-sharing social security diversification permits when there are workers who do not have savings to invest on their own, and when, in the absence of social security diversification, social security benefits have a low correlation with stock returns. This point was made in Geanakoplos, Mitchell, and Zeldes (1999), who also tried to quantify the welfare gain in a special quadratic example.

In the second model (Section 4.6), we retain the risky activity but suppose that there is no safe investment in the original equilibrium. Diversification now raises the safe interest rate, requiring an increase in taxation to pay the government bond interest. This creates welfare effects (from changing returns and changing taxes) in addition to the direct welfare impact of the change in portfolio on the social security benefits. Diversification raises risky investment and so aggregate investment. In Section 4.7, we add infinitely lived assets to the model of Section 4.6. Diversification still raises the safe interest rate. Now, a rise in the safe interest rate lowers the value of infinitely lived assets, hurting the savers holding these assets and benefitting young savers in the future, creating a feedback leading to further investment in the future. This case illustrates the possibility that the purchase of stock and sale of bonds by the social security system might paradoxically lower stock values, even under plausible circumstances.

To clarify the dependence of some of the results on technological assumptions, we consider a model (Section 4.9) in which there is a perfectly safe linear technology but no risky technology. The safe linear technology fixes the equilibrium government bond interest rate. In this case, the price of infinitely lived risky assets goes up after diversification, generating an intergenerational redistribution in the opposite direction to that of the previous model. Moreover, diversification now lowers safe investment and so aggregate investment. This case highlights the possibility that social security diversification might raise the price of equities, benefitting the old savers but reducing the equity returns for all future savers, making them worse off. This drop in welfare might lead them to reduce savings, thereby reducing future investment and output.

Section 4.10 has a general nonlinear model of production that includes all the previous linear models as special cases. Section 4.11 discusses more general defined-benefit systems. Section 4.12 has concluding remarks. Proofs of some propositions are in the appendix.

4.1 Technology

We analyze the equilibrium of a stochastic overlapping-generations economy, where each generation lives for two periods. There is one perishable consumption good in each date-event, which can either be eaten or invested using a productive technology. Young consumers have nonstochastic endowments, which can be interpreted as earnings from inelastically supplied labor with a technology that is linear and nonstochastic in labor.

At each date-event, there are two short-term investment opportunities that transform the single perishable consumption good into (safe or stochastic amounts of) consumption goods in the next period. In Sections 4.1–4.9, we assume a linear short-term technology to avoid the complications from feedback of investment levels on rates of return to productive investments. The safe investment produces $R_0 k_0$ in the period following an investment of k_0, with no durability in the capital, where $R_0 > 1$ is a constant. (Thus, we are assuming a positive safe rate of return.) The risky investment produces Rk in the period following an investment of k, also with no durability in the capital, where $R > 0$ is a random variable. For convenience, we assume the risky returns to be independently and identically distributed each period. Each of these technologies may or may not be used in equilibrium, depending on rates of return.[10] In Section 4.7, we add to the model two types of infinitely lived assets, called land, yielding safe and risky outputs in perpetuity. In Section 4.10, we generalize the model to allow for nonlinear production.

4.2 Consumers

To bring out the difference between social-security–covered workers and wealth holders, we assume there are workers who do not save and savers who are not covered by social security; that is, two representative agents in each birth cohort.[11] We assume that each worker receives w in the first period, with each saver receiving W.

We assume no population growth and normalize the population so that there is a unit measure of (identical) savers and a measure of size n of (identical) workers. The representative saver maximizes expected lifetime utility of consumption, taking prices as given. Expected lifetime utility, V, is equal to $U_1[C_1] + E\{U_2[C_2]\}$, where C_1 is consumption when young and C_2 is consumption when old, and with U_i increasing, concave and twice continuously differentiable. In the model without land, the savers divide exogenous first-period wealth, W, among consumption and (up to) three tangible assets – government bonds, B, and two types of physical capital: k_0, which is the safe asset, and k, which is the risky asset. In addition, the savers pay income taxes, T, in the second period.[12] Thus, we denote expected utility maximization for the representative saver by:

$$V = \max U_1[C_1] + E\{U_2[C_2]\}$$
$$\text{s.t. } W = C_1 + B + k_0 + k$$
$$C_2 = (1+r)B + R_0 k_0 + Rk - T \tag{4.1}$$

where the rate of return, R, is random but taxes are not, as of the time of first-period decisions. If the safe real asset is held in equilibrium, then $1 + r$ is equal to R_0 because the government bond and the safe real asset are perfect substitutes.

---

[10] When a technology is not in use, we suppose that the marginal utility of beginning to use it is strictly less than the marginal cost of beginning to use it. For completeness, we mention that there are (knife-edge) regimes with a technology that is not in use but with the marginal benefit of beginning to use it exactly equal to the marginal cost of beginning to use it. Generically, these regimes will not be observed.

[11] Feldstein (1985) makes a two-types assumption in his classification of agents as rational and myopic. Having savers covered by social security would complicate the notation without changing the analysis.

[12] Taxes are used to pay interest on government bonds. By collecting taxes in the second period of life, they are paid back to the same cohort from which they are collected. Collecting taxes in the first period instead would be equivalent to changing the level of government debt outstanding.

Consumer choice can also be viewed in terms of three (composite) consumer goods – first-period consumption and safe and risky second-period consumption, which we denote as C_1, J, and K.[13] It is, therefore, convenient to imagine that there is a safe financial asset promising one unit of safe consumption and also a risky financial asset promising one unit of risky consumption R, so that J and K can be bought directly.[14] With first-period consumption as numeraire, we denote the price of second-period risky consumption as p_K. The price of one unit of second-period safe consumption is denoted by p_J. When the risky investment is undertaken in equilibrium, $k > 0$, then we must have $p_K = 1$. When safe investment is undertaken in equilibrium, $k_0 > 0$, then we must have $p_J = 1/R_0$. Whether or not real safe investment is undertaken in equilibrium, p_J is always equal to $1/(1+r)$, as long as the supply of government bonds to savers is positive. We now restate the consumer choice problem as:

$$V = \max U_1[C_1] + E\{U_2[J + RK]\} = \max V^*(C_1, J, K)$$
$$\text{s.t. } C_1 + p_J J + p_K K = I = W - p_J T \tag{4.2}$$

Demands for all three consumer goods are functions of the prices of second-period safe and risky consumptions and of net lifetime wealth. We denote them by $C^*[p_J, p_K, I]$, $K^*[p_J, p_K, I]$, and $J^*[p_J, p_K, I]$.

Throughout the paper, we *assume* the function $V^*(C_1, J, K)$ is such that all three of first-period consumption and safe and risky second-period consumptions are normal goods. The normality of the three goods in turn *guarantees* that all three goods are Hicksian substitutes (given the intertemporally additive structure of preferences described in [4.2]). Moreover, a sufficient condition for normality of all three goods is that second-period utility displays decreasing absolute risk aversion (DARA) and increasing relative risk aversion (IRRA). For proofs of these assertions, see Aura, Diamond, and Geanakoplos, 2002.[15]

In contrast, we model workers, who also have two-period lifetimes, as nonsavers. Each worker earns a wage, w, in the first period (with inelastically supplied labor), pays payroll taxes t_w in the first period, and consumes $w - t_w$. In the second period, workers consume social security benefits, b, which may be random, less income

---

[13] Because all trading and production opportunities can be written in terms of these composite commodities, analysis of equilibrium can be done in these terms. Written in this form, the usual properties of compensated demands hold for the vector of consumptions. On the properties of compensated demands in the presence of uncertainty, see Diamond and Yaari (1972) and Fischer (1972). Moreover, analysis can be done in this form without the assumption of expected utility.

[14] When risky real investment is being undertaken, we can interpret the risky financial asset as shares in the output of a risky firm. When there is no real investment being undertaken, then this risky financial asset is like a contingent futures contract. An investor can acquire the right to future risky consumption by buying the risky financial asset (i.e., the shares or the futures contract) without having to actually undertake any risky investment, provided that he can find somebody who is willing to sell the asset.

[15] For the reader interested in nonexpected utility maximization, we must assume that V^* is such that all three goods are normal, *and* that all pairs of goods are Hicksian substitutes.

taxes t. We denote workers' lifetime utility by v and note that it satisfies:

$$v = u_1[c_1] + E\{u_2[c_2]\} = u_1[w - t_w] + E\{u_2[b - t]\} \qquad (4.3)$$

We distinguish two sources of taxes since the first-period payroll tax will be used for social security, whereas the second-period income tax will be used to pay part of the interest on the government debt outstanding.

The lack of randomness in income for young workers, w, guarantees a lack of randomness in the pay-as-you-go component of the financing of social security benefits for contemporaneous old workers, as we shall see in the next section.

4.3 Government and the Social Security System

It is assumed that each period the government rolls over one-period debt with a value of G. The interest payments on this debt are financed by income taxes on older workers and older savers, with the principal rolled over to preserve the debt outstanding:

$$T_t + nt_t = r_{t-1}G \qquad (4.4)$$

where taxes collected in period t are used to pay interest at rate r_{t-1} on debt issued in period $t - 1$. We assume that taxes are divided between savers and nonsavers in the proportions a and $1 - a$, $0 < a < 1$. Using the relationship between r and p_J, $p_J = 1/(1 + r)$, we have the period and steady-state relations:

$$T_t = ar_{t-1}G; \quad t_t = (1 - a)r_{t-1}G/n$$
$$T = arG = a(1 - p_J)G/p_J$$
$$t = (1 - a)rG/n = (1 - a)(1 - p_J)G/np_J \qquad (4.5)$$

Note that income taxes in units of first-period consumption equal $a(1 - p_J)G$.

We model the social security system as a combination of a pay-as-you-go system together with a defined-contribution system without worker choice of portfolio. Equivalently, we can think of the system as a partially funded defined-benefit system where the stochastic returns on stocks are fully used in determining that period's retirement benefits. The social security trust fund holds the value F of government debt, and the value $p_K K^f$ of risky assets (possibly equal to zero at the outset). Denoting the total value of the trust fund by F_0, and supposing the trust fund holds only short-term assets, the trust fund budget set in any period is:

$$F + p_K K^f = F_0 \qquad (4.6)$$

Given the need to maintain the trust fund portfolio, F and $p_K K^f$, and given constant payroll taxes t_w and a stationary population, social security benefits satisfy the period and steady-state relations:

$$b_t = t_w + \left((1 + r_{t-1})F_{t-1} - F_t + \left(RK_{t-1}^f - p_{Kt}K_t^f\right)\right)/n$$
$$b = t_w + (rF + (R - p_K)K^f)/n \tag{4.7}$$

Thus, the expected utility of workers, v, given in (4.3), satisfies the steady-state relations:

$$v = u_1[w - t_w] + E\{u_2[t_w - t + (rF + (R - p_K)K^f)/n\} \tag{4.8}$$

Observe from Equation (4.7) that all the variations in risky asset payoffs held by the trust fund are passed through directly to the current retirees. There is no risk-sharing across generations, as there could be in a defined-benefits plan, either by spreading return risks across several cohorts or by varying the payroll tax rate. The wage and the payroll tax rate are assumed to be constant over time; the retirement benefits, however, are free to vary and will do so if the rates of return earned on the trust fund holdings vary. Similarly, the second-period income tax will change if the interest rate on government debt changes.

A crucial part of our analysis is that if $K^f = 0$, young workers at time $t - 1$ can look forward with certainty to the social security benefits they will receive when they are old at time t. The return r_{t-1} they will get from the trust fund bond investment is already locked in. Furthermore, they can perfectly predict the pay-as-you-go portion of their benefits because, in stationary equilibrium, wages of the young at time t are nonrandom. In reality, of course, future real wages cannot be predicted with certainty. In our judgment, however, they are substantially less random than stock returns.

4.4 Stationary Equilibrium without Land

In stationary equilibrium, prices and young savers' consumption and asset holdings are constant through time and across states of nature. All that varies is output, consumption of the old savers and old workers, and social security benefits. With a single commodity, and stationary and independent productivity shocks, stationary equilibrium will exist. Because wages do not vary, a new steady state is reached starting with the generation born immediately after a permanent policy change.

When savers undertake risky investment, p_K is equal to one. Stationary equilibrium in the model with short-term risky production, but without land, is then defined by prices and quantities (r, C_1, C_2, B, k_0, k) such that given r and taxes T, the choices (C_1, C_2, B, k_0, k) solve the savers' optimization problem (4.1), and such that savers' demand for government bonds equals the supply available to savers:

$$B = G - F = G - F_0 + p_K K^f \tag{4.9}$$

If safe real investment is undertaken in equilibrium, then the interest rate on government bonds equals the return on safe investment. If not, then the government interest rate is determined by market clearance with no additional supply of safe assets.[16]

Alternatively, we can write the market-clearing conditions in terms of the consumption demands C^*, J^*, and K^* introduced in (4.2). This separates the consumption and savings decisions of the savers from the production decisions of firms. From now on, we interpret k_0 to be the safe production chosen by the firms, and we interpret k as the risky production chosen by the firms. Savers' demand for safe second-period consumption must equal the supply of safe second-period consumption to savers, which is equal to the total principal and interest payments of government bonds, less what is held by the social security system, plus the level of safe production, less what is needed to pay taxes.

$$
\begin{aligned}
J^* \left(p_J, p_K, W - a \left(1 - p_J \right) G \right) \\
= \left(G - F_0 + p_K K^f \right) / p_J + R_0 k_0 - a \left(1 - p_J \right) G / p_J \\
= B / p_J + R_0 k_0 - a \left(1 - p_J \right) G / p_J
\end{aligned} \tag{4.10}
$$

where $a \left(1 - p_J \right) G$ is the present discounted value (PDV) of taxes. Using the same variables, we can write market-clearing in the risky good market as

$$
K^* \left(p_J, p_K, W - a \left(1 - p_J \right) G \right) = k - K^f \tag{4.11}
$$

The supply of risky second-period consumption to savers is equal to risky production, less what is held by the social security system.[17]

Market clearance could occur with or without each type of production, depending on rates of return. Profit maximization of the firms gives

$$
\begin{aligned}
p_J = 1/(1 + r) = 1/R_0 \quad \text{if} \quad k_0 > 0 \leq 1/R_0 \quad \text{if} \quad k_0 = 0 \\
p_k = 1 \quad \text{if} \quad k > 0 \leq 1 \quad \text{if} \quad k = 0
\end{aligned} \tag{4.12}
$$

Stationary equilibrium is now defined as a vector (p_J, p_K, k_0, k) such that (4.10)–(4.12) hold. The condition defining the savers' holdings of government bonds B, given by (4.9), still holds, and we continue to use B as a convenient shorthand for the RHS of (4.9). But, Equation (4.9) will not be treated as an independent

---

[16] Because the savers are both the demanders and the suppliers of real investment, the investment markets automatically clear if savers solve (4.1). The consumption market automatically clears as well, once the bond market clears. To check this, we can verify that supply of consumption equals demand,

$$
W + nw + (R_0 - 1)k_0 + (R - 1)k + (R - 1)K^f = C_1 + C_2 + nc_1 + nc_2
$$

The reader can verify that after substituting for C_1 and C_2 from (4.1), c_1 and c_2 from (4.3), taxes from (4.5), and benefits from (4.7), this equation reduces to (4.9).

[17] To complete the picture, we could explicitly model the production decisions of the firms to maximize profit:

$$
\max[p_J R_0 k_0 - k_0] + \max[p_K k - k]
$$

equation because it follows from (4.10)–(4.12) given the saver's budget constraint in (4.2) and trust fund budget constraint in (4.6).

Depending on whether $k_0 > 0$ or $k_0 = 0$, and whether $k = 0$ or $k > 0$, equilibrium can be one of four different types, or regimes.[18] The effect of social security diversification depends crucially on which regime the original equilibrium is in.[19] In each case, we analyze the effect on equilibrium of a change in trust fund investment in risky assets: $d(p_K K^f) = -dF > 0$. Because we are interested mainly in the case where $K^f = 0$, when $d(p_K K^f) = dp_K K^f + p_K dK^f = p_K dK^f$, in what follows we shall take K^f as the exogenous variable, and we shall compute the equilibrium comparative statics by totally differentiating the equilibrium equations with respect to K^f. Because wages do not vary, the economy achieves stationary equilibrium in a single period after a change in the portfolio allocation of the trust fund. If the unanticipated change comes at some date t, then generations born at date t and after will consume as in the new steady state, and generations born at date $t - 2$ and before will consume as in the original steady state. The generation born at date $t - 1$ will consume as if it made consumption and asset choices when young in the original equilibrium but was then forced to pay taxes and liquidate assets at date t at the new steady-state prices.

4.5 Social Security Diversification with Both Safe and Risky Investment

In this section, we assume the economy is such that in equilibrium both physical assets are held, $k_0 > 0$, $k > 0$. In this setting, technology determines prices. That is, the interest rate on government bonds equals the (exogenously fixed) rate of return on the safe asset, and the price of the risky consumption good equals 1, the cost of the risky physical asset. Because prices do not change when the trust fund alters its portfolio, savers are left unaffected. (With the interest rate unchanged, second-period taxes do not change, so the budget set of savers is indeed unaffected.) With unchanging prices, savers demand the same combination of all three consumption goods: first-period, second-period safe, and second-period risky consumptions. Thus, if the trust fund sells some bonds and uses the money to invest in risky production, savers are indifferent to buying the extra bonds and reducing their investment in safe production by the same value, thereby maintaining the equilibrium. Thus, aggregate risky investment goes up, aggregate safe investment goes down, and aggregate investment is unchanged. Because the expected return on risky investment must exceed the return on safe investment (for both to be held by risk-averse savers), expected aggregate output goes up.[20]

---

[18] As mentioned earlier, we shall restrict attention to economies that have no knife-edge stationary equilibria in which $k_0 = 0$ and $p_J = 1/R_0$, or in which $k = 0$ and $p_K = 1$.

[19] Furthermore, small changes in the trust fund create small changes in equilibrium. Equilibrium before and after social security diversification will, therefore, be of the same type.

[20] To see this, note that with $p_K = 1$ and both assets held, the savers' first-order condition is:

$$U_1'[C_1] = E\{U_2'[C_2](1+r)\} = E\{U_2'[C_2]R\}$$

If the trust fund initially has only a small amount of the risky asset, this policy is a (weak) Pareto gain – savers are not affected and workers gain because the workers are not risk averse for the first bit of investment in risky assets. To see this, consider the change in worker expected utility, (4.8), noting that interest rates r and, therefore, taxes t are unaffected. Assuming that K^f is zero, an increase in K^f and matching decrease in F affects expected utility as

$$dv/dK^f = E\{u_2'[c_2](R - 1 - r)\}/n$$
$$= u_2'[c_2]E\{(R - 1 - r)\}/n > 0 \qquad (4.13)$$

The last equality is obtained by noting that second-period consumption of workers is certain; hence, so is second-period marginal utility, so it may be brought outside of the expectation operator. The final inequality follows from the excess expected risky return (see footnote 21). Thus, we have shown:

Proposition 1. *Suppose both the safe and risky assets are held in stationary equilibrium (in positive quantities). Then, increased trust fund investment in risky assets increases risky investment, decreases safe investment, leaves aggregate investment unchanged, and increases expected output.*

If the trust fund initially held no risky assets, then the diversification will lead to a weak Pareto improvement, increasing the utility of all workers (except the old at the time the policy is implemented, who are unaffected) and leaving the utility of all savers unchanged.

The equity premium is defined as the difference between the expected return on the risky investment and the return on the safe investment, $E\{R\} - (1 + r)$. Because the equity premium must be consistent with the portfolio choice of risk-averse savers (who hold a strictly positive quantity of risky assets by hypothesis), it must be positive in equilibrium. As long as the equity premium is positive, there is an expected utility gain to workers from diversification in a model where they bear no other risk.

The crucial step in this argument is the paradoxical claim that workers are *more* risk tolerant *on the margin* than savers. One might suspect that savers are more risk tolerant than workers, all else being equal. That is, it may well be that the worker utility u is a concave transformation of the saver utility U, thereby displaying more risk aversion at any level of consumption. And, workers have lower incomes on average than savers, which also makes them more risk averse if there is decreasing absolute risk aversion. But, all else is not equal. The savers hold the entire risky capital stock of the nation, whereas the workers hold none (if K^f is zero). Our proof that welfare rises after social security diversification only needed that both

---

Because C_2 and R are perfectly correlated, $U_2'[C_2]$ and R are negatively correlated. Hence, the equality of expectations can only hold if $E\{R\} > 1 + r = R_0$.

u and *U* are differentiable, and that workers are not exposed to any stock market risk or other risks correlated with stock market risk.

In reality, workers' retirement income is not completely statistically independent of stock returns. Social security benefits are connected by an explicit formula to real wages. Over career horizons as long as 40 years, there is considerable covariance between real wages and stock returns. The questions then become: How big is worker exposure to stocks, how big is the equity premium, and how risk averse are workers? Addressing these questions in detail is beyond the scope of this paper.[21] Our judgment is that, after properly calibrating the stock exposure implicit in aggregate wages, one would come to the conclusion that the average worker is significantly less exposed to stock returns than savers. At the point at which the trust fund holds no stock, it seems very likely to us that the average worker would be better off by some investing in equity. The converse would hold only if it would be optimal for such a worker just starting to save, to hold a portfolio with no stocks at all.

However, what is best for the average worker may not be best for every worker. Although our model has assumed that all workers are identical, in reality some workers may be far more risk averse, so that for them any additional stock exposure may be bad, preventing social security diversification from being a Pareto gain (Pestieau and Possen 1999). However, in considering a more general setting with heterogeneous workers, the reader should bear in mind that the lowest income workers would be protected by the safety net (i.e., SSI).

By the same logic used in the proof of Proposition 1, further increases in social security risky asset holdings would also be weak Pareto gains until the optimal portfolio for workers was reached, unless the saver's holdings of the safe real investment reached zero first.[22] In considering the optimal level of social security diversification, we note that because social security benefits become more correlated with stock returns as diversification increases, the welfare benefits to further diversification decline. The proof of Proposition 1 is, thus, an argument for limited diversification.

The welfare gain from social security diversification in Proposition 1 is not related to any "unexplained" excess return of stocks over bonds. If savers also were covered by social security, Proposition 1 would show no (ex ante) gain from social security diversification for the typical saver, despite the equity premium (except if some savers were 100 percent in stocks in their portfolio and wanted some of social security to be in stock as well). For every dollar in the social security trust fund that is shifted to equity, the welfare gains described in Proposition 1 apply to that fraction of each dollar that goes to support the benefits of workers with

---

[21] If the workers' and savers' utilities *u* and *U* display similar risk aversion, and both display increasing relative risk aversion, then the poorer workers should have a higher fraction of their wealth invested in stocks than the richer savers.

[22] The social security program is a response to the inadequacy of retirement saving by many workers. Just as mandating savings can raise utility for many workers, adjusting the portfolio can add to utility.

little financial wealth who do not borrow and are, therefore, holding no stocks.[23] If there were no such workers, as is the case in a representative agent model with only rational savers, a small enough change in trust fund portfolio policy would have no effects at all (Smetters 1997; Bohn 1997, 1998).

The welfare gains to nonsavers from social security diversification holds in all of our subsequent models. In later models, the technology is not perfectly elastic. Then, the change in social security portfolio will lead savers to alter their final consumption, forcing equilibrium prices to change, in directions we investigate in the following models. Because workers do not save, the effect of social security diversification on asset prices and taxes is independent of their (marginal) risk tolerance.

4.6 Social Security Diversification with Only Risky Investment

Although the riskiness of aggregate output is plausibly endogenous, as in the bilinear model, it is unrealistic to suppose that technology fixes the returns on all assets, independent of preferences. We now consider an economy with the expected return on risky investment given by technology, but without any safe investments, implying that the return on government bonds is endogenous. That is, in equilibrium: $k_0 = 0$ and $k > 0$. Given the constant marginal returns to risky investments, equilibrium requires $p_K = 1$. The interest rate on government debt is determined by the supply and demand for bonds, with market clearance given in Equation (4.10). Combining the budget constraint in (4.2) with (4.5), (4.9), and (4.10) reduces market clearing to a single equation in a single variable $p_J = 1/(1 + r)$:

$$B = G - F_0 + K^f = W - C^*[p_J, 1, W - a(1 - p_J)G]$$
$$- K^*[p_J, 1, W - a(1 - p_J)G] \qquad (4.14)$$

That is, government bonds not held by social security equal the wealth of savers less what they spend on first-period consumption and what they invest in risky production. Note that with G, F_0, and W all fixed, the response of aggregate investment, $K^* + K^f$, to portfolio policy is minus the response of the consumption of savers, C^*. To analyze the effect of diversification on the interest rate, we differentiate (4.14) with respect to K^f. Because diversification increases the supply of bonds available to savers, we would expect it to lower p_J and raise r. But, the situation is a bit more complicated. Any change in the interest rate (with no change

---

[23] Some workers are unable to hold stocks because they have not saved enough. Others do not hold stocks even though they could. Some of the latter may not be optimizing and would also gain from the diversification, whereas some may not have been willing to bear the cost of learning about stocks and would also gain because they do not have to pay a cost if investment is done centrally. However, workers so risk averse that they should hold no stocks would lose from diversification, as noted earlier. Some workers may mistakenly be overinvested in stocks and also would lose from trust fund diversification if they do not reduce their stockholdings in response to trust fund investment.

in gross debt outstanding) requires a change in income taxes to cover interest costs. Thus, to sign the change in the interest rate, we use a further assumption on the share of taxes paid by savers, beyond our assumptions on demand functions. By changing the interest rate and, therefore, also taxes, social security diversification causes a redistribution between savers and workers, in addition to the gain to workers noted in Section 4.5. To analyze all these changes, we first derive the changes in utilities from an arbitrary change in the interest rate and taxes and, from this relation, we deduce that under our assumptions the interest rate does indeed increase.

4.6.1 Income Taxes, the Interest Rate, and Welfare

A change in the price of safe second-period consumption affects the utility of savers in two ways. One is the change in the cost of safe second-period consumption, which, by the envelope theorem, is $-U_1' J^*$. The second is the change in the PDV of taxes paid. Using the market clearing condition for J^* given by (4.9) and (4.10), the change in utility to savers from a change in p_J is

$$\begin{aligned} \partial V/\partial p_J &= -U_1'\{J^* + d[a(1 - p_J)G)]/dp_J\} \\ &= -U_1'\{[B - a(1 - p_J)G]/p_J - aG\} \\ &= -U_1'[B - aG]/p_J \\ &= -E\{U_2'\}[B - aG]/p_J^2 \end{aligned} \tag{4.15}$$

where we have used the FOC for consumer choice in the last step.

A change in the interest rate on government bonds causes a redistribution of income between taxpayers and interest recipients. Hence, if the shares of marginal second-period taxes paid by savers, a, and workers, $1 - a$, do not match their shares in the holding of government debt (directly by savers and indirectly through social security for workers), $B \neq aG$, a change in the interest rate affects utilities. Recognizing that p_J is the only endogenous price, it follows from (4.15)[24] that the response of expected utility to trust fund portfolio diversification satisfies:

$$\begin{aligned} dV/dK^f &= -E\{U_2'\}\{(B - aG)/p_J^2\}\{dp_J/dK^f\} \\ &= E\{U_2'\}(B - aG)\{dr/dK^f\} \end{aligned} \tag{4.16}$$

Workers are affected by trust fund investment as in Section 4.5 and by the impact of the interest rate on benefits and taxes. Differentiating expected lifetime utility of workers (4.8) with respect to $dK^f = -dF$, noting from (4.5) that $dt/dr = (1 - a)G/n$ and from (4.9) that $F = G - B$, we have:

$$dv/dK^f = E\{u_2'(R - 1 - r)\}/n - E\{u_2'\}(B - aG)(dr/dK^f)/n \tag{4.17}$$

---

[24] And, $dp_J/dr = -p_J^2$.

As was the case in the regime with both investments, the expected utility of workers increases from bearing some risk if they were bearing none before diversification. In addition, the effect on workers from the change in the interest rate has the opposite sign from its effect on savers, as can be seen by comparing (4.16) and (4.17). If a is equal to B/G, then this effect is zero and workers only gain from improved risky investment. When $a = B/G$, we have a (weak) Pareto gain, as in the case with both investments.[25]

Denoting the social evaluation of the marginal utility of second-period safe consumption of a worker relative to that of a saver by m, the impact on a social welfare function for each cohort in steady state (SWF) equals the weighted sum of individual impacts:

$$dSWF/dK^f = m\{ndv/dK^f\} + 1\{dV/dK^f\}$$
$$= mE\{u_2'(R - r - 1)\} - E\{mu_2' - U_2'\}(B - aG)dr/dK^f$$

(4.18)

Thus, there is a direct utility gain from improved risk bearing and a redistributive term, which vanishes if a equals B/G. If there is an income distribution change ($a \neq B/G$), its effect depends on the direction of transfer and the sign of $E\{mu_2' - U_2'\}$. In particular, if other policy tools result in a level of m so that one unit of second-period safe consumption gives the same expected marginal social welfare to every old agent, then the redistribution term drops out and total weighted utility is increased by diversification.

Whether $B < aG$ depends on the size of the trust fund and how tax policy responds to increased interest costs. If $F = 0$, then $B = G > aG$, and an increase in interest rates helps savers, because for every extra dollar in interest receipts received, they pay only $a < 1$ dollars extra in taxes. By contrast, if the trust fund holds all the government bonds, then $B = 0 < aG$, and savers lose from an increase in interest rates.[26] In reality, the social security trust fund pays benefits to nonsavers and savers. But, because of the redistributive nature of the social security benefit rules, nonsavers have a claim on benefits that exceeds their share of payroll taxes. At the end of 2001, the trust fund was $1.2 trillion (OASI plus DI) and increasing rapidly. Once the trust fund is big relative to the outstanding stock of government bonds, interest rate increases can be expected to help workers and hurt savers.

---

[25] Actually, if $a = B/G$, then savers obtain a second-order benefit from trust fund diversification, assuming dr/dK^f is not 0.

[26] To consider who in reality is a receiver of government bond interest payments net of the taxes levied to pay for them, we need to consider which taxes are raised if interest costs are higher. If it is just the income tax increased, then low-income people are not taxed at all. However, if the earned income tax credit is altered along with the income tax (violating our assumption that it is taxes on older workers that are adjusted), then the impact is throughout the income distribution. A realistic case would indeed consider tax changes on young workers and savers as well as on the old. That would have additional effects, which we are not analyzing.

4.6.2 Interest Rate and Aggregate Investment

Increasing the supply of government bonds available to the savers will raise the interest rate if demand slopes down, provided that the indirect effects of the interest rate on demand (through income taxation) do not offset the direct effect. The proof is straightforward and also shows that aggregate investment rises.[27] However, the rise in aggregate investment is smaller than the increase in trust fund investment in risky assets.

We can state these results (which are proved formally in the Appendix) as:

Proposition 2. *Suppose that risky investments, but not safe investments, are undertaken in equilibrium and that* $B \leq aG$. *Then, increased trust fund investment in risky assets increases the interest rate on government debt, and increases aggregate real investment, though by less than the quantity of the trust fund purchases.*

If the trust fund initially held no risky assets, then the diversification increases the expected utility of all workers (except the old at the time the policy is implemented, who are unaffected) and increases the weighted sum of utility of all workers and savers, weighted so that the marginal social utility of second-period consumption is the same for all. If, in addition, $B = aG$, *then trust fund diversification does not affect the utility of young savers in every generation (up to first order, increasing it up to second order). If, instead,* $B < aG$, *then diversification lowers the utility of young savers in every generation.*

Complementing this proposition, we note that if an increase in the government bond interest rate redistributes wealth from workers to savers, $B > aG$, then the interest rate may rise or fall.[28]

4.6.3 Extending the Model to Most Investment Technologies

In the bilinear model of Section 4.5, social security diversification resulted in more investment in the risky technology and less in the safe technology, and so riskier investment and output. This possibility of riskier aggregate investment is necessarily missing in models with just one technology, such as we just considered in Section 4.6. Yet, firms do make investment choices that affect the riskiness of their output. One way to model such choices would be to assume that each firm

---

[27] From (4.15), we see that reducing p_J (i.e., increasing r) lowers the welfare of savers if $B < aG$. Because C and K are normal and Hicksian substitutes for J, a reduction in p_J lowers demands C^* and K^*, and thus by (4.14) raises the demand for B. This confirms that demand for B slopes down, so diversification raises r. The fall in C proves that aggregate investment rises, as noted after (4.14).

[28] So far, we have considered two different models with perfectly elastic and perfectly inelastic supplies of safe assets. We could consider an intermediate model with a downward-sloping demand by foreigners for government debt. This would give a change in the equilibrium interest rate that was between the two cases analyzed. In this case, the increase in the interest rate on government debt would involve increased payments abroad as well as transfers from taxpayers to trust fund beneficiaries.

has two distinct risky technologies (identical across firms) and chooses the overall riskiness of its output by the mix of the two technologies (i.e., an activity analysis model). By the Modigliani–Miller theorem, it would not matter which firm made which production choice as long as the aggregate of investment in each technology was the same. It might be interesting to see whether trust fund diversification into equities (buying the same fraction of each firm) led firms to choose riskier output. We do not pursue this question here.

4.7 Adding Infinitely Lived Assets

In the earlier models, no asset lasts more than one period. Thus, a change in the interest rate does not redistribute wealth across generations. To consider intergenerational redistribution, we now add two infinitely lived assets. A change in policy that changes the prices of the long-lived assets will redistribute wealth between the old, who own the assets at the time the policy is implemented, and all future generations who buy them. We assume fixed quantities of both types of infinitely lived assets, referred to as safe land and risky land. Each unit of safe land provides one unit of consumption, independent of the state of nature, in each period.[29] Each unit of risky land produces the same (realized) output as one unit of the (contemporaneous) risky investment.[30] We denote the supplies of the two assets by L_0 and L, and their prices by p_0 and p. Because of the stationary structure of the economy, in stationary equilibrium, these prices are constant over time. The effects of trust fund diversification are modified by the presence of land, but not drastically changed. As before, the analysis depends on which short-term investments are undertaken in the original stationary equilibrium. The case in which both are undertaken, $k_0 > 0$ and $k > 0$, is exactly like the case without land because no prices change, and it is not repeated here. In the rest of Section 4.7, we reformulate the definition of equilibrium to include land.

In reality, the stock market is made up of both short-term and long-term investments, and so the effect of social security diversification on stock market prices involves both short-term and long-term asset price changes.

4.7.1 Land and the Dynamic Asset Span

Land (of either type) lasts forever and gives new output forever and is sold each period by the older generation to the younger one. Given a stationary economy, and the assumption that land output is independent and identically distributed each

---

[29] This might be a fixed number of government consols, the interest on which is financed by taxation on successive generations.

[30] When the return to risky investment is independent of the level of investment (as assumed in all sections other than Section 4.10), there is no distinction between land that provides output and land that provides capital input.

period, the price of land (just *after* the realization of output) is constant across time, and across realizations of output.[31] The one-period gross return from purchasing land is equal to its dividend that period, plus a constant capital value. The one-period returns on either type of infinitely lived land are, therefore, (endogenous) convex combinations of the returns on risky short-term investments and the safe return on government bonds. Thus, we can incorporate land into our model without introducing a new risk characteristic. We do not need to reformulate the choice problem of savers in terms of the three composite consumer goods.

If a young saver buys one unit of safe land, it costs p_0 and yields safe consumption in the second period (from output and resale) of $1 + p_0$. Because this is a perfect substitute for buying $(1 + p_0)/(1 + r)$ units of the government bond, we have

$$p_0 = (1 + p_0)/(1 + r) \tag{4.19}$$

or

$$p_0 = 1/r = p_J/(1 - p_J) \tag{4.20}$$

Similarly, by spending p on risky land, the consumer gets the risky dividend that can be purchased at a price of p_K (by investing in the short-lived risky asset) and the ability to sell the asset at price p, which has a current value of $p/(1 + r)$. Thus, by arbitrage, we have the equilibrium price of risky land satisfying:

$$p = p_K + p/(1 + r) = p_K + pp_J \tag{4.21}$$

or

$$p = (1 + r)p_K/r = p_K/(1 - p_J) \tag{4.22}$$

Thus, the prices of both kinds of land are determined by the price of the short-term assets. Both land prices increase with the price of second-period safe consumption; equivalently, land prices decrease when the interest rate rises. The total value of land is

$$P = p_0 L_0 + pL = L_0 p_J/(1 - p_J) + L p_K/(1 - p_J) \tag{4.23}$$

The supply of safe consumption because of land is the output from safe land plus the proceeds from the sale of all land, $L_0 + P$, which can also be written as $(L_0 + p_K L)/(1 - p_J)$. We note for later use that

$$dP/dp_J = (P + L_0)/(1 - p_J) \tag{4.24}$$

To keep the analysis simple, we continue to suppose that the trust fund holds only short-term assets.[32]

---

[31] The iid assumption implies that there is never any "news" about future returns, so land values never change.

[32] Any equilibrium in which the trust fund holds L^f acres of risky land is equivalent to an equilibrium in which the trust fund holds L^f units of the risky asset and $L^f pp_J$ bonds. (The dividends are the

4.7.2 Stationary Equilibrium with Land

We now define equilibrium in terms of the three goods C^*, J^*, K^*, as we did earlier. The presence of land does not change the expected utility maximization problem of savers given in (4.2) nor their demand curves. The presence of land does change the supplies of consumption. The supply of safe consumption now includes the output of safe land and the proceeds from the sale of both kinds of land. The supply of risky consumption increases by the output of risky land. Thus, equilibrium Conditions (4.10) and (4.11) become

$$J^*(p_J, p_K, W - a(1 - p_J)G)$$
$$= B/p_J + R_0 k_0 - a(1 - p_J)G/p_J + L_0 + P \qquad (4.25)$$
$$K^*(p_J, p_K, W - a(1-p_J)G) = k - K^f + L \qquad (4.26)$$

4.8 Social Security Diversification with Risky Investment and Land

We suppose the economy with land is such that in stationary equilibrium there is only risky production, $k_0 = 0$ but $k > 0$. Therefore, $p_K = 1$. As in Section 4.6, equilibrium boils down to the market for safe consumption. Rewriting (4.25) using the saver's budget constraint (4.2), and (4.5), (4.9), and (4.23), we have:

$$G - F_0 + K^f + p_J(L_0 + L)/(1 - p_J)$$
$$= W - C^*[p_J, 1, W - a(1 - p_J)G]$$
$$-K^*[p_J, 1, W - a(1 - p_J)G] \qquad (4.27)$$

This differs from (4.14) in Section 4.6 by the addition of the last term on the LHS, representing the supply of safe consumption from the presence of land. As before, we have a single equation in a single variable, p_J. And, with the same assumptions as before, we will again find that diversification causes p_J to go down, equivalent to the interest rate going up.

From (4.26), aggregate investment in short-lived production, k, is trust fund demand for real investment, K^f, plus the demand of savers for risky consumption, K^*, minus the portion of that demand that is satisfied by purchasing risky land, L. Thus, using (4.27), aggregate investment in risky short-term assets can be written:

$$K^f + K^* - L = W - (G - F_0) - C^*[p_J, 1, W - a(1 - p_J)G] - P \qquad (4.28)$$

same, and by [4.21] the bond payoffs pL^f can be used each period to repurchase the same portfolio.) In particular, starting from a portfolio exclusively in short-term assets, a trust fund purchase of L^f acres of risky land (obtained by selling bonds) would have precisely the same effect as the purchase of L^f units of the risky short-term asset (obtained by selling bonds). However, the effect of a further trust fund purchase of land will differ in the two cases because it will change asset prices, giving a different capital gain to the two portfolios.

That is, short-term investment equals the wealth of savers less what they spend on consumption, on bonds, and on land. With W, G, and F_0 all fixed, the response of aggregate investment in short-term assets to social security diversification is minus the sum of the response of consumption of savers, C^*, and the change in the value of total land, P. With the same assumptions as before, we will again find that aggregate investment goes up.

4.8.1 Expected Utility

In the previous models without land, old savers were not affected by social security diversification. But, with the introduction of land, they have something to sell, whose value might be affected by social security diversification. For example, if land prices go down in value (as the interest rate rises), the old savers at the time of the trust fund diversification lose, *ceteris paribus*. Young savers gain, as do savers in every succeeding generation.

We begin with old savers at the time of implementation of the policy change. They are affected only by the change in the value of the land that they hold:

$$dV_{old}/dK^f = U_2'[dP/dp_J]\{dp_J/dK^f\} \qquad (4.29)$$

Because the new stationary equilibrium is achieved immediately after the trust fund purchases, young savers at the time of the purchases are affected exactly the same way as all future savers. This differs from the setting without land, (4.16), only in that the demand for safe consumption (4.25) is met through land as well as bonds, in contrast to (4.10).

$$dV/dK^f = -E\{U_2'\}[(B - aG) + p_J (L_0 + P)]/p_J^2\{dp_J/dK^f\} \qquad (4.30)$$

The first term reflects the within-cohort redistribution between savers and workers as a consequence of different shares in government bonds and in the taxes to pay the interest on the bonds. The second term reflects the across-cohort redistribution from changes in the price of the safe consumption that is purchased from the previous generation by buying land. The formula is expressed in terms of the value of land. Using (4.24), the change in expected utility can be expressed in terms of the change in land value:

$$dV/dK^f = -E\{U_2'\}[(B - aG) + p_J(1 - p_J)dP/dp_J]/p_J^2\{dp_J/dK^f\}$$
$$\qquad (4.31)$$

Now it is clear that changing land values does affect young savers. But, if social security is diversified at time 1, and land prices fall, the young at time 1 do not gain by the whole drop in land prices because the resale value of the land when they get old also falls.

Notice that the expected utility of young savers can increase or decrease, depending on the balance of redistributions between savers and workers, and redistributions between old savers and young savers. If the value of all land, P, exceeds the total of all government bond promises $G/p_J = G(1 + r)$, then social security diversification must improve the welfare of young savers (assuming $dp_J/dK^f < 0$), even though it creates a redistribution from young savers to young workers if $B < aG$. Evidently, young savers gain more from old savers than they lose to young workers. A similar conclusion holds if the value of safe land $p_0 L_0$ is greater than the value of government bonds G outstanding, as can be seen from (4.30), and the equation $p_J(L_0 + P) = p_0(L_0 + L)$.

Equation (4.17) quantifying the effect of trust fund diversification on workers in the risky linear case without land applies without change in this risky linear case with land. As before, the increased exposure to risky stock and the rise in interest rates make workers better off, assuming $B - aG < 0$ and $dp_J/dK^f < 0$. The analysis of a social welfare function is also unchanged.

4.8.2 Interest Rate, Investment, and Land Values

From (4.20) and (4.22), the values of safe land and of risky land each move in the same direction as p_J – that is, in the opposite direction of the change in interest rates. Thus, assuming that diversification raises r, as it did when there was no land, it follows that trust fund purchases of risky short-term investments *reduce* the price of risky land (and also the price of safe land). It is a remarkable and unanticipated property of the current model that the increase in demand for risky land reduces its price! It is often claimed that if social security bought stocks, it would raise the value of the stock market. This conclusion is seen to be more delicate than it sounds. Because the interest rate increases, it is not so surprising, after all, to find a tendency for stock prices to decline, for stock prices depend on discounting future returns. When technology fixes the return on short-term risky investments, the interest-rate effect is the only one impinging on stock prices. We pursue this question of land values further in the next sections.

It remains to show that trust fund purchases of risky investment do indeed increase the interest rate on government debt. An increase in the supply of government bonds available to the savers will raise the interest rate if demand slopes down. The proof requires confirming that the indirect effects of the interest rate on demand (through income taxation and the change in land values) do not offset the direct effect. However, the situation is much subtler than it was without land in Section 4.6 because the welfare of young savers might go up or down. Yet, the effect on interest rates and aggregate investment is unambiguous, as we show in the Appendix.

Proposition 3. *Suppose there is both safe and risky land, that risky investments, but not safe investments, are undertaken in equilibrium and that $B \leq aG$. Then, increased trust fund investment in risky assets increases the interest rate on government debt, and increases aggregate real investment. The increase in aggregate investment* *may be larger or smaller than the trust fund purchase of risky investment. Moreover, the prices of both kinds of land fall. The total value of land therefore falls, though $|dP/dK^f| < 1/p_J$.*

If the trust fund initially held no risky assets, then the diversification increases the expected utility of all workers (except the old at the time the policy is implemented, who are unaffected). Old savers at the time the policy is implemented are hurt. If, in addition, $(aG - B) < p_0(L_0 + L)$, then all other savers are helped. If, however, $(aG - B) > p_0(L_0 + L)$, then all other savers are also hurt. Nevertheless, the diversification increases the weighted sum of utility of all workers and savers, weighted so that the marginal social utility of second-period consumption is the same for all.

From differentiation of the equilibrium condition, we note that the presence of long-lived assets decreases the sensitivity of interest rates to trust fund diversification and, thus, decreases the size of the interest-rate increase. We might interpret the quantitative part of Proposition 3 as follows. Given that a period in this model represents something like 30 years, and that the real interest rate has historically been about 2.3 percent per annum, a crude estimate of p_J is about *1/2*. A \$500 billion transfer of trust fund assets from bonds into stock, maintained there forever, must lower land prices but could not lower land prices by more than \$1 trillion. Moreover, the level of real investment could increase by more than \$500 billion.

4.9 Social Security Diversification with Only Safe Investment and Land

To show that social security diversification could have other effects, depending on the technology, we turn to an economy with one-period safe real investments but no one-period risky investments undertaken in equilibrium, $k_0 > 0$ and $k = 0$. Many of our preceding results are now reversed. Although perhaps extreme, this case illustrates some of the effects of trust fund diversification if there are rapidly diminishing returns to risky investment, so that trust fund diversification reduces the risky investment opportunities available to savers. The interest rate on government bonds is technologically determined by the return on safe real one-period assets, $p_J = 1/(1 + r) = 1/R_0$, and the price of safe land is technologically determined as well. The price p_K of risky consumption and the price p of risky land depend on the evaluation of risky consumption by savers. To reflect this endogeneity, we analyze the effects of an increase in the value of trust fund holdings of risky investments, $p_K K^f$, rather than the quantity K^f. Starting with $K^f = 0$, the two analyses are the same (as $K^f dp_K = 0$).

We could envision someone supplying a short-term risky financial asset promising R without any short-term real risky production. A seller of this asset could simply deliver out of land dividends, without producing any risky output. Thus, we can define social security diversification exactly as before – namely, as the sale of bonds and the purchase of short-term risky securities. Recall that starting from a position with no risky securities, trust fund purchases of short-term risky assets in exchange for bonds have exactly the same effect as the trust fund purchase of risky land in exchange for bonds.

In the absence of risky short-term production, the only source of risky consumption is risky land, and each acre of risky land provides one unit of risky consumption. (Hence, K^* can be interpreted as the savers' demand for risky land.) Market clearing in the market for risky consumption (4.29) now reduces to:

$$K^*(1/R_0, p_K, W - a(1 - 1/R_0)G) = L - K^f \qquad (4.32)$$

Thus, we again have a single equation in a single variable. But, now it is p_K instead of p_J.

4.9.1 Expected Utility, the Price of Risky Consumption, the Price of Land, and Investment

With the interest rate on government bonds fixed by the return on riskless investments, taxes do not change after diversification. Savers' utility changes only on account of a change in price of risky consumption. From the envelope theorem (or Roy's identity) and (4.32), we have:

$$dV/d(p_K K^f) = -U_1'\{L - K^f\}dp_K/d(p_K K^f) \qquad (4.33)$$

Thus, the expected utility of savers moves in the opposite direction from the price of risky investment. With risky second-period consumption being a normal good, the demand is downward sloping and the price p_K must rise to clear the market in response to an increase in trust fund demand for risky consumption. The result is that all savers, starting from the young at the time of social security diversification, lose.

This raises an interesting point for the current privatization debate. Many of today's young are clamoring for diversification on the grounds that stocks earn higher returns than bonds. But, any rational young saver should already be investing so much of his wealth in stock that he is indifferent on the margin between further investments in stocks and bonds. Thus, if prices did not change, the direct effect of social security diversification should be irrelevant to a young saver (even supposing he is covered by social security). However, if the extra demand for risky assets raises p_K (equivalently, if it lowers the expected return savers can get over their life), then Equation (4.33) shows that it reduces their welfare, provided that the riskless rate does not also change.

With young savers worse off and saving less, aggregate real investment also drops, as described in the next proposition (proved in the Appendix).

Proposition 4. *Suppose there is both safe and risky land and that safe investments, but not risky investments, are undertaken in equilibrium. Then, increased trust fund investment in risky assets increases the price of risky consumption, and decreases safe* *and so aggregate real investment. Moreover, social security diversification raises the price of risky land, leaving the price of riskless land unchanged. Therefore, the total value of land rises.*

If the trust fund initially held no risky assets, then the diversification raises the expected utility of all workers (except the old at the time the policy is implemented, who are unaffected). Old savers at the time the policy is implemented are also helped. All young and future savers lose utility as a result of the policy. Nevertheless, trust fund purchases of risky investment increase the weighted sum of utility of all workers and savers, weighted so that the marginal social utility of second-period consumption is the same for all.

4.10 A Concave Technology

The analysis so far was made simpler by the presence of, at most, one endogenous rate of return. The other rate of return and wages were fixed by technology independent of production decisions. When there are no short-term production possibilities or when both technologies are strictly concave, rather than linear, then we need to solve simultaneously two equilibrium equations in two unknown rates of return (wages remaining exogenous). This makes the underlying economic factors harder to see. But, we can still carry out the analysis, as we now show.[33]

We suppose that the safe technology takes the form $f(k_0)$ and that the risky technology takes the form $g(k)R$, where f and g are twice differentiable and concave and R is stochastic. We suppose the productive sectors of the economy are owned entirely by the savers.[34] Each saver receives a rent or profit from ownership of technology, in addition to his wage, as income.[35] This model includes the previous models as special cases.

Generalizing the model does reveal what general qualitative properties persist across all the equilibrium regimes studied earlier. We find that social security diversification always raises the riskless interest rate and lowers the expected

---

[33] A further generalization of the model would have been to introduce labor as a nonseparable input to production. If labor were applied at the same time as capital, for example, at planting time, before uncertainty is resolved, there would be little additional complication. But if labor is applied to production after uncertainty is resolved, for example, at harvest time (so that the capital of one generation combines with the labor of the next), then labor income becomes state dependent and there would be no steady state equilibrium (though perhaps a Markov equilibrium). One could also allow for distinct models of land, depending on whether ownership of land ensures a given level of (possibly stochastic) output each period, or whether the ownership of land provides a given level of capital input to production each period. When the marginal product of capital was given, the two approaches were the same.

[34] That is, each of the unit measure of savers owns access to these technologies in terms of own capital input. Because each saver will invest the same amount, we can do the analysis in terms of aggregates.

[35] This modeling approach differs from that with an externality that could result in the same aggregate output function but without the separation of returns between the return on capital inputs and the return on ownership of technology. This alternative approach would give a larger return to trust fund investment in capital because there would not be an increase in the return to savers from owning technology.

short-term risky return. It decreases safe investment and increases risky investment. Its effect on total investment and total land value could go either way.

To describe equilibrium in terms of budget set (4.2) and the variables C^*, J^*, and K^* requires recognition of the return from owning technologies as part of the definition of income, I. We begin with the productive sector, which is assumed to maximize profits, taking prices as given. Let

$$\prod(p_J, p_K) = \max[p_J f(k_0) - k_0] + \max[p_K g(k) - k] \qquad (4.34)$$

Income for the savers is now defined as

$$I(p_J, p_K) = W - a(1 - p_J)G + \prod(p_J, p_K) \qquad (4.35)$$

With this definition of income, we can define savers' demands C^*, J^*, K^* from budget set (4.2) as before. Stationary equilibrium is now described by a vector (p_J, p_K, k, k_0) satisfying the market-clearance conditions.

$$J^*(p_J, p_K, I(p_J, p_K)) + a(1 - p_J)G/p_J$$
$$= (G - F_0 + p_K K^f)/p_J + L_0 + P + f(k_0) \qquad (4.36)$$

$$K^*(p_J, p_K, I(p_J, p_K)) = L - K^f + g(k) \qquad (4.37)$$

$$\begin{aligned} p_J &= 1/(1 + r) = 1/f'(k_0) \quad \text{if} \quad k_0 > 0 \\ &\leq 1/f'(k_0) \quad \text{if} \quad k_0 = 0 \end{aligned} \qquad (4.38)$$

$$\begin{aligned} p_K &= 1/g'(k) \quad \text{if} \quad k > 0 \\ &\leq 1/g'(k) \quad \text{if} \quad k = 0 \end{aligned} \qquad (4.39)$$

$$P = L_0 p_J/(1 - p_J) + L p_K/(1 - p_J) \qquad (4.40)$$

We confine our attention to "regular economies" that satisfy two restrictions. The first is that if in any equilibrium, either safe or risky investment is not undertaken, then the corresponding price/marginal product condition in (4.38) or (4.39) is a strict inequality. The second restriction is that at every equilibrium, if we linearize the five equations (4.36)–(4.40) and then differentiate with respect to the five variables (p_J, p_K, k, k_0, P), we get an invertible matrix. Because nearly every economy is regular, there is almost no loss of generality in looking only at regular economies.[36]

As in the linear model, there are four equilibrium regimes depending on whether risky or safe investment is undertaken. Nevertheless, because all four of these regimes are consistent with the hypothesis that the economy is regular, we can handle all the cases as part of the same analysis, which proceeds by contradiction. We conclude that the effects of social security diversification on short-term prices

---

[36] That is, if we endow savers with a very small amount s of safe consumption and a very small amount r of risky consumption in their old age, then almost any choice of s and r (precisely, all except for a measure zero set of choices) will give a regular economy.

and investment can be generalized from the special cases of the linear model to the more general concave model of this section.

Proposition 5. *Suppose we have a regular economy with concave short-term production technology and land and $B \leq aG$. Then, increased trust fund investment in risky assets (weakly) raises p_K and k and (weakly) lowers p_J and k_0.*

If the trust fund initially held no risky assets, then the diversification raises the expected utility of all workers (except the old at the time the policy is implemented, who are unaffected). If it also raises the price of land, then it helps old savers and hurts all young and future savers. If, on the other hand, it lowers the total value of land, then it hurts all old savers and may help or hurt young and future savers. Nevertheless, trust fund purchases of risky investment increase the weighted sum of utility of all workers and savers, weighted so that the marginal social utility of second-period consumption is the same for all.

Proposition 5 includes the relevant portions of earlier propositions as special cases. Furthermore, as in the risky linear case and in the safe linear case, one of the prices p_K or p_J is fixed by the technology, Proposition 5 and the formulas for land prices yield the land price results from earlier propositions as well. By contrast, the proof is indirect, and proceeds by finding a contradiction, yielding less insight than the explicit formulas derived in the earlier propositions.

Proposition 5 is qualitative, so we cannot use it in general to sign the effect of social security diversification on aggregate investment, for that involves comparing the magnitudes of the effects on safe and on risky investment or on total land value.

4.11 Defined Benefits

We have restricted attention so far to a defined-contribution social security system for analytical convenience and to make the point that even there, social security diversification in moderation brings potential welfare gains. We show now that, at least for our central risky linear case, we can readily incorporate a defined-benefit structure without changing the comparative statics conclusions.

In our defined-contribution social security system, we supposed that the trust fund maintained a constant value F invested in government bonds and a constant value κ invested in risky securities, distributing any surplus as changes in benefits to the contemporaneous old. If the fund acted only to maintain F, distributing a part of the surplus over F as benefits to the contemporaneous old, and investing the rest in risky equities, then over time the benefits and the size of the trust fund investment in risky equities would change.

Leaving tax rates fixed, the level of benefits would adapt to the level of the trust fund, thereby rising with the return on the portfolio, as does a defined contribution system, but not rising dollar-for-dollar because the returns got spread over future cohorts. In this way, the benefits of a cohort would depend on the realized returns over a longer period of time. With a sensible benefit rule, and a plausible stochastic process for the return on capital, this would raise expected utility for future generations, measured as of the time of implementation of the policy, because a diversified social security system could spread the return risk over many generations. Thus, the gain from a diversified portfolio becomes larger with a good policy for determining benefits.

In any "defined-benefits system" with risky investments, benefits (and/or taxes) must be changed, depending on the returns of the risky investments. The point is to smooth benefits, while recognizing the need to satisfy a nonnegativity constraint should there be a prolonged period of low returns. In the presence of random returns on a nontrivial portion of the trust fund, it is necessary to recognize the probability that the portion of the trust fund invested in risky assets would become negative if both benefits and taxes were unchanged. Thus, every "defined-benefit system" must be changed from time to time. The policies that determine such change need to be modeled in order to consider the value of smoothing that comes from defined benefits. In a model with randomness in other aspects of the economic and demographic environment as well, the change in uncertainty from a diversified portfolio would not be such a salient change in the system.[37]

In the risky linear case, the variations described earlier in the trust fund holding of risky securities and in social security benefits have no effect on any equilibrium price. The extra money invested in risky securities is absorbed by an increase in risky production, with no effect on p_K. The environment of savers is, thus, exactly the same as it was in Section 4.8. The same comparative statics conclusions on prices and quantities for the defined-contribution system of Section 4.8 would, therefore, apply to the defined-benefits system described here, no matter what the precise benefit rule.

4.12 Conclusion

Some proponents of social security diversification say it would help young savers because stocks have traditionally earned a higher return than social security is projected to yield in the future. They have been rightly criticized for sometimes forgetting about the unfunded liability embodied in social security commitments to today's old and for ignoring the riskiness of stock returns.[38] Naturally, our model recognizes both of these considerations and, not surprisingly, it shows that the equity premium would fall after diversification. Our analysis also makes clear that the welfare of young savers depends on at least two more considerations. First, their income taxes will rise (to pay the higher interest on government bonds). Second, the assets they buy and sell will change in value. Young savers, being net

---

[37] If a defined-contribution system is to fulfill its social purpose, it will also need periodic change in response to economic and demographic developments.

[38] This line of criticism is developed in Geanakoplos, Mitchell, and Zeldes (1998, 1999).

buyers of long-term assets, will lose utility if land prices rise. Unless long-term capital values go down substantially after diversification, if their taxes rise by more than their interest receipts, young (and future) savers will be made worse off by social security diversification. By contrast, today's old savers will be made better off if long-term capital values rise.

Proponents of social security diversification also sometimes argue that it will stimulate aggregate investment. We find that it does stimulate risky investment, but it also decreases safe investment. The effect on aggregate investment depends critically on technological assumptions. Investment is driven by the savings of the young. A rise in long-term capital values, which reduces their welfare, tends to reduce their savings and, thus, aggregate investments.

In the risky linear-technology model, to which we devote the most attention, social security diversification *lowers* long-term capital values and increases aggregate investment. In the safe linear model, it raises long-term capital values and lowers aggregate investment. The commonsense conclusion that trust fund diversification would (if it did anything at all) increase real investment and increase stock market value is thus seen to be questionable. In both simple models, one or the other of the commonsense predictions is reversed.

We also have shown that changing the trust fund portfolio policy away from 100 percent government debt raises total welfare (suitably defined), as well as causing welfare redistributions among household types.

The paper assumed that the technology is iid. This leaves out the effect of news about future technologies on current asset prices. This would be an interesting extension. Presumably this would make asset returns riskier and add to the social value of sharing risks more widely and so strengthen the case for investment in equities. The paper assumed that labor is a separable input from capital. Allowing changes in investment to change wages would have created another interesting redistribution.

There are four points to make relative to the current policy debate.[39] First, contrary to some assertions, the heterogeneity of the population implies that trust fund portfolio choice does have real effects on the economy. Second, although it is appropriate to be concerned about the risk associated with a change in portfolio policy, it seems to us unlikely that workers are so risk averse that a portfolio completely invested in Treasury bonds is optimal. This point is reinforced by the ability of the government to spread risk over successive cohorts because social security is a defined-benefit system. That is, if a defined-benefit system is well run, there is a stronger case for trust fund investment in private securities than in the models analyzed here, which assumed a defined-contribution system. Third, the marginal social benefit to diversification declines as the level of diversification

---

[39] For more discussion of diversification, see Munnell and Balduzzi (1998) and Diamond (1999).

increases (exposing workers to more risk), which puts a limit on the amount of socially desirable diversification. Fourth, the models considered here have substituted equity investment for bond investment, holding constant the level of funding of social security. Many proposals for investment in stocks, whether through the trust funds or through individual accounts, use stock investments as a reason to increase or decrease the financing of social security (at least in the short run) relative to what might be proposed without such investment (e.g., see Smetters 1997). Such a change involves intergenerational redistribution that has not been incorporated in the analysis in this paper. Our analysis does apply, however, to proposals that would substitute a portfolio change for cuts in future benefits.

APPENDIX A

Proof of Proposition 2. Equilibrium is given by (4.14). Differentiating (4.14) gives:

$$dp_J/dK^f = -(d\{C^*[p_J, 1, W - a(1 - p_J)G] \\ + K^*[p_J, 1, W - a(1 - p_J)G]\}/dp_J)^{-1} \qquad (4.A.1)$$

With $I = W - (1 - p_J)aG$ as net wealth, and V as utility, and using the Slutsky equation,[40] and the size of the income effect given by (4.15), we have

$$dp_J/dK^f = -1/(C_p^c[p_J, 1, V] + K_p^c[p_J, 1, V] + ((C_I^*[p_J, 1, I] \\ + K_I^*[p_J, 1, I])(-[B - aG]/p_J))) < 0 \qquad (4.A.2)$$

where subscripts p and I refer to partial derivatives with respect to p_J and income I, and superscript c means compensated demand. To see that this expression is less than zero, first note that compensated changes keep expected utility constant and marginal utilities are proportional to prices, implying that $0 = C_p^c + p_K K_p^c + p_J J_p^c = C_p^c + K_p^c + p_J J_p^c$. Because compensated own effects are always negative, $J_p^c < 0$, it follows that $C_p^c + K_p^c > 0$. Because both C and K are normal goods, and $B - aG \leq 0$, the denominator of (4.A.2) is positive. Note that this analysis holds for any $K^f \geq 0$ consistent with equilibrium with positive risky and zero safe investment.

To consider the impact of changing social security portfolio policy on aggregate investment, we need only determine its effect on the consumption of young savers because the consumption of young workers does not change. From (4.11), we know (using Slutsky and the income-effect term from [4.15]) that

---

[40] $dC^*[p_J, 1, W - (1 - p_J)aG]/dp_J$ equals $C_p^c + C_I^*(dV/dp_J)/U_1'[C_1]$ is the change in income that would give the same utility at the old prices as given by the new prices and the new income.

$$dk/dK^f$$
$$= d\{K^* + K^f\}/dK^f$$
$$= -(dC^*[p_J, 1, W - a(1 - p_J)G]/dp_J)(dp_J/dK^f)$$
$$= -\{C_p^c[p_J, 1, V] + C_I^*[p_J, 1, I](-[B - aG]/p_J)\}(dp_J/dK^f)$$
$$= \{C_p^c - C_I^*[B - aG]/p_J\}/\{C_p^c + K_p^c - (C_I^* + K_I^*)[B - aG]/p_J\} > 0$$

$$(4.A.3)$$

We already saw that the denominator is positive. Also, $C_p^c[p_J, 1, V] > 0$, because J and C are Hicksian substitutes if J is normal. Furthermore, $C_I^* > 0$, because C is normal. Thus, if $B \leq aG$, substitution and income effects go the same way. Hence, trust fund diversification lowers C^*, thereby raising total risky investment $K^* + K^f$. Our analysis also shows that $dk/dK^f < 1$, when all the goods are normal, for then $K_p^c > 0$ and $K_I^* > 0$, and the denominator of (4.A.3) is larger than the numerator.

Without land, old savers and old workers at the time diversification is first implemented are not affected. Given a rise in the interest rate, Equations (4.16), (4.17), and (4.18) demonstrate the utility gains.

Proof of Proposition 3. Equilibrium is given by (4.27) or (4.28). Differentiating (4.28), using the Slutsky equation, using the impact of a price change on V, (4.30), and using the derivative of P from (4.24), we have:

$$dp_J/dK^f = -(d(C^* + K^* + P)/dp_J)^{-1}$$
$$= -1/\{C_p^c + K_p^c + (C_I^* + K_I^*)(-(B - aG)/p_J$$
$$- L_0 - P) + dP/dp_J\}$$
$$= -1/\{\{C_p^c + K_p^c\} - \{(C_I^* + K_I^*)(B - aG)/p_J\}$$
$$+ \{-(C_I^* + K_I^*)(L_0 + P) + dP/dp_J\}\}$$
$$= -1/\{\{C_p^c + K_p^c\} - \{(C_I^* + K_I^*)(B - aG)/p_J\}$$
$$+ \{(L_0 + P)(1/(1 - p_J) - (C_I^* + K_I^*))\}\} \qquad (4.A.4)$$

The first terms in the denominator of the last line of (4.A.4) are the compensated demands for first-period consumption and risky second-period consumption with respect to the price of safe second-period consumption and have a positive sum, as noted in the proof of Proposition 2. The next term reflects the redistribution between savers and workers and is positive if savers have a larger share in taxes than in bonds ($B \leq aG$) and have normal demands. The final term reflects the intergenerational redistribution between old savers when the policy is implemented and later cohorts. It is also positive when the demand for safe second-period consumption is normal (which implies that $C_I^* + K_I^* = 1 - p_J J_I^* < 1$) and the price of second-period consumption, p_J, is between zero and one ($r > 0$), as we have assumed. Thus, $dp_J/dK^f < 0$, as was the case without land.

The falls in the prices of land follows from (4.20), (4.22), and the fall in p_J. We can get further information about the size of dP/dK^f by multiplying out the terms in (4.44). In the third line of (4.A.4), define x to solve $-(C_I^* + K_I^*)(L_0 + P) + dP/dp_J = p_J\{dP/dp_J\} + x$. Using (4.24), and the fact that $(C_I^* + K_I^*) < 1$, we know that $x > 0$. Now, multiplying out the terms in (4.44), and using the fact that the rest of the terms in the denominator of (4.A.4) are positive and the fact that $dp_J/dK^f < 0$, gives $-p_J dP/dK^f < 1$.

As noted in (4.28), the level of investment in short-term production possibilities, $K^f + K^* - L$, is equal to the endowment of young savers less their first-period consumption, less the amount spent on purchasing land, less the unified net debt of the government. Note that L is constant. Hence, the change in short-term risky investment is given by the change in the RHS of Equation (4.28). Differentiating (4.28), using the Slutsky equation with the income effect from (4.30), and the derivative of P from (4.24) gives

$$
\begin{aligned}
dk/dK^f &= \{K^* + K^f\}/dK^f = -[d(C^* + P)/dp_J][dp_J/dK^f] \\
&= -\{C_p^c + (C_I^*)(-(B - aG)/p_J + L_0 + P) + dP/dp_J\}[dp_J/dK^f] \\
&= -\{\{C_p^c - (C_I^*)(B - aG)/p_J\} \\
&\quad + \{-(C_I^*)(L_0 + P) + dP/dp_J\}\}[dp_J/dK^f] \\
&= -\{\{C_p^c\} - \{C_I^*(B - aG)/p_J\} \\
&\quad + \{(L_0 + P)(1/(1 - p_J) - C_I^*)\}\}[dp_J/dK^f] > 0 \qquad (4.A.5)
\end{aligned}
$$

The first term C_p^c in the last line is the compensated cross elasticity of first-period consumption with respect to the price of second-period safe consumption. If the demand for riskless second-period consumption is normal, then C^* and J^* are Hicksian substitutes and this term is positive (Aura, Diamond, and Geanakoplos 2002). With normality of demand for first-period consumption and redistribution from savers to workers ($B \leq aG$), the second term is positive. The third term is also positive when the demands for second-period safe and risky consumption are normal ($C_I^* < 1$) and the price of second-period consumption, p_J, is between zero and one ($r > 0$), as we have assumed. Multiplying by the minus sign in front and by $dp_J/dK^f < 0$ gives a positive number.

Replacing $[dp_J/dK^f]$ in the first line of (4.A.5) by the first line of (4.A.4), we get $dk/dK^f = [d(C^* + P)/dp_J]/[d(C^* + K^* + P)/dp_J]$. From this, we see that whether dk/dK^f is above or below one depends on the sign of dK^*/dp_J, which is the sign of $K_p^c - K_I^*\{[(B - aG)/p_J] + (L_0 + P)\}$. The compensated derivative, K_p^c, is positive because the two assets are Hicksian substitutes. Thus, we see that if $-(B - aG) > p_J(L_0 + P)$, then $dk/dK^f < 1$. But, if $-(B - aG) > p_J(L_0 + P)$, and K_p^c is small, then dk/dK^f could be greater than 1. In such a case, the drop in the value of land gives such a big positive income boost to young savers, who are buyers of the land, that they increase their holdings of risky assets K^* even while the competing return on safe assets has gone up.

Given the rise in the interest rate, the utility results follow from the previous equations. We note that the SWF needed for the last conclusion has weights:

$$SWF = mnv_{\text{old}}^0 + V_{\text{old}}^0 + \sum_1^\infty \delta(t)[mnv^t + V^t]$$

The superscript t refers to the generation of birth, and we suppose the diversification takes place at time $t = 1$. The weight m is chosen, as before, so that starting from the original equilibrium, an additional dollar gives the same marginal social utility whether it is given to an old saver or an old worker from the same generation. Finally, we suppose $\delta(t) = 1/(1 + r)^{t-1}$, where r is the interest rate prevailing in the original equilibrium. This also preserves the property that a simple redistribution has no impact on social welfare. To calculate the effect of social security diversification on social welfare, the utility gains must be added across all generations. Using (4.29) and (4.30), and recognizing that $(1 - p_J)$ is equal to $r/(1 + r)$, the change in total land value does not affect social welfare. The sum of all savers' utility gains from the fall in land prices, discounted by the equilibrium interest rate, exactly balances the change in utility of the old from the generation in retirement at the time the policy was implemented.

Proof of Proposition 4. Define $\kappa = p_K K^f$ and consider changes in its value. Differentiating the equilibrium Condition (4.32), and using the Slutsky equation and the income effect from (4.33), we have:

$$dp_K/d\kappa = -(p_K\{dK^*[p_J, p_K, W - p_J T(p_J)]/dp_K - K^f/p_K\})^{-1}$$
$$= -1/\{p_K K_{p_K}^c - p_K K_I^*[L - K^f]\} - K^f\} > 0 \qquad (4.A.6)$$

Because compensated own price effects are always negative, and K^* is a normal good, all the terms in the denominator are negative. Multiplied by the negative sign outside, we get the claimed result. From the connection between p_K and the price of risky land, (4.22), we conclude that the price of risky land also rises. The price of safe land does not change.

Next, we show that aggregate investment declines after trust fund diversification. Rearranging the equilibrium Condition (4.25), using budget set (4.2), and market clearance for risky consumption (4.32) gives:

$$\begin{aligned}
R_0 k_0 &= J^*(p_J, p_K, W - aG(1 - 1/R_0)) + aG(R_0 - 1) \\
&\quad - (L_0 + P) - R_0(G - F_0 + p_K K^f) \\
&= R_0(W - C^*(1/R_0, p_K, W - aG(R_0 - 1)/R_0) - p_K K^*) \\
&\quad - (L_0 + P) - R_0(G - F_0 + p_K K^f) \\
&= R_0(W - C^*(1/R_0, p_K, W - aG(R_0 - 1)/R_0)) \\
&\quad - (L_0 + P) - R_0(G - F_0 + p_K L) \qquad (4.A.7)
\end{aligned}$$

Dividing by R_0, differentiating with respect to κ, noting from (4.23) that $\partial P/\partial p_K = L/(1 - p_J) = L R_0/(R_0 - 1)$, and then using the Slutsky equation with the income effect derived in (4.33), we have:

$$
\begin{aligned}
dk_0/d\kappa &= -(dC^*/dp_K + L/(R_0 - 1) + L)(dp_K/d\kappa) \\
&= -\left(C^c_{p_K} - C^*_I[L - K^f] + L R_0/(R_0 - 1)\right)(dp_K/d\kappa) \\
&= -\left(C^c_{p_K} + L[(R_0/(R_0 - 1)) - C^*_I] + C^*_I K^f\right)(dp_K/d\kappa) < 0
\end{aligned}
$$
$$(4.A.8)$$

To see that the derivative $dk_0/d\kappa$ is negative, note first that because K is normal, C and K are Hicksian substitutes, so $dC^c/dp_K > 0$. By normality of K and J, $C^*_I < 1$. Because $R_0/(R_0 - 1) > 1$, the second term is positive. Finally, because C^* is normal and the trust fund holdings of risky consumption are nonnegative, the last term is positive as well. Thus, the sum in parentheses is positive and, because $dp_K/d\kappa > 0$, safe investment declines.

With a rise in the price of land, the utility of old savers rises when the policy is implemented, as the value of the land they are holding rises. In turn, this lowers the expected utility of young savers and those in future cohorts. Starting from a trust fund invested exclusively in bonds, the expected utility of workers is increased by diversification in the same way as in Proposition 1.

Proof of Proposition 5. Stationary equilibrium is described by a vector (p_J, p_K, k, k_0) satisfying the definitions of profit and income, (4.34), (4.35), and the equilibrium conditions (4.36)–(4.40). (If Condition [4.38] or [4.39] is a strict inequality, then we drop the corresponding production input level, fixing it at 0, and also drop the corresponding equation, and look at the remaining 4×4 or 3×3 matrix.)

We analyze the effect on equilibrium of a change in trust fund investment in risky assets: $d\kappa = -dF > 0$, where κ is the value invested in risky consumption, $p_K K^f$.[41]

We begin as usual by considering welfare effects. Trust fund portfolio diversification will change the prices of consumer goods and land in equilibrium. The price changes also will affect taxes paid. The changes in individual utilities are derived from these changes by the envelope theorem and the market clearance relations.

The old savers at the time of implementation of the policy change hold all the land in the economy, which they sell to the next generation, so

$$
\begin{aligned}
\partial V_{\text{old}}/\partial p_J &= U'_2[dP/dp_J]; \quad \partial V_{\text{old}}/\partial p_K = U'_2[dP/dp_K] \\
dV_{\text{old}}/d\kappa &= U'_2[dP/dp_J](dp_J/d\kappa) + U'_2[dP/dp_K](dp_K/d\kappa) \quad (4.A.9)
\end{aligned}
$$

---

[41] Furthermore, small changes in the trust fund create small changes in equilibrium. Equilibrium before and after social security diversification will, therefore, be of the same type.

Their utility rises or falls, implementation of the policy change as total land value rises or falls.

Because the new stationary equilibrium is achieved immediately after the trust fund purchases, young savers at the time of the purchases are affected exactly the same way as all future savers. Using the envelope theorem and market-clearing equations (4.36) for safe consumption and (4.37) for risky consumption, and the definitions of income taxes (4.5) and profit (4.34), we can derive the response of expected utilities to changes in prices.

$$\partial V/\partial p_J = U_1'\{-J^* + d\Pi/dp_J - d[a(1-p_J)G]/dp_J\}$$
$$= U_1'\{-\{[B - a(1-p_J)G]/p_J + L_0 + P\} - d[a(1-p_J)G]/dp_J\}$$
$$= -U_1'\{[B - aG]/p_J + L_0 + P\} \tag{4.A.10}$$

$$\partial V/\partial p_K = U_1'\{-K^* + d\Pi/dp_K\} = -U_1'\{L - K^f\} \tag{4.A.11}$$
$$dV/d\kappa = (\partial V/\partial p_J)(dp_J/d\kappa) + (\partial V/\partial p_K)(dp_K/d\kappa)$$
$$= -U_1'\{[B - aG]/p_J + L_0 + P\}(dp_J/d\kappa) - U_1'\{L - K^f\}(dp_K/d\kappa)$$

It is interesting that safe output $f(k_0)$ and risky output $g(k)$ both cancel out of (4.A.10) and (4.A.11), respectively. The reason is that the firms effectively trade only with the savers. If the savers own the technology, then there is no welfare effect from price changes via production. If the output becomes more valuable, increasing the profit for the firm, then it becomes more expensive for the savers to buy from the firm.

From the equations for land value and its derivative, (4.23) and (4.24), (4.A.10) and (4.A.11) can also be written as:

$$\partial V/\partial p_J = -U_1'[[B - aG]/p_J + (1-p_J)dP/dp_J]$$
$$\partial V/\partial p_K = -U_1'[(1-p_J)dP/dp_K - K^f] \tag{4.A.12}$$

Assuming that the trust fund does not hold long-term assets, worker utility is not affected by land prices. Hence, we have:

$$dv/d\kappa = E\{u_2'\{((R/p_K) - 1 - r)/n - dt/d\kappa + (F_0 - \kappa)(dr/d\kappa)/n$$
$$- (RK^f/p_k)(dp_K/d\kappa)/n\}\}$$
$$= E\{u_2'\{((R/p_K) - 1 - r + (F - (1-a)G)(dr/d\kappa)$$
$$- (RK^f/p_k)(dp_K/d\kappa)\}\}/n$$
$$= E\{u_2'((R/p_K) - 1 - r)\}/n - E\{u_2'\}(B - aG)(dr/d\kappa)/n$$
$$- E\{u_2'(RK^f/p_k)\}(dp_K/d\kappa)/n \tag{4.A.13}$$

We consider a weighted sum of utilities, denoted SWF:

$$SWF = mnv_{old}^0 + V_{old}^0 + \sum_1^\infty \delta(t)[mnv^t + V^t]$$

with the weights as described in the proof of Proposition 3.

We now turn to the proof of the first part of Proposition 5, which is indirect and proceeds by finding a contradiction.

Recalling that J^* is the demand for safe consumption, define J as the supply of safe consumption, net of tax. Rewriting (4.36), we get:

$$J^*(p_J, p_K, I(p_J, p_K)) = J \equiv [(1-a)G - F_0 + \kappa]/p_J + L_0$$
$$+ P + aG + f(k_0) \tag{4.A.14}$$

Recalling that K^* is the demand for risky consumption, define K as the supply of risky consumption. Similarly rewriting (4.37), we get:

$$K^*(p_J, p_K, I(p_J, p_K)) = K \equiv L + g(k) - \kappa/p_K \tag{4.A.15}$$

Multiplying J^* from (4.A.14) by p_J and K^* from (4.A.15) by p_K and adding, and then using the budget set (4.2), and the definition of I and P from (4.35) and (4.40), and the identity $P = p_J L_0 + p_K L + p_J P$, we get:

$$C^*[p_J, p_K, I(p_J, p_K)] = C \equiv W - [G - F_0] - P - k - k_0 \tag{4.A.16}$$

We think of C^* as the demand for current consumption and C as the supply.

The strategy of proof consists of differentiating the three equations $J^* = J$, $K^* = K$, and $C^* = C$ derived in (4.A.14)–(4.A.16), and the Equation (4.40) defining P, as well as the identity $\kappa = p_K K$, with respect to the six variables $d\kappa$, dp_J, dp_K, dP, dk_0, dk. From the regularity hypothesis, we know that the change in equilibrium values will indeed be differentiable. We will now prove that when $d\kappa > 0$, equilibrium can be restored only if $dp_J \leq 0, dk_0 \leq 0, dp_K \geq 0, dk \geq 0$. We use (4.38) or (4.39) only to conclude that dp_J and dk_0 have the same sign, as do dp_K and dk. Thus, the proof applies to every equilibrium regime. We obtain:

$$dJ = -\{[(1-a)G - F_0 + \kappa]/p_J^2\}dp_J + [1/p_J]d\kappa + dP + f'(k_0)dk_0 \tag{4.A.17}$$

$$dK = g'(k)dk + [\kappa/p_K^2]dp_K - [1/p_K]d\kappa \tag{4.A.18}$$

$$dC = -dP - dk - dk_0 \tag{4.A.19}$$

We also use the welfare effect from (4.A.12):

$$dV = -U_1'\{[[B - aG]/p_J]dp_J + (1 - p_J)dP - K^f dp_K\} \tag{4.A.20}$$

If $dp_J = 0 = dp_K$, then savers' demands do not change, so from (4.A.17) we must have $dk_0 < 0$, and from (4.A.18) $dk > 0$ and we are done. Thus, we assume that not both $dp_J = 0 = dp_K$, and we rule out three cases by contradiction.

Case 1. Suppose $dp_J \geq 0, dk_0 \geq 0, dp_K \geq 0, dk \geq 0$. Because we cannot have both $dp_J = 0$ and $dp_K = 0$, in fact at least one price strictly rises. Then, from

(4.40), $dP > 0$. From (4.A.19), this implies that

$$dC^* = dC < 0 \qquad (4.A.21)$$

Adding dJ and dk from (4.A.17) and (4.A.18), we have that

$$
\begin{aligned}
p_J dJ + p_K dK &= -[((1-a)G - F_0 + \kappa)/p_J]dp_J + d\kappa \\
&\quad + p_J[dP + f'(k_0)dk_0] + p_K g'(k)dk + [\kappa/p_K]dp_K - d\kappa \\
&= -[((1-a)G - F_0 + \kappa)/p_J]dp_J + p_J[dP + f'(k_0)dk_0] \\
&\quad + p_K g'(k)dk + [\kappa/p_K]dp_K > 0 \qquad (4.A.22)
\end{aligned}
$$

provided that $B - aG = [((1-a)G - F_0 + \kappa)] \leq 0$. Observe next that, given that $dp_J \geq 0$, $dp_K \geq 0$, the compensated change

$$dC^c(p_J, p_K, U) \geq 0 \qquad (4.A.23)$$

because all three goods are Hicksian substitutes (see Aura, Diamond, Geanakoplos 2002). To maintain constant utility, the compensated change

$$p_J dJ^c(p_J, p_K, U) + p_K dK^c(p_J, p_K, U) \leq 0 \qquad (4.A.24)$$

Because by (4.A.21), $dC^* < 0$, and by (4.A.23), $dC^c(p_J, p_K, U) \geq 0$, it follows, because C^* is normal, that welfare of the savers must have gone down. Because J^* and K^* are also normal, it follows from (4.A.24) that

$$p_J dJ^* + p_K dK^* < 0 \qquad (4.A.25)$$

But, (4.A.22) and (4.A.25) contradict each other because $dJ = dJ^*$ and $dK = dK^*$.

Before proceeding to Case 2, we remark that we could have deduced (4.A.24) directly from the fact that savers' utility is additively separable between consumption when young and when old. Similarly, (4.A.25) holds for the same reason. Thus, Case 1 does not really need the hypothesis of normality.

Case 2. Suppose $dp_J \leq 0$, $dk_0 \leq 0$, $dp_K \leq 0$, $dk \leq 0$. We get the same contradiction as in Case 1, with all the signs reversed.

Case 3. Suppose $dp_J \geq 0$, $dk_0 \geq 0$, $dp_K \leq 0$, $dk \leq 0$. Because J^* and K^* are Hicksian substitutes, we have

$$dK^* \geq (K_I^*)dI \qquad (4.A.26)$$
$$dJ^* \leq (J_I^*)dI$$

where dI is the change in wealth that would cause the same change in welfare (at constant prices) as caused by the price changes. From (4.A.17), we deduce (assuming that $B - aG \leq 0$) that

$$dJ^* = dJ \geq dP \qquad (4.A.27)$$

and from (4.A.18), we know that

$$dK^* = dK = g'(k)dk + \left[\kappa / p_K^2\right] dp_K - [1/p_K] d\kappa \left[\kappa / p_K^2\right] dp_K \leq 0 \tag{4.A.28}$$

Suppose welfare for the savers went up, or stayed the same, $dI \geq 0$. Then, because K^* is a normal good, we know from (4.A.26) that $dK^* \geq 0$, a contradiction to (4.A.28). Alternatively, suppose that welfare for the savers went down, $dI < 0$, and the total value of land went up or stayed the same, $dP \geq 0$. Then, from (4.A.26), $dJ^* < 0$. But, from (4.A.27), we have that $dJ^* = dJ \geq 0$, contradiction. The only remaining possibility is that $dI < 0$ and $dP < 0$. But, from $dP < 0$ and the welfare effect described in (4.A.21), we deduce that

$$dI = dV/U_1' > K^f dp_K \tag{4.A.29}$$

From the fact that all goods are normal, so that $0 < (K_I^*) < 1/p_K$, and $dp_K \leq 0$, and $dI < 0$, it then follows from (4.A.26) and (4.A.29) that

$$dK^* \geq (K_I^*)dI > dI/p_K > K^f dp_K/p_K = (\kappa/(p_K)^2)dp_K \tag{4.A.30}$$

But now (4.A.28) and (4.A.30) are contradictory.

Using profit maximization for the first time, we cannot get any of the mixed cases, such as where $dp_K > 0$ and $dk < 0$, so the theorem follows after eliminating these three cases.

The welfare part of Proposition 5 follows by combining the welfare implications derived at the beginning of the proof with $dp_J \leq 0$ and $dp_K \geq 0$.

REFERENCES

Abel, Andrew B. 2001. "The Effects of Investing Social Security Funds in the Stock Market When Fixed Costs Prevent Some Households from Holding Stocks." *American Economic Review* 91(1): 128–48.

Advisory Council on Social Security. 1997. *Report of the 1994–1996 Advisory Council on Social Security.* Washington, DC.

Ameriks, John, and Stephen P. Zeldes. "How Do Household Portfolio Shares Vary with Age?" in progress.

Aura, Saku, Peter Diamond, and John Geanakoplos. "Savings in a Two-Period Two-Asset Model." *American Economic Review*, 2002.

Bohn, Henning. 1997. "Risk Sharing in a Stochastic Overlapping Generations Economy." Unpublished. University of California at Santa Barbara.

———. 1998. "Social Security Reform and Financial Markets." In *Federal Reserve Bank of Boston Conference on Social Security Reform*, 41.

———. 1999. "Should the Social Security Trust Fund Hold Equities? An Intergenerational Welfare Analysis." *Review of Economic Dynamics* 2 (3): 666–97.

Diamond, Peter. 1997. "Macroeconomic Aspects of Social Security Reform," *Brookings Papers on Economic Activity* (2): 1–66.

———. 1999. *Issues in Privatizing Social Security.* Cambridge, MA: MIT Press.

Diamond, Peter, and Menahem Yaari. 1972. "Implications of the Theory of Rationing for Consumer Choice under Uncertainty." *American Economic Review* 62 (3): 333–43.

Feldstein, Martin. 1985. "The Optimal Level of Social Security Benefits," *Quarterly Journal of Economics* 100 (2): 303–20.

Financial Economists' Roundtable. 1998. "Statement on Social Security." Unpublished manuscript.

Fischer, Stanley. 1972. "Assets, Contingent Commodities, and the Slutsky Equations." *Econometrica* 40 (2): 371–85.

Geanakoplos, John, Olivia S. Mitchell, and Stephen P. Zeldes. 1998. "Would a Privatized Social Security System Really Pay a Higher Rate of Return?" In R. Douglas Arnold, Michael Graetz, and Alicia H. Munnell (eds.), *Framing the Social Security Debate*. Washington, DC: National Academy of Social Insurance, Brookings Institution Press.

——— 1999. "Social Security Money's Worth." In Olivia S. Mitchell, Robert Myers, and Howard Young (eds.), *Prospects for Social Security Reform*. Philadelphia: University of Pennsylvania Press.

Greenspan, Alan. 1997. Testimony Before the Task Force on Social Security of the Committee on the Budget, U.S. Senate, November 20.

Kennickell, Arthur, Martha Starr-McCluer, and Annika E. Sunden. 1997. "Family Finances in the U.S.: Recent Evidence from the Survey of Consumer Finances." *Federal Reserve Bulletin* 83 (1).

Mitchell, Olivia S., and James F. Moore. 1997. "Retirement Wealth Accumulation and Decumulation: New Developments and Outstanding Opportunities." Working Paper 97-12, The Wharton School, University of Pennsylvania.

Munnell, Alicia H., and Pierluigi Balduzzi. 1998. "Investing the Trust Fund in Equities." Unpublished manuscript, Boston College.

Pestieau, Pierre, and Uri M. Possen. 1999. "Investing Social Security in the Equity Market. Does It Make a Difference?" Unpublished manuscript, University of Liege.

Smetters, Kent. 1997. "Investing the Social Security Trust Fund in Equity: An Options Pricing Approach." Technical Paper 1997-1, Congressional Budget Office, Macroeconomic Analysis and Tax Analysis Divisions.

Social Security Administration. 1996. *Annual Statistical Supplement to the Social Security Bulletin.*

5 Investing Public Pensions in the Stock Market: Implications for Risk Sharing, Capital Formation, and Public Policy in the Developed and Developing World

Policy makers worldwide are contemplating investing public pension assets in the stock market. This is motivated, at least for some, by concerns that existing public systems will be unable to provide benefits to a rapidly aging population without sharp increases in taxes, and by the perception that the higher average return on stocks than on government securities could help alleviate these pressures. Economists also have suggested that including stock market investments in public pension plans could improve risk sharing within and between generations, and perhaps lead to faster market development in developing countries. The purpose of this paper is to assess these arguments, with an emphasis on the considerations that are of special importance to developing markets.

To evaluate the potential value of stock market investments in a public pension system in general, a useful starting point is to identify the main goals such systems are intended to achieve, and a set of principles against which to measure proposed reforms. As discussed in Section 5.1, two of the most important principles are: (1) to minimize its disincentives for work and saving, subject to constraints arising from redistributive and insurance targets; and (2) to maximize transparency and accountability. Investing pension fund assets in the stock market may or may not be consistent with these principles – the answer depends very much on the specifics of how the policy is implemented.

Although there may be legitimate reasons to include stock market investments in public pension systems, there are a number of problems with the simple line of reasoning that emphasizes the higher average rate of return. In Section 5.4, I elaborate on two main points that are well established in the economics literature but bear repeating. First, shifting pension fund investments from government securities to stocks would provide little or no incentive for additional savings, assuming no tax interactions or other policy changes. Hence, aggregate economic growth, and the resources available to pay future pension benefits, would be largely unchanged. Second, raw comparisons between average stock market returns and the returns to pensioners are misleading on several counts. They confuse investment returns with flows determined by program rules, and do not adjust for the risk characteristics of different investments.

The logic that leads to these conclusions is invariant to whether stock market investment is via a government trust fund or via private accounts. That choice, however, may have important implications for the efficiency and transparency of the public pension system. The relative merits of investing through individual accounts versus government accounts are also discussed briefly in the introduction.

Investing public pension system assets in the stock market may, however, shift risk within and between generations. This could improve risk-sharing, but it also could make it worse, depending on what is assumed about the allocation of risk prior to reform and what happens to that distribution of risk as a result of the reform. Furthermore, it could have a political impact, which also is a source of risk. These and other issues surrounding risk and return are discussed in Section 5.4.

Developing countries face a somewhat different demographic outlook than does the developed world and often have a smaller public pension system in place. Those stock markets generally have higher volatility, lower liquidity, a narrower investor base, and less transparency than do developed markets. These issues and other concerns particular to developing countries are discussed in Section 5.5. The pension systems and demographic outlook for East Asia are compared to those for the industrialized countries, and the experience of Latin America in moving toward a prefunded, private-account–based system is discussed. Section 5.6 concludes.

5.1 Principles for Public Pension Fund Design

The question of good pension system design must be addressed in the context of the basic goals that such systems are designed to achieve. In most countries, the public pension system is one element of a broader social security system that provides resources to finance retirement, health care, and disability insurance. One goal is income redistribution – to ensure a minimum level of income for the elderly.[1] Another goal is to provide various types of insurance that may be expensive or unavailable in the private market. For instance, most public systems provide an indexed lifetime annuity to retirees and their spouses that insures against longevity risk. Public pensions also insure spouses and dependent children against the death or disability of the family's primary wage earner.

In practice, most public pension systems in developed countries are more or less universal. They extend beyond the basic goals of redistributing income to the poor elderly and providing insurance, providing pension benefits to middle-class and wealthy retirees as well. Workers and their employers are required to pay

---

[1] In most developed countries, pension systems have redistributed wealth from younger workers to older retirees more broadly. Such a policy may be justified on the grounds that due to economic growth, younger workers as a group are considerably wealthier than the elderly, and such transfers promote fairness.

earmarked taxes, and retirement benefits are tied, often quite loosely, to the value of past taxes collected on behalf of that individual. It is more difficult to articulate clear economic goals that are associated with these types of rules. Clearly, one is to increase national savings beyond what might be achieved with voluntary savings alone. Some would argue that, left to their own devices, people would save too little and later come to regret it. As explained in Section 5.2.1, however, most public systems are implemented in a way that tends to reduce the incentives for private savings, and that may have the effect of actually reducing national savings. Another goal of mandatory universal participation is to avoid the "moral hazard" problem that would be created by providing pension benefits only to those with very low savings. Incentives for private savings are muted by a safety net, particularly for lower income workers. Mandating participation avoids this problem. History suggests that universal coverage is politically as well as economically motivated – universal systems tend to receive greater public support than a pure welfare system.

These goals for redistribution and for ensuring adequate savings are reflected, for instance, in the World Bank's suggestion that pension systems be constructed as three-tiered structures (World Bank 1994). The first redistributive tier establishes a minimal level of poverty reduction and can be funded by general government revenues. The second tier is essentially a mandatory savings system. It is in this second tier that the question of stock market investments arises. The third tier consists of voluntary private savings, which, of course, also may include investments in stocks.

A challenge in any public system is to balance the goal of promoting higher savings rates with the goals of redistributing income and providing insurance. There is no way to completely avoid the conflict between these goals. Imposing the taxes needed to raise money for redistribution discourages work and saving. Providing various types of social insurance makes people better off but also reduces their incentive to work and save. These observations lead quite naturally to one important principle for pension design:

Principle 1: The rules should minimize the disincentives for work and saving, subject to constraints arising from redistribution and insurance targets.

A universal feature of public pension systems is complexity. Intricate rules govern the system's operation and its interaction with the rest of the government and the economy. Because of this, it is often difficult to establish even the most basic facts about who benefits, who loses, and by how much. Even harder to evaluate is the effect of the system on the rest of the economy and, in particular, its influence on work and savings. Adding stock market investments tends to increase complexity, introducing new administrative costs, a new source of risk, the possibility of unintended redistributions, and the potential for greater government intervention in capital markets. This suggests a second important principle for effective pension design:

Principle 2: The rules should maximize transparency and accountability.

Depending on its implementation, a policy that includes stock market invest-ments may or may not be consistent with these basic principles. In the analysis that follows, pension policy options are evaluated with these principles in mind.

5.2 Capital Formation Versus Shell Games

Public pension systems are under growing demographic pressure. In most of the developed world, a slowly growing labor force will have to support a rapidly grow-ing population of retirees who are living longer than ever before. Most economists agree that the best way to alleviate these pressures is to follow policies that will lead to more rapid economic growth and, hence, to a greater availability of goods and services for young and old alike.[2] Within this broader discussion, a policy op-tion that is receiving increasingly serious attention is to invest a portion of public pension contributions in the stock market, either through individual accounts or government trust funds.

Would investments in the stock market increase the rate of capital formation, thereby increasing the future productive resources of an economy? There are several reasons to believe that in developed financial markets such as the United States, Japan, and Europe, increasing the flow of funds into the stock market in itself will have little impact on capital formation. That is, moving a dollar out of private or government bonds and into the stock market has, at most, a secondary effect on aggregate investment. These considerations also apply to developing markets, along with other factors, the discussion of which is postponed until Section 5.5.

Fundamentally, increased investment must be financed by increased saving, and a corresponding reduction in current consumption. Most large public pension systems by design contribute little to aggregate savings; arguably, they reduce savings. In these systems, the debate about whether to invest in stocks or other assets often is a distraction from the more fundamental issue of how to increase the future resources available to the pension system and to the economy in the future. To understand why this is the case, it is first important to distinguish between "pay-go" and "prefunded" systems. In this discussion, I initially focus on stylized systems and abstract from considerations of distribution. Because similar redistributive policies can be implemented under either type of system, this abstraction does not change the main conclusion: that investing in stocks is a meaningful option for a prefunded system but not for a pay-go system.

5.2.1 The Pitfalls of Pay-Go

In a "pay-as-you-go" or "pay-go" system, current workers provide the funding for benefits paid to the current elderly, and depend on the next generation of workers

---

[2] The only alternatives are to cut benefits or to increase taxes, either of which is costly.

to fund their own benefits. No or little capital is accumulated in the process, and so there is a relatively small direct effect on capital formation. Because the accumulated assets in the system are small (particularly when compared to the present value of future pension liabilities), how they are invested cannot have a large impact on the system or the economy. Pay-go systems often are effective in redistributing income but tend to discourage saving and investment.

To understand why a pay-go system is likely to create a drag on the growth of capital, first consider the first generation of pension recipients. This group pays little or nothing into the system but receives a pension for life that is often only loosely tied to work history. What is the effect on the behavior of young workers? First, the additional taxes they must pay to fund those new pension payments discourage work effort and savings. (See Appendix A for a more precise statement of the conditions under which a pension system creates disincentives for work and savings.) The initial effect will be small if there are many workers per retiree because the incremental taxes required will be low. However, any demographic shock that leads to growth in the size of the retiree population relative to the working population increases the requisite taxes and also the disincentives to work or save.

A second and equally important effect of a pay-go system is the reduced incentive for current workers to save for their own retirement. If workers know they can depend on the next generation to partly finance their retirement via the public pension system, they rationally save less on their own account. In sum, a pay-go system unambiguously tends to reduce current and future savings relative to a prefunded system or to no public system at all.

If pay-go systems do not result in capital accumulation, why are countries with pay-go systems such as the United States debating whether to invest pension system assets in the stock market? One reason is that, in pay-go systems, temporary imbalances caused by demographic and economic shocks result in periods of excess revenues and periods of insufficient revenues. The potential for such imbalances is a structural problem inherent in pay-go systems. In the United States, it is also partly the result of deliberate decisions to raise social security taxes relative to current benefits in anticipation of future funding shortfalls. Consequently, the system currently has some of the attributes of a prefunded system. Furthermore, advocates of adopting a more fully prefunded system view mandated private accounts as a way to move toward this goal.

5.2.2 Prefunding Public Pensions

At the inception of a prefunded system, future beneficiaries pay taxes that are accumulated through investments in capital assets. On retirement, the value of the accumulated assets is the funding source for benefit payments. As in a pay-go system, benefits may be loosely or tightly tied to the history of an individuals wage earnings according to program-specific rules.

Current retirees receive no immediate transfers in a pure prefunded system. Similar to a pay-go system, workers face higher taxes (necessary to raise the funding for the system), discouraging work and savings. Also as in the pay-go alternative, workers are likely to save less on their own than they did in the past, knowing that their government pension will cover a portion of their retirement expenses. (Again, see Appendix A for the precise assumptions needed to make this statement true.) It is commonly believed that aggregate savings would nevertheless increase because workers who currently save little or nothing would be forced to save more via the pension system. Relative to an otherwise similar pay-go system, the biggest difference is that the money that would have gone to the first generation of retirees is instead invested. The fact that each generation funds its own retirement makes the system less susceptible to demographic fluctuations but at the possible cost of less risk-sharing across generations.

A useful distinction to make at this point is between "narrow" and "broad" prefunding, as emphasized by Orszag and Stiglitz (1999). In this paper, I use the term "prefunding" in the broad sense that assumes a contribution to aggregate savings. Some commentators have used the term prefunding in the narrower sense of funds earmarked for retirement purposes. Prefunding in the narrow sense may be useful for tracking the amounts individuals have contributed to the system and what they are entitled to as a result. It is not, however, a useful measure of whether an action has been taken to promote savings above what they would otherwise be. To illustrate, consider a transfer of a dollar from a government's general revenues to a "trust fund" earmarked for public pension payments, with all other policies held constant. Such a transfer appears to create an additional dollar of funding because the trust fund is bigger by this amount. But, nothing else has changed; the dollar does not contribute to prefunding in the broader sense because neither government nor private consumption plans change. In contrast, had the government increased taxes by a dollar and invested it in capital, broad prefunding would be increased.[3] In practice, it can be surprisingly difficult to agree on whether and to what extent a given policy promotes broad prefunding.

In sum, a prefunded system only will add to national savings, relative to a system without public pensions, to the extent that it forces or entices people (and their governments) to save more than they would have voluntarily saved. It also will produce higher national savings than a pay-go system because it does not transfer resources to a first generation of elderly who did not contribute. It is not clear, however, that a prefunded system improves social welfare relative to a pay-go system – there is a different set of winners and losers in each case. In a world with pay-go systems already in place, the overhang of existing systems further complicates welfare analysis. Resources that went to pay the first generation of

---

[3] This presumes that, absent the tax, people would have used the dollar for consumption rather than savings.

retirees cannot be recovered, and the transition generation could be forced to pay for their own retirement as well as their parent's retirement. Fortunately for many developing countries with pay-go systems, transition costs would be low because current obligations are relatively modest.

5.2.3 Shell Games

We can now return to the question: For a public pension system with a given store of accumulated assets, what are the implications of investing these assets in the stock market? Particularly for developed markets, an argument will be made that moving funds that would have accumulated in the current pension system into the stock market, without any increase in total savings, is essentially an asset swap or, more pejoratively, a shell game. Such an exchange would have only second-order effects on the system's finances or the economy more broadly, although superficially it might appear to enhance returns. It could, however, have important consequences for the distribution of risk bearing within and between generations. Because of this, some have suggested that shifting risk could, in fact, influence aggregate savings; these issues are discussed in Section 5.4.

Currently, many public pension funds restrict investments to government securities, which offer relatively low returns and commensurately low risk. It is convenient to think of these investments as residing in a government "trust fund" that purchases additional securities whenever dedicated tax revenues exceed pension system expenditures. Conversely, trust fund securities are sold to the public to meet pension obligations when dedicated revenues fall short. If the trust fund were to substitute purchases of risky private securities for purchases of safe government securities, the government would still have to fund any general revenue shortfall in the capital markets by issuing debt to the public instead of to the trust fund. Individual investors would shift private savings from stocks to government securities, in effect doing an asset swap with the pension system.

Immediately after the asset swap, it appears that individuals hold safer, lower-return portfolios than previously, and that the trust fund portfolio has greater risk and return. This, however, is an incomplete analysis of the incidence of risk and return, as can be seen by considering an economy with a "representative consumer." If stock returns are too low to meet the promised pension benefit in the future, the representative consumer will ultimately bear this risk because either his pension benefits must be cut or his taxes increased to meet the shortfall. Similarly, if returns are greater than anticipated, the pension system will have a surplus that will either be used to reduce taxes or pay additional pension benefits, again allocating the risk back to the representative consumer. Pension and tax risk, combined with portfolio risk, are no different than before the asset swap. This is because the overall investment risk in the economy is unchanged. Of course, thinking about pension systems in terms of a representative consumer is unsatisfactory in many ways. In practice, the additional risk and returns assumed by the government can be, to some extent, reallocated across generations, as discussed later. Nevertheless, an asset swap does not affect aggregate risk and return.

In sum, although investing public pension assets in the stock market may alter who owns stock and who owns government securities, this action in itself is unlikely to have a first-order effect on the total amount of capital invested in productive assets. This is akin to the Modigliani–Miller theorem of corporate finance, which says that a firm's cost of capital does not depend on whether it is financed with debt or equity. What matters is the total risk and return of the real investments. The same is true, at least as a first approximation, for an economy as a whole.

5.3 Private Accounts Versus Trust Fund Investments

This discussion has purposefully avoided distinguishing between stocks held in government trust funds and stocks held in mandated private accounts. This is because, in many respects, the economic effects of either are expected to be similar. In practice, however, there are a number of important considerations in choosing between these two alternatives. Although it is beyond the scope of this paper to consider these in detail, it is worthwhile to summarize some of the main issues.

Perhaps the most compelling reason to hold stocks in a government trust fund is to reduce transaction costs. There is evidence (James et al. 1999) that for countries that have instituted private accounts, transactions costs are high, consuming several years of returns for a typical retiree. Centralizing these investments also would avoid any excessive risk-taking or asset-churning by individuals, without the need to impose complicated regulations.

By contrast, the principle of transparency favors investing via private accounts. The financial situation of a trust fund, and its connection to the likely future benefits and taxes, is hard to determine, even for sophisticated analysts. With private accounts, transfers within and across generations can only be implemented by imposing fairly visible taxes, whereas in a trust fund these transfers can be more easily disguised. Because of limited transparency, trust fund investments are arguably more susceptible to political interference of various types as well. There is concern that the government-directed investments would favor particular companies or sectors at the expense of others and that in the event of market disruptions, the government would be more inclined to intervene than otherwise. Corporate governance is also a concern; the government might be too dominant (or too passive), thereby distorting corporate decision making.

Aside from transparency, the most important advantage of a private-accounts system is that it allows individuals to assume risk in exchange for higher returns, but only at their own choosing. In contrast, centralized savings systems with legislated benefits do not accommodate differences in individual risk preferences. It has been argued, for instance, that the U.S. social security system deprives low-income workers from the opportunity to participate in the stock market. The payroll taxes that fund their low-risk public pension crowd out any other saving, leaving them with relatively low-risk and low-return pension benefits. Investing trust fund assets in the stock market and assigning all the risk to beneficiaries could err in the opposite direction, forcing some low-income households to bear more stock market risk than is optimal.

To date, most countries that include stock market investments in the public pension system have opted to do so through private accounts and primarily with defined contributions. Countries that have moved toward investment-based pension systems include Switzerland, Australia, New Zealand, Chile, Malaysia, Argentina, Mexico, and Singapore.

5.4 Evaluating Risk and Return

5.4.1 Comparing Rates of Return

A popular criticism of pay-go systems is that they produce very low "rates of return" for beneficiaries. That is, comparing the present value of taxes paid into the system with the present value of average benefits, the implied rate of return on the taxes paid in is very low and even negative for some beneficiaries. Had the taxes instead been invested in private accounts, the realized returns would, on average, have been much higher.

As emphasized by Geanakoplos et al. (1998) among others, these types of "money's worth" comparisons can be highly misleading. In any pay-go system, the first generation of retirees receives a very high rate of return, at the expense of later generations who receive a correspondingly low rate of return. The main point is that a low rate of return is not an indication of leakage or a large inefficiency in the system; pay-go is simply a zero-sum game between generations. The present value of taxes paid in is equal (net of transaction costs) to the present value of benefits paid out, but the system rules create winners and losers.[4] The key point that emerges from this type of analysis is that in a pay-go system, the windfall gain to the first generation of retirees is a sunk cost that lowers the apparent rate of return for subsequent generations.

Another way to understand this phenomenon is to focus on the fact that in a pay-go system, there are no invested assets. Therefore, there is no rate of return in the sense there would be if benefits were financed from real investment returns. The apparent rate of return is the result of legislative fiat; it could easily be increased to a level that mimics or even exceeds the average return on stocks. The cost of this, however, would be to transfer wealth away from subsequent generations via higher taxes.

---

[4] Another reason that these types of calculations can be misleading is that some of the money is used to support various social insurance programs whose benefits are neglected when looking only at pension returns.

Whether the low returns from a pay-go system are a sign of inefficiency becomes important in evaluating the costs and benefits of transitioning to a prefunded system. Proponents of a switch to prefunding sometimes emphasize that removing the investment inefficiencies associated with pay-go could compensate for transition costs. This analysis suggests that there is little rate-of-return inefficiency to be exploited. The main source of inefficiency is the distorted incentives to work and save, but these also may be present in a prefunded system. If current workers must support current retirees, they are likely to be made worse off by a transition from a pay-go to a prefunded system that also requires them to prefund a considerable portion of their own retirement.

5.4.2 Tracking the Allocation of Risk

As already described, shifting government savings into stock market investments will be largely offset by shifts of private savings into government securities in aggregate. Such shifts, however, may have a significant effect on the distribution of risk and return within and across generations. These effects, and their possible broader implications, are discussed in this subsection.

The allocation of risk and return that results from investing pension fund assets in the stock market will be determined by three main factors: (1) the effect on individual portfolio composition, (2) the effect on benefits, and (3) the effect on tax liabilities. As the example in the previous section showed, with a representative consumer, any changes in portfolio returns are exactly offset by changes in pension benefits and taxes. Therefore, any real effects of such a policy change (assuming the policy causes no other distortions) must be the result of shifts in the distribution of risk and return.

Effect on individual portfolio risk. The initial effect of the government buying stocks financed with the sale of debt is that individuals will, on average, hold more debt and fewer stocks in their portfolios. There also are predictable cross-sectional effects. Stock holdings are concentrated in the portfolios of the relatively wealthy and the old, whereas most middle- and lower-income young families have a small fraction of their wealth in the stock market. If the government were to purchase any sizeable quantity of stocks, it would have to be disproportionately from high wealth and older households.

Effect on benefit risk. Investing pension fund assets in stocks may lead to riskier benefits, but there is no necessary connection. For instance, there are many private firms with defined benefit plans that are partly financed with stocks. Pension plans, whether public or private, fall into two broad categories: defined benefit versus defined contribution. In a defined-benefit plan, a formula determines benefits in a way that is largely independent of investment performance. In a defined-contribution plan, the return on paid-in premiums determines the size of pension benefits.

Many discussions of prefunded systems assume that benefits will be sensitive to realized asset returns, falling into the category of defined-contribution systems. If, however, a government trust fund were invested in stocks, and if realized returns were low, fixed benefits could still be delivered by borrowing or raising taxes. Similarly, in a public system with partially private accounts, a government guarantee of a minimum pension could be financed by borrowing or new taxes. Conversely, pay-go public pensions are generally structured as defined-benefit systems, but the rules could be modified so that benefits were contingent on asset returns. In either case, it is the rules of the system and the vagaries of the political process rather than the underlying investments that determine benefit risk.

Effect on tax risk. If the government assumes stock market risk but does not pass it on to pensioners, the risk will ultimately be transferred to taxpayers. Because retirees generally pay less in taxes, this risk is more likely to fall on the working population. It is difficult, however, to predict the precise timing or incidence of this risk. If, for instance, shortfalls are financed initially by issuing more government debt to the public, it may be many years before that debt is repaid with tax revenue.

Net risk incidence. The change in an individual's net risk position depends on all three of these factors and also on demographic characteristics such as age, wealth, and life expectancy. It is instructive to look at a few stylized proposals that illustrate the sensitivity of the likely incidence of risk to the details of the proposal.

The first proposal is to shift half of the government trust fund into stocks, financed by selling government securities held in the trust fund to the public. Pension benefits are contingent on trust fund returns, so future tax liabilities are unchanged. What are the likely consequences? First, the relatively wealthy elderly will have a less risky position on net and correspondingly lower average returns. This is because their personal portfolios on average will be safer, absorbing the government sales of debt, but their public pension benefits will be riskier. Their public pension represents a small fraction of their retirement income, however, so their net position is likely safer. Second, middle- and low-income elderly will likely have a riskier position and correspondingly higher average returns because the public pension portion of wealth is riskier and their personal portfolios, although safer, are relatively small. The direct effects on much of the working population are small because, by assumption, taxes are largely unchanged. For the minority of young workers with significant stock market wealth, their portfolio will, on average, be less risky.

The second proposal is also to shift half of the government trust fund into stocks, financed with a sale of government securities to the public. However, promised pension benefits are unchanged. Investment shortfalls are made up with higher payroll taxes, and unexpectedly high returns are used to reduce payroll taxes. The incidence of risk and return is quite different than under the first proposal. The relatively wealthy elderly will bear less risk because portfolio risk will likely decrease and pension risk remains the same. The risk borne by the middle- and low-income elderly will be largely as before because the dominant effect is that their pension benefits are unchanged. Because tax revenues are assumed to absorb the additional stock market risk in the trust fund, the working population would face greater exposure to market risk and return.

These examples emphasize the possible cross-sectional differences in the incidence of risk and return under alternative policies. However, it is important to note that some people will be in the position to offset any actions of the public system by varying the composition of their own accounts (e.g., if the government holds another dollar on their behalf in stocks, they reduce their private stock holdings by a dollar). In theory, anyone not up against a borrowing constraint should offset a policy change that alters their risk-return profile because, presumably, they held an optimal asset mix before the change occurred. Such offsetting actions would tend to mitigate any effect of policy changes on equilibrium asset returns.

5.4.3 Risk and Return Revisited

Comparisons of mean returns, without consideration of risk differentials, obviously overstate the apparent advantage of stock market investments. Although it appears easy to avoid naive comparisons that abstract from risk, in practice such adjustments are often neglected.

It is uncontroversial that for any active investor in financial markets, a dollar's worth of bonds has equal value to a dollar's worth of stocks, even though the expected return on stocks is higher. This is because investors (explicitly or implicitly) discount the higher future returns at a higher discount rate, reflecting aversion to the greater (undiversifiable) risk of stocks. The difference in average returns, the "risk premium," has averaged about 7 percent in the United States historically and also has been high in other developed stock markets. As a first approximation, then, the government also should not be able to create value by transferring a dollar from bonds to stocks.

Government accounting practices can disguise the economic equivalence of investing a dollar in stocks and a dollar in bonds. For instance, in the United States, the rules of "credit reform" dictate how the government accounts for programs such as guaranteed student loans in the federal budget. By law, expected future cash flows for these risky investments must be discounted at a risk-free rate.[5] If this method were applied to stock market investments, the implication would be that any proposal that contained stock market investments would, in present value terms, be superior to an otherwise similar proposal where investments were held in bonds. In other words, the market price of risk would be ignored.

A subtler question is whether the government should assign a lower cost to stock market risk than individuals do because it can diversify the risk to a greater extent. If so, there is some justification for using a below-market rate for discounting, although determining the size of the adjustment is problematic. The proper adjustment would depend on exactly how much of an advantage the government is assumed to have, and whether it actually would use its theoretical ability to improve risk-sharing. Considerations of transparency also suggest using the

---

[5] These rules will not necessarily apply to the budgetary treatment of social security investments in the stock market.

observed market premium to set the discount rate for pension system investments in stocks. It is worth emphasizing that any risk the government assumes ultimately falls on the general population. Although it may be able to spread risk broadly across people and, to some extent, across time, it cannot eliminate risk. (See Heaton and Lucas 2001 for a more formal analysis of how pension system rules might affect equilibrium risk-sharing.)

5.4.4 Political Risk

It has been observed (e.g., Brooks and James 1999) that the risks associated with various pension structures are political as well as economic. For instance, a public system that stipulates a defined benefit may fail to deliver one in the face of demographic pressures; political opposition to tax increases may lead to legislated benefit cuts. In the case of some Latin American countries – for instance, Mexico and Argentina – recent pension reforms were a response to the unsustainable promises made under the previously existing systems. A public pension system in which stock market investments put retirees at risk also entails political risk. For instance, in the event of a stock market downturn, the government may shift the risk back to future taxpayers rather than allow retiree benefits to be cut below a minimally acceptable level. Thus, a complete analysis of system risk entails looking beyond program rules and asset structure.

5.5 Considerations for the Developing World

The economic and demographic situation in the developing world is considerably different from that in industrialized countries. Many developing countries have a very limited pension system, and the majority of people rely primarily on their families for support in old age. Financial institutions in general, and stock markets in particular, are less developed in a number of dimensions. Nevertheless, most of the considerations discussed in the previous section are relevant to a developing country seeking to establish or improve its public pension system or contemplating a move toward a prefunded system invested in private assets.

In this section, the focus is on the implications of some of these differences for pension system reform and investing pension system assets in the stock market. Specific examples are drawn primarily from two regions: first, from East Asia, where pension reform is generally a more recent phenomenon but where demographic pressures are increasing; and second, from Latin America, which has experimented with reforms for more than a decade and is often cited as an example for other parts of the developing world to follow.

5.5.1 Demographic Comparisons

Although the demographic outlook differs across countries, increases in life expectancy and a reduction in birth rates implies that most countries worldwide

Table 5.1. *Dependency ratios in selected industrial countries*

	Projected total dependency ratio		
	2010	2030	2050
Canada	0.45	0.60	0.61
France	0.67	0.83	0.91
Germany	0.64	0.77	0.84
Italy	0.66	0.77	0.94
Japan	0.57	0.69	0.83
UK	0.67	0.81	0.86
USA	0.65	0.79	0.79

Source: Tuljapurkar et al. (2000).

will experience the pressures of an aging society. To provide a perspective on the similarities and the differences in these trends, Table 5.1 shows total projected dependency ratios for several industrialized countries, whereas Figure 5.1 shows dependency rates projected for East Asia. A dependency ratio measures the ratio of those 65 and over and under 15 to the working-age population between 15 and 64. The "old dependency ratio" separates out the portion of this ratio attributed to the elderly, and the "youth dependency ratio" is defined similarly. Figures 5.2 and 5.3 illustrate these two components of the dependency ratio separately for the countries of East Asia, showing a rapid increase in the elderly dependency ratio and a decline in the youth dependency ratio. Comparing Table 5.1 and Figure 5.1, with the exception of Hong Kong and Singapore, the total dependency ratios in East Asia are below those for the industrialized countries but are still expected to grow significantly between 2010 and 2050.

5.5.2 Pension Coverage in East Asia

Overall pension coverage in most of the developing world is much less extensive than in industrialized countries. To illustrate the types of arrangements currently in place in East Asia, Table 5.2 summarizes these systems, based on data in Heller (1997).[6] The "average replacement rate" is an estimate of the fraction of the typical worker's salary represented by the average public pension payment and, together with the coverage percentage, suggests the generosity of the benefits and the scope of the system. For comparison, a typical replacement rate for the industrialized countries lies between 50 and 70 percent.

For many of these countries, because existing public commitments are modest and because of the slower growth in dependency ratios, pension system reform may appear to be a secondary priority. However, this relatively quiet period is probably the ideal time to restructure. Experience suggests that when a public

---

[6] Because these systems are still evolving, some of these descriptions may already be out of date.

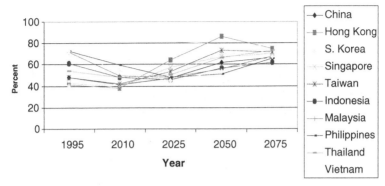

Figure 5.1. Total Dependency Ratio

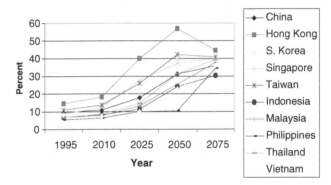

Figure 5.2. Elderly Dependency Ratio

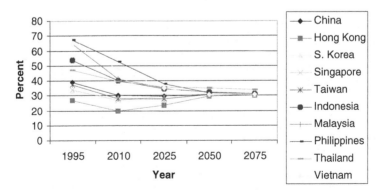

Figure 5.3. Youth Dependency Ratio

Table 5.2. *East Asian pension characteristics*

	Current old age dependency ratio (%)	Labor force coverage of formal public pension schemes (% of labor force)	Public pension outlays (% of GDP)	Implied average replacement rate (1995)	Remarks
China	8.7	28	2.2–2.6 (1995)	41	Covers civil service and state-owned enterprises; defined benefit, pay-go.
Hong Kong	12.7	0	1.0	10	Mostly private and semi-government provident funds. Government budget finances welfare program.
Indonesia	6.5	20	1.0	23	Defined benefit for civil servants and military, mostly pay-go. Some employers have mandatory defined-contribution scheme.
Korea	7.1	80	2.0	39	Defined benefit pay-go, with newer National Pension Fund intended to be fully funded.
Malaysia	6.3	45	2.8	74	Mandatory provident fund with individual accounts; fully funded, with no inflation or longevity insurance, nor redistribution.
Philippines	5.9	20–30 (1990)	1.6	48	First tier is defined-benefit for all government and some private workers. In second tier, some private enterprises offer defined benefit.
Singapore	7.8	67	1.1		Mandatory provident fund. No inflation insurance, nor redistribution. Significant tax subsidy.
Taiwan	9.3	universal		51	Pay-go defined-benefit system instituted in 1950s. Newer employer-based funded accounts.
Thailand	6.0	10 (expected to rise to 67 under new guidelines)	0.6	14	Mandatory provident fund for civil servants, previously defined benefit. A few private-sector provident funds. Sixty percent of investments must be in government securities or bank deposits.
Vietnam	8.1	10	1.7	36	New defined benefit pay-go.

pension system expands in response to an immediate need, such as a rapidly growing poverty rate among the old, political pressures favor immediate transfers over prefunding. This starts a pattern that is costly to change later on and that can be counterproductive for economic growth.

5.5.3 Investing Pension Assets in the Stock Market

For developing markets, both the positive and negative effects of investing pension funds in the stock market are likely to be more pronounced than for industrialized countries. Smaller stock markets generally exhibit higher volatility, lower liquidity, a narrower investor base, less transparency, and possibly lower returns than do developed markets. On the positive side, there is the possibility that the financial markets may be improved by these actions, and that the overall savings rate may be increased.

5.5.3.1 Capital Formation

As for industrialized countries, a primary determinant of the capital stock is the savings rate. Any pension reform that does not alter the overall savings rate is unlikely to have a significant impact on capital formation. For developing countries moving from small pay-go systems to more comprehensive prefunded systems, the overall savings rate may increase because individuals who previously saved little or nothing are compelled to change their actions. To the extent that the public safety net for retirees is expanded, however, it also may create savings disincentives because people who once expected to rely on their own savings now rely on the state. Both of these forces appear to be operating in Chile. Commentators on the Chilean experience have argued that the system provides a larger and more stable source of domestic investment funds than was previously available, and that this is in part responsible for Chile's relatively strong growth over the last two decades. Others have noted that the guaranteed minimum pension appears to be a significant deterrent to savings under the system.[7]

5.5.3.2 Risk, Return, and Diversification

Making a well-diversified investment in a developing stock market is often impossible. A few large companies dominate many smaller markets (e.g., Nokia represents more than half of the Finnish market). Even when most relatively large companies are represented, a few may account for most of the market capitalization. Rather than the stock market, in many countries commercial banks provide most of the investment capital, and channeling savings to the banking sector is the only way to effectively provide broad investment funding to local enterprises. Even in the larger European markets, the diversification gains from investing stocks internationally rather than domestically appear to be significant. All this points to the fact that from a diversification perspective, limiting stock market investments

---

[7] These types of reforms are recent in other developing countries so, apart from Chile, there is little evidence on these effects.

Table 5.3. *Asset allocation restrictions on public pension assets in Latin America*

	Chile	Peru	Argentina	Columbia	Mexico
Year Implemented	1981	1993	1994	1994	1997
Maximum % of portfolio allowed in:					
Domestic equities	30	35	50	30	0
Foreign securities	10	5	10	15	0
Government securities	45	40	50	50	100

Source: Grandolini and Cerda (1998).

to the domestic market would subject citizens of developing countries and, ultimately, their governments to considerably more risk for a given level of return than if they also were allowed to invest abroad. There is also concern about the adequacy of returns, because stock returns have been notably lower in developing markets.

The response to these considerations in the reformed pension systems of Latin America has been to limit the percentage of public pension assets that individuals can allocate to domestic equities and to allow a small fraction of funds to be allocated to foreign securities (see Table 5.3). Nevertheless, the percentage of domestic equity investment permitted, which ranges from 30 percent in Chile and Colombia to 50 percent in Argentina, represents a very risky portfolio strategy that may threaten the sustainability of these systems in the future. These limits reflect the tension between the desire to channel pension assets into domestic investment and the benefits of risk reduction that can only be achieved by investing internationally.

If unrestricted in their individual portfolio choices, some investors would take on considerable risk by holding individual stocks rather than market portfolios. To limit individual risk-taking, the reformed systems of Latin America generally restrict investment choices to diversified funds. To protect against very poor investment performance in these diversified funds, the law also contains a minimum pension guarantee.[8] By contrast, the United Kingdom and Australia provide more investment flexibility to their citizens while also providing a minimum benefit. The appropriate level of flexibility is difficult to determine. As in the developed world, investing public pension funds in stocks would tend to shift financial risk from the wealthy elite to the general population. Because a typical citizen has far fewer resources to fall back on in retirement than his wealthy compatriots and may lack the information or education to make good investment choices, limits on risk-taking may be optimal, at least initially. This philosophy has led to a gradual phase-in of riskier investment options in many of the Latin American countries. Chile, for instance, initially prohibited all stock market investments.

The issue of political risk is also central in developing countries, where the incentive to steer investment funds to preferred constituents may be strong. The

[8] Some commentators have suggested that these minimum guarantees have resulted in very low contribution rates to these systems and so are a strong disincentive to savings.

tight restriction on investment in foreign securities despite their benefits in terms of diversification might be viewed as one manifestation of this risk. Another example is the reform experience of Mexico, as described by the Congressional Budget Office (1999). The system instituted in 1997, which represents a considerable improvement over a previous failed reform, still maintains the requirement that employers contribute 5 percent of wages to a housing fund, which is used to make subsidized loans to workers for building a home. In the past, this fund has produced negative rates of return, reducing workers' retirement income and increasing the risk that the state will have to make up for these losses in the future.

5.5.3.3 Liquidity and Administrative Costs

Whether investing public pensions in a developing stock market would in itself increase market liquidity is unclear. Commentators have pointed out that even in the large U.S. market, if the social security system were to buy a significant fraction of the market, this would reduce liquidity because there would be less stock available for individuals and institutions to trade. To the extent that pension investments are long-term, buy-and-hold decisions, liquidity would be likely to decrease. By contrast, the increased participation in developing markets might enhance liquidity because it would draw more firms seeking capital into the stock market, and increase the pool of potentially active investors.

What is more certain is that the transaction costs associated with trading in illiquid markets are high, and must be taken into account when evaluating the potential returns to pensioners from stock market investments. Chile is the only developing country with a long enough experience with stock market investments to provide data about these costs, although its structure is thought to generate higher costs than necessary. Chile front-loads all costs, taking a fixed percentage of investments to cover administrative costs. Costs at inception were more than 20 percent of the contribution but have fallen to about 15 percent. Simulations suggest that this translates into a reduction in annual returns between 0.5 and 1.5 percent, depending on the assumed contribution pattern and rate of return (James et al. 1999). These fees are comparable to the average fees on U.S. mutual funds, although investors receive fewer services and considerably less diversification in return.

5.6 Conclusion

This paper presents a largely cautionary perspective on investing public pension funds in the stock market, both for developed and developing countries. The allure of using the higher average rates of return on stocks to offset demographic pressures fades when the implications of such an investment strategy are examined more closely. Fundamentally, demographic pressures can only be eased by higher rates of economic growth, which pension policy affects primarily through its influence on savings rates. Switching a fixed amount of investment from government bonds to stocks can be expected to have, at most, a small effect on capital formation and growth. Furthermore, the higher average return on stocks comes with commensurately more risk. How this risk is distributed across various demographic groups can have a significant effect on social welfare. Despite this, many reform proposals do not have a well-articulated plan for how risks will be shared. When managed through individual accounts, stock market investments also may involve relatively high transaction costs that may not be worthwhile for small account holders to bear. Additional risks facing developing countries contemplating investments in their own stock markets include higher volatility, lower liquidity, a narrower investor base, less transparency, and possibly lower returns than in developed markets. The political risk that investment policy may be directed toward other government goals also may be greater.

Although there is no free lunch from investing public pension funds in the stock market, there are potential benefits from such investments. Introducing individual accounts allows people to choose a preferred combination of risk and return, rather than having to accept the implicit risk and return embodied in the laws governing taxes and pension benefits. For developing countries, allowing stock market investments is usually part of a broader reform that tends to expand pension coverage and move in the direction of a prefunded system. Financial markets may be improved by these actions, and the overall savings rate may be increased despite some crowding out of private savings.

Because stock market investments in public pension systems have only a short history, there is little empirical evidence that can be brought to bear on the relative merits of different design choices. These types of reforms are most common in South America, but Chile's 1981 reform predates other reforms in the region by more than a decade. Three tentative conclusions can be drawn from the Chilean experience. First, careful consideration should be given to the administrative structure because transaction costs can be formidable. Second, such a policy can bolster domestic capital markets and growth by creating a larger and more stable pool of domestic savings. Third, the incentive for increased voluntary saving is muted by the provision of a minimum guaranteed pension, although such a guarantee may be welfare-improving overall.

APPENDIX 1. INCENTIVES FOR WORK AND SAVINGS UNDER A PUBLIC PENSION SYSTEM

In this appendix, a simple two-period model is used to illustrate the incentives provided for work and savings by the introduction of a public pension system. In the first period, people work, pay taxes into a pension system, and save for retirement. In the second period, people consume from a combination of pension payments and private savings. Notice that the basic structure and implied incentives could be features of either a pay-go or prefunded system and depend on the rules set by policy makers. In practice, these rules are ultimately constrained by considerations of budget balance, but those constraints are not considered here.

People maximize a lifetime utility function $U(c_1, L) + \beta V(c_2)$, where $\partial U/\partial c_1 > 0$, $\partial^2 U/\partial c_1^2 < 0$, $\partial U/\partial L < 0$, $\partial V/\partial c_2 > 0$, and $\partial^2 V/\partial c_2^2 < 0$. They do this by choosing labor supply and private savings subject to the following constraints:

$$c_1 = wL(1 - \tau) - S \qquad (5.A.1)$$

$$c_2 = S(1 + r) + p_0 + p_1 wL - p_2(wL)^2 \qquad (5.A.2)$$

where c_i is consumption in period i, w is the wage rate, τ is the tax rate, r is the interest rate, S is the amount of private savings, L is labor supplied, and the pension parameters p_i control the sensitivity of the pension payment to the history of a worker's labor income. It is assumed that $p_i \geq 0$ for $i = 1, 2, 3$. Implicit in these constraints are a number of assumptions that reflect the way most pension systems are designed in practice. The tax or mandatory "contribution" is based on wage earnings. The public pension system places a floor on retirement income, p_0. Pension payments increase with earnings history but at a decreasing rate as income grows. The analysis ignores possible general equilibrium effects on wage rates or interest rates.

The first-order necessary conditions for utility maximization imply that:

$$(\partial U/\partial L) + (\partial U/\partial c_1)w(1 - \tau) + \beta(\partial V/\partial c_2)(p_1 w - 2p_2 w^2 L) = 0 \quad (5.A.3)$$

and

$$(\partial U/\partial c_1) = \beta(\partial V/\partial c_2)(1 + r) \qquad (5.A.4)$$

A number of results follow immediately from these conditions under the simplification of quadratic utility, and most also hold under more general utility specifications. To simplify the proofs, I assume that $U(c_1, L) = \alpha_0 c_1 - \alpha_1 c_1^2 - \alpha_3 L - \alpha_4 L^2$ and that $V(c_2) = \alpha_0 c_2 - \alpha_1 c_2^2$, and that $(1 + r) = 1/\beta$. Then, these first-order conditions reduce to:

$$-(\alpha_3 + 2\alpha_4 L) + (\alpha_0 - \alpha_1 c_1)w(1 - \tau) + \beta(\alpha_0 - \alpha_1 c_2)(p_1 w - 2p_2 w^2 L) = 0 \qquad (5.A.5)$$

and

$$(\alpha_0 - \alpha_1 c_1) = \beta(\alpha_0 - \alpha_1 c_2)(\alpha + r) \qquad (5.A.6)$$

Result 1: Under the assumption that $(1 + r) = 1/\beta$, consumption is equal in both periods.

This follows immediately from (5.A.6).

Result 2: For a sufficiently high floor pension amount p_0, there is no (or negative) private saving, and reduced work effort.

This follows from the possibility of consumption satiation, the disutility of working, and Result 1 that consumption is equated across periods. With a large enough anticipated promised lump-sum payment in the second period, it is optimal to borrow against this amount to finance first-period consumption and to forego working.

Result 3: The return from work effort decreases in the tax rate (τ), increases with the positive sensitivity of the pension to work (p_1), and decreases with the progressivity of the pension system (p_2). The net effect of introducing a pension system on labor supply depends on the relative size of these parameters and the relative strength of income and substitution effects in the utility function.

Result 4: An increase in pension system taxes used to finance an increase in the floor pension level of equal value present value to the tax increase decreases labor supply and private savings.

With no change in labor supply, consumption would be the same as in the absence of the change in the pension system. The marginal return from working, however, would be lower. Therefore, equilibrium can only be restored by a reduction in work effort, leading to lower lifetime income. Because time 1 income would lowered relative to time 2 income as a result of lower labor supply and a lump-sum payment increase at time 2, less would be saved at time 1 to equate the marginal utility of consumption across periods.

REFERENCES

Angelis, Theodore. 1998. "Investing Public Money in Private Markets: What Are the Right Questions?" In R. Douglas Arnold, Michael Graetz, Alicia Munnell (eds.) *Framing the Social Security Debate: Values, Politics, and Economics.* Washington, DC: National Academy of Social Insurance.

Brooks, Sarah, and Estelle James. 1999. "The Political Economy of Structural Pension Reform." Paper presented at World Bank Pension Research Conference, Washington, DC.

Congressional Budget Office. 1999. "Social Security Privatization: Experiences Abroad." Washington, DC.

Congressional Budget Office (forthcoming), "A Primer on Social Security," Washington, DC.

Geanakoplos, John, Olivia Mitchell, and Stephen P. Zeldes. 1998. "Social Security Money's Worth." Available as NBER Working Paper Number 6722, and in Olivia S. Mitchell, Robert J. Myers, and Howard Young (eds.), *Prospects for Social Security Reform.* Philadelpha, 1999: University of Pennsylvania Press.

Grandolini, Gloria, and Luis Cerda. 1998. "The 1997 Pension Reform in Mexico." World Bank Working Paper.

Heaton, John, and Deborah Lucas. 2001. "Investing Public Pensions in the Stock Market: Implications for Public Policy, Risk Sharing, and Asset Prices." University of Chicago Working Paper.

Heller, Peter S. 1997. "Aging in the Asian 'Tigers': Challenges for Fiscal Policy." Working Paper of the International Monetary Fund.

James, Estelle, Gary Ferrier, James Smalhout, and Dimitri Vittas. 1999. "Mutual Funds and Institutional Investments: What Is the Most Efficient Way to Set Up Individual Accounts in a Social Security System?" World Bank Working Paper.

Orszag, Peter, and Joseph E. Stiglitz. 1999. "Rethinking Pension Reform: Ten Myths About Social Security Systems." Paper presented at the World Bank Conference on New Ideas About Old Age Security.

Tuljapurkar, Shripad, Nan Li, and Michael Anderson. 2000. "Stochastic Population Forecasts for the G-7 Countries." Mountain View Research, Los Altos, CA.

World Bank. 1994. http://www.cbo.gov/showdoc.cfm?index=3213&sequence=0. There's only one "Primer on Social Security," Published in Sept. 01.

6 The Risk-Sharing Implications of Alternative Social Security Arrangements

In December 1996, the federal Advisory Council on Social Security (1996) outlined three alternatives to the current U.S. social security system. Loosely speaking, each of the proposals can be broken down into reforms geared toward shoring up the anticipated system deficit in 2030, and more fundamental reforms geared toward changing the nature of how the system "saves" for its participants. In this paper, we focus on the latter, with an emphasis on how the proposals affect a fundamental aspect of social security: the tradeoff between the provision of risk-sharing and the distortion of savings incentives.

More specifically, our goal is to run a horse race and understand the fundamentals underlying the outcome. We use a quantitative general equilibrium model to ask which of three pension arrangements are preferable: the current U.S. social security system, the main proposal put forth by the Advisory Council, or the abolition of publicly provided pensions altogether. The winner of this contest will be the alternative that weighs most favorably in terms of the tradeoff between risk-sharing and savings distortions. We focus on four aspects of this tradeoff and quantitatively decompose our results accordingly. On the risk-sharing side, we ask how well the redistributive mechanism inherent in social security provides insurance against uncertain fluctuations in wages. We also examine to what extent the imperfect annuity provided by social security helps insure against "mortality risk": the risk of outliving one's savings. On the distortions side, we focus on the interaction between social security and distortionary capital income taxation and, more important, the effect of social security on aggregate wealth, through the disincentive to save that it imparts on its participants.

Prepared for The Carnegie Rochester Conference on Public Policy, Rochester, New York, April 1998. For helpful comments and suggestions, we thank participants at the Carnegie Rochester Conference, the Penn Macro Lunch Seminar, the Aiyagari Memorial Conference on Dynamic Macroeconomics, and the 1998 NBER Summer Institute. We also thank Andy Abel, Per Krusell, Stan Zin, and, in particular, our discussant, Selo.

The environment in which we ask these questions is a stationary overlapping generations model with productive capital and a large number of heterogeneous agents per generation. Idiosyncratic risk is represented by both an exogenous process for labor productivity and probabilistic death. Agents can trade in a single asset – productive capital – and choose to do so for both life-cycle and precautionary motives. Output is produced by an aggregate production technology to which agents rent capital and labor, the latter being supplied inelastically. The absence of a labor-supply decision will, of course, negate what are undoubtedly important distortions associated with social security payroll taxation. Although we certainly acknowledge this, we feel that our simple setting has the advantage of providing a sharp focus on the specifics of how taxation related to social security affects capital accumulation.

Into this environment we inject an abstract representation of both the U.S. social security system and the Advisory Council's proposal. Social security is run by a government and financed via a payroll tax and the taxation of social security benefits. This government also undertakes an exogenously given level of expenditure, financed through income taxes applied to capital and labor. The distortionary effects of payroll taxation, therefore, travel two channels. First, by taxing (exogenous) labor supply and providing retirement benefits according to a nonlinear benefit function, the system directly affects savings incentives, aggregate capital accumulation and, therefore, market-clearing returns. Second, through the effect on capital accumulation, the social security system indirectly affects the government's operating budget (by changing both the capital income tax base and the labor income tax base) and, therefore, has implications for the income-tax rate required to finance nonpension expenditures. This indirect channel and the "feedback" it generates (e.g., lower capital accumulation implies higher income taxes that further distort capital accumulation) capture, in our opinion, an important aspect of social security finance: the fact that the distortionary effects of fiscal policy and pension policy are tightly intertwined.

A noteworthy aspect of our analysis is the means with which we make welfare comparisons. For the most part, we compare the current U.S. system to some alternative by comparing welfare across alternative steady states, each corresponding to a stationary equilibrium with a different social security system. A critical aspect of these measurements is that they incorporate the so-called social security debt: the gross obligations that a pay-as-you-go system has to existing generations (or, equivalently, the debt associated with providing a transfer to the initial old generation). Our feeling is that, absent adjustments for this notion of indebtedness, comparisons across steady states are misleading. For example, consider a comparison of the U.S. status quo with a world featuring 100 percent privately provided pensions. The welfare of an agent in the former economy will reflect the fact that, unlike an agent in the latter, they must service the debt associated with providing an unfunded transfer to the initial generations (those who were retired when the system began). Given that we are ultimately interested in risk-sharing and marginal savings incentives, we choose to control for these "transfer effects" and, via an adjustment to the government's balance sheet, make social indebtedness comparable across steady states.

An alternative interpretation of our "indebtedness adjustment," one that adds additional support to its attractiveness, is related to the transition between equilibria featuring different social security systems. For example, consider eliminating the current U.S. system while at the same time honoring all existing obligations. One means of accomplishing this is for the government to issue a bond that raises capital sufficient to finance all existing promises. Were this bond to be refinanced perpetually, the cost of meeting these obligations (which is, again, equivalent to the cost of financing the transfer to the initial generations) would be shared by all future generations. In this context, our approach will involve the government doing just that: perpetually taxing agents to finance a bond with face value equal to the "social security debt" in the status quo. Although it is clear that this approach provides only a partial account of the effects of transition (Auerbach and Kotlikoff (1987), De Nardi, İmrohoroğlu, and Sargent (1998), and others, provide an explicit treatment), our feeling is that it has content in this regard.

A problem with examining alternative institutional arrangements by comparing steady states is that many things can change, making it difficult to pin down the essential economics driving the results. This is particularly true in computational economics. In response, we provide a quantitative decomposition of our overall welfare results into components attributable to four economic factors: (i) distortions related to the taxation of capital, (ii) changes in the level of aggregate wealth ("general equilibrium effects"), (iii) the extent to which agents have access to some sort of annuities, and (iv) the degree to which social security allows for the pooling of idiosyncratic labor-market risk. The welfare effect of each of these factors is isolated via a set of computational experiments that, unlike commonly used comparative statics approaches, are progressive in nature, each stripping away an additional contributing factor.

One final aspect of our analysis that deserves mention is how we measure the extent to which agents have any risk to share in the first place. Our overall question is essentially a quantitative one. We ask, given the various parameters associated with the Advisory Council's proposal, how much consumption a hypothetical agent would pay to live in a world with the reformed pension system. The answer will depend critically on how much risk agents are endowed with because the fundamental tradeoff they face is one of distortions versus risk-sharing. In an extreme case, one in which we endow our agents with absolutely no idiosyncratic risk, social security will have no positive attributes but will provide only distortions. With this in mind, we borrow on previous work (Storesletten, Telmer, and Yaron (1998), Storesletten, Telmer, and Yaron (1997)) and attempt to carefully measure labor market risks using data from the Panel Study on Income Dynamics (PSID). By doing so, we feel somewhat more confident that our quantitative welfare comparisons are relevant for the U.S. economy.

Our work is related to the existing literature as follows. The social security framework we use builds on Auerbach and Kotlikoff (1987), Hubbard and Judd (1987), İmrohoroğlu, İmrohoroğlu, and Joines (1995) and, in particular, Huggett and Ventura (1997), who conduct an analysis of the 1986 Boskin plan. Our study is distinct in several respects. Foremost, we focus on the 1996 Advisory Council plans and the effects of a social security system that is partially pay-as-you-go and partially fully funded. Huggett and Ventura (1997) focus is primarily on the Boskin proposal of providing an annuity, which is closely tied to accumulated contributions and is financed on a pay-as-you-go basis. Huggett and Ventura (1997) also incorporate a labor-supply decision, thereby making for a richer examination of the overall effects of distortionary payroll taxation. By contrast, we focus more starkly on the implications for capital accumulation, the incorporation of the "social security debt," and try to more precisely decompose the various channels through which social security provides risk-sharing. Our results are, in some cases, quite different. Huggett and Ventura (1997) find that, in moving from the current system to a Boskin-like one, the aggregate effects are quite small, but that poor (rich) households can experience substantial welfare losses (gains). We find similar effects once we distinguish agents by age and income but find, in some cases, relatively large aggregate welfare gains.

Several other noteworthy papers are Bohn (1997) who looks at aggregate risk-sharing in a Diamond (1965) OLG economy with production; Gertler (1997), who examines the implications for social security of a variety of fiscal policy issues; De Nardi, İmrohoroğlu, and Sargent (1998) and Huang, İmrohoroğlu, and Sargent (1997), who examine transitional dynamics in a much more explicit manner than us; and İmrohoroğlu, İmrohoroğlu, and Joines (1998), who analyze the aggregate effects of having a fixed factor of production in a world with an unfunded social security system.

The remainder of the paper is organized as follows. In the next section, we outline our overlapping generations model, endow it with a fairly general social security structure, and formulate its various equilibrium conditions. In Section 6.2, we provide a brief overview of the current U.S. social security system, discuss the proposals put forth by the federal Advisory Council, and then outline how they are fit into our abstraction. Section 6.3 explicitly discusses what we mean by the term "social security debt" and how we measure it in our theoretical economies. In Section 6.4, we demonstrate how we calibrate our models, including a discussion of measurements from the PSID and how they relate to the risk-sharing aspect of social security. Section 6.5 presents quantitative results and Section 6.6 concludes.

6.1 Overlapping Generations Model

The stationary overlapping generations framework we use builds on the work of Huggett (1996), İmrohoroğlu, İmrohoroğlu, and Joines (1995), and Ríos-Rull (1994), as well as subsequent work in Storesletten, Telmer, and Yaron (1998). The economy is populated by H overlapping generations of agents, where each generation consists of a large number of atomistic, heterogeneous agents. We use h, $h \in \mathcal{H} = \{1, 2, \ldots, H\}$ to index the age cohort to which a particular agent belongs. Agents face both idiosyncratic labor market risk, described later, as well as mortality risk. There are no aggregate shocks. The unconditional probability of surviving up to age h is denoted by ϕ_h, where $\phi_1 = 1$, and $\xi_h = \phi_h/\phi_{h-1}$, $h = 2, 3, \ldots, H$, denotes the probability of surviving to age h, conditional on being alive at age $h - 1$. The fraction of the total population attributable to each age cohort is fixed over time at φ_h and the population grows at rate λ.

Each individual agent is characterized by a preference ordering over consumption distributions, an endowment process, an asset market position, and an entitlement to a particular sequence of social security benefits. Preferences for an unborn agent are represented by

$$E \sum_{h=1}^{H} \beta^h \phi_h u(c_h) \tag{6.1}$$

where β denotes the utility discount factor, c_h denotes the consumption of an h year old agent, u is the standard twice differentiable, strictly concave utility function and the expectation is assumed to be conditional on the state of the economy prior to birth.

Agents of ages 1 through Q are workers, whereas agents of ages $Q + 1$ through H are retirees. Workers are endowed with an exogenous quantity of labor hours (or, equivalently, productive efficiency units), which they supply inelastically to an aggregate production technology. Labor income is then determined as the product of hours worked and the endogenously determined wage rate. The exogenous process for hours worked is the means with which we introduce heterogeneity. The i'th agent of some working cohort, h, will provide an amount of labor, $n_{i,h}$, which is governed by the following stochastic process:

$$\log n_{i,h} = \kappa_h + \alpha_i + z_{i,h} + \varepsilon_{i,h} \tag{6.2}$$

where the parameters κ_h are used to characterize the cohort-specific cross sectional distribution of average income, α_i, and $\varepsilon_{i,h}$ are $i.i.n.d.$ with mean zero and variance σ_α^2 and σ_ε^2, respectively. Finally,

$$z_{i,h} = \rho z_{i,h-1} + \eta_{i,h}, \quad \eta_{i,h} \sim N\left(0, \sigma_\eta^2\right) \tag{6.3}$$

An agent's endowment thus has three random components: a transitory component, $\varepsilon_{i,h}$; a persistent component, $z_{i,h}$; and a "fixed effect," α_i, which is realized at birth and stays with an agent for life. Each component will play an important role, both in terms of interpreting microeconomic data and affecting the allocations in our theory. For example, the amount of cross-sectional variation in the PSID, which we attribute to the fixed effects, will dictate the amount of labor-market risk that an agent faces, conditional on being alive. The latter will have important implications for the risk-sharing role played by financial markets and the extent to which social security enhances risk-sharing opportunities. It also will have important implications for the net value that various age-wealth cohorts associate with the social security system. For notational simplicity, we will hereafter omit i, the agent-specific subscripts.

Output in this world is produced by an aggregate technology to which individuals rent their labor services and capital. The competitively determined wage and capital rental rates are denoted W and R, respectively. The production function takes the form

$$Y = Zf(K, N) \qquad (6.4)$$

where K and N represent per capita capital and labor, respectively; Y represents per capita output; and Z represents secular growth. Given aggregate consumption, C, and the rate of depreciation on aggregate capital, δ, the law of motion for aggregate capital can be written

$$K' = Y - C + (1 - \delta)K \qquad (6.5)$$

Each agent's choice problem is one-dimensional: given knowledge of their idiosyncratic status, they simply choose an amount of assets to accumulate, a_h. Asset holdings are restricted to lie in a set $\mathcal{A}$, which consists of fractions of ownership in the aggregate production technology.

Finally, the model features a government that administers the social security system, consumes a per capita quantity of goods, G, each period, and perpetually refinances a per capita quantity of debt, B, at competitively determined interest rates. The government finances its consumption and its interest payments via a 100 percent estate tax (i.e., it fully captures all "accidental bequests" left behind by those who die prior to age H), as well as proportional taxes on wage and capital income of τ_l and τ_k, respectively. This distinction between tax rates on different sources of income serves, primarily, to uncover the degree to which our results are driven by distortionary capital taxation. The social security system is completely self-financed via the taxation of benefits in addition to payroll taxes levied at rates τ_j, where j is an index corresponding to a number of different retirement accounts that comprise the system. We use the notation τ to represent the vector of tax rates, $[\tau_l \ \tau_k \ \{\tau_j\}]$. A crucial aspect of all these taxes is that they are determined endogenously, in order to achieve budget balance, and that they constitute a fundamental part of what we will call an equilibrium.

Our motivation for including a government in this manner is twofold. First, as discussed in detail in the next section, we pay careful attention to the so-called social security debt: the implicit cost borne by all future generations of providing the initial old generation with unfunded benefits. The debt, B, with which we endow our government is the means with which we will make meaningful comparisons across economies with varying levels of social security indebtedness. Second, a primary feature of our model is the distortionary effect of social security on capital accumulation (i.e., there is no labor-supply decision to be distorted).

Our view is that an important channel with which this takes place is an indirect route, via tax policy. In simple terms, social security affects savings incentives, the resulting changes in the capital stock affect income-tax policy, which itself imparts a further distortion on savings.

6.1.1 The Social Security System

The current U.S. social security system and the various plans for restructuring it all share the idea of taxing agents during their working years while providing benefits during retirement years. The plans differ primarily in terms of the function relating taxation to benefits and the extent to which individuals have control over how their contributions are invested. The plans also differ in the extent to which they represent current period transfers – what we will call a *pay-as-you-go* component – or actual investments on behalf of the contributor – what we will call a *fully funded* component. With this in mind, we formulate a general representation of a social security system that encompasses both components.

The key variable in either system – or some hybrid of both – is accumulated contributions. We use ω_h^p to denote the accumulated contributions of an h-year-old individual toward the pay-as-you-go component of a given system, and ω_h^f to denote the accumulation toward the fully funded component. The vector ω_h is then defined as $\omega_h = [\omega_h^p \ \omega_h^f]$. These accumulation functions, for $j = p, f$, take the following form:

$$\omega_h^j = \begin{cases} \omega_{h-1}^j P_j + \min(\tau_j n_h W, \ \overline{\omega}^j) & h \le Q \\ \omega_Q^j & h > Q \end{cases} \qquad (6.6)$$

where τ_j is a payroll tax rate; $\overline{\omega}^j$ denotes the maximum, per-period contribution level; and P_j denotes the return function that applies to accumulated contributions. As an example, the current U.S. system is represented by a scalar accumulation function, ω_h^p; a single payroll tax, τ_p; and a return function, P_p, which equals the average growth rate in aggregate wages. A hybrid system, comprised of both pay-as-you-go and fully funded components, would append to this an additional accumulation function and tax rate, and a return function, P_f, equal to some market-determined rate of return.

Another important feature shared by most proposals is that benefits are regressive with respect to past contributions. More specifically, benefits are typically bounded from below in some fashion, to accommodate a certain minimum benefit level, and are related to accumulated contributions via a concave function. We denote the lower bound as $\underline{b}^j$ and formulate the benefits function, b^j, as:

$$b^j(\omega_h^j) = \begin{cases} 0 & h \le Q \\ \max[\underline{b}^j, d_j(\omega_Q^j)] & h > Q \end{cases} \qquad (6.7)$$

where d_j is a concave function. For simplicity, we use b_h^j to denote $b^j(\omega_h^j)$, the benefits received by an h-year-old agent from social security arrangement j.

Finally, both the U.S. status quo and the alternative proposal we consider recognize, in one way or another, benefits as taxable income when received after retirement. We use $\bar{b}_h^j$ to denote the taxable component of social security benefits and assume that the applicable tax rate is τ_l, that which applies to wage income. Our formulation of $\bar{b}_h^j$ is stark, especially when considered alongside its complex U.S. counterpart. For our pay-as-you-go systems, a fixed fraction of total benefits are taxable at the labor income-tax rate. For the fully funded system, a lump-sum payment received at retirement is not taxable, but all subsequent income accruing to this payment is. In Section 6.2, we provide a further discussion of benefits taxation and how our treatment captures several salient features of the U.S. status quo and the Advisory Council proposals.

6.1.2 Dynamic Programming Problem

We can now represent the cross-sectional distribution for our economy as a function μ, defined over an appropriate family of subsets of $S = (\mathcal{H} \times \tilde{\mathcal{Z}} \times \mathcal{A})$, where $\tilde{\mathcal{Z}}$ is the product space containing all possible idiosyncratic shocks (permanent and transitory) and all possible values for ω_h. In words, μ is simply a distribution of agents across ages, idiosyncratic shocks, capital holdings, and social security contribution levels. Because our economy does not feature aggregate shocks, we are able to rely on a cross-sectional law of large numbers to ensure that, in any stationary equilibrium, the function μ is fixed.

Recalling that the market-clearing return on capital and the wage rate are R and W, respectively, the decisions of an agent of age h are governed by the following constraints:

$$c_h + a'_{h+1} \leq a_h R - \tau_k a_h (R - 1) + n_h W(1 - \tau_l - \tau_p - \tau_f)$$
$$+ \sum_{j=\{p,f\}} \left(b_h^j - \bar{b}_h^j \tau_l \right) \tag{6.8}$$
$$a'_{h+1} \geq \underline{a} \quad \text{and} \quad a_{H+1} \geq 0$$

where a_h denotes beginning-of-period asset (or capital) holdings and a'_{h+1} denotes end-of-period asset holdings. Our timing convention is that savings decisions are made at the end of the current period, and returns are paid the following period at the realized capital rental rate.

Denoting the value function of an agent of age h as V_h, an agent's choice problem can be represented as:

$$V_h(z_h, a_h, \omega_h) = \max_{a'_{h+1}} \left\{ u(c_h) + \beta \frac{\phi_{h+1}}{\phi_h} E \left[V'_{h+1} \left(z_{h+1}, a'_{h+1}, \omega'_{h+1} \right) \right] \right\} \tag{6.9}$$

subject to equations (6.8).

6.1.3 Equilibrium

Our definition of an equilibrium includes budget balance on both the pay-as-you-go social security account and the government expenditure account. This implies that the payroll-tax rate, τ_p, and one of the income-tax rates, τ_k or τ_l, must arise endogenously and will constitute an important component of the fixed-point problem underlying our solution algorithm. With this in mind, we define an equilibrium to consist of these two endogenously determined tax rates, market-clearing prices R and W, and a set of cohort specific functions, $\{V_h, a'_{h+1}\}_{h=1}^{H}$, such that:

1. The firm's profit maximization problem is satisfied.

$$R = Zf_1(K, N) - \delta + 1 \tag{6.10}$$
$$W = Zf_2(K, N) \tag{6.11}$$

2. Individual optimization problems are satisfied (so that $\{V_h, a'_{h+1}\}_{h=1}^{H}$ satisfy equations (6.9)).
3. Markets clear and aggregate quantities result from individual decisions.

$$K + B = \int_S \left(a_h + \omega_h^f\right) d\mu \tag{6.12}$$

$$N = \int_S n_h \, d\mu \tag{6.13}$$

$$G + K' + \int_S c_h d\mu = ZF(K, N) + (1 - \delta)K \tag{6.14}$$

4. The government budget constraint is satisfied.

$$G + [R - (1 + \lambda)(1 + g)] B = \int_S (\tau_k a_h [R - 1] + \tau_l n_h W) \, d\mu + E \tag{6.15}$$

where λ is the population growth rate, g represents the secular growth in GNP per capita, and E denotes accidental bequests:

$$E = \int_S \varphi_h \frac{(1 - \xi_{h+1})}{1 + \lambda} a_{h+1} \left[(R - 1)(1 - \tau_k) + 1\right] d\mu \tag{6.16}$$

5. The pay-as-you-go component of the social security system is balanced, period-by-period.

$$\int_S [\tau_p n_h W + b_h^p \tau_l] d\mu = \int_S b^p \left(\omega_h^p\right) d\mu \tag{6.17}$$

Conditions 1 and 2 are standard. Condition 3, the aggregate resource constraints, makes clear that individual holdings of financial wealth (bonds plus capital) plus accumulated, fully funded contributions add up to productive capital plus government debt. Condition 4 demonstrates that government budget balance involves choosing the income-tax rates, τ_l and τ_k, so that accidental bequests plus income-tax revenues equal the sum of expenditure, G, plus interest payments on the outstanding debt. The term $(1 + \lambda)(1 + g)$ reflects the fact that government debt, B, will be held constant as a fraction of GNP, which grows at rate $(1 + \lambda)(1 + g) - 1$. Finally, Condition 5 ensures period-by-period social security budget balance. Note that taxable benefits associated with the pay-as-you-go scheme stay within the system. By construction, contributions corresponding to τ_f are allocated to individual, fully funded accounts.

6.2 The Specifics of Social Security

The reform proposals put forth by the federal Advisory Council on Social Security (1996) take the form of three specific alternatives: the Maintenance of Benefits (MB) plan, the Individual Accounts (IA) plan, and the Personal Security Accounts (PSA) plan. The MB plan leaves most of the pay-as-you-go, U.S. status quo in place, focusing instead on changes in taxation and the investment policies governing the social security trust fund, the target being anticipated financing shortfalls in the second third of the next century. The PSA and IA plans dig deeper, each proposing some hybrid system in which a pay-as-you-go mechanism coexists with some form of a fully funded system.

Loosely speaking, each of these proposals can be broken down into reforms geared toward shoring up the anticipated system deficit in 2030 and more fundamental reforms, geared toward changing the nature of how the system "saves" for its participants. The MB plan focuses mainly on the former, whereas the IA and PSA plans turn an increasing amount of attention to the latter. Our analysis is primarily concerned with the more fundamental reforms, although – as we discuss later – we do incorporate the net cost of moving from one system to another and grandfathering-in the new benefits regime. With this in mind, we restrict further attention to the U.S. status quo, the PSA, and an economy in which social security is abolished altogether. We now turn to a more detailed description of each of these arrangements, followed by a description of how we implement them within the context of our theory.

6.2.1 The U.S. Status Quo (SQ)

The current U.S. social security plan is a pay-as-you-go system, designed so that retirement benefits are financed directly from payroll taxation of the existing workforce. The current payroll tax is 12.4 percent, 6.2 percent of which is paid by the employee. Retirement benefits, in 1993 dollars, are based on a 90 percent replacement ratio for the first $5,000 of indexed (previous) annual earnings, 32 percent for the next $25,000, 15 percent for the next $30,000, and 0 percent for any amount above $61,750. The marginal tax rate applied to benefits is increasing in both non-pension income and the overall benefit level. We omit any further description, however, because the actual tax code is marred with exceptions and special clauses. The retirement age is 65 years old and benefits are based on a worker's highest average 35 years of contributions.

Our theoretical implementation of the U.S. status quo, which we denote the "SQ" economy, is formulated as follows. We work backward, taking benefits function d_p and the return function P_p as given, and then solving for the payroll-tax rate, τ_p, which ensures a balanced budget (the fully funded tax rate τ_f, as well as anything else with an f subscript, is zero for this economy). The return function P_p, commonly referred to as the "indexation rate," is set to the rate of growth in real wages, 1.5 percent. The benefit function, d_p, is characterized by the four pairs of cutoff points and replacement rates from the U.S. system which, in order to obtain units that are well defined in our model, we convert to fractions of per capita GNP. For example, the $5,000 level (in 1993 dollars), which determines when the replacement ratio drops from 90 to 32 percent represents 20 percent of GNP per capita. Finally, given this system of benefits and the indexation rate, we solve for the payroll tax rate which, given the income tax rates, τ_l and τ_k, equates contributions plus revenue from benefit taxation with total benefits. As we discuss later, the resulting payroll tax is realistic, at $\tau_p = 10.92$ percent for our benchmark economy.

In contrast to the complex means with which taxable benefits are determined in the United States, we take a simple approach; we treat 25 percent of pay-as-you-go benefits as being taxable and tax them at the income-tax rate. We find that, in terms of expected tax payments and several other simple measures, this function behaves in a qualitatively similar manner with respect to a more realistic implementation. Note, however, that our approach is less progressive than the actual system, which will tend to understate redistribution in our model.

Finally, we provide for a minimum level of benefits of 24 percent of GNP per capita, and a maximum level for accumulated contributions (which determine benefits) of 2.47 times GNP per capita. These values correspond to the notation $\underline{b}^p$ and $\overline{\omega}^p$ from Section 6.1. The former is based on the current U.S. minimum of $572 per month, expressed in annual terms, in 1993 dollars, and as a fraction of GNP per capita (which is roughly $25,000). The latter is based on the current annual maximum contribution level of $61,750, again expressed relative to U.S. GNP per capita. Note that our floor level for benefits is an abstraction relative to the actual system, where the floor for an individual who qualifies for social security is essentially determined by the minimum-wage rate.

6.2.2 Personal Security Accounts (PSA)

The PSA plan put forth by the Advisory Council is essentially a hybrid of a pay-as-you-go system and a fully funded system, with roughly 40 percent of total contributions going toward the latter. Specifically, the proposal envisions a reallocation of 5 percentage points of the current 6.2 percent employee contribution tax toward privately owned retirement accounts. Investment restrictions on these accounts would be minimal and, in contrast to the IA plan, participants would not be required to annuitize their PSA accumulations at retirement. The Council also proposes that any benefits received in lump-sum on retirement go untaxed, although any income accruing to these funds after retirement becomes taxable at regular rates.

The pay-as-you-go component of the PSA proposal would be financed by the taxation of benefits as well as a 7.4 percent payroll tax, which is what is left of the status quo 12.4 percent, after the fully funded component gets its share. Benefits would be paid out as a lump sum, irrespective of contributions, of $410 per month (in 1996 dollars), 100 percent of which would be treated as taxable income. Finally, the PSA proposal includes a "Supplemental Tax" of 1.52 percent until the year 2070 to cover transition costs in moving from the status quo to the new system, something that we ignore.

Our abstract version of the PSA is formulated by setting the fully funded payroll tax rate, τ_f, to 5 percent and computing the accumulated, fully funded contribution accounts, ω_h^f, using the market-determined return function, $P_f = R$. The fully funded component of benefits is then paid out as a lump sum to each agent who retires at age 65. The latter assumption is extremely relative to the (vague) guidelines provided by the Advisory Council, but we find it informative in providing a sharp contrast to the partial annuities of the SQ system. It also will have important implications for overall budget balance and our endogenously determined income tax rates because pension-related capital income over the retirement years becomes taxable.

The pay-as-you-go component of our model follows the Advisory Council in providing an annual, lump-sum benefit payment of 17.5 percent of GNP to each retired agent. This value corresponds to monthly payments of $410, in 1996 dollars. Given these benefits, we solve for a payroll-tax rate, τ_p, to ensure budget balance. This value turns out to be 5.13 percent, which, when added to the fully funded tax rate of 5 percent, makes for an overall payroll tax of 10.13 percent.

Finally, taxation of benefits is straightforward and follows the spirit of the Advisory Council's suggestions. The lump-sum, pay-as-you-go benefits are fully taxable at the income-tax rate. The fixed payment received from the PSA accounts at age 65 is not subject to tax, but any subsequent capital income is fully taxed at the income rate.

6.2.3 Privately Provided Pensions (PP)

An important component of the PSA arrangement is that it represents the privatization of just under half of the publicly provided pension system. Alternatively, it represents a shift from a system of intratemporal transfers between existing generations to one in which pension benefits represent actual savings and investment. The limit of this is simply the abolition of the pay-as-you-go social security system altogether, an economy we refer to as the "PP" economy.

The PP economies we compute are environments with zero payroll taxes, in which agents must provide for retirement consumption themselves. As discussed later, we adjust this economy to have a comparable amount of net indebtedness with respect to the SQ environment. We also subject agents to an income tax rate sufficient to finance both interest rate payments on B, the government debt, and government expenditure, G.

6.3 The Social Security Burden

An inescapable aspect of a pay-as-you-go social security system is the implicit liability associated with providing an unfunded transfer to the initial generations who were retired, or part way through their working years, when the system was introduced. Equivalently, this liability can be thought of as the cost of making good on existing obligations should the government wish to eliminate the social security system altogether. We denote the per capita value of this obligation as D, and refer to it as the "social security debt."

A simple (and well-known) example will make things clear. Consider a deterministic, two-generation world in which pay-as-you-go social security contributions are 1 each period, the population grows at rate q, and the market return on capital is $r > q$. Agents work (and contribute) while young and retire when old. By virtue of the fact that there will always be more contributors than retirees, the system can finance benefits of $1 + q$ each period, thus providing for a return on contributions of q. In this simple world, $D = 1$; the amount of per capita resources required to liquidate the system while making good on existing obligations is simply equal to current-period contributions. An equivalent interpretation is that each member of the initial old generation received a transfer of 1, and this was financed through government borrowing. The "tax" of $r - q$ paid by each subsequent old generation is exactly the amount required to keep the level of debt at 1, per capita.

Although this example is simplistic, it captures the essence of what we mean by the "social security debt." The main difference in our stochastic model with many generations is just more complicated accounting. We proceed in the following manner. Redefine q as the internal rate of return on expected social security contributions. That is, q is the number that results in the following equation being satisfied:

$$\sum_{h=1}^{Q} \phi_h \frac{\tau_p W(1+g)^h E(n_h)}{(1+q)^h} = \sum_{h=Q+1}^{H} \phi_h \frac{E\left(b_h^p\left(\omega_Q^p\right)\tau_l b_h^p\right)}{(1+q)^h}$$

where, recall, ϕ_h is the unconditional probability of surviving to age h. The term in the numerator on the left is simply the product of the payroll-tax rate and the expected wage bill, where we make explicit the growth rate in wages of g. The numerator on the right is the expected, after tax benefit received from retirement age Q until death at age H. Recalling that λ is the population-growth rate, the solution for q turns out to satisfy $1 + q = (1 + g)(1 + \lambda)$, which is essentially the "pay-as-you-go" condition suggested by this example.

Next, we use the internal rate of return, q, to obtain a measure of what the system owes an agent of age h. Define ζ_h as the ratio of the average present value, discounted at rate q, of what an h year has contributed to what a retired agent has contributed:

$$\zeta_h = \frac{\sum_{j=1}^{h} \phi_j \tau_p WE(n_j)(1+g)^j(1+q)^j}{\sum_{j=1}^{Q} \phi_j \tau_p WE(n_j)(1+g)^j(1+q)^j}$$

Given this, we interpret the existing obligation of the system toward the average agent of age h as a promise to pay a retirement annuity equal to ζ_h percent of what they would have received under the status quo. The relevance of the "average agent" in this context is that we are interested in systemwide obligations, which, by the cross-sectional law of large numbers, can be expressed in terms of the cross-sectional mean. Note also that the "survivor's premium" is incorporated in these calculations in that the shares, ζ_h, incorporate survival probabilities.

All that remains is to sum up the system's obligations toward all age cohorts and discount back to the current period at the market-interest rate, r. The latter – the fact that we discount at rate r and not q – is important: it effectively implies that the government is able to finance its obligations at below-market rates of return, something intrinsic to the pay-as-you-go system. The sum of obligations, weighted by cohort size, φ_h, is what we label the social security debt, D:

$$D = \sum_{h=1}^{Q} \varphi_h (1+g)^{Q+1-h} \sum_{j=Q+1}^{H} \frac{\phi_j}{\phi_h} \frac{\zeta_h E\left(b_j^p\left(\omega_Q^p\right) - \tau_l \bar{b}_j^p\right)}{(1+r)^{j-h}}$$

$$+ \sum_{h=Q+1}^{H} \varphi_h \sum_{j=h}^{H} \frac{\phi_j}{\phi_h} \frac{E\left(b_j^p\left(\omega_Q^p\right) - \tau_l \bar{b}_j^p\right)}{(1+r)^{j-h}} \tag{6.18}$$

The first term in this expression is the present discounted value of obligations toward cohorts that are currently working. The second term is analogous but applies to cohorts that are currently retired. The term $(1+g)^{Q+1-h}$ incorporates the fact that contributions are growing larger over the working years (at the rate of growth in wages, g) but that benefits are held fixed after retirement.

Aside from being of interest in its own right, the social security debt, D, is useful in helping us compare environments with differing levels of social security in a sensible way. Our approach is simply to choose B – the constant level of debt that the government must perpetually refinance – so that each of the economies we study features a comparable level of consolidated indebtedness. The thought experiment we have in mind is as follows. Consider, for example, moving from an economy endowed with the U.S. status quo social security system to one with no system whatsoever. We interpret B as the total amount of borrowing that the government must undertake in order to fulfill the obligations associated with the transition. This level of debt is then rolled over every period, effectively forcing all future generations to pay the cost of transition (or, equivalently, the cost of the transfer to the initial old). In Section 6.5, when we incorporate this debt adjustment, we provide more explicit details on how it is computed (e.g., which discount factor, r, is used).

Incorporating the level of indebtedness in this fashion is, in our opinion, an important aspect of our analysis. To not do so would ignore the costs of transition as well as confound the welfare effects of risk-sharing with those of redistribution. In regard to the former – the transitional dynamics – our approach is certainly inferior to one that explicitly models the transition (see, for example, De Nardi, İmrohoroğlu, and Sargent (1998)). It does, however, capture some aspect of moving from one system to another in that the government is (implicitly) prohibited from defaulting on existing obligations.

6.4 Calibration

The fundamental source of idiosyncratic risk in our economy is the process for labor efficiency units, n_h. It is the variation attributable to this process that will be the primary target of the risk-sharing technology afforded by the social security system. A plausible quantitative characterization of n_h is, therefore, crucial for our question, which essentially asks how well alternative arrangements provide for risk-sharing otherwise not available via decentralized financial markets. We begin this section by describing how we obtain such a characterization and then move on to explicitly describe how we calibrate our model.

6.4.1 Measuring Idiosyncratic Risk

In previous work (Storesletten, Telmer, and Yaron (1998), Storesletten, Telmer, and Yaron (1997)), we have argued that the PSID is an attractive data set for measuring the types of labor-market risks (through the window of the process (6.2)) faced by a wide cross-section of the U.S. population. If anything, the argument for using the PSID is strengthened in relation to a study of the risk-sharing aspects of social security. It is well known that the PSID is not representative of the relatively wealthy segment of the U.S. population. However, it also seems reasonable that social security is relatively unimportant for this collection of households. With this in mind, we provide a brief summary of our previous findings, supplemented with a parameterization that we feel is better suited for the social security question.

Our departure point is that we choose to use labor-market earnings to calibrate the n_h process, despite the fact that it is better interpreted hours worked. The main reasons for doing so are to avoid measurement issues related to indivisible labor supply, which our model abstracts from, and to allow for the straightforward incorporation of the many types of transfers that will comprise an integral component of our interpretation of a household's "endowment." In addition, we verify that the statistical properties of the endogenous process for labor income in our model are very similar to those of hours worked (because our theoretical wage process is relatively stable), thereby providing a sense in which we actually have calibrated theoretical income to PSID income.

More specifically, we define a household's "endowment" as the combined labor-market earnings of all members, plus any transfers received such as unemployment insurance, workers compensation, transfers from nonhousehold family members, and so on. We include transfers because our model abstracts from the implicit insurance mechanisms that these payments often represent. That is, we wish to measure the amount of income variation that impinges on household financial decisions *net* of risks, which are insured against by programs such as unemployment insurance. Along a similar vein, we study the household as a single unit in order to measure household risk net of things like substitution in labor supply between household members in response to some shock.

Our panel of PSID households is constructed as follows. We use data from the surveys dated 1969 through 1992. Because each survey pertains to household data from the previous year, we refer to the time dimension of our panel as being 1968 through 1991. Beginning with the 1968 survey, we construct a sequence of 22 overlapping panels, each with a three-year time horizon. Each subpanel (beginning with years 1969 through 1989) consists of data on households who reported strictly positive total household earnings (inclusive of transfers) for that year and the next two consecutive years. For example, our 1970 panel is essentially a longitudinal panel on 1,663 households over the years 1970, 1971, and 1972. We choose to depart from the more standard longitudinal panel for two primary reasons. First, our sequence of three-year panels contains a sufficient time-series dimension so as to allow for the identification of all parameters of interest. Second, the selection of three-year panels mitigates a number of problems that one might associate with a "flat" longitudinal panel (e.g., a panel with 24 time-series observations on each household), such as survivorship bias, a necessarily small cross-sectional sample size, and the fact that average age increases by one year, for each survey year.

Two final transformations we apply are to deflate nominal income using the CPI and, in order to incorporate differing family size, to divide total household earnings by the number of household members. The end result is 22 overlapping panels, each with time dimension of three years. The cross-sectional distribution of age is quite stable over each of the panels, with an average (across years) mean and standard deviation of 44.05 and 14.71, and a standard deviation for the means of 1.04. The number of households is substantially larger than would be possible

Table 6.1. *Idiosyncratic Endowment Process: Parameter Estimates*

Description	σ_α^2	ρ	σ_η^2	σ_ε^2
No Fixed Effects	–	0.935	0.061	0.017
Time Series Moments	0.125	0.935	0.061	0.017
Cross-Sectional Moments	0.326	0.980	0.019	0.005

Notes: Entries describe point estimates for the idiosyncratic endowment process described in the text:

$$u_{it} = \alpha_i + z_{it} + \varepsilon_{it} \quad \varepsilon_{it} \sim N\left(0, \sigma_\varepsilon^2\right)$$

$$z_{it} = \rho z_{i,t-1} + \eta_{it} \quad \eta_{it} \sim N\left(0, \sigma_\eta^2\right) \quad \alpha_i \sim N\left(0, \sigma_\alpha^2\right)$$

The GMM estimates in the first row are reproduced from Storesletten, Telmer, and Yaron (1998), whereas those in the second and third rows incorporate agent-specific "fixed effects" in the manner described in the text. Specifically, for the parameters labeled "Time Series Moments," the values of ρ, σ_η, and σ_ε are our GMM estimates and the value of σ_α is chosen so that the average dispersion across age-cohorts matches that of the data (Figure 6.1). For the parameters labeled "Cross-Sectional Moments," we choose σ_α^2 to match the initial variance in the data, σ_η^2 to match the slope of the profile (or, equivalently, the endpoint), and ρ to match its curvature. The value for σ_ε is chosen to keep the ratio of the variance of the persistent shock to the transitory shock the same as that associated with our GMM estimates.

in a longitudinal sample, with a mean and standard deviation of 2,019 and 220 observations. Further details on the exact composition of our panel are available in Storesletten-Telmer-Yaron-98.

In Table 6.1, row 1, we reproduce point estimates from our previous paper for the following time-series process:

$$y_{it} = g_{it}(y_t) + u_{it} \tag{6.19}$$

$$u_{it} = z_{it} + \varepsilon_{it}, \quad \varepsilon_{it} \sim N\left(0, \sigma_\varepsilon^2\right) \tag{6.20}$$

$$z_{it} = \rho z_{i,t-1} + \eta_{it}, \quad \eta_{it} \sim N\left(0, \sigma_\eta^2\right) \tag{6.21}$$

where y_{it} is the logarithm of the i'th household's labor-market endowment and $g_{it}(y_t)$ is the portion of y_{it} comprising aggregate shocks as well as deterministic components of household-specific earnings, such as unobservable "fixed effects" and deterministic variation attributable to household age, education level, and so on. In Storesletten, Telmer, and Yaron (1998), we discuss our particular parameterization of g (which follows closely a number of studies in the labor-market dynamics literature), provide estimates, and discuss how sensitive our results are to alternatives. The first row of Table 6.1 shows that the autocorrelation coefficient is relatively large, at 0.935, and that the conditional standard deviation of the persistent shock process is roughly 90 percent larger than that of the transitory shocks.

The process (6.19) explicitly rules out any agent-specific "fixed effects," which one might think of as a household-specific intercept term in the equation describing z_{it}. For the purposes of Storesletten, Telmer, and Yaron (1998) (which asks questions related to asset pricing), such an omission was unimportant, particularly from a theoretical perspective (we did, however, check the sensitivity of our estimates by differencing our data). For risk-sharing social security, however, our feeling is that allowing for an intercept term, which is tantamount to decomposing cross-sectional variation into a stochastic component and a deterministic component, conditional on being born, may be crucial. Consider, for example, the welfare benefits of alternative social security arrangements for agents belonging to differing age cohorts. These benefits are likely to be mitigated for all those but the unborn, should a substantial portion of the overall cross-sectional variation in the economy be deterministic, after birth.

We incorporate fixed effects by altering the equation for the shock u_{it} as follows:

$$u_{it} = \alpha_i + z_{i,t} + \epsilon_{it} \quad \epsilon_{it} \sim N\left(0, \sigma_\eta^2\right) \quad \alpha_i \sim N\left(0, \sigma_\alpha^2\right) \tag{6.22}$$

Next, we "estimate" the magnitude of σ_α using information on how cross-sectional variation differs by age within our panel. In Figure 6.1, we report estimates of the age-dependent, cross-sectional variance from the PSID (the solid line), as well as the associated population moments from the process (6.19), amended with fixed effects as in (6.22). The dashed-dot line (the lower one) shows how our model without fixed effects matches the pattern in cross-sectional dispersion. We clearly miss a substantial amount of the cross-sectional variation in the data, something that the incorporation of fixed effects will rectify. We take two approaches. First, we simply choose the variance of the distribution from which an agent draws his or her intercept term at birth so that the average, theoretical cross-sectional variance matches that of the data. Values represented by this procedure are reported in Table 6.1, row 2. The resulting age-profile for cross-sectional variance is represented by the dotted line in Figure 6.1.

The second method we employ is essentially exactly identified GMM, using age-dependent cross-sectional variances to identify ρ, σ_α, and σ_η (we set the value of σ_ε so that the ratio of the variance of the persistent shock to the transitory shock is the same as that associated with our GMM estimates). Loosely speaking, we chose σ_α to match the cross-sectional variation associated with the youngest age-cohort, σ_η to match the slope required to hit the variation associated with agents just ready to retire (the 60-year-olds), and ρ to match the curvature of the age-profile. The values that result are reported in the third row of Table 6.1 and the theoretical age-profile is represented by the dashed line in Figure 6.1. Note that the implied value for ρ is substantially higher, at 0.98, which corresponds to the fact that the increase in cross-sectional variance as a cohort ages dies out at what appears to be a very slow rate. In addition, the implied fraction of an unborn agent's labor-market risk, which is associated with a fixed effect (obtained at birth), increases substantially – something we expect to have an important effect on our welfare calculations.

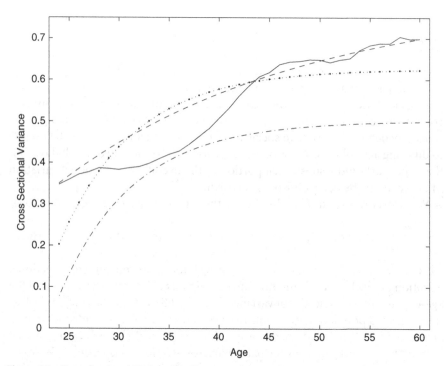

Figure 6.1. Cross Sectional Variance by Age
The solid line represents estimates of the cross-sectional variance of PSID labor-market income (inclusive of "transfers"), described in detail in Storesletten, Telmer, and Yaron (1997). The dash-dot line represents population moments associated with the time series process (6.19), evaluated at parameter estimates obtained by GMM (the first row of Table 6.1). The dotted line represents the incorporation of "fixed effects," where we choose the variance of the distribution from which these parameters are drawn in order to match average dispersion across ages (the second row of Table 6.1). The dashed line incorporates fixed effects by choosing parameter values in order to match the initial cross-sectional dispersion, and the slope and curvature of the age-profile (the third row of Table 6.1). Specifically, we choose σ_{α}^2 to match the initial variance, σ_{η}^2 to match the slope (or, equivalently, the endpoint), and ρ to match the curvature. The value for σ_{ε} is chosen to keep the ratio of the variance of the persistent shock to the transitory shock the same as that associated with our GMM estimates.

6.4.2 Implementation

We interpret one period in our model as corresponding to one year of calendar time. The aggregate production technology is Cobb-Douglas:

$$Y = ZK^{\theta}N^{1-\theta} \qquad (6.23)$$

Following much of the business-cycle literature, we set θ equal to 0.4 (which corresponds to capital's share of national income of 40 percent) and allow for a 7.8 percent annual depreciation rate on the aggregate capital stock. The secular growth rate in GNP per capita, by which we normalize all individual quantities in our model, is chosen to be 1.5 percent per year.

Turning to the characteristics of individual agents, preferences are identical (up to age-dependent mortality risk) and are described by Equation (6.1). We parameterize the period utility function with the standard isoelastic specification:

$$u(c) = \frac{c^{1-\gamma} - 1}{1 - \gamma} \tag{6.24}$$

We set γ to 2 and the utility discount factor, β, to 1.011 (for details on the interaction between mortality rates and the discount factor, which results in $\beta > 1$, see Hurd (1989)). Demographic variables are chosen to correspond to simple properties of the U.S. workforce. Agents are "born" at age 22, retire at age 65, and are dead by age 100. "Retirement" is defined as having one's labor income drop to zero. Mortality rates are chosen to match those of the U.S. females in 1991 and population growth is set to 1.0 percent.

The process for idiosyncratic labor income, Equation (6.2), is implemented as a discrete approximation to the autoregressive time-series model and is parameterized using our point estimates from Table 6.1. To highlight the implications of the fixed effects, α_i, we begin by setting them to zero for our benchmark economy. In subsequent experiments (Section 6.3), we allow them to be nonzero and implement them as an i.i.d. two-state binomial process, with variance chosen to match our estimates in Table 6.1. The age-dependent intercept terms, κ_h, are chosen so that the age-dependent mean of the logarithm of labor income in our theory matches our measure from the PSID. The transitory shocks, ε_h, follow a two-state binomial process with equally likely probabilities and a standard deviation of 0.1304. This results in $\varepsilon_h \in \{-0.1304, 0.304\}$. The persistent process is approximated with a two-state Markov chain.

The only remaining item is the portfolio constraint. In each of the economies we study, borrowing is disallowed: $\underline{a} = 0$.

6.5 Quantitative Results

For much of our analysis, we will think of an economy endowed with the current U.S. social security system as the benchmark with which to evaluate other alternatives. We treat income from capital and labor equivalently, so that $\tau_l = \tau_k$, and refer to this economy as the 'status quo' (SQ). In Table 6.2, under the column labeled "SQ," we report a number of aggregate features of this economy, to which we now turn.

To begin with, our benchmark economy is broadly consistent with several simple features of the aggregate U.S. economy. The capital-to-output ratio is 3.10, consumption is approximately half the magnitude of output, and the government consumes just under 20 of aggregate production. Just as importantly, the critical

Table 6.2. *Properties of Economies with Alternative Social Security Systems* (not adjusted to equalize net indebtedness)

	SQ	PSA	PP
Output, Y	1.636	1.813	2.118
Capital, K	5.067	6.556	9.665
Consumption, C	0.802	0.826	0.810
Government consumption, G	0.311	0.311	0.311
Income-tax rate, $\tau_l = \tau_k$ (%)	19.959	18.998	14.090
Payroll-tax rate, τ_p (%)	10.923	10.128	
Before-tax return, R (%)	5.111	3.262	0.964
After-tax return, $R(1 - \tau_k)$ (%)	4.091	2.642	0.828
Accidental bequests, E	0.063	0.072	0.119
Pay-as-you-go benefits (net of tax)	0.107	0.056	
Fully funded benefits		0.064	
Social security debt	2.165	1.515	
Government net worth	−2.165	−1.515	
Publicly held capital		1.358	
Government-issued bonds, B			
Private financial wealth	5.066	5.199	9.668
IRR on total contributions (%)	2.515	3.209	
IRR on fully funded contributions (%)		3.262	
IRR on pay-as-you-go contributions (%)	2.515	3.173	
Welfare Losses, relative to SQ (%)			
Proportional (ψ_0)		−7.323	−0.881
Proportional (ψ_1), $z_1 =$ high		−4.562	4.286
Proportional (ψ_1), $z_1 =$ low		−8.933	−3.895
Additive (ψ_0')		−4.233	−0.435
Additive (ψ_1'), $z_1 =$ high		−3.771	2.880
Additive (ψ_1'), $z_1 =$ low		−4.387	−1.637
Mean Utility (V_0)	−86.460	−80.129	−85.698

Notes: Entries correspond to per capita values (except for the various "rates") for economies featuring the status quo U.S. social security system (SQ), a system with 100 percent privately provided pensions (PP), and the Personal Security Accounts system (PSA). Government debt in these economies *has not* been adjusted to make net indebtedness comparable across steady states. The notation ψ_h denotes the welfare loss, expressed as a proportion of per-period consumption, associated with the average agent of age h moving from the SQ economy into one of the alternatives. The notation ψ_h' is identical, except that the welfare loss is expressed as an additive increment to per-period consumption. IRR denotes "internal rate of return." All remaining notations are defined in the text.

aspects of the social security system line up with the U.S. status quo in a reasonable manner. The endogenously determined rates for income and social security taxes – recall that we fix benefits and solve for tax rates to ensure budget balance – are realistic at roughly 20 and 11 percent, respectively. The internal rate of return on social security contributions, 2.51 percent, is substantially smaller than the after-tax return on capital, 4.09 percent, and matches the growth rate in GNP (recall the discussion in Section 6.3). Accidental bequests, or what we sometimes refer to as "estate taxes," are roughly 3.8 percent of GNP. Finally, our measure of the gross magnitude of the social security debt (defined in Section 6.3) is 1.32 times the size of output, a number that is conservative but in the right ballpark relative to previous studies, such as Feldstein (1997) and De Nardi, İmrohoroğlu, and Sargent (1998). These papers explicitly incorporate an anticipated increase in the average age of the population (i.e., the retiring Baby Boomers) and, not surprisingly, find that implicit obligations are larger than in our economy, which is characterized by a stationary demographic structure.

It is important to note that we have chosen quantitative values for our model's parameters in order to obtain a realistic *status quo* economy. When we consider alternatives – for instance, an economy with only private pensions – it will often be the case that, absent changes in these parameters, aggregate prices and quantities will be unrealistic as a result of fairly dramatic swings in the level of private savings. In these cases, we make a conscious choice to not adjust parameter values, the idea being that holding them fixed results in more direct, meaningful comparisons across economies.

6.5.1 Welfare Comparisons Across Alternative Economies

Having described the basic features of our benchmark economy, we now ask how the alternative social security arrangements measure up in terms of welfare as well as a number of aggregate statistics.

Our approach toward obtaining welfare comparisons is standard. We denote the value function for an h-year-old agent living in an economy with the SQ social security system as $V_h(\cdot)$. Similarly, $W_h(\cdot)$ denotes this agent's value function, were they to live in an economy endowed with an alternative social security system. The welfare loss associated with moving from the SQ to the alternative is measured as the proportional gain in consumption, received in the alternative, which makes them indifferent between the two. That is, this welfare loss is the number x, which results in the following equations being satisfied:

$$V_h(\cdot) = W_h(\cdot ; x) \tag{6.25}$$

where $W_h(\cdot ; x)$ solves

$$W_h(\cdot ; x) = \max_{a'_{h+1}} \left\{ u(c[1 + x]) + \beta \frac{\phi_{h+1}}{\phi_h} E \ W_{h+1}(\cdot ; x) \right\} \tag{6.26}$$

subject to Equations (6.8). The average welfare loss for age cohort h can now be expressed as the number ψ_h, which results in average utility being equated:

$$\int_{\tilde{Z} \times A} V_h(\cdot) d\mu = \int_{\tilde{Z} \times A} W_h(\cdot ; \psi_h) d\mu \tag{6.27}$$

where $W_h(\cdot\ ;\ \psi_h)$ is defined exactly as earlier but with the proportional change in consumption held equal across all agents of age h. We also find it instructive to compute these welfare measures in an additive fashion. We denote ψ_h^I as the number that results in the previous equations being satisfied, but where the first argument in the maximand is replaced by $u(c + x)$.

What will be crucial about the computation of each of these welfare measures are the prices at which their associated maximization problems are solved. To begin with (in this section of the paper), W_h will be computed vis-à-vis market-clearing prices from the steady state associated with the alternative social security system. That is, V_h and W_h will constitute a comparison *across* different steady states, thereby incorporating the effects of changing equilibrium prices and aggregate quantities into our welfare assessments. In subsequent analysis, when being able to abstract from general equilibrium effects will prove instrumental, W_h will correspond to a problem solved vis-à-vis prices from the reference point equilibrium: the SQ economy. These cases will represent welfare comparisons *within* the benchmark, steady-state equilibrium.

Given a methodology for making welfare assessments, we now turn to our results. To begin with, primarily for illustrative purposes, we compare alternative steady states *without* the adjustment for net indebtedness discussed in Section 6.3. These comparisons, although useful in a pedagogical sense, are misleading in that they confound risk-sharing with redistribution and ignore any notion of how an economy might transit from one system to another. Accordingly, we conclude this section by incorporating the social security debt and studying steady states in which the initial level of government debt, B, is chosen to make net social indebtedness comparable.

Table 6.2 reports properties of the stationary steady state corresponding to our three alternative economies: the status quo (SQ), an economy with private pensions (PP), and an economy with the Personal Security Account (PSA) social security system. Our welfare measures indicate that, without an adjustment for the social security debt, an unborn agent experiences a welfare gain in living in the PP and PSA economies of 0.88 and 7.32 percent, respectively. Note, however, that not only are these measures misleading in that an indebtedness adjustment has not been made, but also in that the PP economy is dynamically inefficient. In each of our economies, population growth is 1 percent and growth in GNP per capita is 1.5 percent. GNP, therefore, grows at 2.5 percent, which exceeds the PP economy's before-tax return on capital of 0.96 percent. The latter is simply a manifestation of the relatively large capital stock – 9.66 in the PP world versus 5.07 in the SQ world – which is itself driven by forcing agents to provide for 100 percent of their own retirement benefits in addition to accumulating a substantially larger precautionary buffer stock. The net result is that, in the PP economy without debt adjustments, an increase in per capita consumption can be attained by simply taxing capital and reducing savings. It is, therefore, no surprise that the PSA welfare measures indicate a substantially larger gain than their PP counterparts.

It is also interesting to note that the main finding of İmrohoroğlu, İmrohoroğlu, and Joines (1995) – that a social security system can help alleviate a dynamic inefficiency problem – is consistent with our result in this context.

We incorporate indebtedness in the following manner. First, as was discussed in Section 6.3, we obtain a measure of gross obligations in the form of a sequence of promised annuities, which correspond to the SQ economy. We then envision the government issuing a bond, which raises financing sufficient to meet these obligations. An important question, therefore, involves the appropriate rate of return on capital, which will be applied to these government funds. The higher this rate, the lower the requisite amount of borrowing that needs to be undertaken. Were we to explicitly model the transition between steady states, the appropriate rate would be determined within the model. However, because we only compare alternative steady-states, the appropriate return is ambiguous. Our approach is to use the return associated with the non-SQ economy: the economy we envision a transition toward. An impressionistic way to think of this is that once the social security system is changed from the status quo, prices and aggregate capital immediately jump to their new steady-state values.

We report results from economies with social security debt adjustments in Table 6.3. The level of debt associated with the SQ, evaluated at SQ prices, is 2.17, or 1.32 times GNP. To finance these obligations, when moving to a system with privately provided pensions, the government needs to borrow 2.95, or 1.60 times GNP. The extra amount here, relative to the debt in the SQ economy, corresponds to the higher capital stock and, therefore, the lower return on capital in the PP economy of 3.02 percent (versus 5.11 percent in the SQ). Along similar lines, capital in the PSA economy is slightly larger than in the SQ. The before-tax return on capital is, therefore, slightly lower, at 4.32 percent. The requisite amount of borrowing, keeping in mind that only half of the pay-as-you-go obligations are being eliminated, is 1.19, or roughly 70 percent of GNP.

The welfare implications are quite different once we incorporate the debt adjustment. Table 6.3 shows that an unborn agent would pay 3.74 percent of per-period consumption to move from the status quo to a debt-adjusted world with only private pensions. They would pay 4.03 percent to move to an economy with a PSA pension system. Note that the former – the value associated with the PP economy – is *larger* than the welfare gain before the debt adjustment. This might seem erroneous when taken at face value, the idea being that welfare should be higher before incorporating the cost of providing an unfunded transfer to the initial old generation. What's going on, however, is that the act of adding societal debt serves to decrease aggregate capital and pull the economy over the dynamically inefficient barrier. Welfare is, therefore, increased. In the case of the PSA, incorporating the debt adjustment does have the predictable effect of reducing welfare: the gain from switching goes from 7.32 to 4.03 percent once society is forced to live up to existing obligations.

Table 6.3. *Properties of Economies with Alternative Social Security Systems* (adjusted to equalize net indebtedness)

	SQ	PSA	PP
Output, Y	1.636	1.706	1.840
Capital, K	5.067	5.631	6.804
Consumption, C	0.802	0.813	0.828
Government consumption, G	0.311	0.311	0.311
Income-tax rate, $\tau_l = \tau_k$ (%)	19.959	20.158	13.923
Payroll-tax rate, τ_p (%)	10.923	10.054	
Before-tax return, R (%)	5.111	4.319	3.018
After-tax return, $R(1 - \tau_k)$ (%)	4.091	3.448	2.598
Accidental bequests, E	0.063	0.080	0.131
Pay-as-you-go benefits (net of tax)	0.107	0.052	
Fully funded benefits		0.077	
Social security debt	2.165	1.192	
Government net worth	−2.165	−2.417	−2.954
Publicly held capital		1.505	
Government-issued bonds, B		1.225	2.954
Private financial wealth	5.066	5.350	9.757
IRR on total contributions (%)	2.515	3.719	
IRR on fully funded contributions (%)		4.319	
IRR on pay-as-you-go contributions (%)	2.515	3.218	
Welfare Losses, relative to SQ (%)			
Proportional (ψ_0)		−4.027	−3.747
Proportional (ψ_1), $z_1 =$ high		−3.128	−2.545
Proportional (ψ_1), $z_1 =$ low		−4.550	−4.448
Additive (ψ_0')		−2.254	−1.997
Additive (ψ_1'), $z_1 =$ high		−2.584	−1.912
Additive (ψ_1'), $z_1 =$ low		−2.146	−2.027
Mean Utility (V_0)	−86.460	−82.979	−83.221

Notes: Entries correspond to per capita values (except for the various "rates") for economies featuring the status quo U.S. social security system (SQ), a system with 100 percent privately provided pensions (PP), and the Personal Security Accounts system (PSA). Government debt in these economies *has* been adjusted to make net indebtedness comparable across steady states. The notation ψ_h denotes the welfare loss, expressed as a proportion of per-period consumption, associated with the average agent of age h moving from the SQ economy into one of the alternatives. The notation ψ_h' is identical, except that the welfare loss is expressed as an additive increment to per-period consumption. IRR denotes "internal rate of return." All remaining notations are defined in the text.

6.5.2 Decomposing the Welfare Gains

The overall welfare gains associated with social security reform – 3.75 percent of consumption from abolishing the system or 4.03 percent from privatizing half of it – characterize the outcome of the simple horse race we put forth at the outset of our study. Understanding the economics behind our results is, however, more involved: there are a number of forces at work, each of which can conceivably pull in a different direction. The primary candidates are (i) the interaction between distortionary capital taxation and how the pension system alters the total level of publicly and privately held capital; (ii) "general equilibrium effects": the impact of alternative pension arrangements on the overall level of capital and on market-clearing prices; (iii) the extent to which a social security arrangement provides some form of an annuity, thereby aiding in the hedging of mortality risk; and (iv) changes in the income risk-sharing technology available to agents. To decompose our overall results into components attributable to each of these effects, we conduct a number of additional experiments, each involving a set of economies in which progressively fewer of the effects are at work. In simple terms, we first eliminate capital-taxation effects, then general-equilibrium effects, then annuity effects, which finally leaves us with only risk-sharing effects. The differences we find each step of the way constitute the contribution associated with the factor most recently removed. This is, admittedly, a mouthful. The following notation should serve to clarify matters.

Exhibit 6.1. *Summary of Experiments Underling Welfare Decompositions*

Notation for welfare loss	Eliminated effects ψ	Comments
ψ	None	Benchmark welfare comparisons (Table 6.3)
ψ_a	Capital taxation ($\tau_k = 0$)	Comparison across steady states
ψ_b	Capital taxation ($\tau_k = 0$) Equilibrium effects	Comparison within steady state ψ_c
ψ_c	Capital taxation ($\tau_k = 0$) Equilibrium effects	Comparison within steady state Agents given access to perfect annuities
	Imperfect annuity effects	

Our decomposition uses these definitions coupled with the following identity:

$$\underbrace{\psi}_{\text{total welfare loss}} = \underbrace{(\psi - \psi_a)}_{\text{tax effect}} + \underbrace{(\psi_a - \psi_b)}_{\text{equilibrium effect}} + \underbrace{(\psi_b - \psi_c)}_{\text{annuity effect}} + \underbrace{\psi_c}_{\text{risk-sharing effect}} \qquad (6.28)$$

The idea behind all this is straightforward. Consider the welfare loss associated with moving from the SQ economy to some alternative, say the PP economy. First, ψ represents the overall welfare loss (from Table 6.3), which we are attempting to decompose. Each of the four economic factors we have highlighted play some role in generating this number. Second, ψ_a represents an analogous welfare loss, only computed using economies in which capital-income is not taxed. Therefore, of the four original contributing factors, only three remain. The contribution of capital-income taxation can thus be associated with the difference between the former and the latter: $\psi - \psi_a$. Along a similar vein, if we compute the welfare loss in an environment devoid of both capital-income taxation and equilibrium effects, then the difference between this value and that which excludes only capital taxation constitutes the contribution of equilibrium effects. This difference is labeled $\psi_a - \psi_b$. The story is complete once we eliminate mortality risk, leaving us with the contribution of imperfect annuity effects, $\psi_b - \psi_c$, as well as the residual: the pure contribution of income risk-sharing effects, ψ_c.

The following table provides a quantitative breakdown of how each of the economic factors we focus on contributes toward our bottom line.

Exhibit 6.2. *Welfare Decomposition* (welfare losses as a percentage of per-period consumption)

Contributing factor	PSA	PP
Distortionary capital taxation	0.027	0.717
General equilibrium effects	−3.662	−6.832
Provision of annuities	−0.677	0.758
Income risk-sharing	0.285	1.610
Total	−4.027	−3.747

The main message of this decomposition is simple. The lion's share of the welfare gain associated with social security reform derives from the general equilibrium effects. As we demonstrate explicitly later, this is a manifestation of the fact that, as a whole, society saves more under either of the PP or PSA arrangements, leading to lower interest rates, a higher capital stock, and a higher level of aggregate output and consumption. Income risk-sharing effects also are important, as evidenced by the 1.6 percent loss associated with the PP alternative, whereas effects directly attributable to the provision of annuities and capital income tax distortions play a relatively minor role.

We now provide a more explicit description of the experiments and economic intuition that underly each of these results.

6.5.3 Capital Taxation Effects

The economies we use to isolate capital taxation effects are essentially identical to those represented in Table 6.3, except that all government expenditure is financed through labor-income taxation: $\tau_k = 0$ rather than $\tau_k = \tau_l$ as before. That is, we compute three new steady states, each corresponding to either the SQ, the PSA, or the PP social security system, where $\tau_k = 0$ in all cases. The welfare numbers of interest, reported along with aggregate statistics in Table 6.4, are computed by comparing utility in these three steady states, and are thus free of any effects related to capital-income taxation.

The main message of Table 6.4 is that the effects of capital-income taxation are not large in magnitude. In the SQ economy, for instance, the increase

Table 6.4. *Properties of Economies with Alternative Social Security Systems* (adjusted to equalize net indebtedness, zero captial taxation: $\tau_k = 0$)

	SQ	PSA	PP
Output, Y	1.669	1.729	1.828
Capital, K	5.328	5.822	6.692
Consumption, C	0.802	0.810	0.821
Government consumption, G	0.317	0.317	0.317
Labor income-tax rate, τ_l (%)	24.670	24.145	18.440
Payroll-tax rate, τ_p (%)	10.788	9.802	
Before-tax return, R (%)	4.728	4.078	3.126
After-tax return, $R(1 - \tau_k)$ (%)	4.728	4.078	3.126
Accidental bequests, E	0.070	0.087	0.133
Pay-as-you-go benefits (net of tax)	0.108	0.050	
Fully funded benefits		0.074	
Social security debt	2.298	1.190	
Government net worth	−2.298	−2.523	−2.924
Publicly held capital		1.468	
Government-issued bonds, B		1.333	2.924
Private financial wealth	5.328	5.687	9.616
IRR on total contributions (%)	2.515	3.694	
IRR on fully funded contributions (%)		4.078	
IRR on pay-as-you-go contributions (%)	2.515	3.377	
Welfare Losses, relative to SQ (%)			
Proportional (ψ_0)		−4.054	−4.464
Proportional (ψ_1), $z_1 =$ high		−3.027	−3.049
Proportional (ψ_1), $z_1 =$ low		−4.645	−5.279
Additive (ψ_0')		−2.198	−2.383
Additive (ψ_1'), $z_1 =$ high		−2.460	−2.333
Additive (ψ_1'), $z_1 =$ low		−2.115	−2.400
Mean Utility (V_0)	−88.307	−84.727	−84.365

Notes: Economies are identical to those in Table 6.3, except that capital income taxation has been abolished: $\tau_k = 0$. Entries correspond to per capita values (except for the various "rates") for economies featuring the status quo U.S. social security system (SQ), a system with 100 percent privately provided pensions (PP), and the Personal Security Accounts system (PSA). Government debt in these economies *has* been adjusted to make net indebtedness comparable across steady states. The notation ψ_h denotes the welfare loss, expressed as a proportion of per-period consumption, associated with the average agent of age h moving from the SQ economy into one of the alternatives. The notation ψ_h' is identical, except that the welfare loss is expressed as an additive increment to per-period consumption. IRR denotes "internal rate of return." All remaining notations are defined in the text.

in steady-state output because of an elimination of the distortion is a mere 2 percent. The associated increase in the capital stock is 5 percent, which generates a decrease in the return on capital from 5.11 to 4.73 percent. The welfare effects of capital-taxation are also not large. Removing the tax implies a small increase in the gain associated with the PSA proposal – from 4.03 up to 4.05 percent – and a moderate increase associated with private pensions – from 3.75 up to 4.46 percent. As is outlined earlier, these changes in welfare gains can be interpreted as the incremental contribution of capital-income taxation toward our overall results. We associate a 0.027 percent effect with the PSA proposal and a 0.717 percent effect with the PP, both of which are tabulated in Exhibit 6.2.

6.5.4 General Equilibrium Effects

What we mean by "general equilibrium effects" are the implications of changes in our model's institutional structure for the level of aggregate resources and for market-clearing prices. For example, to foreshadow what will turn out to be a driving force behind capital accumulation, the existence of annuities turns out to mitigate the desire to save among the working population in our economy. An important implication, one that is external to each individual's decision problem, is that the steady-state level of aggregate capital will be lower than it would be, absent annuities. One might, therefore, think of the "externality" associated with annuities markets as the aggregate effect of each agent's decision to save less. That these effects are an important component of what alternative social security systems bring to the table seems obvious. They are certainly implicit in much of the current public policy debate in the United States, where social security reform is often seen as a remedy for what many feel is an undesirably low savings rate.

In Table 6.5, we isolate equilibrium effects by holding prices and aggregate quantities fixed across our experiments. The equilibrium effects are then computed as the difference between the fixed-price results and our previous results (Table 6.4), in which endogenous variables were allowed to change.

More specifically, our reference point is an economy endowed with the SQ social security system, in which the capital income-tax rate is set to zero. In this environment, we confront one atomistic agent with an alternative social security system but hold prices and aggregate quantities identical to those associated with the reference point equilibrium. In addition, to make the comparison meaningful, we tax this atomistic agent so that their net tax burden is comparable to that of an agent facing the SQ system. This is accomplished by computing the present value, in the SQ world, of total payroll, income, and estate taxes paid less total social security benefits received. The atomistic agent, facing one of the alternative systems, is then forced to pay payroll taxes at a rate that implies an equivalent net tax burden.

Table 6.5 shows the results of these experiments. The first column, labeled SQ, corresponds to an economy identical to that reported in Table 6.4. The remaining two columns characterize life under an alternative regime, in which prices are held identical to those underlying the first column. We see, for example, that

Table 6.5. *Properties of Alternative Social Security Systems, Evaluated at SQ Prices* (adjusted to equalize net tax burden, zero capital taxation: $\tau_k = 0$)

	SQ	PSA	PP
Tax burden	−9.810	−9.810	−9.810
Average private financial wealth	5.328	5.708	9.133
Accidental bequests	0.070	0.093	0.138
NPV of cohort consumption	19.046	19.046	19.046
Labor income-tax rate, τ_l (%)	24.670	24.670	24.670
Payroll-tax rate, τ_p (%)	10.788	11.727	1.900
IRR on total contributions (%)	2.515	3.358	
IRR on fully funded contributions (%)		4.728	
IRR on pay-as-you-go contributions (%)	2.515	2.324	
Welfare Losses, relative to SQ (%)			
Proportional (ψ_0)		−0.392	2.368
Additive (ψ_0')		−0.204	1.216
Mean Utility V_0	−88.307	−87.961	−90.398

Notes: Entries correspond to confronting an agent with alternative social security systems, whereas holding prices fixed at the level associated with the U.S. status quo (SQ). PP represents privately provided pensions, and PSA the personal security account system. The notation ψ_h denotes the welfare loss, expressed as a proportion of per-period consumption, associated with the average agent of age h moving from the SQ economy to some alternative. The notation ψ_h' is identical, except that the welfare loss is expressed as an additive increment to per-period consumption. The tax burden represents the net present value of lifetime taxes paid less benefits received, the measurement of which is discussed in detail in the text. The units in which the tax burden, privately held capital, and estate taxes are denominated in are essentially per capita, and are directly comparable. IRR denotes "internal rate of return." NPV denotes "net present value." All remaining notations are defined in the text.

the agent forced to live without publicly provided pensions actually pays a small payroll tax (1.9 percent) despite not receiving any social security benefits. The implication is that the net taxes avoided by opting out of the social security system are not quite offset by the increased estate taxes paid as a result of having to save more for retirement. In regard to welfare, an agent suffers a loss of 2.37 percent in moving from the SQ to PP economy and a gain of 0.39 percent in moving to the PSA. Our decomposition methodology, therefore, associates a welfare gain of 6.83 percent of consumption with the general equilibrium effects involved in moving from the SQ to the PP economy (tabulated in Exhibit 6.2). This value is simply the difference between the gain when equilibrium effects are removed, −2.37 percent, and the gain when they are present: 4.46 percent. Likewise, the welfare gain associated with the PSA is 3.66 percent, owing to a gain of 4.05 percent inclusive of equilibrium effects and a gain of 0.39 percent without them.

The key to understanding these relatively large general equilibrium effects – as well as the main punchline in our paper – is understanding the increase in the capital stock, which is associated with making agents provide for their own pensions. In Table 6.4, we see that this increase is substantial: absent capital-income taxation, aggregate capital increases by just under 10 percent for a move to the PSA system and just over 25 percent for a move to the PP. In simple terms, the welfare gains owe to being born into a richer economy. As we'll see shortly, and as we alluded to earlier, a critical aspect of this increase in societal wealth will turn out to be the interaction between savings and the provision of annuities.

6.5.5 Imperfect Annuity Effects

We isolate effects related to mortality risk by modifying the market for capital to include perfect annuities. This is accomplished through a simple reformulation of the budget constraint, which essentially transfers economy-wide estate taxes from the government back to the private sector. The budget constraint, Equation (6.8), is replaced by:

$$c_h + a'_{h+1}\xi_{h+1} \le a_h R - \tau_k a_h (R - 1) + n_h W(1 - \tau_l - \tau_p - \tau_f)$$
$$+ \sum_{j=\{p,f\}} \left(b_h^j - \tilde{b}_h^j \tau_l\right). \tag{6.8'}$$

The only change is that the conditional probability of surviving to age $h + 1$, given that one survives to age h, is multiplied against the savings term on the left side of the equation. The idea is that, because one may not survive to capture the benefit of saving, the sacrifice in terms of current consumption is reduced (in an actuarily fair manner). A number of authors – Blanchard and Fischer (1989), for instance – refer to this reduction as the "survivor's premium."

Table 6.6 shows what happens when we add perfect annuities to the fixed-price environment with zero capital taxation. Eliminating estate taxation as a means of public finance makes for a substantial increase in the income-tax rate required to balance the budget in the SQ economy. The tax rate increases from 24.7 percent without annuities (Table 6.5) to 31.7 percent with annuities (Table 6.6). In addition, the adjustment we apply to equate the net tax burden across experiments (recall the earlier discussion) has the PP agent paying a 5.6 percent payroll tax – despite receiving zero benefits – and the PSA agent paying 12.6 percent, a slight premium (2 percent) above the rate applicable in the SQ economy. Again, each of these tax adjustments owes to the fact that the alternative in question involves paying less in net transfers through a reduced size of the pay-as-you-go system.

Finally, the welfare implications of reform, having eliminated capital taxation effects, general equilibrium effects, and annuities effects, are that an agent suffers a 1.6 percent welfare loss from the abolition of social security and a 0.29 percent loss from switching to the PSA. Using the methodology that is, hopefully, familiar

Table 6.6. *Properties of Alternative Social Security Systems, Evaluated at SQ Prices* (adjusted to equalize net tax burden, perfect annuities, zero capital taxation: $\tau_k = 0$)

	SQ	PSA	PP
Tax burden	−10.375	−10.375	−10.375
Average private financial wealth	5.218	5.080	7.495
Accidental bequests	–	–	–
NPV of cohort consumption	17.471	17.471	17.471
Labor income-tax rate, τ_l (%)	31.667	31.667	31.667
Payroll-tax rate, τ_p (%)	10.587	12.596	5.592
IRR on total contributions (%)	2.515	3.175	
IRR on fully funded contributions (%)		4.889	
IRR on pay-as-you-go contributions (%)	2.515	1.941	
Welfare Losses, relative to SQ (%)			
Proportional (ψ_0)		0.285	1.610
Additive (ψ_0')		0.131	0.749
Mean Utility V_0	−94.128	−94.522	−95.771

Notes: Economies are identical to those in Table 6.5, except that agents have access to perfect annuity markets. Entries correspond to confronting an agent with alternative social security systems, whereas holding prices fixed at the level associated with the U.S. status quo (SQ). PP represents privately provided pensions, and PSA the personal security account system. The notation ψ_h denotes the welfare loss, expressed as a proportion of per-period consumption, associated with the average agent of age h moving from the SQ economy to some alternative. The notation ψ_h' is identical, except that the welfare loss is expressed as an additive increment to per-period consumption. The tax burden represents the net present value of lifetime taxes paid less benefits received, the measurement of which is discussed in detail in the text. The units in which the tax burden, privately held capital, and estate taxes are denominated in are essentially per capita, and are directly comparable. IRR denotes "internal rate of return." NPV denotes "net present value." All remaining notations are defined in the text.

by now, this translates into a 0.76 percent loss attributable to changes in annuities markets for the PP economy and a 0.67 percent gain associated with the PSA economy.

6.5.6 Income Risk-Sharing Effects

The final economic factor we wish to isolate is labor-income risk-sharing. That is, social security is redistributive both in the sense that payroll taxes are proportional and that benefits are regressive with respect to contributions. The floor on benefits also can play a key role, both in our model and the real world.

The good news is that our work here is done. The fixed-price comparisons in Table 6.6, where capital taxation is eliminated and perfect annuities are added, isolates the risk-sharing effect in an absolute sense because three of the four candidates we postulated at the outset have been removed. To reiterate, we find that an agent living in a world with private pensions would pay 1.6 percent of per-period consumption in order to have access to the income risk-sharing technology inherent in the SQ social security system. The analogous number for an agent living in the PSA economy is 0.29 percent.

An informative context in which to consider the magnitude of these findings is the total amount of idiosyncratic variation faced by an agent and how much they would pay to eliminate it. For example, we calculate that in an economy with privately provided pensions, zero income taxation, and no mortality risk (i.e., perfect annuities), an agent would pay roughly 26 percent of per-period consumption to eliminate all idiosyncratic labor-income variation. Although this number might seem large, it is actually consistent with previous studies, at least in a methodological sense. Lucas (1987), for instance, calculates that a rough estimate of the welfare gain from eliminating business cycles is given by one half the product of the risk-aversion coefficient and the variance of aggregate consumption. We use a risk-aversion coefficient of 2, so Lucas's measure suggests that welfare gains from removing variation are roughly on the order of the variance removed. The unconditional variance of consumption in our benchmark economy is approximately 0.16 and 0.32 for agents of age 22 and 65, respectively – numbers that are not unrealistic given evidence from panel data studies (see Deaton and Paxson (1994), for instance). Welfare gains on the order of 26 percent are, therefore, plausible, given the amount of idiosyncratic variation with which we start.

Our results on risk-sharing can, therefore, be thought of in the following loose, but we think informative, manner. An agent would pay 26 percent of per-period consumption to be able to eliminate idiosyncratic risk. Of these 26 percentage points, the risk-sharing component of social security delivers 1.6, or about 6 percent, of the potential gains. The PSA delivers significantly less (just over 1 percent of the potential gains), reflecting the fact that its fully funded component represents a movement away from redistribution and toward a stronger link between benefits and accumulated contributions. Although these numbers might seem small in an absolute sense, it is important to keep in mind that the overall size of the system is such that only 12 percent of total wage receipts are incorporated. In light of this, being able to deliver on 6 percent of the total by taxing only 12 percent of the total seems substantial.

6.5.7 The Interaction of Annuities and Aggregate Savings

The upshot of our welfare decomposition is that the lion's share of the gains we attribute to social security reform are due to what we have labeled "general equilibrium effects": changes in equilibrium prices and aggregate quantities that result from changes in our model's institutional structure. Table 6.3 demonstrates this in a fairly obvious manner: aggregate capital in the reformed economies increases by 11 percent in the case of the PSA economy and by 34 percent in the case of the PP economy. A substantial portion of the associated welfare gain is, therefore, a simple result of being born into a richer economy. We now demonstrate that a critical ingredient driving this increase in aggregate capital is the savings response of an individual, having lost access to the annuities which social security provides.

In Table 6.7, we report results from an experiment analogous to that in Table 6.4, but in which perfect annuities have been added in the same manner as described earlier. Specifically, the comparison in Table 6.7 is conducted across alternative steady states (with zero capital taxation) in which the need to hedge mortality risk has been eliminated. The idea is that, should we see a smaller increase in aggregate capital relative to our previous experiments, we can attribute much of the aggregate wealth effect in those experiments to the removal of annuities.

Table 6.7 shows that this is exactly the case. The increase in aggregate capital, vis-à-vis the SQ economy with perfect annuities, is 2.7 percent for the PSA and 1.9 percent for the PP. The increases in aggregate consumption and output are also small, especially when compared to the increases reported in Table 6.4. In addition, a smaller capital stock, relative to the economies that exclude annuities (Table 6.4, makes for lower wages and, therefore, a lower payroll tax base. The payroll tax rate must, therefore, be higher – 31.7 percent in Table 6.7 versus 21.7 percent in Table 6.4 – which itself provides a further drag on disposable income and welfare.

Taken at face value, the implication of these results is that the provision of annuities makes agents worse off. Although this is true in a literal sense, we would argue that it confuses the direct effect of annuities – something that our decomposition has shown to be beneficial to agents – with the external effect on aggregate savings. In isolation, an individual agent prefers to have his or her retirement wealth annuitized, thereby avoiding estate taxes and making for a smoother consumption profile over the life-cycle. However, the collective implication of annuities is a reduction in aggregate savings, which makes for lower steady-state capital, output, and consumption, as well as higher taxes.

Finally, one might think of our results, loosely speaking, as an example of what incomplete-markets theorists (see Geanakoplos (1990), for instance) have known for a long time: that adding a market to an incomplete-markets setting need not increase welfare. In the incomplete-markets literature, many such results are driven by changes in the endogenously determined space spanned by an agent's budget constraint, the endogeneity arising from relative prices effects in multigood settings. Our example is less rich in two senses. First, our environment features only a single good. Second, in incorporating annuities, we don't really "add a market," we simply enhance what the existing market structure is capable of. Nevertheless, the fact that society as a whole can accumulate capital in our setting, and that this directly affects the asset return process, makes "the span" of our asset markets every bit as endogenous as that in richer models. The resulting externality – the fact that individuals do not incorporate the effect of their savings decision on everyone else's investment opportunities – lies at the heart of the welfare implications we derive.

Table 6.7. *Properties of Economies with Alternative Social Security Systems* (adjusted to equalize net indebtedness, perfect annuities, zero capital taxation: $\tau_k = 0$)

	SQ	PSA	PP
Output, Y	1.655	1.673	1.667
Capital, K	5.217	5.360	5.315
Consumption, C	0.802	0.804	0.804
Government consumption, G	0.314	0.314	0.314
Labor income-tax rate, τ_l (%)	31.667	34.209	36.403
Payroll-tax rate, τ_p (%)	10.586	9.165	
Before-tax return, R (%)	4.887	4.683	4.746
After-tax return, $R(1 - \tau_k)$ (%)	4.887	4.683	4.746
Accidental bequests, E			
pay-as-you-go benefits	0.105	0.042	
(net of tax)			
Fully funded benefits		0.083	
Social security debt	2.188	0.914	
Government net worth	−2.188	−2.251	−2.231
Publicly held capital		1.564	
Government-issued bonds, B		1.337	2.231
Private financial wealth	5.217	5.133	7.546
IRR on total contributions (%)	2.515	4.249	
IRR on fully funded contributions (%)		4.683	
IRR on pay-as-you-go contributions (%)	2.515	3.817	
Welfare Losses, relative to SQ (%)			
Proportional (ψ_0)		−1.090	0.339
Proportional (ψ_1), $z_1 =$ high		−1.519	−0.997
Proportional (ψ_1), $z_1 =$ low		−0.849	1.086
Additive (ψ_0')		−0.509	0.159
Additive (ψ_1'), $z_1 =$ high		−1.113	−0.716
Additive (ψ_1'), $z_1 =$ low		−0.331	0.429
Mean Utility (V_0)	−94.248	−93.226	−94.567

Notes: Economies are identical to those in Table 6.5, except that agents have access to perfect annuity markets. Entries correspond to per capita values (except for the various "rates") for economies featuring the status quo U.S. social security system (SQ), a system with 100 percent privately provided pensions (PP), and the Personal Security Accounts system (PSA). Government debt in these economies *has* been adjusted to make net indebtedness comparable across steady states. The notation ψ_h denotes the welfare loss, expressed as a proportion of per-period consumption, associated with the average agent of age h moving from the SQ economy into one of the alternatives. The notation ψ_h' is identical, except that the welfare loss is expressed as an additive increment to per-period consumption. IRR denotes "internal rate of return." All remaining notations are defined in the text.

6.5.8 Fixed Effects

Up to this point, the process we've used for idiosyncratic shocks has not included the "fixed-effect" terms from Equation 6.22, Section 5.1. A simple way of thinking about why these terms might be important involves the way they effectively redistribute total labor-market uncertainty toward the earlier part of the life-cycle. To understand this, first consider the process without fixed effects. In this case, uncertainty is spread out uniformly over the earning years (in a conditional sense), a pattern that might be effectively hedged through the *contingent* aspect of buffer-stock savings and dissavings (i.e., save on receiving a good shock, dissave on receiving a bad one). A redistributive social security system, by contrast, lacks a strong contingent transfer mechanism and, as we have seen, eliminates (incrementally) only a small fraction of the total idiosyncratic variation faced by agents.

In contrast, consider the case in which fixed effects constitute an important component of total labor-market uncertainty. The ability to make a lifelong sequence of state contingent savings decisions now looks less appealing. Social security, by contrast, looks more promising as a risk-sharing vehicle; in some sense, it represents an uncontingent transfer from rich young agents to old poor agents. One might expect, therefore, to find that the risk-sharing benefits of social security are enhanced in the presence of fixed effects. This will, of course, be especially true for the unborn who are the only cohort for which fixed-effect variation represents uncertainty.

We examine these suppositions in the context of our model by adding fixed-effects as described in Sections 5.1. Specifically, we modify the idiosyncratic risk process to include fixed effects according to the parameter values from the second line of Table 6.1. We then conduct several experiments designed to isolate pure risk-sharing effects (i.e., Table 6.6): fixed-price comparisons with perfect annuities and zero capital taxation. The results are reported in Table 6.8. Under the heading "Fixed Effects," we report welfare losses from both types of reform, in which unborn agents face fixed-effects risk. We also report comparable results from economies with zero fixed-effects but in which the conditional variance of the persistent shocks has been increased so that the unconditional variance of labor income equals that faced by an unborn agent in the fixed-effects economies. The latter make for meaningful comparisons because the addition of fixed effects serves to add variation in an unconditional sense (see Figure 6.1).

Our findings confirm the intuition spelled out earlier. Relative to an economy with no fixed effects and an equal amount of overall variation, an unborn agent suffers a substantially greater welfare loss because of pension reform, should their income process feature a fixed effect. The loss with respect to the PP economy increases from 2.5 to 3.4 percent. The loss for the PSA experiment increases from 0.6 to 2.1 percent. Note that, in each case, the welfare loss associated with the

Table 6.8. *Incorporating Fixed Effects: Properties of Alternative Social Security Systems, Evaluated at SQ Prices* (adjusted to equalize net tax burden, perfect annuities, zero capital taxation: $\tau_k = 0$)

Welfare losses, relative to SQ	Fixed	Effects	High	Variance
Proportional ψ	PSA	PP	PSA	PP
(ψ_0)	2.107	3.377	0.620	2.511
$(\psi_1, \alpha = \text{low}, z = \text{low})$	3.846	6.580	1.251	3.702
$(\psi_1, \alpha = \text{low}, z = \text{high})$	1.473	2.393	−0.592	0.233
$(\psi_1, \alpha = \text{high}, z = \text{low})$	0.735	0.721	1.251	3,702
$(\psi_1, \alpha = \text{high}, z = \text{high})$	−0.160	−0.937	−0.592	0.233

Notes: Welfare losses incorporate a "fixed effect" into the idiosyncratic income process, as described in Section 6.3. Entries correspond to confronting an agent with alternative social security systems while holding prices fixed at the level associated with the U.S. status quo (SQ). PP represents privately provided pensions, and PSA the personal security account system. Columns labeled "Fixed Effects" modify the income process according to the second row of Table 6.1. Columns labeled "High Variance" set the fixed-effects terms to zero but increase the variance of the persistent shock innovations so as to equate the unconditional variance (from the perspective of an unborn agent) with that of the fixed-effects economies. The notation ψ_h denotes the welfare loss, expressed as a proportion of per-period consumption, associated with the average agent of age h moving from the SQ economy to some alternative. The notation $\psi_1(\alpha, z)$ denotes the welfare loss for an agent of age 1 who received a fixed-effect shock of α and an initial persistent shock of z.

economy with no fixed-effects is larger than that from Table 6.6. This is simply a result of increasing the conditional variance in the manner we have described.

Finally, the welfare losses contingent on age also conform to one's priors. For example, an agent who receives a high fixed-effect shock and a high initial-period persistent shock gains by almost 1 percent of consumption from the abolition of public pensions. In contrast, an agent who gets a low fixed-effect shock and a low persistent shock suffers a loss of 6.6 percent from the same reform.

Our examination of fixed effects, both here and in a related paper (Storesletten, Telmer, and Yaron (1997)), suggests several important points. First, they can provide for a fairly different picture of how much idiosyncratic variation is in the data and how it is distributed over the life-cycle. Second, these differences can have substantial implications for the risk-sharing benefits associated with both financial markets and publicly instituted transfer schemes such as social security. Finally, fixed effects are likely to be important for any questions that are age-dependent – for example, a more explicit breakdown of the winners and losers in the transition to a new pension system.

6.6 Conclusion

Our main finding is that agents value the risk-sharing benefits associated with social security but, once general-equilibrium effects are incorporated, not more than the costs associated with its impact on savings incentives. In terms of the federal Advisory Council on Social Security's (1996) proposals, we associate a welfare benefit of 4.02 percent of annual consumption with moving from the status quo to a system of comparable size, but one in which roughly half of worker contributions are earmarked for "personal security accounts (PSAs)": privately owned, defined-contribution accounts that are invested in capital markets. We associate a slightly lower welfare gain – roughly 3.73 percent of annual consumption – with abolishing social security altogether. A crucial aspect of these welfare comparisons is that they incorporate the "social security debt": the obligations associated with the status quo system that we assume the government does not renege.

The primary force driving these welfare gains is a kind of externality associated with retirement savings. Social security provides a participant with an imperfect annuity. When that annuity is removed – either completely or partially – individuals save more during their working lives to ensure against the possibility of outliving their resources during retirement. The collective effect of this increase in savings, something that is external to each individual's choice problem, is an increase in aggregate capital, output, and consumption. This increase in aggregate resources lies at the heart of the welfare gains we uncover.

We argue that this finding – that the provision of annuities can reduce welfare – is not unlike a classic set of results from the literature on general equilibrium with incomplete markets; the endogenous nature of the set of investment opportunities generates an externality that can make changes in the market structure welfare-decreasing. Our example of this is stark in that it abstracts from privately provided (imperfect) annuities that are, to some extent, available in actual financial markets. Nevertheless, it makes a point that often is overlooked in the debate on social security reform: that the savings response to a change in the system can very much depend on how the availability of annuities is altered. Our results suggest that the quantitative magnitude of this response is substantial.

It is important to note that welfare increases are not necessarily *un fait accompli* in our analysis. Despite its adverse effects on savings incentives, social security plays a valuable role as a risk-sharing technology, both in relation to income risk and mortality risk. We quantitatively isolate these effects through experiments that abstract from changing equilibrium prices and aggregate quantities. We find that, for instance, the risk-sharing role of the U.S. status quo system, when compared to a world without publicly provided pensions, is worth 2.37 percent of annual consumption from the perspective of an unborn agent. This same agent would pay roughly 34 percent of annual consumption to eliminate idiosyncratic risk altogether, so social security gets them almost 7 percent of the way there. Although 7 percent might not seem large, one must keep in mind that it is delivered by taxing just 12 percent of the overall wage bill.

Our analysis does not model the transition between steady states, something that is clearly important in assessing exactly who the winners and losers of any reform would be. Despite this, one can draw some loose implications of what an explicit account of the transition might yield. First, based on our results that abstract from equilibrium effects, an agent who lives through the early part of the transition, in which the level of aggregate capital will be similar to that of the status quo economy, will suffer slightly as a result of moving to a PSA system and will suffer substantially if publicly provided pensions are abandoned altogether. These welfare losses are essentially a manifestation of losing access to a valuable risk-sharing technology while not participating in the beneficial aspects of the reformed steady state. It is important to note that this statement is made *net* of the influences of a changing tax burden and/or financing the obligations associated with the status quo. Second, based on comparisons that do incorporate equilibrium effects, agents who live through the later part of the transition, or those who live in an economy resembling the new steady state, will benefit substantially from either a privatization of a portion of the status quo system or an abolition of the system altogether. These agents will tend to regret the absence of a societal risk-sharing mechanism, but this regret will be far outweighed by the removal of distortionary capital-income taxation and the higher level of aggregate capital and per-capita consumption they will enjoy.

Our overall message is that the benefits or losses associated with social security reform must trade off the gains we associate with the new steady state – primarily that agents will be borne into a richer economy – with the losses borne by those who live through the transition. This points to the importance of the work of Auerbach and Kotlikoff (1987), De Nardi, İmrohoroğlu, and Sargent (1998), and others who explicitly model the transition and are better able to evaluate this tradeoff. A point that such work might take from our study is that the institutional characteristics of annuities markets are likely to play a quantitatively important role, both in relation to transitional issues and the properties of the reformed steady state.

REFERENCES

Advisory Council on Social Security, (1996), *Report of the 1994–1996. Advisory Council on Social Security*, Volumes 1 and 2.

Auerbach, A. J. and L. Kotlikoff, (1987), *Dynamic Fiscal Policy*, Cambridge University Press.

Blanchard, O. J. and S. Fischer, (1989), *Lectures on macroeconomics*, MIT Press, Cambridge, MA.

Bohn, H., (1997), Risk sharing in a stochastic overlapping generations economy, UCSB working paper.

De Nardi, M., S. İmrohoroğlu, and T. Sargent, (1998), Projected u.s. demographics and social security, Working Paper, University of Chicago.

Deaton, A. and C. Paxson, (1994), Intertepmoral choice and inequality, *Journal of Political Economy* 102, 437–467.

Diamond, P., (1965), National debt in a neo-classical growth model, *American Economic Review* 55, 1126–1150.

Feldstein, M., (1997), Transition to a fully funded pension system: Five economic issues, NBER working paper No 6149.

Geanakoplos, J., (1990), An introduction to general equilibrium with incomplete asset markets, *Journal of Mathemathical Economics* 19, 1–38.

Gertler, M., (1997), Government debt and social security in a life cycle economy, NBER working Paper No. 6000.

Huang, H., S. İmrohoroğlu, and T. J. Sargent, (1997), Two computational experiments to fund social security, *Macroeconomic Dynamics* 1, 7–74.

Hubbard, G. and K. Judd, (1987), Social security and individual welfare: precautionary savings, liquidity constraints and the payroll tax, *American Economic Review* 77, 630–646.

Huggett, M., (1996), Wealth distribution in life-cycle economies, *Journal of Monetary Economics* 38, 469–494.

Huggett, M. and A. Ventura, (1997), The distribution effects of social security, Unpublished Manuscript, ITAM.

Hurd, M. A., (1989), Mortality risks and bequests, *Econometrica* 57, 173–209.

İmrohoroğlu, A., S. İmrohoroğlu, and D. H. Joines, (1995), A life cycle analysis of social security, *Economic Theory* 6, 83–114.

İmrohoroğlu, A., S. İmrohoroğlu, and D. H. Joines, (1998), Social Security in an overlapping generations economy with land, Working Paper, Department of Finance, Marshall School of Business, University of South California.

Lucas, R. E., (1987), *Models of Business Cycles*, Basil Blackwell.

Ríos-Rull, J. V., (1994), On the quantitative importance of market completeness, *Journal of Monetary Economics* 34, 463–496.

Storesletten, K., C. I. Telmer, and A. Yaron, (1997), Consumption and risk sharing over the life cycle, GSIA working paper no. 1997-E228, Carnegie Mellon University.

Storesletten, K., C. I. Telmer, and A. Yaron, (1998), Asset pricing with idiosyncratic risk and overlapping generations, GSIA working paper no. 1998-E226, Carnegie Mellon University.

7 Asset Market Effects of the Baby Boom and Social Security Reform

Several articles in the popular press have linked the rise in U.S. stock prices in the 1990s to growing demand for financial assets as the Baby Boomers save for retirement. These accounts often warn that the Baby Boomers may earn returns on their retirement saving far below historical returns because they will have to sell their financial assets to a smaller generation of young investors.[1]

In the academic literature, however, there is little consensus on the asset market effects of the Baby Boom. For example, Poterba (2001a) finds little evidence of a robust empirical link between demographic change and real returns on financial assets in the United States and elsewhere. He concludes that a "market meltdown" is unlikely in the years ahead, especially because most investors do not abruptly sell off their financial assets once retired. In contrast, Abel (2001) argues that the Baby Boom may cause substantial movements in the real price of capital, even if agents have a bequest motive.

The building momentum for privatizing Social Security raises the question of how the transition should be financed. From an *ex post* perspective, a better understanding of which generations benefit from the asset market effects of the Baby Boom and which generations lose is key for the current policy debate over who should pay for the transition. From an *ex ante* perspective, some argue that a defined-benefit (DB) pension system may be optimal in terms of intergenerational insurance because it can offset movements in wages and asset returns that disadvantage large cohorts, by taxing smaller cohorts more heavily. In fact,

---

[1] For popular accounts on the possible link between the stock market and the age distribution, see Passell (1996), Colvin (1997), Sterling and Waite (1998), and Dent (1998).

Research Department, International Monetary Fund, 700 19th Street, NW, Washington, DC, 20431(e-mail: rbooks2@imf.org). This is an expanded version of the paper published in the *American Economic Papers & Proceedings,* May 2002, bearing the same title. Special thanks go to Christopher Sims. I am also grateful to Thomas Helbling, Ayhan Kose, Maya MacGuineas, Ashoka Mody, Kenichi Ueda, and participants at the January 2002 AEA session on "Social Security Reform" for their comments.

Bohn (2001) finds that adverse wage and asset return effects may be so large that, even with a DB system the size of Social Security and Medicare, the Baby Boomers are worse off in terms of welfare than smaller cohorts around them.

Against this background, this paper explores the quantitative impact of the Baby Boom on stock and bond returns. It augments a real business-cycle model with overlapping generations (OLG) and a portfolio decision over risky capital and safe bonds, which are in zero net supply. Agents live for four periods: childhood, young working age, old working age, and retirement. The model has two exogenous sources of uncertainty – technology shocks and population growth – both of which are calibrated to match long-run data for the United States. A numerical solution is obtained and used to simulate the asset market effects of past and projected changes in the U.S. population structure.

Before turning to the simulation results, it is natural to ask how the model compares to reality. A brief look at its asset-pricing implications provides some perspective. The model falls far short in matching the historical equity premium.[2] The lack of a substantial risk premium in the model is closely related to agents' portfolio behavior. Young workers short-sell the safe bond and invest in risky capital, whereas old workers invest most of their retirement savings in bonds. Agents behave this way because wages in the model are much less volatile than the return on capital, so that wage income effectively buffers consumption against adverse technology shocks. In retirement, agents no longer supply labor – their implicit holdings of the nontraded asset, human capital, are run down. As a result, old workers seek to reduce consumption risk in retirement by investing most of their financial wealth in bonds. On one level, this portfolio behavior is consistent with empirical evidence that U.S. households shift the composition of their financial wealth from risky to less risky assets as they approach retirement.[3] But, on another level, in the asset-pricing dimension, it means that the model fails to match the historical equity premium. This is because young workers, through their ability to freely short-sell bonds, are able to arbitrage into risky capital, which has the effect of raising the risk-free rate to just below the expected return on capital. Following Constantinides et al. (2002), Brooks (2003) extends the model

---

[2] Attempts to explain the equity premium in models with nontrivial production sectors have not been on the whole successful. Jermann (1998) finds that capital-adjustment costs and habit persistence in preferences can together generate a realistic equity premium and a reasonable risk-free rate. In the present model, in which every period approximates 20 years, adjustment costs to capital would be little more than a modeling device.

[3] This portfolio behavior – the shift toward bonds as agents approach retirement – parallels Jagannathan and Kocherlakota (1996). Storesletten, Telmer, and Yaron (2001) generate a U-shaped profile for bond holdings over the life-cycle, in an OLG model in which the volatility of persistent idiosyncratic shocks to wage income is negatively correlated with the return on risky capital. When they hold the volatility of idiosyncratic shocks constant, they generate a monotonically increasing bond portfolio share over the life-cycle, as in this paper. Yoo (1994) uses Survey of Consumer Finances (SCF) data to analyze age patterns in asset allocation. He finds that within each cross-section, the share of financial wealth in equities increases over the working life and declines after retirement. Poterba and Samwick (1997) find a similar hump-shaped pattern for equity holdings, again using SCF data.

to include exogenous borrowing constraints, which prevent young workers from short-selling bonds and capture well-recognized difficulties for young workers in collateralizing loans with future wages, for reasons of moral hazard and adverse selection. In this setting, young workers drop out of financial markets, forcing old workers to hold risky capital in retirement. This *constrained* model matches the historical equity premium because old workers demand a substantial premium to hold the risky asset in retirement.[4]

Does this mean that portfolio behavior in the *unconstrained* model – in particular, the ability of young workers to freely short-sell bonds – is unrealistic? Poterba (2001b) notes that stock market participation has been rising steadily, to a point where more than 50 percent of U.S. households now hold equity. A likely reason for this rise is financial innovation, which has been making it easier for households to borrow. Simultaneously, the equity premium is estimated to have fallen substantially over the last decade. This suggests that, going forward, the *unconstrained* model in this paper represents a useful benchmark in which to investigate the asset-market effects of the Baby Boom.

Turning now to the simulation results, the model predicts that the return Boomers can expect on their retirement savings will be around 100 basis points below the return to current retirees. This effect is driven by a rise in capital formation as the Baby Boomers save in preparation for retirement, which reduces both the expected return on capital and the risk-free rate. In addition, the model forecasts that the risk premium on capital will be about half its current level when the Baby Boomers retire. This is because the model estimates that the current risk premium is about triple its steady-state level, driven up by the fact that the Baby Boomers have relatively few children and, therefore, had only a limited desire to borrow in young working age. Because borrowing in the model generates the supply of safe bonds, and because current retirees want to hold as much of their retirement wealth in bonds as possible, the risk-free rate generated by the model is currently low relative to the return on capital to clear the bond market. The model predicts that, in the absence of further shocks to the birth rate, the risk premium on capital will return to its steady-state level in coming years.

The predicted 100 basis point decline in the return on the Baby Boomers' retirement savings is fairly small.[5] How to interpret the effect on the risk premium is complicated by the fact that the model does not match the historical equity premium. In absolute terms, the effect is small, with the risk premium falling from

---

[4] Brooks (2003) can be seen as an extension of Constantinides et al. (2002), who show that borrowing constraints generate a realistic equity premium in a partial equilibrium OLG model without production or demographic risk. Endogenous production is critical to capture the general equilibrium effects on capital formation and asset returns of demographic change.

[5] This magnitude is consistent with the existing literature. For example, Börsch-Supan and Winter (2001) use population forecasts to project the capital-labor ratio and, hence, the real return on capital in a perfect foresight OLG model. They generate a decline in the real return on capital for Germany of around 100 basis points and around 20 basis points for the OECD countries as a whole.

a current level of 27 basis points to 17 basis points in the years ahead. Controlling for the lack of sufficient volatility in the model, the effects are quite large however. The Sharpe ratio of the model's risk premium rises from 22 percent in steady state to a current level of 47 percent, before falling to a predicted 30 percent when the Baby Boomers retire. Compared to a Sharpe ratio for the historical equity premium of around 40 percent, these effects are not insignificant.

Even though the Boomers are forecast to earn returns on retirement saving about 100 basis points below current returns, the simulation reveals that they are nonetheless better off in terms of lifetime consumption than their parents or children. This is because asset returns move in Boomers' favor during their working lives and because they have relatively few children, which boosts their consumption and ability to save early on. Together, these effects outweigh the impact of poor asset returns in retirement.[6]

In terms of the current debate over social security reform, this result questions the apparent political consensus to exempt the pension benefits of those retiring soon, some of the older Baby Boomers among them, from helping to finance the transition from the current system through benefit cuts. In addition, the Baby Boomers are better off even in a model without DB social security, though the margin by which they are better off declines. This suggests that defined-contribution social security, in which benefits rather than payroll taxes move to balance the system, may in fact be optimal in terms of intergenerational insurance.

The paper is structured as follows. Section 7.1 introduces the model, and Section 7.2 discusses its calibration. Section 7.3 presents the results. Section 7.4 concludes.

7.1 The Model

The representative agent lives for four periods: childhood, young working age, old working age, and retirement. In childhood, agents are not active decision makers and depend on their parents for consumption. In young working age, agents supply labor inelastically. Out of after-tax wages, they consume for themselves and their children and make a portfolio decision over risky capital and safe bonds, which are in zero net supply. In old working age, agents again supply labor inelastically. They earn returns on their savings in addition to the after-tax wage and consume only for themselves, their children having left the household. They also decide on what mix of stocks and bonds to hold going into retirement. In retirement, agents no longer supply labor and consume down their savings, there being no bequests. They receive a retirement benefit, which is financed out of payroll taxes levied on the workforce.

---

[6] Bohn (2001) uses a three-period OLG model with childhood, working age, and retirement to show that movements in the capital-labor ratio generally disadvantage large cohorts. His result is robust to the inclusion of a DB social security system, provided that the pension system is not unrealistically large. This model differs from Bohn's principally in that it incorporates an additional working period and a risk-free asset, which allows workers to supply capital in addition to supplying labor.

More formally, the representative young worker in period t maximizes expected lifetime utility in (7.1) subject to the budget constraints in young working age (7.2), old working age (7.3), and retirement (7.4).

$$V_t = \lambda(1+n_t)\frac{\left(c_t^0\right)^{1-\theta}}{1-\theta} + \frac{\left(c_t^1\right)^{1-\theta}}{1-\theta} + \beta E_t\left[\frac{\left(c_{t+1}^2\right)^{1-\theta}}{1-\theta}\right] + \beta^2 E_t\left[\frac{\left(c_{t+2}^3\right)^{1-\theta}}{1-\theta}\right]$$

$$\tag{7.1}$$

$$(1+n_t)c_t^0 + c_t^1 + s_{et}^1 + s_{bt}^1 = w_t(1-\eta_t) \tag{7.2}$$

$$c_{t+1}^2 + s_{et+1}^2 + s_{bt+1}^2 = w_{t+1}(1-\eta_{t+1}) + (1+r_{et+1})s_{et}^1 + (1+r_{ft})s_{bt}^1 \tag{7.3}$$

$$c_{t+2}^3 = (1+r_{et+2})s_{et+1}^1 + (1+r_{ft+1})s_{bt+1}^1 + bw_{t+2} \tag{7.4}$$

Young workers care about their children's consumption c_t^0 with a discount factor λ but do not have a bequest motive.[7] β reflects their subjective rate of time preference, whereas θ is their coefficient of relative risk aversion. Young workers determine their own consumption c_t^1, that of their children $(1+n_t)c_t^0$, and make a portfolio decision over risky capital (s_{et}^1) and safe bonds (s_{bt}^1). When making this portfolio decision, the period $t+1$ bond return is known at t and is denoted r_{ft}. In contrast, the return on capital is not observed until period $t+1$ and is, therefore, denoted r_{et+1}. Young workers' disposable income is $w_t(1-\eta_t)$, where η_t is the payroll tax rate. In old working age, agents receive a return on their portfolio of financial assets, selected in young working age, in addition to the after-tax wage. In retirement, they receive a retirement benefit, which is determined by the exogenous replacement rate b.

Output is generated by a constant-returns-to-scale neoclassical production function. Factor markets are efficient so that capital and labor are rewarded their marginal products:

$$r_{et} = \alpha A_t K_{t-1}^{\alpha-1} L_t^{1-\alpha} - \delta \tag{7.5}$$

$$w_t = (1-\alpha)A_t K_{t-1}^{\alpha} L_t^{-\alpha} \tag{7.6}$$

δ is the depreciation rate and α determines the share of output rewarded to capital. The age distribution in period t consists of N_{t-1} young workers, N_{t-2} old workers, and N_{t-3} retirees. The period t child cohort is determined by $N_t = (1+n_t)N_{t-1}$, where n_t represents cohort growth. The labor force is given by $L_t = N_{t-1} + N_{t-2}$, whereas the period $t+1$ capital stock is determined by the stock-holding decision of young and old workers in period t:

$$K_t = N_{t-1}s_{et}^1 + N_{t-2}s_{et}^2 \tag{7.7}$$

---

[7] This specification of preferences is adopted from Higgins and Williamson (1996) and is similar to Bohn (2001).

The risk-free rate r_{ft} moves to satisfy the equilibrium condition that bonds are in zero net supply across generations:

$$0 = N_{t-1}s^1_{bt} + N_{t-2}s^2_{bt} \tag{7.8}$$

The model abstracts from government activity with the exception of a pay-as-you-go social security system. Given an exogenous replacement rate b, payroll taxes move to balance the pension system, rising with the retiree-to-worker ratio: $\eta_t = bN_{t-3}/(N_{t-1} + N_{t-2})$. Effectively, this is a DB pension system where the retirement benefit to period t retirees is indexed to period t wages.[8]

The model has two exogenous sources of aggregate uncertainty: a technology shock A_t and cohort size N_t. Both are assumed to follow lognormal AR (7.1) processes such that:

$$\begin{bmatrix} \ln A_t \\ \ln N_t \end{bmatrix} = \begin{bmatrix} c_1 \\ c_2 \end{bmatrix} + \begin{bmatrix} a_{11} & a_{12} \\ a_{21} & a_{22} \end{bmatrix} \begin{bmatrix} \ln A_{t-1} \\ \ln N_{t-1} \end{bmatrix} + \begin{bmatrix} \varepsilon^a_t \\ \varepsilon^n_t \end{bmatrix} \tag{7.9}$$

where $\varepsilon_t = [\varepsilon^a_t, \varepsilon^n_t]$ is a two-dimensional i.i.d. process that is $N(0, \Sigma)$.

7.2 Calibration

The model is calibrated so that each period represents about 20 years. The subjective discount factor β and the discount factor applied to the utility of children λ are each set at 0.44, which corresponds to an annual rate of 0.96. The relative risk-aversion parameter θ equals 2. The share of output rewarded to capital α is 0.33, while depreciation occurs at 5 percent per year so that $\delta = 0.65$. b is chosen so that the payroll tax rate is 15 percent in equilibrium. This implies a replacement rate of 30 percent.[9]

As noted earlier, the model has two exogenous sources of aggregate uncertainty: total factor productivity A_t and cohort size N_t. The role of the former is to differentiate the risky from the riskless asset, while the latter captures the risk that agents may be born into a large or small cohort. Figure 7.1 plots the U.S. population between ages 0 and 19 for the period 1880 to 2040, whereas Figure 7.2 plots historical data for U.S. total factor productivity (TFP) over the period 1880 to 2000. Both series are centered 20-year averages and rebased to eliminate scale differences.

---

[8] This Social Security system is modeled after Bohn (2001), who shows that a DB system is more efficient *ex ante* in insuring agents against demographic risk. Neither a defined-contribution system (where η is exogenous and b endogenous) nor a privatized pension system ($b = \eta = 0$) impose higher taxes on the young when the retiree-to-worker ratio rises, whereas the DB system does. In testing the sensitivity of the asset market implications of the model, a DB specification is, therefore, more interesting.

[9] Bohn (2001) calibrates his pension system to have a payroll tax rate of 15 percent. Estimates for the average replacement rate of actual social security benefits vary. Aaron et al. (2001), for example, report an average replacement rate of 42 percent.

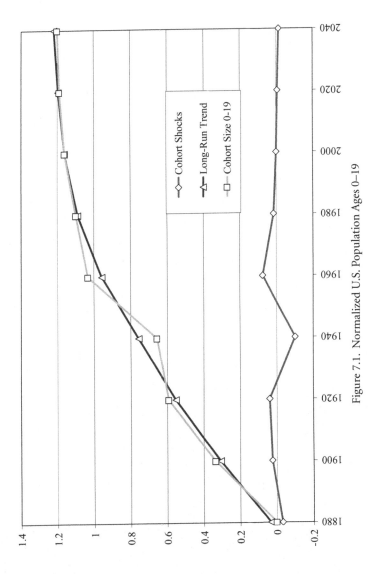

Figure 7.1. Normalized U.S. Population Ages 0–19

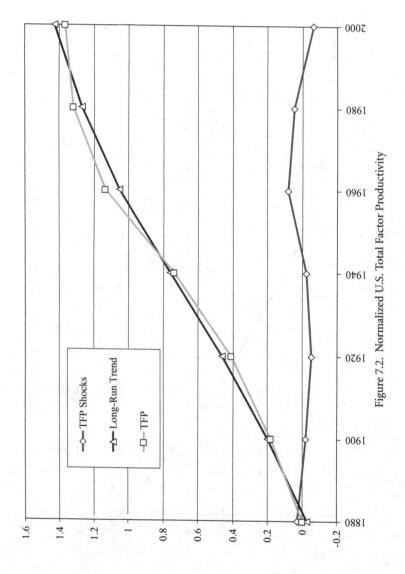

Figure 7.2. Normalized U.S. Total Factor Productivity

Annualized cohort growth has fallen steadily from 2 percent in the 1880 period to 0.4 percent in 1980. This decline in cohort growth reflects a long-run trend toward lower fertility, which is forecast to continue and cause the U.S. population to stabilize around 2040. Figure 7.1 shows that the postwar Baby Boom follows a prewar baby bust in 1940 and is followed in turn by a postwar baby bust. During the prewar baby bust, annualized cohort growth fell sharply from 1.3 percent around 1920 to 0.3 percent as households postponed having children because of the Great Depression and World War II. The postwar Baby Boom thus represents a catching up, with annualized cohort growth rising to an annualized rate of 1.9 percent in the period around 1960, before resuming its long-run trend toward declining fertility, exacerbated temporarily by the postwar baby bust. Figure 7.2 shows that long-run TFP has followed a wavelike pattern, as noted by Gordon (2000).[10]

Because the model is stationary, cohort size is defined relative to a long-run trend, which is approximated here through a nonlinear trend that captures the long-run decline in fertility. Figure 7.1 shows the detrended population series, which clearly captures the prewar baby bust in 1940, the Baby Boom in 1960, and the postwar baby bust in 1980. Figure 7.2 depicts a similar long-run trend for the TFP series, along with the detrended series.[11]

The most serious challenge to the calibration is the estimation of the unconditional moments for the exogenous shocks. With each period representing approximately 20 years, even a century-long time series provides only five nonoverlapping observations. Against this background, bivariate first-order autoregressions in the detrended series suggest that TFP and cohort shocks are of roughly equal magnitude at long horizons. Setting to zero all estimates that are not significantly different from zero, the second-moment matrix for the shocks is:

$$\Sigma = \begin{bmatrix} 0.07^2 & 0.00 \\ 0.00 & 0.07^2 \end{bmatrix} \tag{7.10}$$

The bivariate first-order regressions also suggest that productivity shocks are more persistent, whereas population shocks are almost uncorrelated over time. a_{11} is,

[10] Both series are rebased from one and shown in natural logs to eliminate scale differences. Annual U.S. population data are spliced together from three sources. Historical data are taken from "Historical Statistics of the United States: Colonial Times to 1970," published by the U.S. Bureau of the Census. For the period 1950 to 1990, data are taken from the United Nations "World Population Prospects: The 1992 Revision." From 1995 on, data are from the World Bank "World Population Projections: The 1994–95 Edition." Historical TFP data are spliced together from Kendrick (1961) and Jorgenson and Stiroh (1999). This annual series goes from 1869 to 1996, so that the period 2000 TFP observation only represents six annual observations.

[11] The long-run trend depicted is generated using the Hodrick-Prescott filter, with the value of the smoothing parameter determined endogenously to capture a very long-run trend. For the population series, this implied a smoothing parameter of one, to capture the curvature of the series implied by the long-run fertility decline. Because the TFP series is approximately trend stationary, the value for the smoothing parameter was not as important. A value of 1 was chosen for consistency with the population series.

therefore, set to 0.5 below, whereas a_{22} is set to zero. All other parameters are set to zero in the simulation because they do not differ significantly from zero in the regressions.

7.3 Simulating the Asset Market Effects of the Baby Boom

The model is solved numerically using the parameterized expectations approach (PEA) of Den Haan and Marcet (1990), by parameterizing agents' period $t + 1$ conditional expectations as polynomials of the period t state variables, and using Monte Carlo simulations to solve for the coefficients, such that the forecast error is orthogonalized on information at t. The computational appendix contains a detailed explanation of this solution method.

Before turning to the simulation results, it is natural to ask how the model compares to reality. A brief look at its asset-pricing implications provides some perspective. The model generates a risk premium on capital over the risk-free rate of 0.13 percent annualized, compared with 8.9 percent per annum for the excess return of the S&P 500 over U.S. Treasury Bills.[12] One reason why the model fails to match the historical equity premium is that the risky asset differs in an important way from equity. Risky capital is a composite asset that aggregates over different claims on productive capital such as stocks and corporate bonds. As a result, it is not a levered asset, unlike equity, and, therefore, not risky enough. Allowing for this, following Storesletten et al. (2001), the Sharpe ratio for the risk premium on capital amounts to 22 percent in the stochastic steady state, compared to 40 percent for the historical equity premium. Thus, even in risk-adjusted terms, the model falls short in matching the historical equity premium.

An important reason for this is that the model generates portfolio behavior whereby young workers short-sell the safe bond and invest in risky capital, whereas old workers invest most of their retirement savings in bonds. Young workers' ability to freely short-sell bonds allows them to arbitrage into risky capital, which has the effect of raising the risk-free rate to just below the expected return on capital. Following Constantinides et al. (2002), Brooks (2003) extends the model to include borrowing constraints, which prevent young workers from borrowing against future wage income by short-selling bonds and capture well recognized difficulties for the young in collateralizing loans with future wages, for reasons of moral hazard and adverse selection. In this setting, young workers drop out of financial markets, forcing old workers to hold risky capital in retirement. This *constrained* model matches the historical equity premium because old workers demand a substantial premium to hold the risky asset in retirement.

---

[12] Stock and bond market data are taken from Ibbotson Associates (2001). Table 4-1 presents annual inflation-adjusted returns for the S&P 500 and U.S. Treasury Bills for the period 1926–2000. Arithmetic means are used to compute sample average returns on both assets.

Does this mean that portfolio behavior in the *unconstrained* model – in particular, the ability of young workers to freely short-sell bonds – is unrealistic? Poterba (2001) notes that stock-market participation has been rising steadily, to a point at which more than 50 percent of U.S. households now hold equity. A likely reason for this rise is financial innovation, which has been making it easier for households to borrow. Simultaneously, the equity premium is estimated to have fallen substantially over the last decade. This suggests that, going forward, the *unconstrained* model in this paper represents a useful benchmark in which to investigate the asset-market effects of the Baby Boom.

Against this background, the discussion now turns to simulating the asset-market effects of the Baby Boom. As suggested by Figure 7.1, key changes in the U.S. age distribution consist broadly of a pre–World War II baby bust, the postwar Baby Boom, and a subsequent baby bust. In the simulation, the prewar baby bust occurs in the 1940 period when the child cohort is 10 percent smaller than its parent cohort, which is in steady state, as are all older cohorts. The Baby Boom occurs in 1960, when the child cohort is 10 percent larger than in steady state. In 1980, the postwar baby bust brings the size of the child cohort back to steady state, where it stays thereafter. This population shift is calibrated to closely match past and projected population changes, although it assumes that the age distribution is in steady state before and after the transition. Figure 7.3 plots the size of the child cohort over this bust-boom-bust, and Figure 7.4 plots the annualized expected returns on risky capital and the safe bond, conditional on this population shift.[13]

Returns on both assets remain in steady state in 1940 because both capital and labor are predetermined. However, the prewar baby bust reduces youth dependency below steady state. Young workers' per-capita consumption in 1940 rises, as does their ability to save. The resulting rise in capital formation, together with the decline in the labor force, pushes the capital-labor ratio 6 percent above steady state in 1960, driving returns on both assets below steady state. The birth of the Baby Boomers in 1960 raises youth dependency sharply. Young workers seek to offset the impact on consumption and investment by issuing bonds. In fact, their desire to borrow exceeds demand for bonds by old workers and, in 1980, the risk-free rate rises by more than the return on capital, which is driven up as the capital-labor ratio falls below steady state. During 1980, the Boomer cohort has a small number of children (the postwar baby bust). This decline in youth

---

[13] The returns in Figure 7.4 are generated by using the approximation to agents' decision rules at convergence to simulate the same population shift 3,000 times, each time for a new TFP shock sequence. Averaging across simulations generates expected returns on both assets, conditional on the population shift. The Baby Boom in the simulation occurs in 1960 because of the way the data are aggregated into 20-year averages. The results are qualitatively unchanged for different aggregations of the data. Annualized mean returns in Figure 7.4 are constructed as $100 \times [(1 + \mu^{20})^{(1/20)} - 1]$, where μ^{20} are the arithmetic means of the 20-year holding-period returns.

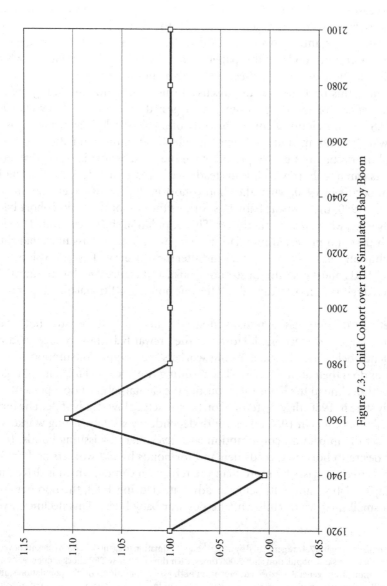

Figure 7.3. Child Cohort over the Simulated Baby Boom

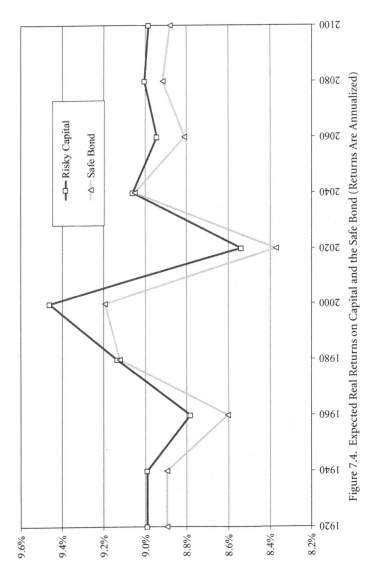

Figure 7.4. Expected Real Returns on Capital and the Safe Bond (Returns Are Annualized)

dependency raises Boomers' per-capita consumption, which reduces their desire to borrow below demand by old workers. As a result, the risk-free rate in 2000 remains almost unchanged from 1980, even as the return on capital rises still further, driven up by a capital-labor ratio that is 13 percent below steady state. During 2000, the Baby Boomers want to invest in bonds for retirement. This generates a large demand for bonds, whereas young workers in 2000 are eager to borrow against higher after-tax wages in 2020. This combination of eager lenders and willing borrowers causes capital formation to rise, which – together with the exit of the Boomers from the workforce – raises the capital-labor ratio 15 percent above steady state in 2020. This drives returns on stocks and bonds 92 and 82 basis points, respectively, below their 2000 levels, and 47 and 55 basis points, respectively, below steady state. Beyond 2020, the age distribution gradually returns to steady state, as do asset returns.

Overall, Baby Boomers earn returns on retirement saving about 100 basis points below current returns. In terms of lifetime consumption, however, Figure 7.6 shows that they are 2.3 percent better off than if the age distribution had remained in steady state, whereas their parents and children are 3.3 and 2.3 percent worse off, respectively.[14] This reflects the fact that, by shorting the riskless asset, workers in the model are able to supply capital in addition to labor. It turns out that the expected return on this levered portfolio, the risk premium on capital, moves to benefit Boomers so that, unlike in Bohn (2001), asset returns do not move against large cohorts consistently. In addition, the model captures the fact that the Baby Boomers have relatively few children, which boosts their per-capita consumption and ability to save early on. Together, these effects more than offset the impact of poor asset returns in retirement. Of course, the fact that the Boomers do better than their parents or offspring could be because of the DB pension system, which dampens the decline in after-tax wages over their working lives. However, even without Social Security, they come out ahead, although the margin by which they do so declines.

Over the simulation period, the risk premium on capital rises from near zero in 1980 to about triple its steady-state level in 2000, driven up by the fact that the Baby Boomers have relatively few children and, therefore, only a limited desire to borrow as young adults. The model predicts that, in the absence of further shocks to the birth rate, the observed risk premium will fall to half its current level by the time the Boomers retire, as it returns toward steady state in coming years. Mapping these effects on the risk premium into reality is complicated by the fact that the model does not match the historical equity premium. As noted earlier,

---

[14] The deviations in Figure 7.6 are given by generation at year of birth so that, for example, the Baby Boomers' deviation from steady state is in the 1960 column. Figure 7.5 complements Figure 7.6, showing the consumption responses in percent deviation from steady state by age and generation. Figure 7.5 shows consumption deviations by year of birth for each generation in each age bracket (relative to steady-state consumption in that age bracket); that is, 1940 for the prewar baby bust, 1960 for the postwar Baby Boom, and 1980 for the postwar baby bust.

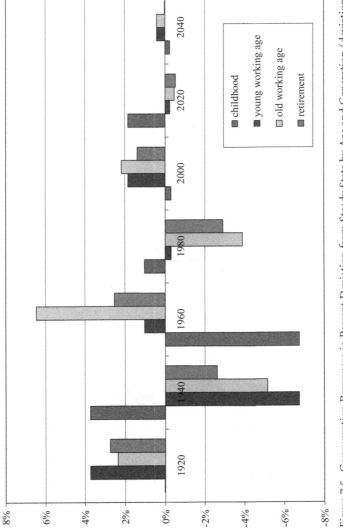

Figure 7.5. Consumption Responses in Percent Deviation from Steady State by Age and Generation (deviations shown by year of birth: prewar bust, 1940; postwar Boom, 1960; postwar bust, 1980)

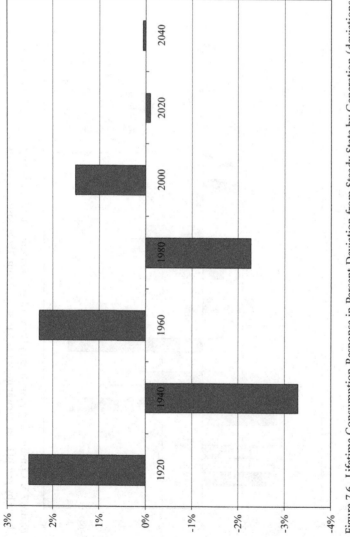

Figure 7.6. Lifetime Consumption Response in Percent Deviation from Steady State by Generation (deviations shown by year of birth: prewar bust, 1940; postwar Boom, 1960; postwar bust, 1980)

this is partly because the model fails to generate returns on capital that are sufficiently volatile, compared with historical data on real equity returns. Adjusting for this, the risk premium effects are quite large. The Sharpe ratio of the model's risk premium rises from 22 percent in steady state to a current level of 47 percent, before falling to a predicted 30 percent when the Baby Boomers retire. Compared to a Sharpe ratio for the historical equity premium of around 40 percent, these effects are quite large.

From a policy perspective, this result is important because the transition costs of different reform proposals are typically evaluated taking the historical equity premium as given. But, because demographic change may affect the equity premium going forward, this approach may misrepresent the true cost of reform.

7.4 Conclusion

Even though Baby Boomers can expect returns on retirement saving about 100 basis points below current returns, this does not imply that they will be worse off than their parents or children. In fact, the general equilibrium analysis in this paper shows that they will be better off, a result that obtains with or without a DB pension system calibrated to match the size of social security and Medicare. From an *ex ante* perspective, this suggests that the ability of DB social security to offset movements in the capital-labor ratio that go against large cohorts may be overrated in practice, especially given the likely welfare loss from the crowding out of private capital formation. From an *ex post* perspective, this result questions the apparent political consensus to exempt the benefits of older Baby Boomers who are near retirement from reform.

An important caveat to these results is that the model does not match the historical equity premium. As discussed earlier, this stems from the ability of young workers to freely short-sell bonds and arbitrage into risky capital, which raises the risk-free rate to just under the expected return on capital. Following Constantinides et al. (2002), Brooks (2003) extends this model to include borrowing constraints, which prevent young workers from borrowing against future wages by shorting bonds. This *constrained* model generates a substantial risk premium on capital because, young workers being unable to short-sell bonds, old workers are forced to hold risky capital going into retirement and demand a substantial risk premium to compensate them for the additional risk.[15] It is possible that the asset market and welfare effects of the Baby Boom are different, and possibly much larger, in this *constrained* setting that more closely resembles historical data. This question is left for future research.

[15] For a similar parameterization, the *constrained* model generates a risk premium on capital of close to 3 percent per annum, which is the benchmark that Constantinides et al. (2002) argue models with only aggregate capital (rather than levered equity) should match.

COMPUTATIONAL APPENDIX

Maximizing expected utility, period t young workers choose c_t^0, c_t^1, s_{et}^1, and s_{bt}^1, such that

$$c_t^0 = \lambda^{1/\theta} c_t^1 \tag{7.A.1}$$

$$\left(c_t^1\right)^{-\theta} = \beta E_t \left\lfloor \left(c_{t+1}^2\right)^{-\theta} (1 + r_{et+1}) \right\rfloor \tag{7.A.2}$$

$$\left(c_t^1\right)^{-\theta} = \beta (1 + r_{ft}) E_t \left\lfloor \left(c_{t+1}^2\right)^{-\theta} \right\rfloor \tag{7.A.3}$$

$$(1 + n_t) c_t^0 + c_t^1 + s_{et}^1 + s_{bt}^1 = w_t (1 - \eta_t) \tag{7.A.4}$$

are satisfied, taking factor returns and the return on the riskless asset as given. Period t old workers choose c_t^2, s_{et}^2, and s_{bt}^2 such that

$$\left(c_t^2\right)^{-\theta} = \beta E_t \left\lfloor \left(c_{t+1}^3\right)^{-\theta} (1 + r_{et+1}) \right\rfloor \tag{7.A.5}$$

$$\left(c_t^2\right)^{-\theta} = \beta (1 + r_{ft}) E_t \left\lfloor \left(c_{t+1}^3\right)^{-\theta} \right\rfloor \tag{7.A.6}$$

$$c_t^2 + s_{et}^2 + s_{bt}^2 = w_t (1 - \eta_t) + (1 + r_{et}) s_{et-1}^1 + (1 + r_{ft-1}) s_{bt-1}^1 \tag{7.A.7}$$

are satisfied, again taking factor returns and the return on the riskless asset as given. Consumption of the period t retiree cohort is given by:

$$c_t^3 = (1 + r_{et}) s_{et-1}^2 + (1 + r_{ft-1}) s_{bt-1}^2 + b w_t \tag{7.A.8}$$

(7.A.1) through (7.A.8) represent a system of eight equations that characterize individual consumption (c_t^0, c_t^1, c_t^2, c_t^3) and investment behavior (s_{et}^1, s_{bt}^1, s_{et}^2, s_{bt}^2) for given wage and return distributions. In equilibrium, consumption and investment decision rules that maximize expected utility at the individual level must be consistent with the equilibrium conditions for the stock and bond markets.

The model has only two active decision makers: young and old workers. Both make their consumption-investment decision based on total wealth, which for young workers is simply after-tax wage income.

$$w_t^1 = w_t (1 - \eta_t) \tag{7.A.9}$$

Total wealth of old workers consists of the after-tax wage, in addition to stock and bond holdings plus returns.

$$w_t^2 = w_t (1 - \eta_t) + (1 + r_{et}) s_{et-1}^1 + (1 + r_{ft-1}) s_{bt-1}^1 \tag{7.A.10}$$

w_t^1 and w_t^2 are the distribution of wealth across working-age cohorts and are endogenous state variables. In addition, the age distribution with the exception of the retiree cohort, which will not live to see the next period, represents an exogenous state variable. Given that the TFP shock is serially correlated, the set of period t state variables is given by:

$$\Theta_t = \left\lfloor w_t^1, w_t^2, N_t, N_{t-1}, N_{t-2}, A_t \right\rfloor \tag{7.A.11}$$

Using the PEA to replace the conditional expectations in (7.A.2), (7.A.3), (7.A.5), and (7.A.6) with polynomials in the state variables yields:

$$\left(c_t^1\right)^{-\theta} = \beta \Psi(\Theta_t, \tau) \tag{7.A.12}$$

$$\left(c_t^1\right)^{-\theta} \left(s_{et}^1\right)^2 = \beta(1 + r_{ft})\Omega(\Theta_t, \gamma) \tag{7.A.13}$$

$$\left(c_t^2\right)^{-\theta} = \beta \Lambda(\Theta_t, \xi) \tag{7.A.14}$$

$$\left(c_t^2\right)^{-\theta} (s_{et}^2)^2 = \beta(1 + r_{ft})\Gamma(\Theta_t, \omega) \tag{7.A.15}$$

It is worth noting that the expectations in (7.A.13) and (7.A.16) have not been parameterized in the traditional manner. Both equations have been multiplied by functions of the respective equity holdings. This modification is based on Marcet and Singleton (1999) and addresses an indeterminacy in the system of Euler equations and aggregate equilibrium conditions that arises in models that solve for equilibrium holdings of two or more assets.

Given two sequences of length T for the technology shock and the age distribution, assuming starting values for w_t^1 and w_t^2, and given values for τ, γ, ξ, and ω, it is then possible to solve out the model for T periods. The PEA begins with exactly this step. It draws two sequences of length T for the technology shock and the age distribution and solves out the model for the T periods. The PEA then turns to fitting the conditional expectations in (7.A.2), (7.A.3), (7.A.5), and (7.A.6), solving for the coefficients in the polynomial approximations that minimize the mean squared error between the actual realization in $t + 1$ and the expectation at t of that realization based on Θ_t. The particular version of the PEA implemented here proceeds in a step-by-step approach. Fitting the conditional expectation in (7.A.12), a nonlinear least squares estimation for τ is performed:

$$\min_{\tau} \frac{1}{T-1} \sum_{t=1}^{T-1} \left[\left(c_{t+1}^2\right)^{-\theta} (1 + r_{et+1}) - \Psi(\Theta_t, \tau)\right]^2 \tag{7.A.16}$$

At the n'th iteration, a new value τ_{n+1} is generated according to $\tau_{n+1} = \lambda\tau_n + (1 - \lambda)\tau_e$ where τ_e is the estimate for τ from the nonlinear least squares estimation. Given τ_{n+1}, γ_n, ξ_n, and ω_n, the system is solved out again for T periods and the algorithm proceeds to fit the other conditional expectations in turn. This procedure is repeated until the algorithm reaches a fixed point in τ, γ, ξ, and ω. Rather than performing a computationally expensive nonlinear least squares estimation to find τ_e, the paper takes a first-order approximation of $\Psi(\Theta_t, \tau_n)$ around τ_n following Den Haan and Marcet (1990). Rearranging terms τ_e is then the coefficient vector in an OLS regression.

The functional form for Ψ is chosen as $\exp(f(w_t^1, w_t^2, \ln N_t, \ln N_{t-1}, \ln N_{t-2}, \ln A_t; \psi))$. The simulation results in the paper are for a second-order polynomial approximation without cross terms, so that 13 coefficients are estimated per Euler equation. Solving the model with higher-order terms is difficult using this solution method because of multicollinearity problems. Brooks (2003) confirms that the results are consistent with higher-order approximations, using a projection-based method following Judd (1998) and Chebychev polynomials in the parameterized expectations to mitigate multicollinearity problems.

REFERENCES

Aaron, Henry, Allan Blinder, Alicia Munnell, and Peter Orszag. 2001. "Perspectives on the Draft Interim Report of the President's Commission to Strengthen Social Security." Unpublished manuscript.

Abel, Andrew. 2001. "Will Bequests Attenuate the Predicted Meltdown in Stock Prices When Baby Boomers Retire?" *Review of Economics and Statistics* 83(4): 589–95.

Bohn, Henning. 2001. "Social Security and Demographic Uncertainty: The Risk-Sharing Properties of Alternative Policies." In J. Y. Campbell and M. Feldstein (eds.), *Risk Aspects of Investment-Based Social Security Reform*. Chicago: University of Chicago Press, pp. 203–41.

Börsch-Supan, Axel, and Joachim Winter. 2001. "Population Aging, Savings Behavior, and Capital Markets." NBER Working Paper 8561.

Brooks, Robin. 2003. "The Equity Premium and the Baby Boom." Unpublished manuscript. International Monetary Fund, Washington, DC.

Colvin, Geoff. 1997. "How to Beat the Boomer Rush." *Fortune*, August 18, pp. 59–63.

Constantinides, George, John Donaldson, and Rajnish Mehra. 2002. "Junior Can't Borrow: A New Perspective on the Equity Premium Puzzle." *Quarterly Journal of Economics* 117(1): 269–96.

Den Haan, Wouter, and Albert Marcet. 1990. "Solving the Stochastic Growth Model by Parameterizing Expectations." *Journal of Business & Economic Statistics* 8: 31–4.

Dent, Harry S., Jr. 1998. *The Roaring 2000s*. New York: Simon and Schuster.

Gordon, J. 2000. "Interpreting the One Big Wave in U.S. Long-Term Productivity Growth." In Bart van Ark, Simon Kuipers, and Gerard Kuper (eds.), *Productivity, Technology, and Economic Growth*. Boston, MA: Kluwer Publishers, pp. 19–65.

Higgins, Matthew, and Jeffrey Williamson. 1996. "Asian Demography and Foreign Capital Dependence." NBER Working Paper 5560.

Ibbotson Associates. 1999. "Stocks, Bonds, Bills, and Inflation: 1999 Yearbook."

Jagannathan, R., and N. Kocherlakota. 1996. "Why Should Older People Invest Less in Stocks than Younger People?" *Federal Reserve Bank of Minneapolis Quarterly Review*, 11–23.

Jorgenson, D., and K. Stiroh. 1999. "Information Technology and Growth." *American Economic Review* 89(2): 109–15.

Judd, Kenneth. 1998. "Numerical Methods in Economics." Cambridge, MA: MIT Press.

Kendrick, J. 1961. *Productivity Trends in the United States*. Princeton, NJ: Princeton University Press.

Marcet, A., and K. Singleton. 1999. "Equilibrium Asset Prices and Savings of Heterogeneous Agents in the Presence of Incomplete Markets and Portfolio Constraints." *Macroeconomic Dynamics* 3: 243–77.

Passell, Peter. 1996. "The Year Is 2010. Do You Know Where Your Bull Is?" *New York Times* (March 10), Section 3, 1–6.

Poterba, James. 2001a. "Demographic Structure and Asset Returns." *Review of Economics and Statistics* 83(4): 565–84.

Poterba, James. 2001b. "The Rise of the Equity Culture: U.S. Stock Ownership Patterns, 1989–1998." Unpublished manuscript. Cambridge, MA: MIT.

Poterba, James, and Andrew Samwick. 1997. "Household Portfolio Allocation Over the Life-Cycle." National Bureau of Economic Research Working Paper 6185.

Sterling, William, and Stephen Waite. 1998. *Boomernomics: The Future of Your Money in the Upcoming Generational Warfare.* New York: Balantine Publishing Group.

Storesletten, K., C. Telmer, and A. Yaron. 2001. "Asset Pricing with Idiosyncratic Risk and Overlapping Generations." Unpublished manuscript.

Yoo, Peter. 1994. "Age Distributions and Returns of Financial Assets." Federal Reserve Bank of St. Louis Working Paper 94-002B.

8 Demographic Structure and Asset Returns

The Baby Boom generation, those born in roughly the two decades following World War II, has had and will continue to have important effects on the U.S. economy. In its youth, this group placed high demands on infrastructure for education and other types of training. The entry of this large cohort into the labor market may have been associated with an increase in the aggregate unemployment rate. The Baby Boom cohort is now in its prime earning years, and it will begin to reach retirement age in just over a decade. Concern has now begun to focus on the preparations that this cohort has made for retirement and on the burden that this cohort will place on government programs such as Social Security and Medicare.

How the aging of the Baby Boom will affect financial markets is an important issue for assessing whether this cohort is saving enough for retirement. Popular accounts, such as Passell (1996), Sterling and Waite (1998), and Dent (1998), sometimes suggest that the rise in U.S. stock prices during the 1990s was partly attributable to the growing demand for financial assets as Baby Boomers began to save for retirement. Demographic explanations for recent share-price movements are typically accompanied by a warning about what may happen in the future, when the Baby Boomers reach retirement age and begin to draw down their wealth. Siegel (1998, 41) summarizes this argument when he writes, "The words 'Sell? Sell to whom?' might haunt the Baby Boomers in the next century. Who are the buyers of the trillions of dollars of Boomer assets? The [Baby Boomer generation] . . . threatens to drown in financial assets. The consequences could be disastrous not only for the Boomers' retirement but also for the economic health of the entire population." Schieber and Shoven (1997) develop the same argument in their analysis of the link between demographic structure and the pattern of inflows and outflows from defined-benefit pension plans. Although cautious, they nevertheless suggest that "when the pension system begins to be a net seller [of assets] . . . in the third decade of the next century . . . this could depress asset prices, particularly since the demographic structure of the United States does not differ that greatly from Japan and Europe..." (p. 25).

Although the potential link between demographic structure and asset returns is widely discussed, there have been few systematic studies of the historical relationship between asset prices, population age structure, and asset returns. This paper presents new empirical evidence on these links. It focuses on the returns on Treasury bills, long-term government bonds, and corporate stock in the United States over the last three quarters of a century, and it also presents some evidence from Canada and the United Kingdom. It considers how the level of asset prices, as well as the returns earned by investors, has varied with shifting demographic structure.

The paper is divided into seven sections. The first develops a stylized model indicating how demographic changes can affect rates of return on various assets, and it summarizes previous theoretical research on demographic structure and asset returns. The second section describes the age structure of asset holdings in the current U.S. economy. It considers the age pattern of net worth, net financial assets, and corporate stock holdings. This section also describes the historical and prospective age structure of the U.S. population. Section 3 summarizes previous empirical research on the links between demographic structure and asset returns.

The fourth section presents the core empirical findings on the time-series relationships between returns and population age structure. The results do not suggest any robust patterns linking demographic structure and asset returns. This finding for the United States is supported by analysis of data from the United Kingdom and Canada. Section 5 combines information from the age structure of asset demands, and from the changing age structure of the population over time, to create a "predicted asset demand" variable that can be related to both asset returns and the level of asset prices. This analysis yields some evidence that higher asset demand is associated with higher asset prices, as measured by the price-to-dividend ratio for common stocks.

Section 6 investigates whether changing demographic structure affects returns through its impact on the risk tolerance of potential investors. This section presents survey evidence suggesting that households become more risk averse only at ages that are traditionally associated with retirement, and it raises questions about previous claims that age-related risk aversion affects aggregate returns.

A brief concluding section considers several factors that might contribute to a weak relationship between asset returns and demographic structure in a single nation. It also suggests several directions for future empirical as well as theoretical work on the financial-market consequences of population aging.

8.1 Theoretical Analysis of Population Age Structure and Asset Returns

Much of the interest in demographic change and asset markets stems from popular accounts of the rapid rise in U.S. share prices during the 1990s. Such accounts suggest that as the Baby Boom cohort entered its prime earning years and began saving for retirement, their asset demand drove up asset prices. It is possible to formalize this logic in a simple model that highlights the many strong assumptions that are needed for this conclusion. Abel (2001) develops more rigorous formulation, and indicates when the general conclusion of weak asset prices is likely to hold.

Assume that individuals live for two periods, and that they work when young (y) and retire when old (o). Normalize their production while working to one unit of a numeraire good, and assume that there is also a durable capital good that does not depreciate and that is in fixed supply. If the saving rate out of labor income is fixed at s for young workers, then demand for assets in any period will be $N_y^* s$. With a fixed supply of durable assets (K), the relative price of these assets in terms of the numeraire good (p) will satisfy

$$p^* K = N_y^* s \tag{8.1}$$

An increase in the size of the working cohort will drive up asset prices, and the arrival of a small cohort of working age will lead to a decline in asset prices. In such a setting, as a large birth cohort works its way through the life-cycle, it will purchase assets at high prices, and sell them at low prices, thereby earning a low return on investments.

The foregoing logic is simple, and it seems compelling in many popular accounts, but it neglects many important realities of asset pricing. First, it fixes the saving rate of young workers, rather than deriving it from an optimizing model with endogenous saving and rational, forward-looking behavior. Rational expectations pose an important challenge to those who argue that demographic factors account for the recent increase in asset values in economies like the United States. The fact that a growing share of the U.S. population would enter the prime saving years of 40–64 during the 1990s was predictable at least two decades ago. Forward-looking investors should have anticipated the rising demand for capital and bid up share prices and the prices of other durable assets before the Baby Boomers reached their saving years.

Second, the foregoing model does not allow for endogenous production of capital. In a more realistic setting, the price of capital goods would affect the growth of the capital stock. Abel (2001) shows that allowing for a supply curve for capital goods can affect the conclusions. His results illustrate that the precise impact of a demographic change is likely to be model-specific, and that it is in particular sensitive to specific choices regarding the specification of demand and supply.

Third, the analysis does not consider how a changing age structure might affect other aspects of the economy, such as the rate of productivity growth or, more directly, the marginal product of capital. Cutler et al. (1990) suggest that links between age structure and the rate of productivity improvement, if they exist, can swamp many other channels linking demographic change to equilibrium factor returns.

Several recent studies have used intertemporal general equilibrium models, with varying degrees of richness along each of these dimensions, to study whether shifting age structures can significantly affect equilibrium asset returns and asset prices. These studies are *not* directed at the question of whether demographic factors can explain the recent runup in U.S. asset values but, rather, at issues involving lower-frequency movements in asset values, returns, and demographic structure. Such studies may be relevant for discussions of the potential returns available to the Baby Boom cohort over the next few decades. The most detailed studies, which include Yoo (1994a), Brooks (2000), and Abel (1999, 2001), present simulation or analytic results suggesting that demographic change can affect equilibrium returns. These studies leave open the question of whether demographic effects are large enough to be detectable in historical data.

The various studies of equilibrium asset returns and population age structure adopt different modeling strategies, but they reach broadly similar conclusions. Yoo (1994a) calibrates a model in which overlapping generations of consumers live for 55 periods, working for the first 45, and he simulates a "Baby Boom." He finds that a rise in the birth rate, followed by a decline, first raises then lowers asset prices, but he also discovers that the effects are quite sensitive to whether or not capital is in variable supply. With a fixed supply of durable assets, asset prices in the "Baby Boom economy" rise to a height of roughly 35 percent above their level in the baseline case. This effect is attenuated, to a 15 percent increase in asset prices, in a production economy. In both settings, asset prices reach their peak about 35 years after the Baby Boom commences. In the endowment economy, equilibrium asset returns change by roughly 85 basis points per year relative to their values in the absence of a "Baby Boom," whereas in the production economy, the effect is roughly 40 basis points per year.

Brooks (2000) also presents simulation evidence on the impact of a "Baby Boom," but he develops a more stylized model in which consumers live for four periods. His model incorporates both risky and riskless assets, however, so it is possible to explore how demographic shocks affect the risk premium. Rapid population growth that persists for half a generation (two periods) and which is followed by below-average population growth affects the equilibrium level of both risky and riskless asset returns. The riskless return rises when the "Baby Boom generation" is young and working, and it falls by roughly the same amount when the large cohort reaches retirement age, because older households prefer riskless to risky assets. Equilibrium returns on the risky asset change by roughly half as much as the riskless return, so the equilibrium equity risk premium declines in the early stage of the "Baby Boom," and then increases when the large cohort is old. The simulation results suggest that these effects are modest in size. A simulation designed to roughly approximate the postwar Baby Boom in the United States suggests that riskless returns rise from about 4.5 percent per year, in the initial baseline, to 4.8 percent per year when the large population cohort is in its peak saving years. Risk-free returns subsequently fall to just over 4.1 percent when the large cohort reaches retirement. The model also yields intriguing predictions about the relative movements in riskless and risky rates, with a decline in the risk premium when the large birth cohort begins saving and a rise in this premium when it retires.

The third study of demographic change and asset values, Abel (1999), also uses an overlapping generations model, but it develops analytical rather than simulation results on the impact of demographic change. Abel (1999) modifies Diamond's (1965) overlapping generations neoclassical growth model to allow for random population growth and for adjustment costs in producing capital. The latter permits a shift in population growth to affect the equilibrium price of capital goods. The key analytical finding is that a "Baby Boom" drives up the price of capital, but that the price of capital subsequently reverts toward its long-run mean. Thus, the price of capital goods will rise when the "Baby Boom" cohort is in the labor force and decline as this cohort reaches retirement age. The analytical results highlight the dependence of the asset price effect on the parameters of both the consumer's utility function and the production function that is associated with the production of capital goods.

Abel (2001) builds on this framework to explore how introducing a bequest motive would alter the basic analysis. A bequest motive could explain the empirical findings reported herein on the slow decumulation of assets after households reach retirement age, although it is not the only possible explanation for such findings. For at least some specifications of the bequest motive, the slow draw-down of assets during retirement does not overturn the basic conclusion that a decline in the population growth rate is associated with a decline in the equilibrium price of capital. This implies that showing that households do not draw down their assets does not provide conclusive evidence against the view that a demographic shock like the "Baby Boom" could lead to an increase, and then a decline, in asset prices.

These studies confirm the basic insight that shocks to the rate of population growth can affect equilibrium asset returns in well-specified general equilibrium models. The simulation results from Yoo (1994a) and Brooks (2000) nevertheless suggest that the effects of plausible-sized demographic shocks may be relatively modest in magnitude. These findings motivate the empirical work on asset returns, asset prices, and demographic structure that comprises the balance of this paper.

8.2 Age Patterns in Asset Ownership

The theoretical analysis in each of the papers described previously, with the exception of Abel (1999), assumes that there are pronounced age patterns in the ownership of financial assets. This can take two forms: differences in the amount of wealth that households hold at different ages and differences in the *composition* of wealth that households hold at different ages. In overlapping generations models in which consumers are born, acquire assets, and then die, and in which consumers do not have bequest motives, assets are accumulated as the household ages and then they are decumulated before death. In practice, although there is little doubt that households accumulate assets early in life and through middle-age, Hurd's (1990) summary suggests that there is less agreement on the rate at which assets are decumulated in retirement. Researchers also disagree on the reason for slow decumulation, in particular on the relative importance of bequest motives and precautionary saving demands in accounting for this pattern. Studying how asset profiles vary as households age provides evidence on how rapidly assets are likely to be sold off as the "Baby Boom" cohort ages.

8.2.1 Age-Wealth Profiles in the Survey of Consumer Finances

Many previous studies have computed age-wealth profiles, or age-saving profiles, and tested for evidence of stylized "life-cycle" behavior. Relatively few of these studies have focused on the high net worth households who account for the majority of net worth in the U.S. economy, however. Data on these households is provided by the repeated cross sections of the Survey of Consumer Finances (SCF). The SCF provides the most comprehensive information on asset ownership in the United States. The Federal Reserve Board commissioned the first "modern" SCF in 1983, and the survey has been carried out every three years since then. Kennickell, Starr-McLuer, and Sunden (1997) provide a detailed description of the SCF, along with summary tabulations from the most recent survey.

The SCF can be used to measure average levels of asset holdings for individuals in different age groups. The basic unit of observation in the survey is the household, and most households include several adult members. To construct age-specific asset profiles, I have allocated half of the assets held by married couples to each member of the couple. Thus, if a married couple in which the husband is 62 and the wife is 57 holds $250,000 in financial assets, this will translate into $125,000 held by a 62-year-old and $125,000 held by a 57-year-old.

Many previous studies of age-wealth profiles, including those by Yoo (1994b) and Bergantino (1998), focus on cross-sectional age-wealth profiles. Such wealth profiles describe the average asset holdings of individuals of different ages *at a point in time*. Such data can be used to summarize the potential evolution of asset demand as the population age structure changes only under the assumption that the "cohort effects" for all of the age groups are identical. Shorrocks (1975) is one of the first studies to recognize the need to move beyond cross-sectional data in studying age-wealth profiles.

To illustrate the difficulty with cross-sectional age-wealth profiles, the asset holdings by individuals of age a at time period t, A_{at}, can, in principle, be decomposed as follows:

$$A_{at} = \alpha_a + \beta_t + \gamma_{t-a} \qquad (8.2)$$

where α_a is the age-specific asset demand at age a, β_t is the time-period-specific shift in asset demand, and γ_{t-a} is the cohort-specific asset demand effort for those

Table 8.1. *Cross-section estimates of age-specific asset demands, 1995 Survey of Consumer Finances*

Age of individual	Common stock holdings	Net financial assets	Net worth
15–19	$ 0	$ 1,610 (2,832)	$ 10,144 (5,406)
20–24	384 (73)	−1,340 (1,660)	7,635 (5,308)
25–29	3,073 (510)	4,322 (1,339)	19,798 (2,984)
30–34	4,666 (1,515)	7,806 (3,334)	30,666 (8,891)
35–39	7,438 (4,399)	13,692 (8,019)	53,767 (12,171)
40–44	14,593 (3,584)	26,564 (6,168)	90,606 (18,701)
45–49	21,762 (4,554)	42,442 (9,915)	131,932 (26,660)
50–54	29,965 (20,628)	59,083 (25,660)	169,574 (42,454)
55–59	38,319 (17,943)	65,781 (27,798)	186,505 (54,645)
60–64	29,416 (16,167)	63,066 (28,842)	178,648 (54,312)
65–69	29,219 (16,605)	82,538 (37,538)	189,068 (65,026)
70–74	31,367 (30,067)	76,835 (45,798)	190,729 (70,800)
75 & Up	34,558 (26,645)	84,806 (42,151)	167,279 (62,174)
All Ages	18,272 (3,407)	38,351 (5,475)	106,399 (9,612)

Note: Common stock holdings include assets held through defined-contribution pension accounts. Net financial assets subtracts consumer and investment debt from gross financial assets. Net worth is the sum of net financial assets, the gross value of owner-occupied housing, and holdings of other assets such as investment real estate, less the value of housing mortgage debt. Standard errors are shown in parentheses.

who were born in period $t - a$. With a single cross-section of asset demands by age, it is not possible to separate any of these effects. With panel data or repeated cross-sections, it is possible to estimate two of the three effects, but it is not possible to recover all three. Because birth cohort is a linear combination of age and time, there is a fundamental identification problem with recovering all three effects.

There are good reasons to expect both cohort effects and time effects in asset demands. For example, individuals who lived through the Great Depression may have lower levels of lifetime earnings, and correspondingly lower levels of net worth at all ages, than individuals who were born in more recent years. This could lead to cohort effects. Alternatively, a revaluation of assets, such as a sharp increase in asset values in the 1990s, may raise the wealth of all individuals in a given period. This would result in time effects. This makes it natural to compare cross-sectional age-wealth profiles with profiles estimated with some allowance for time or cohort effects.

Table 8.1 presents a cross-sectional age-wealth profile from the 1995 Survey of Consumer Finances. It reports average holdings of common stock, net financial assets, and net worth for individuals in different five-year age groups. Not surprisingly, there are important age-related differences in the levels of assets and in net worth. The table focuses on mean holdings, which are much higher than median holdings at all ages. Average holdings of net financial assets rise with an individual's age for those between their early 30s and those in their early 60s. There is a decline in the rate of increase in financial asset holdings for individuals at older ages, but there is no evident *decline* in net financial assets when one compares those above age 75 with those in somewhat younger age groups.

A similar pattern emerges with respect to both corporate stock and net worth. Older individuals exhibit larger asset holdings than younger ones, but there is only a limited downturn in average asset holdings at older ages. There is some downturn in holdings of corporate stock, where the age-specific ownership peaks between the ages of 55 and 59 at \$38,319, and declines by nearly \$10,000 for those in the next two age categories. The imprecision of the age-specific asset holdings makes it difficult, however, to reject the null hypothesis that stock holding is constant at ages above 55. Net worth, which includes financial assets as well as holdings of owner-occupied real estate, other real property, equity in unincorporated businesses, and assets held through defined-contribution pension plans, rises up to age 55 and then stays relatively constant for the remainder of an individual's lifetime.

The confounding effects of age and cohort effects make it difficult to interpret findings like those in Table 8.1. If older cohorts have lower lifetime earnings than younger cohorts, and if the accumulation of financial assets is correlated with lifetime earnings, then we could observe lower asset holdings at older ages even if households did not draw down assets in their old age. Alternatively, if older households had higher lifetime earnings on average than their younger counterparts, or if older households had lived through a period of particularly favorable asset market returns, then it would be possible to observe a rising age-asset profile at all ages, even if older households did reduce their asset holdings as they aged.

Ameriks and Zeldes (2000) present simple examples of how a given age-wealth profile, and even a given set of age-wealth profiles over time, can be consistent with very different underlying patterns of asset accumulation over the life-cycle as a result of different combinations of time and cohort effects. In light of the fundamental identification problem noted herein studies that move beyond cross-sectional comparisons of asset holdings at different ages must choose between a cohort-effects and a time-effects specification. Allowing for cohort effects offers the best chance of detecting a traditional hump-shaped, life-cycle pattern of asset holdings in cross-sectional data such as those in Table 8.1. Because cohort effects allow for different wealth levels for households at different ages, they can reconcile a flat age-wealth cross-sectional profile with a declining cohort-specific pattern. Allowing for time effects, however, would not recover such a pattern because all cohorts are constrained to experience the same asset shock in each period.

To provide the best possible opportunity for evidence of prospective asset decumulation to emerge from the SCF data, I use repeated cross-sections of the SCF from 1983, 1986, 1989, 1992, and 1995 to estimate age profiles of asset ownership allowing for different lifetime asset levels for different birth cohorts. The empirical specification models A_{it}, the level of an asset stock (or of net worth)

Table 8.2. *Age-specific asset demands estimated allowing for age and cohort effects, Surveys of Consumer Finances, 1983–1995*

Age of individual	Common stock holdings	Net financial assets	Net worth
15–19	$ 0 (0)	$ 2,285 (2,823)	$ 11,042 (5,391)
20–24	470 (134)	2,170 (2,939)	13,656 (6,337)
25–29	1,477 (214)	4,477 (3,010)	25,471 (6,848)
30–34	3,391 (367)	9,402 (3,126)	37,706 (6,648)
35–39	5,906 (908)	14,325 (3,352)	60,758 (7,166)
40–44	10,795 (1,175)	20,236 (4,789)	86,808 (7,939)
45–49	18,631 (1,996)	37,122 (4,668)	123,683 (10,136)
50–54	23,913 (2,805)	57,396 (6,634)	151,981 (15,641)
55–59	32,515 (3,882)	71,884 (7,505)	177,522 (17,133)
60–64	31,004 (4,857)	80,931 (8,757)	189,134 (19,670)
65–69	30,822 (5,791)	92,262 (9,901)	201,509 (22,973)
70–74	28,219 (7,186)	92,366 (11,707)	173,796 (25,961)
75+	24,722 (7,482)	92,239 (12,091)	144,316 (27,026)

Notes: Estimates are based on regression models that relate real holdings of various assets by age cohorts in different survey years to a set of cohort "intercepts" and indicator variables for various age groups. Standard errors are shown in parentheses. See text for further discussion.

held by individuals in age group a in period t as:

$$A_{it} = \Sigma \, \alpha_j^* AGE_{ijt} + \Sigma \, \gamma_c^* COHORT_{it} + \varepsilon_{it} \qquad (8.3)$$

where α_j denotes the age effect on asset ownership and γ_c denotes a birth-cohort specific intercept term that captures the level of assets held by different birth cohorts. Both sets of parameters are estimated *conditional* on the assumption that there are no time effects on asset demand.

Assets in different years of the SCF are inflated or deflated to constant 1995 dollars using the Consumer Price Index. The equations are estimated by ordinary least squares, and the sample size varies across years of the SCF. There are 30,553 individuals in the combined SCF data files for these years, with 30,394 observations reporting all of the variables that are needed to estimate Equation (8.3). Net financial assets are defined inclusive of assets in defined-contribution pension accounts, and equity for 1983 includes an imputation of half of the assets in self-directed defined-contribution pension accounts.

The α_j coefficients in Equation (8.3) can be used to predict how an individual's asset holdings will change as they age. Poterba and Samwick (2001) present detailed findings, using this method, for a range of different asset classes. Ameriks and Zeldes (2000) also analyze repeated cross-sections of the SCF, along with a panel data set of TIAA-CREF participants, to study how the equity share of household portfolios change as households age.

Table 8.2 presents the estimates of the age effects, the $\{\alpha_i\}$ coefficients, from Equation (8.3) for three asset categories, whereas Table 8.3 shows the

Table 8.3. *Cohort-specific intercepts for asset demands, Surveys of Consumer Finances,*
1983–1995

Birth-year cohort for individual	Common stock holdings	Net financial assets	Net worth
1971–1975	$ −102 (136)	$ −2,673 (2,991)	$ −4,317 (6,333)
1970–1974	624 (236)	−881 (2,982)	−4,720 (6,631)
1965–1969	−9 (94)	−1,220 (2,897)	−36 (6,002)
1960–1964	−178 (255)	−703 (3,111)	−821 (6,822)
1955–1959	−1,137 (321)	−3,671 (3,079)	−4,923 (6,766)
1950–1954	−507 (1,335)	−5,512 (3,891)	8,425 (7,523)
1945–1949	−2,394 (1,250)	−5,444 (4,292)	−1,250 (8,342)
1940–1944	−2,087 (2,767)	−11,024 (5,414)	−3,230 (11,829)
1935–1939	−8,917 (3,057)	−26,819 (7,314)	−15,385 (17,616)
1930–1934	−2,771 (4,730)	−15,294 (8,478)	−3,741 (19,196)
1925–1929	−6,984 (5,351)	−24,458 (9,312)	−19,281 (20,572)
Before 1925	1,714 (6,593)	−21,686 (10,756)	−720 (25,601)
R2	0.008	0.017	0.041

Notes: Estimates are based on regression models that relate real holdings of various assets by age cohorts in different survey years to a set of cohort "intercepts" and indicator variables for various age groups. Robust standard errors are shown in parentheses. Sample size is 30,394 observations. See text for further discussion.

cohort-specific intercepts. The patterns in the age-effect coefficients in Table 8.2 are quite similar to those of the cross-sectional wealth-holding coefficients in Table 8.1. The results suggest that allowing for cohort effects has a surprisingly small impact on the estimated age structure of asset holdings. Although holdings of common stock and total financial assets increase as individuals age, the decline in assets as individuals enter old age is again much less pronounced than the increase in asset holdings during middle age. For equities, for example, real holdings of common stock peak between the ages of 55 and 59, at $32,515. They decline to $28,219 for those between the ages of 70 and 74 and further to $24,722 for those over the age of 75.

For net financial assets, there is virtually no decline in old age, with peak holdings between the ages of 70 and 74; for net worth, the peak occurs between 65 and 69 with a notable decline at ages above 75. For household net worth, which may be the most relevant variable in determining the demand for assets, the point estimates of the age-effects decline after age 65, but the standard errors are large enough to admit a relatively wide range of age-wealth profiles. The point estimate of the net-worth level for individuals aged 75+ is roughly one quarter lower than that for households in their mid-60s. The large standard errors in Table 8.2 are a reflection of the very large underlying dispersion of asset wealth, which makes it difficult to precisely estimate age patterns in asset holdings.

The limited decline in financial asset holdings as individuals age suggests that the rush to sell financial assets that underlies most predictions of "market meltdown" in 2020 or 2030 may be somewhat muted. The results in Tables 8.1 and 8.2 do suggest that there are substantial increases in asset holdings as households move through their 30s and 40s, which supports the view that the aging of the Baby Boom cohort during the last two decades could have raised the demand for financial assets.

The coefficient estimates in Table 8.2 suggest that corporate stock as a share of net financial assets rises as individuals age, but that this share declines after individuals reach retirement age. The systematic growth in equity ownership during the last two decades, however, makes it particularly difficult to attribute this to a hump-shaped pattern of age effects for equity ownership. Ameriks and Zeldes (2000) show that over the 1989–1995 period, when one fits a model that includes age and time effects, the pattern of estimated age effects is virtually flat. With age and cohort effects, however, there is an upward-sloping profile to age effects for the share of equity in the total portfolio. The age profile of equity shares may be particularly important for discussions of how population aging may affect the equity premium, although it may be less central for discussions of overall asset returns.

Table 8.3 presents the estimated cohort-specific intercepts from Equation (8.3). There are surprisingly small differences across cohorts for net worth, equities, and net financial assets, and the standard errors associated with most of the cohort effects are large relative to the differences in the cohort-specific coefficients. For example, one cannot reject the null hypothesis that the age-specific net worth profile for individuals born between 1925 and 1929 is the same as that for individuals born between 1945 and 1949. The large dispersion in wealth at various ages is reflected in the low R^2 values for models such as Equation (8.3). The model has the greatest explanatory power with respect to net worth and, even in that case, cohort and age effects explain less than 5 percent of the variation in real net worth.

The foregoing results suggest rapid growth in asset holdings during the early part of a household's working career. They suggest somewhat less rapid decumulation of assets in retirement, but they do indicate, particularly with respect to net worth, some decline. One recent study using SCF data, Sabelhaus and Pence (1998), finds somewhat greater dissaving after retirement than the estimates in Table 8.2 suggest. This is in part because of different "mortality adjustments" for older households. Tables 8.1 and 8.2 report asset holdings for individuals, not households. At most ages, dividing household assets equally across adult members of the household is a natural way to generate an age-asset holding profile. For older individuals, however, mortality can have an important effect on the measured trajectory of asset holding, for at least three reasons.

First, mortality may be correlated with net worth. Attanasio and Hoynes (2000) find that high-income households have lower mortality rates than their lower net-worth counterparts. Those who survive to advanced ages may, therefore, be a selected group, biased toward a higher net-worth part of the population. This is very likely to result in upward bias in the age-wealth profile.

Second, when one member of a married couple dies, the couple's assets typically flow to the surviving spouse. This can raise the net worth of the survivor relative to what it would have been when this individual's spouse was still alive. Because other research suggests that surviving spouses draw down their assets faster than married couples, however, the net effect of this bias may be modest. Reestimating the age effects in Table 8.2 with the wealth of each widow or widower divided by two lowered the *level* of the age-wealth profile but did not affect the proportionate decumulation at older ages.

Third, when an older person dies and leaves their assets to a group of heirs, this may affect the demand for assets, but the effects are complex. If the recipients of bequests continue to hold the assets, rather than using them to finance consumption, the death of the decedent may not have a pronounced effect on the desired stock of wealth. How long assets are held after the recipients of bequests receive them is an open issue. Holtz-Eakin, Joulfaian, and Rosen (1993) present some evidence that individuals who receive large inheritances are more likely to leave the labor force than those with comparable preinheritance incomes who do not receive bequests. This provides some support for the notion that bequests are used to support higher levels of consumption. The absence of other data on consumption spending by bequest recipients, however, makes it difficult to address this issue quantitatively.

The calculations of age-wealth profiles in Tables 8.1 and 8.2 omit defined-benefit pension assets. Schieber and Shoven's (1997) analysis of population aging and asset demand emphasizes the mechanical accumulation, and then decumulation, of assets that occurs as individuals age in a defined-benefit pension regime. In most cases, the value of the assets that are accumulated in defined-benefit plans peaks at the date when an individual retires. As benefits are paid out, the actuarial present value of the remaining payouts declines, and the assets needed to provide these benefits decline. This implies that there is a substantial force of accumulation and then decumulation as a large birth cohort ages. Such effects may have been more important historically then they will be prospectively, at least in the United States, as current trends suggest an important shift away from defined-benefit and toward defined-contribution pension plans.

8.2.2 Changing Demographic Patterns, Past and Future

To translate the age-wealth profiles reported in Tables 8.1 and 8.2 into measures of aggregate asset demand, one needs information on the demographic structure of the population. Table 8.4 presents summary statistics on various measures of the age structure of the U.S. population for every tenth year between 1920 and 2050. The historical data are drawn from Census Bureau *Population Reports P-25* publications, whereas the forecasts beginning in year 2000 are based on Census projections.

Table 8.4. *Historical and forecast values for indicators of demographic structure, 1920–2050*

Year	Median age	Average age of those 20+	Percent of population 40–64	(Population 40–64)/ population 65+	(Population 40–64)/ population 20+
1920	25.3	40.3	22.2	4.8	0.375
1930	26.5	41.2	24.1	4.4	0.392
1940	29.1	42.2	26.5	3.9	0.404
1950	30.2	43.5	27.0	3.3	0.409
1960	29.4	45.3	26.5	2.9	0.431
1970	27.9	45.2	26.3	2.7	0.423
1980	30.0	44.5	24.7	2.2	0.362
1990	32.8	45.1	25.7	2.1	0.361
2000	35.7	46.6	30.4	2.4	0.426
2010	35.7	46.6	30.4	2.4	0.456
2020	37.6	49.2	30.5	1.8	0.416
2030	38.5	50.5	28.0	1.4	0.382
2040	38.6	51.0	27.9	1.4	0.381
2050	38.1	51.1	27.6	1.4	0.379

Source: U.S. Census Bureau historical data and projections from CPS Reports P25-1130. Average age over 20 computed using the midpoint in five-year age intervals as the average age for all persons in that interval, and assuming that the average age for persons 85 and older is 90.

The data in Table 8.4 show that between 1970 and 2000, the median age of the U.S. population increased by nearly eight years. It is projected to increase by more than two years more between 2000 and 2050. The median age in 2000 is more than 10 years greater than median age in 1900. The two periods of most rapid increase in median age during the last century were 1920–1940 and 1960–1990. The average age of the adult population rose by 4.2 years between 1930 and 1960, or by less than the median age. In the last three decades, the average age of adults has risen less than 1.5 years. This summary measure of population age structure shows both increases and decreases during the postwar period.

The fraction of the population in the "asset accumulating years," 40–64, often is cited as a key variable in discussions of asset demand and demographic structure. Table 8.4 shows that this fraction rose by roughly four percentage points, to 30.4 percent, between 1970 and 2000. Looking forward, this fraction is expected to decline by nearly three percentage points between 2000 and 2050. The population share in this age group exhibits substantial long-term and short-term variation. It was 19.4 percent in 1900, compared with 30.4 percent today, and it has changed by nearly five percentage points since 1990. It was 27 percent in 1950, 24.7 percent in 1980, and 25.7 percent in 1990.

Table 8.4 shows that there was a rapid change between 1950 and 2000 in the median age of the entire population, with a smaller change in the average age of those over the age of 19. In the next 50 years, however, the most dramatic change will be in the average age of those in the 20+ age group. Today, the population between the ages of 40 and 64 is 2.3 times as large as the population over the age of 65. By 2050, this ratio, which is sometimes called the elderly dependency ratio, will have declined to 1.4. As a share of the adult population, those between the ages of 40 and 64 account for 42.6 percent of the population in 2000, up from 36.1 percent in 1990, but similar to the 42.3 percent value for 1990. The record of past experience is important because it suggests that the prospective demographic changes that the United States will experience in the next three decades are not outside the range of experience in the past century.

8.2.3 Integrating Age-Specific Asset Demands with Changing Age Structure: "Projected Asset Demand"

To illustrate the impact of population aging on the demand for financial assets, it is possible to construct a measure of projected asset holdings per capita in each year, based on the age-specific structure of asset demands in a given year. This measure is defined by:

$$(\text{PROJECTED ASSET DEMAND})_t = \Sigma\,\alpha_i^* N_{it} \qquad (8.4)$$

where α_i denotes the age-specific asset holdings from Table 8.2, and N_{it} denotes the actual or projected number of individuals of age i in year t. Mankiw and Weil (1989) used a similar strategy to construct their measure of demography-affected housing demand, with estimates of age-specific housing demand based on Census data. Bergantino (1998) followed a similar approach in estimating demand for both housing and corporate stock based on a cross-section household wealth survey.

Table 8.5 reports the projected demand for common stock, financial assets, and net worth for each year between 1925 and 2050, based on the age-specific asset-demand coefficients reported in Table 8.2. (These are estimates that correct for cohort effects.) The table shows that projected asset demand rises over the four-decade period between 1980 and 2020. Projected asset holdings per capita plateau after that date, reflecting the relatively flat profile of age-specific asset ownership between middle age and death. This finding contrasts with the "asset market meltdown" scenarios that predict a sharp decline in asset demand in the decades after 2020. Because there is only modest dissaving at older ages in Table 8.2, the aging of the Baby Boom cohort does not result in a significant decline in asset demand.

The data in Table 8.5 also show a modest decline in the projected per capita holdings of both common stock and net worth between 1960 and 1980. This reflects the growing importance of young households, with relatively small asset holdings, during this time period. Between 1925 and 1950, each of the three projected asset demand series display substantial increase.

Table 8.5. *"Projected asset demand" per capita, persons aged 15 and greater ($1995)*

Year	Common stock holdings	Net financial assets	Net worth
1925	10.359	26.120	74.790
1926	10.419	26.275	75.121
1927	10.476	26.433	75.433
1928	10.487	26.533	75.492
1929	10.583	26.742	76.059
1930	10.652	26.942	76.451
1931	10.750	27.204	76.969
1932	10.846	27.457	77.474
1933	10.937	27.701	77.957
1934	11.022	27.931	78.411
1935	11.100	28.150	78.833
1936	11.171	28.353	79.219
1937	11.236	28.547	79.580
1938	11.308	28.760	79.988
1939	11.366	28.938	80.313
1940	11.423	29.107	80.631
1941	11.505	29.334	81.099
1942	11.600	29.593	81.623
1943	11.683	29.831	82.116
1944	11.765	30.059	82.592
1945	11.892	30.411	83.328
1946	12.013.	30.749	84.029
1947	12.121	31.061	84.654
1948	12.229	31.369	85.278
1949	12.351	31.714	85.975
1950	12.457	32.031	86.608
1951	12.584	32.384	87.328
1952	12.704	32.724	88.024
1953	12.817	33.053	88.676
1954	12.929	33.387	89.313
1955	13.039	33.710	89.927
1956	13.125	33.968	90.403
1957	13.192	34.184	90.769
1958	13.222	34.299	90.884
1959	13.275	34.479	91.130
1960	13.332	34.665	91.405
1961	13.378	34.820	91.606
1962	13.319	34.709	91.165
1963	13.288	34.652	90.887
1964	13.260	34.614	90.627
1965	13.231	34.575	90.368
1966	13.188	34.502	90.041
1967	13.146	34.428	89.726
1968	13.099	34.342	89.397
1969	13.041	34.238	89.009

Year	Common stock holdings	Net financial assets	Net worth
1970	12.982	34.156	88.611
1971	12.914	34.039	88.167
1972	12.844	33.924	87.769
1973	12.777	33.817	87.386
1974	12.715	33.721	87.015
1975	12.665	33.661	86.698
1976	12.603	33.563	86.334
1977	12.569	33.527	86.143
1978	12.536	33.491	85.984
1979	12.504	33.465	85.834
1980	12.474	33.444	85.706
1981	12.450	33.430	85.633
1982	12.454	33.477	85.774
1983	12.471	33.538	85.963
1984	12.475	33.571	86.086
1985	12.475	33.599	86.183
1986	12.468	33.607	86.246
1987	12.514	33.720	86.616
1988	12.575	33.869	87.056
1989	12.638	34.029	87.520
1990	12.726	34.250	88.102
1991	12.773	34.360	88.444
1992	12.900	34.655	89.186
1993	12.991	34.859	89.720
1994	13.093	35.076	90.294
1995	13.173	35.240	90.760
1996	13.258	35.403	91.227
1997	13.371	35.654	91.811
1998	13.511	35.968	92.506
1999	13.632	36.231	93.110
2000	13.749	36.491	93.695
2001	13.860	36.739	94.248
2002	14.014	37.073	94.953
2003	14.148	37.393	95.603
2004	14.274	37.688	96.210
2005	14.390	37.968	96.754
2010	14.953	39.584	99.600
2020	15.697	42.603	103.756
2030	15.709	43.896	103.957
2040	15.660	44.138	103.066
2050	15.690	44.202	103.248

Notes: Each column reports the value of $\Sigma \alpha_i^* N_{it}$, where α_i denotes age-specific asset holdings (for five-year age groups) based on the cohort-corrected wealth accumulation models reported in Table 8.2. N denotes the actual or projected number of individuals in a given age range in a given year. Tabulations apply to individuals aged 15 and greater. See text for further details.

Time series like those in Table 8.5 can be used to study the historical relationship between demographic shifts and the returns on various financial assets. High values of projected asset demand should be associated with low required returns and high asset prices. Calculations like those that underlie the estimates in Table 8.5 should be viewed with caution, however. Using a static age-wealth profile, like the estimates of the $\{\alpha_i\}$ parameters in Table 8.2, does not allow for rational forward-looking consumers to adjust their saving and asset holdings in response to expected changes in asset returns. Of course, analyses that predict future asset prices on the basis of currently forecastable demographics assume that there is a relatively stable relationship between asset demand and demographic structure.

8.3 Previous Empirical Evidence on Asset Returns and Population Age Structure

Several previous studies have considered how changing demographic structure affects asset prices and asset returns. The best known is Mankiw and Weil's (1989) analysis of house prices and the age structure of the U.S. population. It shows that demand for owner-occupied housing rises sharply when households pass through ages between 25 and 40, and finds a strong time-series correlation between a demographic housing demand variable and real house prices in the postwar period. The study forecast that the reduced housing demand that would result from aging of the U.S. population in the decades after 1990 would lead to substantially lower house prices. The last decade has not witnessed the sharp decline in real prices that study predicted, although it is difficult to interpret this experience as a clear refutation. Housing demand is increasing in household net worth, and the sharp increase in household net worth during the last decade has surely led to higher demand for housing than would otherwise have occurred.

A number of studies have specifically considered issues relating to the "asset market meltdown" scenario. The first systematic study of age structure and asset returns, by Bakshi and Chen (1994), includes a variable measuring the average age of the U.S. population in a standard Euler equation that relates the growth rate of consumption to either T-bill or stock returns. This specification is motivated by claims that risk tolerance declines as households age, as in Brooks's (1998) model described earlier. The authors assume that the utility function of the representative consumer is given by:

$$U(C_t, M_t) = C_t^{1-\gamma-\lambda^*M_t}/(1-\gamma-\lambda^*M_t) \qquad (8.5)$$

where M_t denotes the average age of the population, and C_t denotes aggregate per-capita consumption. Allowing for nonzero values of λ improves the fit of the intertemporal Euler equation associated with (8.5), and the authors interpret this as evidence of age-dependent risk aversion. This finding implies that changes in population age structure would affect equilibrium asset returns.

Whereas Bakshi and Chen (1994) constrain demographic change to affect asset returns in a tightly parameterized way, a second study, Yoo (1994b), allows for a more flexible relationship. This study relates real returns on stocks, bonds, and Treasury bills to five explanatory variables corresponding to the share of the population in different age groups. Some of the empirical results presented herein are similar, although they impose greater structure on the demographic variables to avoid "overfitting" with many slowly trending time series on population shares. Yoo (1994b) focuses on the 1926–88 period, and finds that a higher fraction of the population in the prime saving years is associated with a lower real return on Treasury bills. The results for other asset classes are less definitive, and large standard errors make it impossible to draw firm inferences about the link between demographic structure and returns on longer maturity assets.

Two related studies focus on U.S. stock returns over a shorter time period. Macunovich (1997) follows a strategy similar to that in Yoo (1994b), although she includes an even richer set of demographic variables in regression equations that seek to explain the postwar fluctuation in the real return on the Dow Jones Industrial Average. She considers nearly a dozen population-age share variables, and overfitting appears to be a substantial problem. Poterba (1998) shows that specifications like those used by Macunovich (1997) lead to implausible out-of-sample predictions for the real return on stocks, with both very large positive and very large negative returns. This suggests that the underlying regression models may be overfitting within-sample trends.

Erb, Harvey, and Viskanta (1997), another study of the postwar U.S. experience, focuses on the sample period 1970–95 and finds a positive correlation between the fraction of the population between the ages of 25 and 45 and real stock returns. This contrasts with Yoo's (1994b) statistically insignificant, but negative, effect of the share for this population age group. They also show that there is a positive relationship in both developed and developing countries between stock returns and the change in the average age of a country's inhabitants. Although this finding suggests a possible link from demographic structure to asset returns, other interpretations are also possible. In many developing nations, average age may proxy for changes in underlying economic conditions that reduce morbidity and mortality. It is not clear whether such demographic changes should be viewed as the driving force behind asset market movements or whether they, in turn, reflect other factors at work in developing nations.

Goyal (1999) explores the link between population age structure and the net cash outflows, defined as dividends plus net share repurchases, from the corporate sector. The study finds that an increase in the fraction of the population in the retirement years is associated with an increase in net payouts from the corporate sector and a decline in the equity premium. However, the study also considers the impact of prospective changes in population age structure and concludes that they are likely to have, at most, a modest impact on asset returns.

Finally, two other studies, by Brooks (1998) and Bergantino (1998), focus on the link between demographic structure and the level of asset prices. Brooks (1998) relates the level of real equity prices for OECD nations to the ratio of the population aged 40–64 to that outside this age range. For 11 of 14 countries in the sample, there is a positive relationship between this demographic variable and the real stock price. A key question in evaluating these results is how to normalize share prices. For some of the smaller nations in the sample, such as Denmark, Belgium, and the Netherlands, it is also unclear whether domestic demographic variables should have much impact on domestic share prices.

Bergantino's (1998) study extends Mankiw and Weil's (1989) research strategy. It studies house prices and stock returns in the United States and estimates of age-specific asset demands using cross-sectional data. The study then considers the effect of changes in the level of demographic demand on changes in house and share prices and finds a a clear relationship between the level of age-specific asset demand and the level of stock prices. These effects are clearest in multiyear differences of prices, which tend to emphasize the low-frequency variation in the demographic demand variable. Bergantino (1998) interprets these findings as strong support for an important demographic demand effect on stock prices. He uses his model to calculate the share of post war equity price movements that can be attributed to demographic factors and to predict the future evolution of equity values. Given the size of demographic changes, he concludes that these changes have had and will have a large impact on stock-price levels.

The balance of previous work seems to suggest that demographic factors are correlated with the level of asset prices, although each of the empirical specifications is open to some question. One of the generic difficulties that plagues all of these studies concerns effective sample size. This is a manifestation of a more general problem – discussed, for example, in Campbell, Lo, and MacKinlay (1996) and in Ferson, Sarkissian, and Simin (2000) – of testing for low-frequency patterns in asset returns. Given the slowly evolving character of population age structure, even annual data may overstate the effective degrees of freedom associated with studies of demography and asset markets. There is one Baby Boom shock in the postwar U.S. demographic experience, and as the Baby Boom cohort has approached age 50, real stock-market wealth has risen rapidly. This is consistent with some variants of the demographic demand hypothesis. Whether 50 years of prices and returns on this experience represent 1 observation or 50 is, however, an open question.

Against the background of these prior studies, the current paper presents a battery of new empirical findings. First, it examines the U.S. time series on asset returns and relates real returns on stocks, bonds, and bills to a broader range of demographic variables than previous studies. It also explores the sensitivity of the empirical findings to different data subsamples, and presents related evidence for Canada and the United Kingdom. Second, it considers the relationship between the level of stock prices, measured by the price-to-dividend ratio, and various measures of demographic structure. Third, it uses the "projected asset demand variable" described previously to explore how demographic demand is related to asset returns. Finally, this study revisits Bakshi and Chen's (1994) estimates of how the representative consumer's coefficient of relative risk aversion depends on demographic variables, using both survey data on household preferences with respect to risk as well as aggregate time-series data.

8.4 New Evidence on Population Age Structure and Asset Returns

The theoretical models discussed earlier do not offer clear guidance on which measure of population age structure should affect asset prices and asset returns. Rather than trying to make an arbitrary choice among such variables, this section presents empirical results that exploit a range of different potential measures of demographic structure. Each measure is included in a bivariate regression in which an asset return is the dependent variable.

8.4.1 Evidence for the United States

This section considers the relationship between real returns on three assets – Treasury bills, long-term government bonds, and large corporate stocks (as measured by the return on the S&P index) – and several measures of population age structure. Real returns are computed by subtracting actual inflation rates for each year (based on the year-end to year-end change in the Consumer Price Index) from the pretax nominal return on each asset. The analysis focuses on the period 1926–99, for which Ibbotson Associates (2000) provides reliable and comparable data on returns. For each of the three asset classes, I consider the link between demography and asset returns for the postwar period (1947–99) as well as for the 1926–75 sample. Considering several different asset categories provides information on returns on both relatively low-volatility assets (Treasury bills) and more risky assets. It also has the potential to provide information on how demographic factors affect the equity risk premium. Considering several different assets also allows for the possibility that age-related patterns in the demand for particular assets (e.g., equities) lead to more pronounced demographic effects for some assets than for others, and thus to movements in the risk premium for some assets.

Table 8.6 presents the estimated δ_j coefficients from regression models of the form:

$$R_{i,t} = \kappa + \delta_j^* Z_{j,t} + \varepsilon_{i,t} \tag{8.6}$$

where $R_{i,t}$ denotes the real return on asset i in year t, and $Z_{j,t}$ denotes the value of one of the demographic summary statistics described previously.

The results provide, at best, limited support for a link between asset returns and demographic structure. For common stocks, only one of the fifteen estimated coefficients, that on median age for the 1947–99 period, is statistically significantly

Table 8.6. *Demographic structure and real returns on stocks, bonds, and bills: Annual regression estimates*

Asset return and sample period	Median age	Average age of those 20+	Percent of population 40–64	(Population 40–64)/ population 65+	(Population 40–64)/ population 20+
Independent variable measuring demographic structure					
1926–1999					
Treasury Bills	−0.001 (0.002)	0.000 (0.004)	−1.303 (0.350)	−0.002 (0.006)	−0.392 (0.187)
Long-term Government Bonds	0.004 (0.006)	−0.006 (0.008)	−1.732 (0.959)	0.000 (0.015)	−1.158 (0.474)
Common Stock	0.014 (0.011)	0.003 (0.015)	1.464 (1.877)	−0.001 (0.030)	−0.070 (0.948)
1947–1999					
Treasury Bills	0.004 (0.002)	0.021 (0.005)	−0.553 (0.396)	−0.040 (0.009)	−0.291 (0.155)
Long-term Government Bonds	0.015 (0.007)	0.023 (0.020)	−1.180 (1.336)	−0.082 (0.032)	−1.131 (0.510)
Common Stock	0.023 (0.011)	0.027 (0.030)	2.851 (2.016)	−0.018 (0.052)	−0.045 (0.816)
1926–1975					
Treasury Bills	−0.021 (0.004)	−0.004 (0.004)	−2.573 (0.496)	0.015 (0.010)	−0.253 (0.465)
Long-term Government Bonds	−0.023 (0.008)	−0.017 (0.007)	−3.111 (0.980)	0.046 (0.016)	−1.440 (0.785)
Common Stock	0.010 (0.026)	−0.008 (0.020)	−0.287 (3.073)	0.027 (0.050)	−0.034 (2.313)

Note: Each equation presents the results of estimating an equation of the form

$$R_t = \alpha + \beta^*(\text{DEMOGRAPHIC VARIABLE})_t + \varepsilon_t$$

Standard errors are shown in parentheses. Equations are estimated using annual data for the sample period indicated. Dickey and Fuller (1979) tests, allowing for an estimated mean, applied to the five explanatory variables for the 1926–99 sample period yield t-statistics of 1.804, −2.356, −1.018, −5.271, and −0.572, respectively.

different from zero, and the associated coefficient estimate suggests that increasing the median age raises equity returns. There is some evidence in the fixed-income markets, and particularly the Treasury bill market, for a link between population age structure and asset returns. This result is consistent with the findings in Yoo (1994b). The variable measuring the fraction of the population between the ages of 40 and 64 has the greatest explanatory power in the equations for Treasury bill and long-term government bond returns, although the coefficients vary as we alter the sample period. The results are not very sensitive to whether this population age group is compared to the total population or the population over the age of 19. In most cases, the estimated coefficients are negative, suggesting that an increase in the fraction of the population in the key asset accumulating years reduces required returns, thereby lowering observed returns. The finding that other measures of demographic structure do not appear to covary with real returns should nevertheless be borne in mind to avoid the risk of overinterpreting the findings for the population share aged 40–64.

Although the point estimates of how the population age share between 40 and 64 is correlated with short-term real rates and bond returns are consistent with the theoretical models discussed earlier, the estimated effects are large and may be viewed as implausible. The percentage of the population between the ages of 40 and 64 rose by nearly 0.05 (five percentage points) between 1975 and 2000. The point estimates of the δ_j coefficient for the full sample, -1.30 on real bill yields and -1.73 on real bond yields, imply that a demographic change of this magnitude would reduce real bill yields by 650 basis points, and real bond yields by 900 basis points. These effects seem larger than actual experience with respect to changes in real interest rates. They also are much larger than the modest predictions from the simulation models developed by Brooks (2000) and Yoo (1994a). The very large values of these predicted effects raise the possibility that the demographic variables are capturing other omitted variables, rather than the relationship between notional asset demand and equilibrium returns.

The large predicted effects of demographic changes are also difficult to explain in light of what appear to be relatively high real interest rates at the end of the sample period. The average realized short-term real interest rate in the United States, defined as the nominal short-term rate minus the actual inflation rate was 1.3 percent in the five years centered on 1980, and 1.9 percent in the five years centered on 1995. In the United Kingdom, where the term structure of indexed bond yields permits direct observation of real interest rates, the 10-year real interest rate averaged less than 3 percent in 1982 and 1983, the first years when indexed bonds were traded, and between 3 and 4 percent in the mid-1980s. This real rate averaged more than 4 percent during the early 1990s, and there has been some decline in the late 1990s. In the United States, inflation-indexed bonds have only been available for several years, but long-term real yields of more than 4 percent are high by historical standards. These observations do not support the notion that real interest rates are low, at least by historical standards, even though we currently observe a large age cohort in its prime working years.

The problem of drawing inferences about how low-frequency demographic variation affects asset returns is illustrated by the results for different subsamples. When the sample begins in 1947, the resulting point estimates of the effect of the 40–64 population share on bill and bond returns are substantially smaller than the estimates for the longer sample period. For the 1926–75 sample period, the

Table 8.7. *Unit root test statistics for residuals from models relating returns to demographic variables, 1926–1999*

Asset return and sample period		Independent variable measuring demographic structure			
	Median age	Average age of those 20+	Percent of population 40–64	(Population 40–64)/ population 65+	(Population 40–64)/ population 20+
Treasury Bills	−3.805	−3.824	−3.973	−3.846	−3.932
Long-term Government Bonds	−7.981	−7.927	−8.150	−7.890	−8.490
Common Stock	−8.613	−8.380	−8.469	−8.373	−8.372

Notes: Each entry reports the value of the Dickey and Fuller (1979) test statistic, allowing for an unknown mean, applied to the *residuals* corresponding to the regression equations in the first panel of Table 8.6. The critical (95 percent) value for these test statistics is −2.91, based on tables in Fuller (1976).

estimated effects are larger than those for the full sample. For some of the other demographic variables, which do not have statistically significant effects for the long sample period, the signs of the coefficient estimates also change when the sample changes.

Econometric analyses like those reported in Table 8.6 must be viewed with caution because the explanatory variables evolve slowly. Dickey and Fuller (1979) test statistics (including a constant term) for the presence of a unit root in the five demographic time-series reject the null hypothesis of a unit root in only one case, that of the population aged 40–64 relative to the population aged 65 and older. When the explanatory variables have unit roots, the "spurious regression problem" described by Granger and Newbold (1974) may result in incorrect statistical inferences.

To evaluate the potential importance of this problem, the residuals from the estimating equations that underlie the coefficients in Table 8.6 were tested for the presence of a unit root. This is a variant of a test suggested in Engle and Granger (1987). If the null hypothesis of a unit root in the residuals cannot be rejected using Dickey-Fuller type tests, then the underlying regression model may be misspecified.

Table 8.7 reports the Dickey-Fuller test statistics for the residuals from the 15 regression models reported in the first panel of Table 8.6. These are the models that use data from the full 1926–99 sample period. The t-statistics that are shown reject the null hypothesis of a unit root for each of the specifications; the critical values are approximately −2.91 for the 5 percent tail and −3.20 for the 2.5 percent tail. The estimated t-values in Table 8.7 are all substantially smaller than these critical values.

The results in Table 8.6, supported by the specification tests of Table 8.7, suggest several conclusions. First, to the extent that there is a correlation between

Table 8.8. *"Long-horizon" evidence on demographic structure and real returns on stocks, bonds, and bills, 1926–1995*

	Independent variable measuring demographic structure				
Asset return	Median age	Average age of those 20+	Percent of population 40–64	(Population 40–64)/ population 65+	(Population 40–64)/ population 20+
Treasury Bills	−0.002	−0.001	−2.187	−0.001	−0.441
	(0.005)	(0.006)	(0.579)	(0.011)	(0.330)
LT Gov't Bonds	0.007	−0.008	−2.576	0.001	−1.291
	(0.009)	(0.011)	(1.428)	(0.021)	(0.551)
Common Stock	0.007	−0.008	0.023	0.013	−0.221
	(0.009)	(0.012)	(1.717)	(0.022)	(0.706)

Note: Each equation presents the results of estimating an equation of the form

$$R_t = \alpha + \beta^*(\text{DEMOGRAPHIC VARIABLE})_t + \varepsilon_t$$

The equations are estimated using data for five-year *nonoverlapping* intervals from the period 1926–1995. There are a total of 14 nonoverlapping observations. Standard errors are shown in parentheses. For the "level" specification, the dependent and independent variables are five-year averages of the underlying annual variables. For the demographic change specifications, the independent variables are the average annual change over the five-year measurement interval.

population age structure and returns on assets in the United States, the effect is most pronounced for Treasury bills. This may, in part, reflect the greater volatility of returns in other asset markets, which makes it more difficult to detect the impact of demographic change or other factors. Nevertheless, the real returns on corporate stocks for the last 75 years do not display a clear link with population age structure. Second, the demographic effect appears to be much larger in the prewar period than in the postwar period. Studying the impact of the postwar Baby Boom cohort on asset markets does not provide strong evidence of a link between demography and returns, even in the Treasury bill market. Finally, many measures of population age structure exhibit very little correlation with asset returns, so one must be careful in interpreting a finding that some demographic variable is correlated with returns.

Given the low-frequency variation in population age structure, annual returns may introduce substantial noise to any relationship with demographic structure. I, therefore, constructed five-year returns for nonoverlapping five-year periods between 1926 and 1995. (When one additional year of data, for 2000, becomes available, it will be possible to add another five-year return.) Such multiperiod returns will tend to emphasize the low-frequency variation in asset returns. Table 8.8 presents the results of estimating models like those in Table 8.6 with these nonoverlapping return observations. The results are quite similar to those in Table 8.6. There is, once again, evidence of a negative correlation between the percent of the population between the ages of 40 and 64 and the real return on T-bills and long-term government bonds. There is still no evidence of an impact of population age structure on real equity returns. There is no evidence that the other demographic variables, such as the median age of the population or the average age of the adult population, are correlated with any of the asset-return measures. The point estimates of the coefficients on the percent aged 40–64 variable are even larger with the long-period returns than with annual returns. This means that the concerns raised herein about the large predicted effects of demographic change arise with even more force for these estimates.

The analysis so far has studied the relationship between returns and demographic structure, which is the approach of most of the previous empirical studies. However, theoretical models such as Abel (1999) suggest that when a large age cohort begins to purchase assets for retirement, this should bid up the price of capital. This would suggest that the *level* of stock-market values should be high at such a time, on the grounds that stock prices reflect the purchase price of existing capital assets. This issue can be tested by studying the relationship between stock prices, normalized for example by corporate dividends, and the demographic variables considered in Table 8.6. Both Brooks (1998) and Bergantino (1998) pursue empirical strategies motivated by these insights. The end-of-year level of the price-to-dividend ratio on the S&P500, available on a Web site maintained by Robert Shiller, provides the dependent variable for these calculations.

Table 8.9 reports the results of regression equations of the form

$$(P/D)_{,t} = \kappa + \delta_j^* Z_{,t} + \varepsilon_{,t} \tag{8.7}$$

where Z_t denotes various demographic variables. The results suggest that several demographic variables *do* exhibit a strong association with the price-dividend ratio. In the first row of Table 8.9, the null hypothesis of no relationship between the demographic variable and the price-dividend (P/D) ratio is rejected for all five demographic measures. The estimated coefficients are sometimes inconsistent across specifications, however. In the third column, an increase in the share of the population between ages 40 and 64 has a positive effect on the P/D ratio, whereas in the fourth column, an increase in this population age group relative to those over the age of 65 has a negative effect. The estimates in the next two rows fit the same regression models, Equation (8.7), for different subsamples. The coefficient estimates vary substantially in most cases as the sample period changes. Despite these concerns, the point estimates in the first three rows of Table 8.9 suggest the possibility of large potential effects of demographic changes on asset prices.

Regression models like those that underlie the estimates in the first three rows of Table 8.9 are more subject to the "spurious regression" problem than the equations in Table 8.6 because the P/D ratio is a more slowly evolving time series than the return measures that were the dependent variables in Table 8.6. To address the possibility of spurious regression findings, the fourth row of Table 8.9 reports Dickey-Fuller test statistics that test the null hypothesis of a unit root in the

Table 8.9. *Demographic structure and price-dividend ratios, annual regression estimates*

Asset return and sample period	Independent variable measuring demographic structure				
	Median age	Average age of those 20+	Percent of population 40–64	(Population 40–64)/ population 65+	(Population 40–64)/ population 20+
Coefficient	3.302	4.969	532.284	−6.885	68.641
Estimates,	(0.524)	(0.739)	(96.929)	(1.628)	(57.557)
1926–1999					
Coefficient	3.613	13.216	719.114	−9.384	75.771
Estimates,	(0.715)	(1.447)	(123.211)	(3.787)	(62.052)
1946–1999					
Coefficient	−0.578	2.879	48.225	−6.196	312.952
Estimates,	(0.786)	(0.472)	(94.172)	(1.245)	(54.889)
1926–1975					
Dickey–Fuller	−0.456	0.262	−0.492	1.175	1.610
Test for					
Residuals,					
1926–1999					
Coefficient	0.625	10.244	644.998	49.888	148.922
Estimates,	(3.270)	(6.378)	(273.614)	(17.692)	(167.271)
Differenced					
Model, 1926–1999					

Note: Each equation in rows one through three presents the results of estimating an equation of the form

$$(P/D)_t = \alpha + \beta^*(\text{DEMOGRAPHIC VARIABLE})_t + \varepsilon_t$$

Standard errors are shown in parentheses. Equations are estimated using annual data for the sample period indicated. The entries in the fourth row are Dickey-Fuller t-test statistics, with an unknown mean, applied to the residuals from the regression models in the first row. The estimates in the last row correspond to a regression model of the form

$$\delta(P/D)_t = \alpha' + \beta'^*\delta(\text{DEMOGRAPHIC VARIABLE})_t + \varepsilon'_t$$

residuals from the equations reported in the first row. It is not possible to reject the null hypothesis of a unit root in any case. This suggests that the underlying regression equations may be misspecified.

In light of this finding, the last row of Table 8.9 reports coefficient estimates for the full sample period from a differenced version of Equation 8.7:

$$\delta(P/D)_{,t} = \kappa' + \delta'_{j*}\delta Z_{,t} + \varepsilon'_{,t} \tag{8.7'}$$

In this case, the coefficient estimates for the demographic variables (δ'_j) are statistically significantly different from zero in only two of the five equations. These correspond to the cases in which the independent variable is the percent of the population between the ages of 40 and 64, and the population aged 40–64 as a share of the population aged 65+. In these cases, however, the point estimates of the coefficients seem implausibly large. Consider the increase of 0.05 in the percentage of the population aged 40–64 that took place between 1980 and 2000. The coefficient estimate in the third column of the last row in Table 8.9 suggests that this demographic shift would be associated with an increase of more than 30 in the P/D ratio.

The results in Table 8.9 suggest two conclusions. First, regressions relating the P/D ratio to demographic variables may be subject to "spurious regression bias." The coefficients from these models are sensitive to differencing, and to altering the sample period of estimation. Second, however, there is some evidence, even from differenced models that address the spurious regression problem, that the P/D ratio is higher when a larger share of the population is between the ages of 40 and 64. The point estimates of these effects are implausibly large, but more plausible ranges may fall within the 95 percent confidence interval for the coefficients. This finding provides more support than any of the earlier findings for the possibility that demographics are related to asset prices.

8.4.2 Evidence for Canada and the United Kingdom

In an effort to overcome the problem of "only one Baby Boom" in the United States, I also estimated equations like (8.6) with data from two other nations with well-developed capital markets: the United Kingdom and Canada. The desire to obtain greater demographic variation also motivates Brooks's (1998) focus on stock-price levels in the OECD nations and Erb, Harvey, and Viskanta's (1997) focus on demographics and stock returns in a broad sample of countries. Given the widely disparate sizes of the capital markets and especially the equity markets in different nations, however, it can be difficult to evaluate the results from cross-sectional studies that treat all countries in the same way. Rather than following this strategy, I apply the "one-country time-series approach" to these two other nations.

I focus on equity-market returns for the period 1961–97 in Canada and 1961–96 in the United Kingdom Data on equity-market returns for these samples are computed from information provided by Morgan Stanley–Capital International. Returns are measured in local currency for both nations. Data on Treasury bill returns, on returns to holding long-term bonds, and on the Consumer Price Index in each country were drawn from the IMF database. Returns on fixed-income instruments were available for the period since 1950, so the sample for Canada is 1950–97, whereas that for the United Kingdom is 1950–96. Demographic data were tabulated from various issues of the *United Nations Demographic Yearbook*, updated as necessary using data from the U.S. Census International Database and the United Kingdom *Annual Abstract of Statistics*.

Table 8.10 presents regression results relating the population share between the ages of 40 and 64 and various real return measures for each of these countries.

Table 8.10. *Percent of the population aged 40–64 and asset returns, Canada and the United Kingdom*

Asset category	Canada	United Kingdom
Treasury Bills (50–97 Canada, 50–96 U.K.)	0.766	−0.333
	(0.234)	(0.334)
Long-Term Government Bonds (50–97 Canada, 50–96 U.K.)	0.893	−0.164
	(0.206)	(0.274)
Corporate Stock (61–97 Canada, 61–96 U.K.)	0.903	−2.174
	(1.588)	(3.048)

Notes: Each equation presents the results of estimating an equation of the form

$$R_t = \alpha + \beta^*(\text{Population Share } 40\text{–}60)_t + \varepsilon_t$$

Standard errors are shown in parentheses. See text for further discussion.

The results do not match those for the United States, and they further weaken the claim that demographic structure and asset returns exhibit systematic linkages. In Canada, the share of the population between the ages of 40 and 64 exhibits a positive correlation with all three real return measures. The effect is statistically significantly different from zero for both long-term government bonds and Treasury bills. (In the United States, the coefficients were negative and statistically significantly different from zero.) For the United Kingdom, the point estimates of the coefficients for the real bill and real bond returns are negative, but the coefficient estimates are not statistically significantly different from zero in either case. There is no evidence for either country of a strong relationship between real stock returns and the share of the population between the ages of 40 and 64. Other results, not reported here, confirm the generally weak relationship between other measures of demographic structure and real asset returns in Canada and the United Kingdom.

8.5 Demography-Based "Projected Asset Demand," Asset Returns, and Asset Prices

The empirical results in the last section consider the links between population age structure, asset returns, and asset levels, but they do not utilize the detailed information on the age-wealth profile that emerges from the analysis of the SCF. To do so, I also analyzed how asset returns and asset prices are related to the "projected asset demand variable" that was defined in Equation (8.4). Because this variable combines information on the age-specific evolution of asset holdings with information on the age structure of the population in various years, it offers a more formal link between household-level data on wealth-age profiles and the aggregate analysis of asset demand.

Table 8.11 reports the result of estimating regression models in which the real returns on bills, bonds, and stocks are related to the level of the projected asset

Table 8.11. *"Projected asset demand" and asset returns*

Asset return	Common stocks	Net financial assets	Net worth
1926–1999			
Treasury Bills	−0.004	−0.001	−0.001
	(0.006)	(0.002)	(0.001)
Long-Term Government Bonds	−0.018	−0.004	−0.003
	(0.014)	(0.004)	(0.003)
Corporate Stock	0.010	0.002	0.003
	(0.027)	(0.009)	(0.005)
1946–1999			
Treasury Bills	0.031	0.017	0.005
	(0.012)	(0.004)	(0.002)
Long-Term Government Bonds	0.013	0.021	0.003
	(0.041)	(0.014)	(0.007)
Corporate Stock	0.094	0.030	0.019
	(0.062)	(0.021)	(0.010)

Notes: Each entry reports the regression coefficient and standard error (in parentheses) from a regression with the real asset return as the dependent variable and the indicated demographic demand variable as the independent variable. See text for further discussion. Dickey-Fuller tests applied to the explanatory variables for the 1926–99 period yield t-statistics of −3.49, −4.16, and −2.97 for projected common-stock holdings, projected net-financial assets, and projected net worth, respectively.

demand variable. The table reports two different sets of estimates, corresponding to the 1926–99 and postwar (1946–99) sample periods. The pre-1975 sample is excluded on the grounds that the age-specific asset holding data, which are drawn from household surveys in the 1980s and 1990s, are less likely to apply to that sample period. The results are all based on the age-specific asset profiles that were estimated with cohort effects, and they consider separately the predictive power of the age-specific patterns of corporate-stock ownership, net financial-asset ownership, and net worth.

The results suggest very limited linkage between *any* of the projected demand variables and the realized patterns of asset returns. This is particularly true for the full sample estimates. Only three of the estimated coefficients, those relating the T-bill return to the three projected demand variables for the postwar period, are statistically significantly different from zero. The coefficients for T-bills for the longer sample period are not statistically distinguishable from zero. The net demand for financial assets at various ages should provide important information on the aggregate demand for financial assets as the population ages. The weak empirical findings in Table 8.11 cast doubt on whether the coefficients on the 40–64 age share in the earlier tables reflect age-specific asset demand effects or other factors.

To inform the possibility of spurious regressions in the regressions that include the projected asset demand variables, Table 8.12 presents Dickey-Fuller test statistics similar to those in Table 8.7 but now for the full-sample regression models in

Table 8.12. *Unit root test statistics for residuals from "projected asset demand" and asset return models, 1926–1999*

Asset return	Common stocks	Net financial assets	Net worth
Treasury Bills	−3.801	−3.810	−3.801
Long-Term Government Bonds	−8.022	−7.938	−7.997
Corporate Stock	−8.392	−8.385	−8.411

Notes: Each entry reports the value of the Dickey-Fuller (1979) test statistic, allowing for an unknown mean, applied to the *residuals* corresponding to the regression equations in the first panel of Table 8.11. The critical (95 percent) value for these test statistics is −2.91, based on tables in Fuller (1976).

Table 8.11. In all nine cases, three return measures related to three possible asset demand measures, the null hypothesis of a unit root in the residuals from the regression model, can be rejected.

It is also possible to use the projected demographic demand for assets to explore whether projected wealth holdings are related to the level of stock prices. This exercise is similar to the empirical analysis, using various measures of population age structure that was described in Equation (8.7). Table 8.13 presents the results of regressing the price-to-dividend ratio on projected asset demand. The full-sample findings, as well as those from the postwar subsample, suggest that an increase in projected asset demand is associated with an increase in the P/D ratio. This finding is robust to the choice between projected asset demand measured

Table 8.13. *"Projected asset demand" and price-dividend ratios*

Sample period	Common stocks	Net financial assets	Net worth
Coefficient Estimates, 1926–1999	7.830	2.507	1.453
	(1.402)	(0.436)	(0.249)
Coefficient Estimates, 1947–1995	24.506	9.338	4.088
	(3.487)	(1.058)	(0.579)
Dickey-Fuller Test Statistics, 1926–1999	0.586	0.577	0.484
Coefficient Estimates from Differenced Model, 1926–1999	17.104	6.036	2.640
	(9.247)	(4.024)	(1.587)
Dickey-Fuller Test Statistics, Differenced Model, 1926–1999	−9.540	−9.419	−9.474

Notes: Each entry in the first two rows presents the results of estimating an equation of the form

$$(P/D)_t = \alpha + \beta^*(\text{PROJECTED ASSET DEMAND})_t + \varepsilon_t$$

Standard errors are shown in parentheses. Equations are estimated using annual data for the sample period indicated. The entries in the third row are Dickey-Fuller t-test statistics, with an unknown mean, applied to the residuals from the regression models in the first row. The estimates in the second-to-last row correspond to a regression model of the form

$$\delta(P/D)_t = \alpha' + \beta'^*\delta(\text{PROJECTED ASSET DEMAND})_t + \varepsilon_t'$$

and the entries in the final row are Dickey-Fuller test statistics for the residuals from this equation.

using age-specific net worth, net financial assets, or common stocks. As in some of the earlier specifications, the results again appear quite sensitive to the choice between the full sample and the most recent subsample, with the coefficient estimates doubling or tripling as a result of this sample change.

As with some of the earlier estimates, however, the coefficients imply larger demographic effects than theoretical analyses of demography and asset prices suggest. Consider, for example, the estimates of the link between projected net worth and the P/D ratio for the full sample period. The estimated coefficient of 1.435 implies that the change in projected net worth between 1980 and 2000 (93.7 − 85.7 = 8) could have raised the P/D ratio by 11.2. This seems like a large change in the P/D ratio to ascribe to a single factor, but it does suggest that the change in desired wealth holdings associated with demographic changes in the last two decades may explain some of the variation in P/D ratios.

The equations reported in the first two rows of Table 8.13, like those in Table 8.9, may be misspecified. To address this question, the third row of Table 8.13 reports Dickey-Fuller test statistics for the presence of unit roots in the residuals from the regression models estimated for the full sample period. The null hypothesis of a unit root is not rejected in any case. As in the previous set of regression models for P/D ratios, I difference the underlying specification and reestimate a model linking changes in the P/D ratio to changes in the projected asset demand variable. The results are shown in the penultimate row of Table 8.13. The statistical significance of the coefficient estimates declines when the variables are differenced, although the point estimates continue to suggest a positive effect of projected asset demand on the P/D ratio. For the projected demand for common stock variable, the coefficient estimate is statistically distinguishable from zero at the 90 percent but not the 95 percent confidence level. The last row of Table 8.13 shows that applying the Dickey-Fuller test to the residuals from the differenced models clearly rejects the null hypothesis of a unit root in this specification. The results in Table 8.13 broadly confirm the findings of Bergantino (1998) and Brooks (1999). They illustrate that it is possible to find statistical support for a link between demographic structure and asset prices.

The results in Table 8.13 raise an important question about why projected asset demand measures are correlated with the price-to-dividend ratio whereas simple measures of demographic structure, such as the population share between the ages of 40 and 64, are not. A key difference between the projected asset demand variables that constitute the explanatory variables in Table 8.13 and the simpler measures of demographic structure that were in earlier tables is that the projected asset demand variables place roughly equal weight on retired individuals and prime-age workers. This is because the age-wealth profiles do not show substantial decline in old age. Thus, the variables that seem to track at least the level of equity prices do not distinguish between prime-age workers and older individuals. This observation has important implications for evaluating the "asset market meltdown" hypothesis. Because projected asset demand *does not decline* in the period between 2020 and 2050, as Table 8.5 illustrates, the empirical results in Table 8.13 do not imply that asset values will fall when the Baby Boom cohort reaches retirement age. This is the implication of these results, even though they are consistent with demographic changes such as those in the last two decades affecting asset values.

8.6 Demographic Structure and Risk Aversion of the Representative Consumer

The foregoing results raise questions about whether there is a robust relationship between population age structure and asset returns. They also beg the question of whether by imposing still further structure on the empirical analysis, it might be possible to obtain more definitive results. One previous study that imposed substantial structure on the problem of how demographic change might affect asset demands, the study by Bakshi and Chen (1994), did find statistically significant effects of the average age of the population older than 19 in an Euler equation setting. This section revisits their findings.

Data from the SCF can be used to test the maintained hypothesis that age is related to risk tolerance. SCF survey respondents are asked whether they are prepared to accept "substantial risk in pursuit of substantially above-average returns," "above average risk in return for above-average returns," "average risk for average returns," or virtually no risk in pursuit of higher investment returns. Table 8.14 shows the resulting breakdown of responses, tabulated by the age of the head of the household responding to the SCF. The table is divided into two parts. The first shows the responses of the self-selected subset of individuals who hold corporate stock, whereas the second shows the responses for the entire population. Not surprisingly, the investors who hold some stocks are more prepared to take risk than are their non–equity-investing counterparts. There are also substantial differences between the fraction of households headed by individuals who are younger than 65 and the fraction headed by individuals older than 65 that are willing to take some risk in return for higher average returns.

The data in Table 8.14 do not suggest any clear age patterns in risk tolerance at younger ages. This is consistent with Barsky et al.'s (1997) results based on survey questions in the Health and Retirement Survey. Their analysis suggests that risk tolerance is greatest at older and young ages, with the most risk-averse group in middle age. The findings in Table 8.14, as well as similar findings in other studies, suggest that simple summary measures like the average age in the adult population may not fully capture the link between demographic structure and risk tolerance. In contrast to the data on age-specific asset holdings, which do not draw a strong distinction between prime-age workers and retirees, the data in Table 8.12 on risk aversion do suggest differences between these groups.

Table 8.14. *Age-specific patterns of risk tolerance, 1995 survey of consumer finances*

Age of household head	"Take substantial risk to earn substantial reward"	"Take above-average risk for above-average reward"	"Take average risks for average returns"	"Not willing to take any financial risks"
Population That Holds Stocks or Equity Mutual Funds				
<25	3.9%	34.5%	41.9%	19.7%
25–34	9.8	34.2	45.5	10.6
35–44	5.6	26.4	54.2	13.8
45–54	4.8	24.8	58.6	11.8
55–64	1.7	22.2	62.1	14.0
65–74	4.1	12.8	56.7	26.4
75–84	3.2	7.0	33.2	56.6
>85	0.0	12.4	33.1	54.5
TOTAL	5.0	23.2	52.7	19.1
Entire Population				
<25	6.3%	14.0	39.8	39.9
25–34	4.3	20.3	38.4	37.0
35–44	4.5	17.0	42.5	36.0
45–54	3.8	14.5	42.0	39.8
55–64	2.2	10.7	38.1	49.0
65–74	2.0	5.9	29.1	62.9
75–84	1.2	3.1	23.5	72.1
>85	0.0	5.0	14.8	80.3
TOTAL	3.5	13.6	37.3	45.6

Source: Author's tabulations using the 1995 Survey of Consumer Finances.

The foregoing discussion of previous literature noted that Bakshi and Chen (1994) assume that the utility function of the representative investor is given by:

$$U(C_t, M_t) = C_t^{1-\gamma-\lambda^*Mt}/(1 - \gamma - \lambda^*M_t) \qquad (8.8)$$

where M_t denotes the average age of the population and C_t denotes aggregate per-capita consumption. They use the average age of the adult population over the age of 19 as their focal variable in studying how age structure affects asset returns.

If preferences are given by (8.9), then the standard intertemporal Euler equation generalizes to

$$E_t[(C_{t+1}/C_t)^{-\gamma-\lambda^*Mt}(1 + r_t)] = 1 \qquad (8.9)$$

Thus, Bakshi and Chen (1994) argue, testing the null hypothesis that $\lambda = 0$ provides a parametric test of whether age factors affect the equilibrium determination of asset returns.

Choosing this parametric approach to testing for demographic effects on asset pricing, rather than the approach in earlier sections that is not constrained by functional form, has potential pitfalls. Say the particular functional form for the

Table 8.15. *Sensitivity of Euler equation results to alternative demographic summary variables*

Demographic summary measure	Return = T-bill rate		Return = return on S&P 500	
	γ	λ	γ	λ
Average Age of Persons Over 19	−3.89 (1.67)	0.11 (0.04)	−10.99 (8.60)	0.34 (0.19)
Percent of Population 40–64	0.02 (0.49)	2.95 (1.52)	0.39 (2.61)	12.57 (8.38)
Percent of Population Aged 55+	2.87 (0.96)	−7.94 (3.32)	8.62 (4.57)	−18.08 (15.91)

Notes: Coefficient estimates from NLIV estimation of Equation (8.10) in the text. Sample period 1959–94, with real per-capita consumption of nondurables as the consumption measure. Standard errors are shown in parentheses. See text for further discussion of specification and the set of instrumental variables.

Euler equation turns out to be invalid. This might be because some households face liquidity constraints, because aggregation across households fails, or because of other factors. In these cases, the age variable may have some explanatory power in tracking the movements of consumption growth and asset returns, but this may not reflect an age-structure effect on risk tolerance and, hence, asset returns. Bakshi and Chen (1994) estimate (8.8) for the 1945–90 period and find that λ is positive and statistically significantly different from zero. For a range of other sample periods, including 1926–90 and 1900–45, they cannot reject the null hypothesis that $\lambda = 0$.

Table 8.15 presents estimates of both γ and λ from the equation:

$$E_t[(C_{t+1}/C_t)^{-\gamma-\lambda^* Z_{j,t}}(1 + r_t)] = 1 \qquad (8.10)$$

where $Z_{j,t}$ is one of the demographic variables considered in the previous sections. This includes the average age of the adult population, the variable considered by Bakshi and Chen (1994), as well as the population share between the ages of 40 and 64.

The equations are estimated for the sample period 1959–94. These equations are based on data on personal consumption expenditures in the National Income and Product Accounts. The consumption measure is nondurable consumption, which avoids problems of durability that may contaminate the Euler equation specification. The equations are estimated by nonlinear instrumental variables, with the second and third lags of real per-capita consumption and the real return, as well as a constant, a time trend, and the contemporaneous, first, and second lag of the applicable demographic variable, as instruments.

The results in Table 8.15 confirm the findings reported by Bakshi and Chen (1994). When population age structure is measured using the average age of the adult population, the estimate of λ is positive and statistically significantly different from zero. This is particularly evident when the Treasury bill return is used as the rate of return variable in the Euler equation, but it is also true when the stock-market return is used. These estimates suggest that as the population becomes older, the relative risk aversion of the representative consumer increases.

The results from other specifications, which include alternative demographic variables, are not as encouraging with respect to the age-dependent risk-aversion interpretation. When the demography variable (Z) is the population share between the ages of 40 and 64, there is again evidence of increasing risk-aversion as this age group expands. This is consistent with some of the findings in Barsky et al. (1997) but not with the evidence from the risk-aversion questions in the SCF that suggested that this age group was not more risk averse than other age groups. The evidence from including the fraction of the population over the age of 55 is even more discouraging for the age-dependent risk-aversion view. The SCF data suggest that there is a clear increase in the risk aversion of older households, relative to their younger counterparts, yet the coefficient estimate (λ) on this demographic variable is negative and statistically significant for Treasury bills, and negative (but not significant) for stocks. These results suggest that risk aversion of the representative consumer declines as the fraction of the population over the age of 55 increases. This finding is not consistent with the model that Bakshi and Chen (1994) use to motivate their analysis, and it contrasts with evidence from household surveys that ask about risk preferences.

8.7 Conclusion

The empirical results in this paper suggest that it is difficult to find a robust relationship between asset returns on stocks, bonds, or bills and the age structure of the U.S. population over the last 70 years. The correlations that do emerge are stronger between Treasury-bill returns, and long-term government bond returns, and demographic variables, than between stock returns and these demographic variables. Most measures of demographic structure, however, do not show a statistically significant correlation with asset returns. These findings stand in contrast to the results of general equilibrium models for asset returns, which suggest a clear link between age structure and returns. One possible interpretation of these findings is that, even though changes in age structure do affect asset demand, these effects are simply too small to be detected among the other shocks to asset markets.

The empirical findings do provide some evidence that the level of asset prices, measured as the price of corporate equities relative to corporate dividends, is related to demographic structure. The evidence is strongest when age-specific asset demands are used to construct time-varying "projected asset demands" at different dates and when these "projected asset demands" are then related to P/D ratios. There is substantial variation in the estimated effect of "projected asset demand" on asset prices as the estimation sample varies, but for both postwar and longer sample periods, there is some evidence of a link between demographic structure and the P/D ratio.

Neither the findings on returns nor the findings on the level of asset prices are consistent with the view that asset returns will decline sharply when the Baby Boom cohort reaches retirement age. Most of the empirical results suggest very little relationship between population age structure and asset returns. Moreover, the variable that does appear to be related to share price levels, the "projected asset demand" variable, is not projected to decline when the Baby Boomers reach retirement because asset decumulation in retirement takes place much more gradually than asset accumulation during working years. The results suggesting at best a weak link between population age structure and P/D ratios indicate that future work is needed to isolate and empirically measure the channels through which demographic changes may affect asset prices.

Any attempt to assess the future link between asset returns and demographic structure must also consider the potentially important role of integrated world-capital markets. Such markets make the link between population age structure in any nation, and the asset market returns in that nation, substantially weaker than such a link would be in a closed economy. For textbook "small open economies," required returns are exogenous, and they are determined in world, not domestic, capital markets. For such nations, if demography affects returns at all, it is global demographic structure that should matter. Shifts in the demographic structure of a single nation would affect the amount of capital owned by that country's residents but not the return earned on such capital.

The degree to which world-capital markets are integrated and, hence, the importance of this modeling assumption remains an open question. Feldstein and Horioka (1980), Frankel (1991), and Taylor (1996) document substantial correlation between national saving and national investment rates. These relationships make the effect of a change in a country's domestic saving rate and desired asset holdings on the equilibrium return on its capital stock an open issue. With respect to risky assets, particularly corporate equity, the evidence on capital-market integration is even less clear. Despite large cross-border gross investment flows, there is still a substantial home bias in equity ownership. French and Poterba (1991) present evidence showing that more than 90 percent of the equity assets of investors in the United States and Japan are held in their domestic equity markets.

Prospectively, the integration of capital markets in currently emerging economies with those of currently established economies may be an important factor determining the demand for financial assets. Siegel (1998, 41) succinctly presents the issue when he writes, "The developing world emerges as the answer to the age mismatch of the industrialized economies. If their progress continues, they will sell goods to the Baby Boomers and thereby acquire the buying power to purchase their assets."

The empirical findings reported here suggest several directions for future work. One is expanding the current analysis to consider asset accumulation in defined-benefit pension plans and in funded government Social Security systems. The "projected asset demand variable" developed herein includes only those assets that individuals purchase directly or hold through defined-contribution pension plans. It excludes accumulations on their behalf in defined-benefit plans. These accumulations are a substantial share of total household asset holdings, and they display a somewhat mechanical accumulation and decumulation profile as a result of population aging. Miles (1999) presents calculations for the United Kingdom and for Europe that suggest the potential importance of including pension saving in calculation age-wealth profiles.

A second issue, which may be too subtle to study with existing data, concerns the timing of any asset market reactions to demographic shocks. The "news" about demography is revealed when cohorts are born, not when they reach their prime saving years. Yet, multiperiod overlapping generations models suggest that the equilibrium path of asset prices, and not just the initial level of such prices, is affected by demographic shocks. Detailing the structure of the asset market response to a demographic shock, and then testing for the presence of such effects in actual data, would represent an important improvement on the reduced-form regression strategies used in this paper.

Finally, the current analysis has ignored a wide range of nondemographic factors that may affect equilibrium real returns and asset prices. Monetary policy is an obvious example. If the monetary authority can affect the real interest rate on Treasury bills and long-term government bonds through its policy actions, then postulating a link between population age structure and equilibrium returns must make an implicit assumption about how the monetary authority would respond to changing age structure. This raises a whole host of questions about other control variables that might be included in regression specifications like those reported in this paper. These questions have implications for the design of empirical tests, and they might lead to the addition of variables other than demographic factors in the real-return models. These issues also raise important questions about optimal policy and how the monetary authority (let alone the fiscal policy makers) should react to changing demographic structure.

REFERENCES

Abel, Andrew B. 1999. "The Effects of a Baby Boom on Stock Prices and Capital Accumulation in the Presence of Social Security." Mimeo, Wharton School, University of Pennsylvania.

———. 2001. "Will Bequests Attenuate the Predicted Meltdown in Stock Prices When Baby Boomers Retire?" NBER Working Paper 8131. Cambridge, MA.

Ameriks, John, and Stephen P. Zeldes. 2000. "How Do Household Portfolio Shares Vary with Age?" Mimeo, Columbia University, Graduate School of Business.

Attanasio, Orazio, and Hilary Hoynes. 2000. "Differential Mortality and Wealth Accumulation." *Journal of Human Resources* 35: 1–29.

Attanasio, Orazio, and Giovanni Violante, 2000. "The Demographic Transition in Closed and Open Economies: A Tale of Two Regions." Inter-American Development Bank Working Paper 412, Washington, DC.

Bakshi, Gurdip, and Zhiwu Chen. 1994. "Baby Boom, Population Aging, and Capital Markets." *Journal of Business* 67: 165–202.

Barsky, Robert, F. Thomas Juster, Miles Kimball, and Matthew Shapiro. 1997. "Preference Parameters and Behavioral Heterogeneity: An Experimental Approach in the Health and Retirement Survey." *Quarterly Journal of Economics* 62: 537–80.

Bergantino, Steven. 1998. *Life-Cycle Investment Behavior, Demographics, and Asset Prices.* Doctoral Dissertation, Massachusetts Institute of Technology, Department of Economics.

Bohn, Henning. 1998. "Will Social Security and Medicare Remain Viable as the U.S. Population Ages?" Mimeo, University of California, Santa Barbara, Department of Economics.

Brooks, Robin J. 1998. *Asset Market and Saving Effects of Demographic Transitions.* Doctoral Dissertation, Yale University, Department of Economics.

Brooks, Robin. 2000. "Life-Cycle Portfolio Choice and Asset Market Effects of the Baby Boom." Mimeo, International Monetary Fund, Washington, DC.

Campbell, John Y., Andrew W. Lo, and A. Craig MacKinlay. 1996. *The Econometrics of Financial Markets.* Princeton, NJ: Princeton University Press.

Cutler, David, James Poterba, Louise Sheiner, and Lawrence Summers. 1990. "An Aging Society: Challenge or Opportunity?" *Brookings Papers on Economic Activity* 1: 1–74.

Dent, Harry S., Jr. 1998. *The Roaring 2000s.* New York: Simon & Schuster.

Diamond, Peter. 1965. "National Debt in a Neoclassical Growth Model." *American Economic Review* 55: 1125–50.

Dickey, David A., and Wayne A. Fuller. 1979. "Distribution of Estimators for Autoregressive Time Series with a Unit Root." *Journal of the American Statistical Association* 74: 427–31.

Engle, Robert F., and C. W. J. Granger. 1987. "Cointegration and Error Correction: Representation, Estimation, and Testing," *Econometrica* 55: 251–76.

Erb, Claude B., Campbell R. Harvey, and Tadas E. Viskanta. 1997. "Demographics and International Investments." *Financial Analysts Journal* (July/August): 14–28.

Feldstein, Martin, and Charles Horioka. 1980. "Domestic Savings and International Capital Flows." *Economic Journal* 90: 314–29.

Ferson, Wayne E., Sergei Sarkissian, and Timothy Simin. 2000. "Spurious Regressions in Financial Econometrics." Mimeo, University of Washington.

Frankel, Jeffrey. 1991. "Quantifying International Capital Mobility in the 1980s." In B. D. Bernheim and J. Shoven (eds.), *National Saving and Economic Performance.* Chicago: University of Chicago Press, pp. 227–69.

French, Kenneth, and James Poterba. 1991. "Investor Diversification and International Equity Markets." *American Economic Review* 81: 222–6.

Fuller, Wayne. 1976. *Introduction to Statistical Time Series.* New York: John Wiley & Sons.

Goyal, Amit. 1999. "Demographics, Stock Market Flows, and Stock Returns." Mimeo, Anderson Graduate School of Management, UCLA.

Granger, C. W. J., and Paul Newbold. 1974. "Spurious Regressions in Econometrics." *Journal of Econometrics* 2: 111–20.

Hamilton, James D. 1994. *Time Series Analysis.* Princeton, NJ: Princeton University Press.

Holtz-Eakin, Douglas, David Joulfaian, and Harvey Rosen. 1993. "The Carnegie Conjecture: Some Empirical Evidence." *Quarterly Journal of Economics* 108: 413–35.

——— 1990. "Research on the Aged: Economic Status, Retirement, and Consumption." *Journal of Economic Literature* 28: 565–637.

Ibbotson Associates. 2000. *Stocks, Bonds, Bills, and Inflation: 2000 Yearbook.* Chicago: Ibbotson Associates.

Kennickell, Arthur B., Martha Starr-McLuer, and Annika Sunden. 1997. "Family Finances in the United States: Recent Evidence from the Survey of Consumer Finances." *Federal Reserve Bulletin* (January): 1–24.

Kennickell, Arthur B., Martha Starr-McLuer, and B. J. Surette. 2000. "Recent Changes in U.S. Family Finances: Results from the 1998 Survey of Consumer Finances." *Federal Reserve Bulletin* 86 (January): 1–29.

Macunovich, Diane. 1997. "Discussion of 'Social Security: How Social and Secure Should It Be?'" in Steven Sass and Robert Triest (eds.), *Social Security Reform: Links to Saving, Investment, and Growth*. Boston: Federal Reserve Bank of Boston, pp. 64–76.

Mankiw, N. Gregory, and David Weil. 1989. "The Baby Boom, the Baby Bust, and the Housing Market." *Regional Science and Urban Economics* 19: 235–58.

Meyers, Mike. 2000. "After the (Baby) Boom." *Minneapolis St. Paul Star-Tribune* (February 8).

Miles, David. 1999. "Modeling the Impact of Demographic Change Upon the Economy." *Economic Journal* 109: 1–36.

Passell, Peter. 1996. "The Year Is 2010. Do You Know Where Your Bull Is?" *New York Times* (March 10), Section 3, 1–6.

Poterba, James. 1998. "Population Age Structure and Asset Returns." NBER Working Paper 6774.

Poterba, James, and Andrew Samwick. 1995. "Stock Ownership Patterns, Stock Market Fluctuations, and Consumption." *Brookings Papers on Economic Activity* 1995: 2, 295–371.

2001. "Household Portfolio Allocation over the Life-Cycle." in S. Ogura, T. Tachibanaki, and D. Wise (eds.), *Aging Issues in the U.S. and Japan*. Chicago, University of Chicago Press, pp. 65–103.

Sabelhaus, John, and Karen Pence. 1998. "Household Saving in the '90s: Evidence from Cross-Section Wealth Surveys." Mimeo, U.S. Congressional Budget Office, Washington, DC.

Schieber, Sylvester, and John Shoven. 1997. "The Consequences of Population Aging on Private Pension Fund Saving and Asset Markets," in S. Schieber and J. Shoven (eds.), *Public Policy Toward Pensions*. Cambridge, MA: MIT Press, pp. 219–45.

Shorrocks, Anthony F. 1975. "The Age-Wealth Relationship: A Cross-Section and Cohort Analysis." *Review of Economics and Statistics* 57: 155–63.

Siegel, Jeremy. 1998. *Stocks for the Long Run, Second Edition*. New York: McGraw-Hill.

Sterling, William, and Stephen Waite. 1998. *Boomernomics: The Future of Your Money in the Upcoming Generational Warfare*. New York: Ballantine Publishing Group.

Taylor, Alan. 1996. "International Capital Mobility in History: The Saving-Investment Relationship." NBER Working Paper 5743.

Yoo, Peter S. 1994a. "Age-Dependent Portfolio Selection." Federal Reserve Bank of St. Louis. Working Paper 94-003A.

1994b. "Age Distributions and Returns of Financial Assets." Federal Reserve Bank of St. Louis. Working Paper 94-002B.

9 Will Bequests Attenuate the Predicted Meltdown in Stock Prices When Baby Boomers Retire?

There are many potential explanations of the phenomenal increase in stock prices in the United States during the past several years. One popular explanation is that as Baby Boomers save for retirement, their aggregate demand for capital is very large, which drives up the price of capital. This explanation then goes on to predict that when the Baby Boomers retire, they will sell large amounts of capital and drive down its price. Jim Poterba uses the term "asset market meltdown hypothesis" to refer to this predicted decline in stock prices.

In the previous chapter Poterba examines data on asset holdings in several cross sections of the Survey of Consumer Finances (SCF) and raises an important challenge to the asset market meltdown hypothesis. He points out that recent theoretical models of a market meltdown assume that Baby Boomers will sell all of their assets during their retirement years,[1] and he argues that this assumption is inconsistent with the data on asset holdings in the SCF. Subject to the difficulty of disentangling time effects, cohort effects, and age effects, Poterba concludes from his Tables 8.1 and 8.2 that although consumers rapidly accumulate assets while they are of working age, they decumulate assets during retirement much less rapidly than would be predicted by a simple life-cycle model with no bequest motive and no lifetime uncertainty. He extrapolates from these results to conclude that the Baby Boomers will not sell all of their assets during retirement, and he further concludes that the asset market meltdown hypothesis is incorrect in its prediction that the price of capital will fall.

---

[1] Abel (2000) and Brooks (1999) both assume that consumers know precisely when they will die and do not have bequest motives so that they optimally choose to have zero wealth at the time of death.

This paper was prepared as a discussion of "Demographic Structure and Asset Returns," presented by James Poterba as the Review of Economics and Statistics Lecture, Cambridge, Massachusetts, March 20, 2000. I thank Bill Dupor, Yoel Lax, Nick Souleles, and Amir Yaron for helpful discussion.

Poterba also looks for empirical evidence of an effect of demographic variables on asset prices and returns. He finds a very weak effect of demographic variables on asset *returns*, but he finds a more substantial effect of demographic variables on stock *prices* using data he generates on "projected asset demands." Poterba calculates projected asset demands by combining age-specific asset holdings from his Table 8.2 with actual and projected age-specific populations in each year. He finds (Table 8.13) some evidence of a positive relationship between projected asset demands and the price-dividend ratio over various historical sample periods dating back to 1926. Looking forward, the projected asset demands reported in his Table 8.5 increase over the next two decades and then remain fairly constant for the succeeding three decades. Because projected asset demands do not fall when the Baby Boomers retire, Poterba rejects the asset market meltdown hypothesis while maintaining the notion that the Baby Boom contributed to the increase in stock prices.

Poterba has demonstrated that, in contrast to the predictions of a life-cycle model with no bequest motive and no lifetime uncertainty, the projected demand for assets will not decline sharply when the Baby Boomers are retired. I will accept this conclusion, but I argue here that the failure of the demand for capital to fall in the future does not imply that the price of capital will not fall. Specifically, taking account of the supply of capital, as well as its demand, the equilibrium price of capital may fall when Baby Boomers retire, even if the the demand for capital by retired Baby Boomers remains high.

In this paper, I present a general equilibrium overlapping generations model with convex adjustment costs, which generate an endogenous price of capital as in Abel (2000). I include a bequest motive so that consumers will choose not to consume all of their wealth during retirement. The inclusion of a bequest motive provides a framework for addressing the extent to which the predicted meltdown in asset prices is attenuated by taking account of the fact that consumers do not consume all of their wealth during retirement. The equilibrium of the model has the following properties: (1) the price of capital rises when a large cohort of consumers – Baby Boomers – is young and working, which is consistent with Poterba's Tables 8.5 and 8.13; (2) the price of capital is anticipated to fall when Baby Boomers retire; (3) young Baby Boomers optimally choose to hold capital even with the anticipation that its price will fall; (4) consumers do not completely decumulate their assets during retirement, consistent with Poterba's Tables 8.1 and 8.2; and, yet, (5) the dynamic behavior of the equilibrium price of capital is unaffected by the strength of the bequest motive, so that assets held by old consumers for the purpose of making bequests do not attenuate the predicted drop in the price of capital when Baby Boomers retire.

I develop and analyze the formal overlapping generations model in Section 9.2. Before presenting this formal model, in Section 9.1 I present Poterba's heuristic model and augment it to include the supply of capital as well as the demand for capital. The discussion in Section 9.1 provides an intuitive preview of the formal results in Section 9.2.

9.1 A Heuristic Model

Poterba presents a simple stylized, or heuristic, model to illustrate the effects of demographic variables on the price of capital. I begin by presenting this model, with slightly modified notation.

Consider a closed economy with overlapping generations of consumers who live for two periods. All consumers who are born in the same period are identical. Let N_t be the number of consumers born at the beginning of period t. They inelastically supply one unit of labor when they are young, and they do not work when they are old, so the amount of labor employed in period t is N_t. Let

$$\eta_{t+1} \equiv \frac{N_{t+1}}{N_t} \tag{9.1}$$

be the birth rate in period $t + 1$, and assume that the birth rate is a serially uncorrelated random variable.

To make the analysis transparent, Poterba makes additional simplifying assumptions. He assumes that the capital stock cannot be augmented by investment and does not depreciate. Therefore, K_t, the aggregate capital stock held at the beginning of period t, remains constant over time. He also assumes that in each period, the wage income of each young consumer equals one unit of output[2] and that young consumers save a constant fraction s of their wage income. Therefore, the aggregate saving of the cohort of young consumers born at the beginning of period t is $N_t s$. All of this saving is used to purchase K_{t+1}, the aggregate capital stock to be carried into period $t + 1$, at a price of q_t per unit of capital in period t. Therefore,

$$q_t K_{t+1} = N_t s \tag{9.2}$$

which is equivalent to Poterba's Equation (9.1).

Equation (9.2) can be interpreted as the demand for capital, K_{t+1}, at the end of period t as a function of the price of capital, q_t, given N_t and s. If the capital stock remains constant, as in Poterba's stylized model, then the price of capital can be determined directly from this demand curve. In particular, the price of capital, q_t, is proportional to N_t, the number of workers in the economy. Thus, an increase in N_t will increase the price of capital, q_t, as the large cohort of workers bids up the price of the fixed capital stock. Poterba goes on to claim that when the large cohort of workers retires and sells its capital, it will drive down the price

---

[2] The aggregate production function implicitly underlying this model is $Y_t = N_t + f(K_t)$, where Y_t is aggregate output. With this specification of the production function, the marginal product of labor always equals one, regardless of the level of the capital stock.

of capital. This claim is based on the implicit assumption that a Baby Boom in period t, which generates a large cohort of workers, N_t, will be followed by a decrease in the size of the working population in the following generation. That is, Poterba assumes that N_{t+1} is smaller than N_t. Equivalently, he assumes that if the birth rate in period t, η_t, is large, then the birth rate in the following period, η_{t+1}, must not only be small, it also must be less than one.[3] This assumption requires strong negative serial correlation in the birth rate across successive generations.[4] However, if the economy has a fluctuating birth rate that always exceeds one so that the population of workers always grows over time, then in the stylized model introduced by Poterba and represented by Equation (9.2), the price of capital increases in every period.

In the presence of a growing population, the price of capital in Equation (9.2) can be prevented from growing in every period by allowing the capital stock to grow over time. To preview the rational expectations general equilibrium model that I present in Section 9.2, suppose the aggregate supply curve of capital slopes upward so that the (gross) growth rate of the capital stock, $\frac{K_{t+1}}{K_t}$, is an increasing function of the price of capital. In particular, suppose that

$$K_{t+1} = \kappa K_t q_t^\lambda \tag{9.3}$$

where $\kappa > 0$ and $\lambda > 0$.[5] Equation (9.3) represents the supply of capital, K_{t+1}, at the end of period t as a function of the price of capital, q_t, for a given value of K_t.

To determine the equilibrium price of capital, I solve the demand and supply curves in Equations (9.2) and (9.3) simultaneously. First, divide both sides of Equation (9.3) by N_{t+1}, and use the definition of the birth rate, η_{t+1}, in Equation (9.1) to obtain

$$k_{t+1} = \kappa k_t \frac{1}{\eta_{t+1}} q_t^\lambda \tag{9.4}$$

where $k_{t+1} \equiv K_t/N_t$ is the capital-labor ratio in period t. To express the capital-labor ratio k_t as a function of q_t, use Equation (9.3) to substitute for K_{t+1} in Equation (9.2), and use the definition of k_t to obtain

$$k_t = \frac{1}{\kappa} s q_t^{-(1+\lambda)} \tag{9.5}$$

To obtain an expression for the dynamic behavior of the price of capital, q_t, substitute Equation (9.5) into Equation (9.4) to obtain

$$\ln q_t = \frac{1}{1+\lambda} \ln q_{t-1} - \frac{1}{1+\lambda} \ln \kappa + \frac{1}{1+\lambda} \ln \eta_t \tag{9.6}$$

[3] A birth rate equal to one in the model corresponds to one child per person, which is equivalent to two children per woman.

[4] In contrast, if the birth rate is i.i.d. across successive generations, an increase in N_t, which increases q_t, is no more likely to be followed by a decrease in the number of workers or in the price of capital in the following period than at any other time.

[5] If λ were equal to zero, and if κ were equal to one, the capital stock would be constant over time, as in Poterba's model.

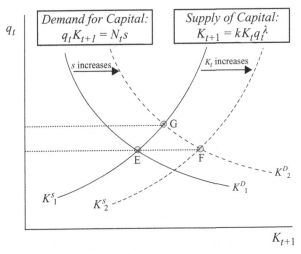

Figure 9.1. Supply and Demand for Capital

Because $\lambda > 0$, if the birth rate, $\ln \eta_t$, is serially uncorrelated with unconditional mean $E(\ln \eta)$, then $\ln q_t$ follows a stationary AR(1) process with unconditional mean $\frac{1}{\lambda}(E\{\ln \eta\} - \ln \kappa)$. Thus, starting from the unconditional mean price of capital, an increase in the birth rate η_t causes an increase in the price of capital q_t. Consistent with the asset-market meltdown hypothesis, the price of capital, $\ln q_{t+1}$, is anticipated to fall toward its unconditional mean in the following period.

In the heuristic model presented here, as well as in the general equilibrium models in Abel (2000) and Brooks (1999), consumers spend all of their resources in the final period of life, contrary to the empirical findings reported by Poterba in his Tables 1 and 2. Poterba argues that because consumers continue to hold assets throughout old age, the aggregate demand for capital does not fall when the Baby Boomers age, and, hence, contrary to the asset-market meltdown hypothesis, the price of capital will not plunge when the Baby Boomers are retired. I was intrigued by Poterba's argument that the meltdown would be attenuated by the fact that people hold substantial assets until death, and I set out to examine the extent of this attenuation in the context of a rational expectations general equilibrium model that I present in Section 9.2. To address this issue, I assume that consumers have bequest motives and, thus, hold assets at the time of death. In the specification I use in Section 9.2, the equilibrium dynamics of the price of capital are completely unaffected by the presence of a bequest motive and the consequent holding of assets at the time of death. Therefore, a bequest motive does not attenuate the predicted decline in stock prices when the Baby Boomers retires.

Before proceeding to the general equilibrium model, I use the analysis in the current section to illustrate the invariance of the price of capital to the strength of the bequest motive. Figure 9.1 illustrates the demand and supply curves for capital, K_{t+1}, in period t as a function of the price of capital, q_t. The solid downward-sloping curve, K_1^D, is the demand for capital in Equation (9.2) in the absence of a bequest motive. The solid upward-sloping curve, K_1^S, is the supply of capital in Equation (9.3) in the absence of a bequest motive. Thus, in the absence of a bequest motive, equilibrium in the market for capital in period t is represented by point E.

Now consider an otherwise-identical economy with a bequest motive. The amount of saving and, hence, the demand for capital in period t will be higher in the economy with a bequest motive than in the economy without a bequest motive. Thus, the demand for capital in an economy with a bequest motive is represented by K_2^D, which is to the right of K_1^D.[6] If the supply curve of capital were invariant to the strength of the bequest motive (which is implicitly assumed by Poterba), the equilibrium in the economy with a bequest motive would be represented by point G, where the price of capital is higher than in the absence of a bequest motive. However, an economy with a bequest motive will have a higher capital stock in each period than an otherwise-identical economy without a bequest motive. Therefore, in period t, the capital stock, K_t, is higher in the presence of a bequest motive than in its absence and, hence, the supply curve of capital in the economy with a bequest motive, K_2^S, is to the right of the supply curve in the absence of a bequest motive, K_1^S. The equilibrium in the economy with a bequest motive is represented by point F, where K_2^D and K_2^S intersect, with a higher capital stock but the same price of capital, as at point E. In the parametric rational expectations general equilibrium model in Section 9.2, I show that the equilibrium price of capital, q_t, is invariant to the strength of the bequest motive, which means that rightward shifts of the supply and demand curves in Figure 9.1 are of the same size. Because the equilibrium price of capital is not affected by strength of the bequest motive, the asset-market meltdown is not attenuated by the introduction of a bequest motive.

9.2 A General Equilibrium Model with a Baby Boom and an Endogenous Price of Capital

In this section, I present a rational expectations general equilibrium model in which the wage income of workers is determined endogenously, and the asset demands of young and old consumers maximize expected lifetime utility. This model is a simplified version of the model in Abel (2000), except that it includes a bequest motive so that consumers will not completely decumulate their assets in old age.

As in Section 9.1, consider a closed economy with overlapping generations of consumers who live for two periods. At the beginning of period t, N_t identical consumers are born, and they each inelastically supply one unit of labor in period

---

[6] The economy with a bequest motive can be viewed as having a higher value of saving per worker, s, than does the economy without a bequest motive.

t and earn wage income w_t, which I derive after introducing the production technologies. These consumers do not work in period $t + 1$ when they are old.

9.2.1 Production Technologies

There are two production technologies. One technology, which I call the consumption goods technology, produces output that can be either consumed or used as an input to the other technology, which is the capital adjustment technology.

The consumption goods technology uses capital and labor to produce output. Let K_t be the aggregate capital stock at the beginning of period t, let Y_t be the aggregate output of the consumption goods technology in period t, and assume that

$$Y_t = AK_t^\alpha N_t^{1-\alpha}, \quad \text{where } 0 < \alpha < 1 \text{ and } A > 0 \tag{9.7}$$

The capital adjustment technology uses output from the consumption goods technology together with capital to produce capital for use in the following period. Suppose that the capital adjustment technology is

$$K_{t+1} = a I_t^\phi K_t^{1-\phi} \tag{9.8}$$

where $a > 0$, $0 < \phi < 1$, and investment, I_t, is the aggregate quantity of output from the consumption goods technology used in the capital adjustment technology. Because the curvature parameter ϕ is strictly between zero and one, the capital stock in period $t + 1$ is an increasing and concave function of investment, I_t. The concavity of this function captures convex costs of adjustment.

The price of capital at the end of period t, q_t, is the amount of consumption goods in period t that must be used to produce an additional unit of capital for use in period $t + 1$. Thus, $q_t = (\frac{\partial K_{t+1}}{\partial I_t})^{-1}$, which can be calculated using Equation (9.8) to obtain[7]

$$q_t = \frac{1}{a\phi} \left(\frac{I_t}{K_t} \right)^{1-\phi} \tag{9.9}$$

The value, in terms of consumption goods in period t, of the capital stock carried into period $t + 1$ equals the product of q_t from Equation (9.9) and K_{t+1} from Equation (9.8), which is

$$q_t K_{t+1} = \frac{1}{\phi} I_t \tag{9.10}$$

---

[7] Equations (9.8) and (9.9) imply that $\frac{K_{t+1}}{K_t} = a^{\frac{1}{1-\phi}} (\phi q_t)^{\frac{\phi}{1-\phi}}$, which implies that in Equation (9.3) $\lambda = \frac{\phi}{1-\phi}$ and $\kappa = a^{\frac{1}{1-\phi}} \phi^{\frac{\phi}{1-\phi}}$.

Factor markets are perfectly competitive so that each factor of production earns its marginal product. Thus, using Equation (9.7), the wage rate in period t, w_t, is

$$w_t = (1 - \alpha) \frac{Y_t}{N_t} \tag{9.11}$$

Because capital is used in both the consumption goods technology and the capital adjustment technology, capital earns rentals in both technologies. The rental earned by a unit of capital in the consumption goods technology in period t is $\alpha \frac{Y_t}{K_t}$. The rental earned by a unit of capital in the capital adjustment technology in period t is the marginal product of capital in that technology, $\frac{\partial K_{t+1}}{\partial K_t}$, multiplied by the current price of next period's capital, q_t. This rental can be calculated using Equations (9.8) and (9.9) to obtain $\frac{1-\phi}{\phi} \frac{I_t}{K_t}$. Therefore, the total rental to capital is

$$v_t = \alpha \frac{Y_t}{K_t} + \frac{1 - \phi}{\phi} \frac{I_t}{K_t} \tag{9.12}$$

The (gross) rate of return on capital held from period $t - 1$ to period t, R_t, equals the rental on capital, v_t, divided by the price paid for the capital in period $t - 1$, q_{t-1}. Therefore,

$$R_t = \frac{\alpha Y_t + \frac{1-\phi}{\phi} I_t}{q_{t-1} K_t} \tag{9.13}$$

9.2.2 Consumer Behavior

A consumer born at the beginning of period t chooses consumption when young, c_t, consumption when old, x_{t+1}, and a bequest, b_{t+2}, to be divided equally among the consumer's η_{t+1} children at the beginning of period $t + 2$ when the consumer's children are beginning the second period of life. Each consumer born at the beginning of period t receives a bequest $\frac{b_{t+1}}{\eta_t}$ at the beginning of period $t + 1$. Thus, the present value of the lifetime resources of a consumer born at the beginning of period t is

$$\theta_t \equiv w_t + \frac{1}{R_{t+1}} \frac{b_{t+1}}{\eta_t} \tag{9.14}$$

The lifetime budget constraint of a consumer born at the beginning of period t is

$$c_t + \frac{1}{R_{t+1}} x_{t+1} + \frac{1}{R_{t+1}} \frac{1}{R_{t+2}} b_{t+2} = \theta_t \tag{9.15}$$

A consumer born at the beginning of period t has the utility function

$$U_t = \ln c_t + \beta E_t \{\ln x_{t+1}\} + \gamma E_t \{\ln b_{t+2}\} \tag{9.16}$$

where $0 < \beta \leq 1$, $\gamma \geq 0$, and $E_t\{\ \}$ denotes the expectation conditional on information available in period t. The consumer chooses c_t, x_{t+1} and b_{t+2} to maximize the utility function in Equation (9.16), subject to the budget constraint in Equation (9.15). It can be shown that the optimal value of consumption when young is[8]

$$c_t = \frac{1}{1 + \beta + \gamma}\theta_t \tag{9.17}$$

At the beginning of period $t + 1$, all of the capital in the economy, K_{t+1}, is held by the N_t consumers who were born at the beginning of period t. They acquired some of this capital by saving when they were young, and they inherited the remaining portion of their capital. The rental accruing to the aggregate capital held by these consumers is $v_{t+1}K_{t+1}$, where v_{t+1} is the rental to capital in Equation (9.12). Therefore, each owner of capital has resources equal to

$$v_{t+1}\frac{K_{t+1}}{N_t} = \frac{1}{N_t}\left(\alpha Y_{t+1} + \frac{1-\phi}{\phi}I_{t+1}\right) \tag{9.18}$$

The owners of this capital (who were born at the beginning of period t) are in the final period of their lives in period $t + 1$, and they choose consumption, x_{t+1}, and a bequest, b_{t+2}, to maximize $\beta \ln x_{t+1} + \gamma E_{t+1}\{\ln b_{t+2}\}$, subject to $x_{t+1} + \frac{1}{R_{t+2}}b_{t+2} = \frac{\alpha Y_{t+1} + \frac{1-\phi}{\phi}I_{t+1}}{N_t}$. The optimal values of x_{t+1} and b_{t+2} are

$$x_{t+1} = \frac{\beta}{\beta + \gamma}\frac{1}{N_t}\left(\alpha Y_{t+1} + \frac{1-\phi}{\phi}I_{t+1}\right) \tag{9.19}$$

and

$$\frac{b_{t+2}}{R_{t+2}} = \frac{\gamma}{\beta + \gamma}\frac{1}{N_t}\left(\alpha Y_{t+1} + \frac{1-\phi}{\phi}I_{t+1}\right) \tag{9.20}$$

Decreasing the time subscript by one unit in Equation (9.20) implies that a consumer born at the beginning of period t receives a bequest with present value (as of the beginning of period t) equal to

$$\frac{1}{R_{t+1}}\frac{b_{t+1}}{\eta_t} = \frac{\gamma}{\beta + \gamma}\frac{1}{N_t}\left(\alpha Y_t + \frac{1-\phi}{\phi}I_t\right) \tag{9.21}$$

The present value of lifetime resources of a consumer born at the beginning of period t can be calculated by substituting the wage from Equation (9.11) and the bequest received from Equation (9.21) into Equation (9.14) to obtain

$$\theta_t = (1 - \alpha)\frac{Y_t}{N_t} + \frac{\gamma}{\beta + \gamma}\frac{1}{N_t}\left(\alpha Y_t + \frac{1-\phi}{\phi}I_t\right) \tag{9.22}$$

---

[8] Define $\varphi_{t+1} \equiv (\theta_t - c_t)R_{t+1}$ and $V_{t+1}(\varphi_{t+1}) \equiv \max_{x_{t+1}, b_{t+2}} \beta \ln x_{t+1} + \gamma E_{t+1}\{\ln b_{t+2}\}$, subject to $x_{t+1} + \frac{b_{t+2}}{R_{t+2}} = \varphi_{t+1}$. The optimal values of x_{t+1} and b_{t+2} are $x_{t+1} = \frac{\beta}{\beta+\gamma}\varphi_{t+1}$ and $b_{t+2} = \frac{\gamma}{\beta+\gamma}\varphi_{t+1}R_{t+2}$. Therefore, $V_{t+1}(\varphi_{t+1}) = (\beta + \gamma)\ln \varphi_{t+1} + \beta \ln \frac{\beta}{\beta+\gamma} + \gamma \ln \frac{\gamma}{\beta+\gamma} + \gamma E_{t+1}\{\ln R_{t+2}\}$. The optimal value of c_t maximizes $\ln c_t + E_t\{V_{t+1}(\varphi_{t+1})\}$, which is the value of c_t that maximizes $\ln c_t + (\beta + \gamma)E_t\{\ln \varphi_{t+1}\}$ or, equivalently, the value of c_t that maximizes $\ln c_t + (\beta + \gamma)\ln(\theta_t - c_t)$. The first-order condition for this maximization is $\frac{1}{c_t} = \frac{\beta+\gamma}{\theta_t-c_t}$, which implies $(1 + \beta + \gamma)c_t = \theta_t$.

9.2.3 Aggregate Behavior

Let $\Theta_t \equiv N_t \theta_t$ denote the aggregate present value of lifetime resources of the cohort born at the beginning of period t. Equation (9.22) implies

$$\Theta_t \equiv N_t \theta_t = \left(1 - \frac{\beta}{\beta + \gamma}\alpha\right) Y_t + \frac{\gamma}{\beta + \gamma}\frac{1 - \phi}{\phi} I_t \tag{9.23}$$

Let $C_t \equiv N_t c_t$ be the aggregate consumption in period t of the cohort of young consumers. Equations (9.17) and (9.23) imply

$$C_t = \frac{1}{1 + \beta + \gamma}\left[\left(1 - \frac{\beta}{\beta + \gamma}\alpha\right) Y_t + \frac{\gamma}{\beta + \gamma}\frac{1 - \phi}{\phi} I_t\right] \tag{9.24}$$

Let $X_t \equiv N_{t-1} x_t$ be the aggregate consumption in period t of the cohort of N_{t-1} old consumers (who were born at the beginning of period $t - 1$). Equation (9.19) implies

$$X_t = \frac{\beta}{\beta + \gamma}\left(\alpha Y_t + \frac{1 - \phi}{\phi} I_t\right) \tag{9.25}$$

The aggregate consumption of all consumers in period t is calculated by adding C_t from Equation (9.24) to X_t from Equation (9.25) to obtain

$$C_t + X_t = \frac{1}{1 + \beta + \gamma}\left[(1 + \alpha\beta) Y_t + (1 + \beta)\frac{1 - \phi}{\phi} I_t\right] \tag{9.26}$$

Recall that Y_t is the aggregate output of the consumption goods technology in period t, and I_t is the amount of this output used as an input to the capital adjustment technology rather than consumed. Thus,

$$I_t = Y_t - C_t - X_t \tag{9.27}$$

Now substitute aggregate consumption from Equation (9.26) into Equation (9.27) to obtain[9]

$$I_t = \psi Y_t \tag{9.28}$$

where

$$0 < \psi \equiv \phi\frac{(1 - \alpha)\beta + \gamma}{1 + \beta + \gamma\phi} < 1 \tag{9.29}$$

---

[9] Equations (9.28) and (9.29) may be derived alternatively as follows. The cohort of consumers born at the beginning of period t owns the entire capital stock, K_{t+1}, at the beginning of period $t + 1$. It acquires capital by saving $(1 - \alpha)Y_t - C_t$, and (see Equation [9.21]) it inherits capital that has a present value at the end of period t equal to $\frac{\gamma}{\beta + \gamma}(\alpha Y_t + \frac{1 - \phi}{\phi} I_t)$. Therefore, the value at the end of period t of the capital stock carried into period $t + 1$ is $q_t K_{t+1} = (1 - \alpha)Y_t - C_t + \frac{\gamma}{\beta + \gamma}(\alpha Y_t + \frac{1 - \phi}{\phi} I_t)$. Now use Equation (9.10) to substitute $\frac{1}{\phi}I_t$ for $q_t K_{t+1}$, and use Equation (9.24) for C_t to obtain $\frac{1}{\phi}I_t = (1 - \alpha)Y_t - \frac{1}{1 + \beta + \gamma}[(1 - \frac{\beta}{\beta + \gamma}\alpha)Y_t + \frac{\gamma}{\beta + \gamma}\frac{1 - \phi}{\phi} I_t] + \frac{\gamma}{\beta + \gamma}(\alpha Y_t + \frac{1 - \phi}{\phi} I_t)$. Simplifying this equation yields $I_t = \phi\frac{(1 - \alpha)\beta + \gamma}{1 + \beta + \gamma\phi} Y_t$.

The investment-output ratio ψ depends on the strength of the bequest motive γ. In the special case in which $\gamma = 0$, the investment-output ratio is $\psi = \phi \frac{\beta}{1+\beta}(1-\alpha)$ as in the laissez-faire special case in Abel (2000, Section 5). To determine the effect of γ on ψ, differentiate the expression for ψ in Equation (9.29) with respect to γ to obtain

$$\frac{\partial \psi}{\partial \gamma} = (1 - \psi)\frac{\phi}{1 + \beta + \gamma\phi} > 0 \qquad (9.30)$$

Equation (9.30) implies that when comparing two economies with identical technologies, and preferences that are identical except for the value of γ, the economy with a stronger bequest motive (higher γ) will have a higher investment-output ratio, ψ.

9.2.4 The Dynamic Behavior of Aggregates

The investment-capital ratio, $\frac{I_t}{K_t}$, is an important factor affecting the growth rate of the capital stock as well as the price of capital. Use Equation (9.7) to substitute for Y_t in Equation (9.28) and divide both sides by K_t to obtain

$$\frac{I_t}{K_t} = \psi A k_t^{\alpha-1} \qquad (9.31)$$

where $k_t \equiv \frac{K_t}{N_t}$. Now divide both sides of the capital adjustment technology in Equation (9.8) by N_t, and use the expression for the investment-capital ratio in Equation (9.31) to obtain

$$k_{t+1}\eta_{t+1} = a\psi^\phi A^\phi k_t^{1-(1-\alpha)\phi} \qquad (9.32)$$

Take logarithms of both sides of Equation (9.32) to obtain an AR(1) process for $\ln k_{t+1}$

$$\ln k_{t+1} = [1 - (1-\alpha)\phi]\ln k_t + \ln a + \phi \ln \psi + \phi \ln A - \ln \eta_{t+1}. \qquad (9.33)$$

Because $0 < \alpha < 1$ and $0 < \phi < 1$, $\ln k_{t+1}$ follows a stationary AR(1) process if the birth rate, $\ln \eta_{t+1}$, is serially uncorrelated. To analyze the impact of a bequest motive on the accumulation of capital, recall from Equation (9.30) that the investment-output ratio, ψ, is an increasing function of the bequest motive parameter γ. Equation (9.33) implies that an increase in γ, which increases ψ, will increase the average value of the capital-labor ratio but will not affect the variance or serial correlation of $\ln k_{t+1}$. More precisely, an increase in γ increases the mean of the stationary distribution of $\ln k_{t+1}$ but has no effect on any autocovariances of $\ln k_{t+1}$.

The equilibrium value of the (logarithm of the) price of capital is determined by substituting Equation (9.31) into Equation (9.9) and taking logarithms of both sides of the equation to obtain

$$\ln q_t = -\ln \phi a + (1 - \phi) \ln \psi + (1 - \phi) \ln A - (1 - \alpha)(1 - \phi) \ln k_t. \quad (9.34)$$

Use Equation (9.34) lagged one period to obtain an expression for $\ln q_{t-1}$. Then subtract $[1 - (1 - \alpha)\phi] \ln q_{t-1}$ from $\ln q_t$, and use Equation (9.33) to obtain

$$\ln q_t = [1 - (1 - \alpha)\phi] \ln q_{t-1} - (1 - \alpha)(\phi \ln \phi + \ln a)$$
$$+ (1 - \alpha)(1 - \phi) \ln \eta_t \qquad (9.35)$$

If the birth rate, η_t, is serially uncorrelated, then the (logarithm of the) equilibrium price of capital, $\ln q_t$, follows a stationary AR(9.1) process, with the same serial correlation as $\ln k_{t+1}$, and this AR(9.1) process is independent of the strength of the bequest motive γ. Suppose that in period $t - 1$ the price of capital equals its unconditional mean, and that the realization of the birth rate, η_t, is unusually large. According to Equation (9.35), this Baby Boom in period t causes the price of capital, q_t, to increase. If the birth rate is serially uncorrelated, the price of capital is rationally anticipated to fall back toward its unconditional mean in period $t + 1$. The magnitude of the anticipated drop in the price of capital – or asset-market meltdown – when the Baby Boomers retire in period $t + 1$ is independent of the strength of the bequest motive. Therefore, the introduction of a bequest motive does not attenuate the asset-market meltdown.

9.3 Conclusion

Poterba's examination of age-specific asset holdings in the SCF leads him to conclude that consumers accumulate assets while they are of working age, but they hold on to these assets during retirement much more than would be predicted by a simple life-cycle model without lifetime uncertainty and without a bequest motive. He uses age-specific asset holdings, together with age-specific population data and projections, to calculate a time series of projected asset-demand. He finds evidence that the price-dividend ratio of stocks in the United States has been positively related to his projected asset-demand variable in various historical sample periods. Looking into the future, Poterba's projected asset-demand variable increases over the next 20 years and then remains fairly constant. Because the projected asset demand does not decline when the Baby Boomers retire, Poterba rejects the asset-market meltdown hypothesis, which predicts a decline in stock prices when the Baby Boomers retire.

I have taken at face value Poterba's finding about age-specific asset holdings and his finding of a positive effect of his projected asset demand on stock prices in historical data. I also have taken at face value his finding that projected asset demand will not fall when the Baby Boomers retire. However, to understand the behavior of the price of capital, it is important to take account of the supply of capital as well as the demand for capital. To analyze the interaction of the supply and demand for capital, I have developed a rational expectations general equilibrium model with a bequest motive. This model is consistent with Poterba's observations that retired consumers continue to hold a substantial amount of assets at the time of death and that a Baby Boom can drive up the price of capital. However, contrary to Poterba's conclusion, there is an anticipated decline in the price of capital when Baby Boomers retire, and this decline is not attenuated by the introduction of a bequest motive.

My finding that the equilibrium price of capital is invariant to the bequest motive is a consequence of the particular parametric specification of preferences and technology that I use. I regard this invariance result as a rhetorical device to make the point that one cannot predict the price of capital by focusing on the demand for capital while ignoring its supply. The effect of asset demands by retirees on asset prices in a more general context remains an open question worthy of further study. In considering the role of asset demands by retirees in a more general framework, different motives for these asset demands might be analyzed. Instead of using the bequest motive specified in this paper, positive asset demands by retirees can be generated by a bequest motive based on altruism. Alternatively, precautionary saving to guard against longevity risk in the absence of perfect annuity markets would be a way to generate a demand for assets by retired consumers. Another direction for exploration is to examine alternative forms of the aggregate supply curve of capital, especially because this paper has illustrated the potentially important role of the supply of capital in determining the equilibrium price of capital.

REFERENCES

Abel, Andrew B. 2000. "The Effects of a Baby Boom on Stock Prices and Capital Accumulation in the Presence of Social Security." Mimeo, Wharton School of the University of Pennsylvania.
Brooks, Robin. 1999. "What Will Happen to Financial Markets When Baby Boomers Retire?" Mimeo, International Monetary Fund.
Poterba, James M. 2000. "Demographic Structure and Asset Returns." Mimeo, Massachusetts Institute of Technology.

10 Aging and the Private Versus Public Pension Controversy: A Political-Economy Perspective

Aging can tilt the political power balance toward downscaling the welfare state; see, for instance, Razin, Sadka, and Swagel (2002). One of the well-publicized proposals on how to reduce the size of the welfare state is to shift from pay-as-you-go (PAYG) national pensions to individual retirement accounts. In this chapter, we develop a simple political-economy model in which we analyze how aging can be a driving force behind such a reform. Also, we examine how rigid balanced-budget rules that do not make exceptions for fundamental structural changes in social security (e.g., the Stability and Growth Part in the European Union) can impede this reform.

The economic viability of national old-age security systems has been increasingly deteriorating. Although the recent 2000 population census in the United States reveals some encouraging signs that the aging process is checked through increasing fertility rates and migration of young people, the demographic picture for Europe is cloudy. As vividly put by *The Economist* (August 3, 2002, p. 23):

> As its people grow fewer, Europe's state pensions systems will go deeper into the red. Germany and Italy are trying to push the private-sector alternative. It is not easy...

More concretely, for Germany (op. cit):

> Seven-tenths of German pensions come from a state scheme with roots in Bismarck's day. It is financed mainly by a levy on wages, 19.1% this year, half paid by workers and half by employers. But, as all over Europe, the demographics are grim. Today, there are 2.8 Germans aged 20–59 to support each pensioner. By 2030 there could be half as many. And the state can't just fork out money to fill the gap.

And similarly, in Italy (op. cit):

> The government's strategy is to get private pension schemes and funds, now embryonic, working properly first. Then, it hopes, it will be politically able to tackle the financing of the pay-as-you-go state system. But Italy cannot afford to wait. Its state's

spending on pensions is more than 14% of GDP, almost double the European Union average. Every year, payouts far exceed contributions by workers and employers.

Indeed, the aging of the population raises the burden of financing the existing PAYG, national pension (old-age security) systems, because there is a relatively falling number of workers that have to bear the cost of paying pensions to a relatively rising number of retirees. Against this backdrop, there arose proposals to privatize social security, as a solution to the economic sustainability of the existing systems. This, by and large, means a shift from the current PAYG systems to individual retirement accounts (or fully funded systems). A supposedly added benefit to such a shift is the better return on the contributions to individual accounts than to a PAYG national pension system. If privatized pensions can offer better rates of return than national pensions, transition from the latter to the former may be smooth. However, a careful scrutiny of the pensions' rate-of-return argument reveals that it is flawed. We follow now Krugman (2002) to demonstrate the weakness of the argument.

We imagine an overlapping-generations model with just one young (working) person and one old (retired) person in each period – each individual lives for two periods. Suppose there is a PAYG, national pension system by which the worker contributes one euro to finance the pension benefit of one euro paid to the retiree. Each young person contributes one euro when young and working and receives one euro upon retirement. Evidently, the young person earns zero return on her contribution to the national PAYG, old-age security system. If, instead, the young person were to invest her one euro in an individual account, she would have earned the real market rate of return of, say, 100%, allowing her a pension of two euros at retirement. (Recall that the average length of time between the first period of her life, in which she works, and the second period of her life, in which she is a pensioner, could be something like 30 years; a real rate of return of 100 percent between these two periods is not exorbitant.) Is the young person better off with this transition from a PAYG system to an individual retirement account? Not if the government still wishes to honor the existing "social contract" (or political norm) to pay a pension benefit of one euro to the old at the time of the transition. To meet this liability, the government can issue a debt of one euro. The interest to be paid by the government on this debt at the market rate of 100 percent will be one euro in each period, starting from the next period *ad infinitum*. Hence, the young person will be levied a tax of one euro in the next period when old, to finance the interest payment. Thus, her net-of-tax balance in the individual account will only be one euro, implying a zero net-of-tax return in the individual account – the same return as in the national PAYG system. And what if the individual invests the one euro in the equity market and gets a better return than the 100 percent, which the government pays on its debt? If the capital markets are efficient, the higher equity return (relative to the government bond rate) reflects nothing else but a risk premium. That is, the equity premium is equal to the risk premium through arbitrage. Therefore, equity investment offers no gain in risk-adjusted return over government bonds.[1,2,3] And if markets are inefficient, then the government can, as a general policy, issue debt in order to invest in the equity market, irrespective of the issue of replacing social security by individual retirement accounts.

Nevertheless, the increased fragility of national PAYG pension systems, caused by the aging of the population, raises doubts among the young about whether the next generations will continue to honor the implicit intergenerational social contract, or the political norm, according to which, "I pay now for the pension benefits of the old, and the next young generation pays for my pension benefits, when I get old." These doubts are not unfounded for, after all, there will indeed be more pensioners per each young worker of the next generation and, hence, each one of the young workers will have to pay more to honor the implicit social contract. With such doubts, the political power balance may indeed shift toward scaling down the PAYG system, encouraging the establishment of supplemental

---

[1] Greg Mankiw (*Fortune Magazine*, March 15, 1999) puts this argument as follows: "Having trouble saving for your retirement? Try this simple solution: Borrow some money at 7%, buy stocks that return 10%, and pocket the 3% difference. Still running short? Don't worry – just do it again.

This is, of course, ridiculous advice. Buying equities with borrowed money is a risky stratgegy, and no one should do it without understanding those risks.

So, let's consider the downside. Suppose the federal government put some of the social security trust fund in equities. Now suppose that the next decade turns out less like the early 1990s and more like the early 1930s, when the Dow Jones Industrial Average fell from 381 to 41 – or like Japan today, where the stock market is still at less than half the level it reached a decade ago. What would happen?

Clearly, social security would be in big trouble. Not only would Baby Boomers be starting to retire, automatically boosting government spending on retirement programs, but the market collapse would likely coincide with a recession, reducing tax revenue. With the trust fund drained by low stock prices, social security benefits would almost certainly be cut a lot.

Although the downside risk is far from negligible, it could still be a risk worth taking. Buying stocks rather than bonds does work out, on average, and we would be irrational to avoid risk at all costs. But there are several reasons to think it's a bad bet.

First, it seems an unlikely coincidence that the proposal (to go long on equities and short on government bonds) comes on the heels of several years (the 1990s) of truly exceptional stock returns. If we take a look at history, however, the stock market isn't nearly as imprressive. In the 19th century, the average premium for investing in stocks over bonds was less than 3 percent.

Second, the stock market's historical performance reflects a large amount of good luck. We live in the world's richest country, at the end of the most prosperous century ever; it should come as no surprise that the market has done so well. The future may give us a similarly lucky draw, but let's not count on it.

Third, some economists see the large historical equity premium as an anomaly that's already been corrected. Most measures of stock market valuation are now at historical extremes. Perhaps this is because investors, realizing stocks were undervalued in the past, have corrected the problem. If so, stocks are unlikely to keep outperforming bonds by the same margin."

[2] Galasso (2000) indeed calculated the returns of the PAYG social security "investment" for the U.S. median voter in the 1964 to the 1996 presidential elections. He found that these overperformed the Dow Jones Industrial Average (DJIA) for the early part of this period but underperformed the DJIA in the later part of this period.

[3] See, however, Diamond and Geannakoplos (forthcoming) for a useful analysis of the portfolio diversification advantages from investing retirement savings in the equity market in certain circumstances.

individual retirement accounts.[4] Such accounts are, by their very nature, fully funded, so that they are not directly affected by the aging of the population.[5] Naturally, the existing old generation opposes any scaling down of the PAYG system because it stands to lose pension benefits (without enjoying the reduction in the social security contributions). This opposition can, however, be softened, or altogether removed, if the government creates a budget deficit in order to support the social security system and allow it not to scale down the pension benefits to the current old, so as to fully offset the reduction in social security contributions, or even allow it to maintain these benefits intact. (Of course, this deficit will be carried over to the future, with its debt service smoothed over the next several generations.) However, here may stand in the way some self-imposed restrictions such as those imposed by the Stability and Growth Pact in the EU, which put a ceiling on the current fiscal deficit. As put by Tabellini (2003):

> The current formulation of the Stability and Growth Pact is problematic.... The Pact now emphasizes the budget deficit, but neglects the longer term generational imbalances. For instance, consider a pension reform that gradually but permanently reduces pension outlays in the future, but immediately cuts social security contributions so as to relax political constraints. A transition from a pay-as-you-go towards a fully funded private pension system could have this effect. Such a reform could run against the Stability Pact as currently formulated, no matter how desirable from an economic point of view.

In any event, the current systems are, by and large, insolvent because of the aging of the population. So either social security taxes are increased exorbitantly or, as we point out in the overview, government debt could, according to some projections, reach 150 percent of national income in the EU at large by 2050 and 250 percent in Germany and France. Recall that the debt target ceiling in the Pact is only 60 percent!

In this paper, we develop an analytical model in which a PAYG, old-age security system is designed as a political-economy equilibrium. We then investigate how the aging of the population can shift the equilibrium toward scaling down this fiscal system (thereby encouraging the emergence of individual retirement accounts). We further examine how lifting the ceiling on fiscal deficits can politically facilitate such a scaling down of PAYG systems and whether such a constitutional reform could come about through the political process.

---

[4] The welfare state may also come under attack because of international tax competition brought about by globalization; see, for instance, Sinn (1990), Lassen and Sorensen (2002), and Wilson and Wildasin (forthcoming). By contrast, Rodrik (1998) advances an opposite hypothesis that exposure to foreign trade, another facet of globalization, generates greater income uncertainties; consequently, the public demand for social insurance rises.

[5] Naturally, the aging of the population has some bearing on individual retirement accounts, too, through the general-equilibrium effects on the return to capital (stemming from the induced change in the capital-labor ratio).

10.1 Political-Economy Design of Social Security

We continue to employ a standard overlapping-generations model in which each generation lives for two periods: a working period and a retirement period. As before, we assume a stylized economy in which there are two types of workers: skilled workers who have high productivity and provide one efficiency unit of labor per unit of labor time, and unskilled workers who provide only $q < 1$ efficiency units of labor per unit of labor time. Workers have one unit of labor time during their first period of life but are born without skills and, thus, with low productivity. Each worker chooses whether to acquire an education and become a skilled worker or else remain unskilled. After the working period, individuals retire, with their consumption funded by private savings and social security pension, discussed later. As before, there is a continuum of individuals, characterized by an innate ability parameter, e, which is the time needed to acquire an education.

The transfer b is now paid only to the retirees, so that the cutoff level of the education-cost parameter is given by:

$$(1 - \tau)w(1 - e^*) - \gamma = (1 - \tau)qw$$

which yields the same formula as before:

$$e^* = 1 - q - \frac{\gamma}{(1 - \tau)w} \tag{10.1}$$

To obtain analytical results, we continue to employ a specification in which factor prices are exogenously determined. Thus, we assume a linear production function in which output (Y) is produced using labor (L) and capital (K):

$$Y = wL + (1 + r)K \tag{10.2}$$

with capital fully depreciating at the end of the production process.

As before, the population grows at a rate of n. Each individual's labor supply is assumed to be fixed, so that the income tax does not distort individual labor supply decisions at the margin. But, the total labor supply does again depend on the income tax rate because this affects the cut-off ability, e^*; thus, the mix of skilled and unskilled individuals in the economy. At present, the total labor supply is given by:

$$L = \left\{ \int_0^{e^*} (1 - e)dG + q[1 - G(e^*)] \right\} N_0(1 + n) \equiv \ell(e^*)N_0(1 + n) \tag{10.3}$$

where $N_0(1+n)$ is the size of the working-age population at present (N_0 is the number of young individuals born in the preceding period), and $\ell(e^*) = \int_0^{e^*} (1 - e)dG + q[1 - G(e^*)]$ is the average (per worker) labor supply at present. As before, G is the cumulative distribution function of e, with $G(0) = 0$ and $G(1) = 1$.

There is a PAYG, old-age social security system by which the taxes collected from the young (working) population are earmarked to finance a pension-benefit to the old (retired) population. Thus, the benefit (b), paid to each individual at present, must satisfy the following PAYG budget constraint:

$$bN_0 = \tau wL = \tau w\ell(e^*)N_o(1+n)$$

where τ is the social security tax at present. Dividing through by N_o yields an explicit formula for the pension benefit:

$$b = \tau wl(e^*)(1+n) \tag{10.4}$$

In each period, the benefit of the social security system accrues only to the old, whereas the burden (the social security taxes) are borne by the young. Then, one may wonder why would not the young, who outnumber the old with a growing population, drive the tax and the benefit down to zero in a political-economy equilibrium. We appeal to a sort of an implicit intergenerational social contract, which goes like this:[6]

> I, the young, pay now for the pension benefits of the old; and you, the young of the next generation, will pay for my pension benefit, when I grow old and retire.

With such a contract in place, the young at present are willing to politically support a social security tax, τ, which is earmarked to pay the current old a pension benefit of b, because they expect the young generation in the next period to honor the implicit social contract and pay them a benefit αb. The parameter α is assumed to depend negatively on the share of the old in the population. If the current young will each continue to bring n children, then the share of the old will not change in the next period and α is expected to be one. But if fertility falls, the share of the old in the next period will rise relative to the present and α is expected to fall below one.

Because factor prices are constant over time, current saving decisions will not affect the rate of return on capital that the current young will earn on their savings. Hence, the dynamics in this model are redundant. For any social security tax rate, τ, Equations (10.1) and (10.2) determine the functions $e^* = e^*(\tau)$ and $b = b(\tau)$.

---

[6] Recent models (Bohn [forthcoming]) have used an explicit game-theoretic reasoning to address the issue of the survivability of the PAYG social security system. This literature demonstrates the existence of an equilibrium in an overlapping-generations model with social security as a sequential equilibrium in an infinitely repeated voting game. The critical support mechanism is provided by trigger strategies. As put by Bohn:

> The failure of any cohort to adhere to the proposed equilibrium triggers a negative change in voters' expectations about future benefits that destroys social security. Since survival and collapse are discrete alternatives, trigger strategy models provide a natural definition of what is meant by social security being viable.

> To support social security as a sequential equilibrium, there is a very simple condition that must be fulfilled: For the median voter, the present value of future benefits exceeds the value of social security contributions until retirement. This condition is easily satisfied in our overlapping-generations model.

Denote by $W(e, \tau, \alpha)$ the lifetime income of a young e-individual:

$$W(e, \tau, \alpha) = \begin{cases} (1-\tau)w(1-e) - \gamma + \alpha b(\tau)/(1+r) & \text{for } e \leq e^*(\tau) \\ (1-\tau)wq + \alpha b(\tau)/(1+r) & \text{for } e \geq e^*(\tau) \end{cases}$$

$$(10.5)$$

In each period, the political-economy equilibrium for the social security tax, τ (and the associated pension benefit, b), is determined by majority voting among the young and old individuals who are alive in this period. The objective of the old is quite clear: so long as raising the social security tax rate, τ, generates more revenues and, consequently, a higher pension benefit, b, they will vote for it. However, voting of the young is less clear-cut. Because a young individual pays a tax bill of $\tau w(1-e)$ or τwq, depending on her skill level, and receives a benefit of $\alpha b/(1+r)$, in present value terms, she must weigh her tax bill against her benefit. She votes for raising the tax rate if $\partial W/\partial \tau > 0$ and for lowering it if $\partial W/\partial \tau < 0$. Note that:

$$\partial^2 W(e, \tau, \alpha)/\partial e \partial \tau = \begin{cases} w & \text{for } e < e^*(\tau) \\ 0 & \text{for } e > e^*(\tau) \end{cases}$$

$$(10.6)$$

As before, if $\partial W/\partial \tau > 0$ for some e_o, then $\partial W/\partial \tau > 0$ for all $e > e_o$; similarly, if $\partial W/\partial \tau < 0$ for some e_o, then $\partial W/\partial \tau < 0$ for all $e < e_0$. This implies that if an increase in the social security tax rate benefits a particular young (working) individual (because the increased pension benefit outweighs the increase in the tax bill), then all young individuals who are less able than her (i.e., those who have a higher cost-of-education parameter, e) also must gain from this tax increase. Similarly, if a social security tax increase hurts a certain young individual (because the increased pension benefit does not fully compensate for the tax hike), then it must also hurt all young individuals who are more able than her.

As was already pointed out, the old always opt for a higher social security tax. But as long as $n > 0$, the old are outnumbered by the young. To reach an equilibrium, the bottom end of the skill distribution of the young population joins forces with the old to form a pro-tax coalition of 50 percent of the population, whereas the top end of the skill distribution of the young population forms a counter antitax coalition of equal size. The pivot in determining the outcome of majority voting is a young individual with an education-cost index denoted by e_M, such that the young who have an education-cost index below e_M (namely, the antitax coalition) form 50 percent of the total population. The political-economy equilibrium tax rate maximizes the lifetime income of this median voter.

Formally, e_M is defined as follows. At present, there are $N_o(1+n)G(e_M)$ young individuals with cost-of-education parameter $e \leq e_M$ (more able than the median voter) and $N_o(1+n)[1 - G(e_M)]$ young individuals with cost-of-education parameter $e \geq e_M$ (less able than the median voter). There are also N_o retired individuals at present who always join the pro-tax coalition. Hence, e_M is defined implicitly by:

$$N_0(1+n)G(e_M) = N_o(1+n)[1 - G(e_m)] + N_o$$

Dividing this equation by N_o and rearranging terms yield the cost-of-education parameter for the median voter:

$$e_M = G^{-1}\left[\frac{2+n}{2(1+n)}\right] \tag{10.7}$$

As before, the political equilibrium tax rate, τ, denoted by $\tau_o(e_M, \alpha)$, maximizes the lifetime income of the median voter:

$$\tau_o(e_M, \alpha) = \arg\max_{\tau} W(e_M, \tau, \alpha) \tag{10.8}$$

This equilibrium tax rate is implicitly defined by the first-order condition:

$$\frac{\partial W[e_M, \tau_0(e_M, \alpha), \alpha]}{\partial \tau} \equiv B[e_M, \tau_0(e_M, \alpha), \alpha] = 0 \tag{10.9}$$

and the second-order condition is:

$$\frac{\partial^2 W[e_M, \tau_0(e_M, \alpha), \alpha]}{\partial \tau^2} \equiv B_\tau[e_M, \tau_0(e_M, \alpha), \alpha] \lessgtr 0 \tag{10.10}$$

where B_τ is the partial derivative of B with respect to its second argument.

10.2 Social Security under Strain: Aging Population

The aging population puts the PAYG, old-age social security systems under strain. The burden of financing the pension benefits to the old falls on fewer young shoulders when population ages, as we have already pointed out. Thus, if the fertility of the current young falls below the fertility rate (n) of their parents, then the share of the old in the next period will rise and α will fall.

To find the effect of aging on social security, we investigate the effect of a decline in α on the equilibrium social security tax rate, $\tau_o(e_M, \alpha)$. Differentiate Equation (10.9) totally with respect to α to conclude that

$$\frac{\partial \tau_o(e_M, \alpha)}{\partial \alpha} = -\frac{B_\alpha[e_M, \tau_0(e_M, \alpha), \alpha]}{B_\tau[e_M, \tau_0(e_M, \alpha), \alpha]} \tag{10.11}$$

where B_α is the partial derivative of B with respect to its third argument. Because B_τ is nonnegative (see the second-order condition [10.10]), it follows that the sign of $\partial \tau_o/\partial \alpha$ is the same as the sign of B_α. It also follows from Equation (10.9) that $B_\alpha = \partial^2 W/\partial \alpha \partial \tau$. Employing Equation (10.5), we find that:

$$B_\alpha[e_M, \tau_o(e_M, \alpha), \alpha] = \frac{\partial^2 W[e_M, \tau_o(e_M, \alpha), \alpha]}{\partial \alpha \partial \tau} = \frac{1}{1+r}\frac{db[\tau_0(e_M, \alpha)]}{d\tau} \tag{10.12}$$

Naturally, no one will vote for raising the social security tax if $db/dt < 0$ because, in such a case, the pension-benefit falls when the social security tax is raised. Put differently, a political-economy equilibrium will never be located on the "wrong" side of the Laffer curve, where a tax rate hike lowers revenue. This also can be seen formally. From Equation (10.5),

$$B(e, \tau, \alpha) = \frac{\partial W(e, \tau, \alpha)}{\partial \tau} = \begin{cases} -w(1-e) + \dfrac{\alpha}{1+r} \dfrac{db(\tau)}{d\tau} & \text{for } e \leqq e^*(\tau) \\[2ex] -wq + \dfrac{\alpha}{1+r} \dfrac{db(\tau)}{d\tau} & \text{for } e \geqq e^*(\tau) \end{cases}$$

(10.13)

so that, when the lifetime income of the median voter is maximized – that is, when $B = 0$ (see Equation [10.9]) – we have

$$\frac{db[\tau_0(e_M, \alpha)]}{d\tau} = \begin{cases} w(1-e_M)(1+r)/\alpha & \text{if } e_M \leqq e^*(\tau) \\ wq(1+r)/\alpha & \text{if } e_M \geqq e^*(\tau) \end{cases} \geq 0 \qquad (10.14)$$

Thus, it follows from Equations (10.12) and (10.14) that $B_\alpha[e_M \, \tau_0(e_M, \alpha), \alpha] \geq 0$ and, hence, from Equation (10.11) that

$$\frac{\partial \tau_0(e_M, \alpha)}{\partial \alpha} > 0 \qquad (10.15)$$

We conclude that when the young population expects reduced social security benefits because of the aging of the populations (i.e., when α falls), the public indeed votes for scaling down the social security system already at present (i.e., for lowering τ and b). As a result, the young resort to supplemental old-age savings, such as individual retirement accounts. Naturally, the old are worse off as a result of reducing b. But, they are outvoted by the young, whose attitude for lowering τ has turned stronger following the reduction in the social security benefits that they will get.

10.3 Relaxing the Ceiling on Fiscal Deficits

The old, naturally, continue to oppose the (partial) transition from a PAYG, old-age social security system to individual retirement accounts because they lose some of their pension benefits. They also have a strong moral claim that they contributed their fair share to the social security system when they were young, but they receive at retirement less than what they paid when they were young. Their opposition, strengthened perhaps by being morally justified, can be accommodated, in part or in full, if the government is allowed to make a *debt-financed* transfer to the social security system so as to allow the system to pay pension benefits in excess of the social security tax revenues. This deficit is carried forward to the future and its debt-service is smoothed over the next few generations so that its future tax implications for the current young generation is not significant. This, of course, requires relaxation of some restrictions of the sorts imposed by the Stabilization and Growth Pact in the European Union during the transition from social security to individual retirement accounts.

For simplicity, suppose that the government makes a transfer at the exact amount that is required to keep the pension benefits of the current old intact, despite the reduction in the social security tax rate. Specifically, when τ falls, then the term b in Equation (10.4) that is financed by this τ falls as well. But, we assume that the government compensates the old generation so as to maintain the total pension benefits intact. Therefore, despite the fall in b, the old are indifferent to the reduction in τ (and, consequently, the reduction in b). Thus, the outcome of the majority voting is now effectively determined by the young only. The median voter is now a median among the young population only. This median voter has a lower cost-of-education index than before; that is, e_M will fall.

To find the effect of the fall in e_M on the political-economy equilibrium social security tax rate, $\tau_0(e_M, \alpha)$, we follow the same procedure as in the preceding section, and conclude that:

$$\frac{\partial \tau_0}{\partial e_M} = -\frac{B_{e_M}[e_M, \tau_0(e_M, \alpha), \alpha]}{B_\tau[e_M, \tau_0(e_M, \alpha), \alpha]} \tag{10.16}$$

As before, the sign of $\partial \tau / \partial e_M$ is the same as the sign of B_{e_M} because $B_\tau \leq 0$. Note that $B_{e_M} = \partial^2 W / \partial e_M \partial \tau$ (see Equation [10.9]) so that it follows from Equation (10.5) that:

$$B_{e_M}[e_M, \tau_0(e_M, \alpha), \alpha] = \begin{cases} w & \text{for } e_M < e^*(\tau) \\ 0 & \text{for } e_M > e^*(\tau) \end{cases} \tag{10.17}$$

Thus, we conclude that $\partial \tau / \partial e_M$ is nonnegative: it is positive when the median voter is a skilled individual (i.e., when $e_M < e^*$), and zero when the median voter is an unskilled individual (i.e., when $e_M > e^*$). Hence, a decline in e_M decreases (or leaves intact) the social security tax $\tau_0(e_M, \alpha)$ and the associated benefit b.

The rationale for this result is straightforward. All unskilled people have the same lifetime income, regardless of their cost-of-education parameter, e. Therefore, the attitude toward the (τ, b) – pair is the same for all of them. Hence, the change in the median voter has no consequence on the outcome of the majority voting when this median voter is an unskilled individual. For skilled individuals, lifetime income increases when the education-cost parameter, e, declines. Because the social security system is progressive with respect to the cost-of-education parameter, the net benefit from it (i.e., the present value of the expected pension benefit minus the social security tax) declines, as lifetime income increases (i.e., as e falls). Therefore, a decline in the cost-of-education parameter of the median voter, e_M, lowers the political-economy equilibrium social security tax and pension benefit.

Thus, making the fiscal constraints of the sorts imposed by the Stability and Growth Pact in the European Union more flexible may facilitate the political-economy transition from a national PAYG, old-age social security system to a fully funded private pension system. Such a transition improves the viability of the national system but at a cost of a lesser degree of redistribution (which is an inherent feature of a national system).[7]

10.4 Conclusion

The idea of the Stability and Growth Pact is to prevent governments from running loose fiscal policies at the expense of other euro-area countries. This spillover effect could happen through higher interest rates if the ECB offset the fiscal laxity with tight monetary policy or through higher risk premium on euro-area government bonds. But, the Pact, as it is rigidly constructed, neglects long-term fiscal considerations and creates political-economy impediments to social security reforms that, if implemented, can improve the fiscal balance in the future.

We emphasize in this paper that the aging population shakes the public finances of PAYG, old-age social security systems. We demonstrate how in a political-economy framework these deteriorated balances lead to the downsizing of the social system, and the emergence of supplemental individual retirement accounts. Indeed, in Razin, Sadka, and Swagel (2002), we demonstrate the existence of a negative correlation between the dependency ratio (which increases with the aging of the population) and labor tax rates, in a 1970s–1990s sample that includes 12 Western European countries and the United States. Similarly, a negative correlation is found between the dependency ratio and per-capita social transfers (of which old-age social security captures the lion's share). These findings are consistent with the hypothesis of this paper that aging puts political-economic pressure so as to downsize PAYG, old-age national systems.

---

[7] There is a majority of the voters who may benefit from the budget deficit cum social security reform. The majority consists of the entire group of the old and those skilled working young who contribute to the PAYG social security system more than the benefit (in present value) they expect to get when they retire. The minority of the votes are those who are less skilled and thereby contribute to the PAYG social-security system less than the benefit they expect to get upon retirement. Thus, we may envisage a two-stage voting process. In the first stage, the vote is cast on whether to allow budget deficit so as to be able to implement the social security reform. The majority will vote yes. In the second stage, the vote is on the tax-benefit rates of the post-reform PAYG social security system. The transition from the existing large PAYG social security system to the individual retirement accounts becomes smoother in this two-stage political economy process.

REFERENCES

Cooley, Thomas, and Jorge Soares. 1999. "A Positive Theory of Social Security Based on Reputation." *Journal of Political Economy* 107: 135–60.

Galasso, Vincenzo. 2000. "The U.S. Social Security: A Financial Appraisal for the Median Voter." CEPR Discussion Paper No. 2456.

Krugman, Paul. 2002. "Notes on Social Security." www.wws.princeton.edu/~pkrugman/.

Lassen, David D., and Peter Birch Sorensen. 2002. "Financing the Nordic Welfare States: The Challenge of Globalization to Taxation in Nordic Countries." A report prepared for the Nordic Council of Ministers, June.

Razin, Assaf, Efraim Sadka, and Philip Swagel. 2002. "The Aging Population and the Size of the Welfare State." *Journal of Political Economy* 110 (4): 900–18.

Rodrik, Dani. 1998. "Why Do More Open Economies Have Bigger Governments?" *Journal of Political Economy* 106 (5): 997–1032.

Sinn, Hans-Werner. 1990. "Tax Harmonization and Tax Competition in Europe." *European Economic Review* 34: 489–504.

Tabellini, Guido. 2003. "Principles of Policy Making in the European Union: An Economic Perspective." *CESifo Economic Studies*, 49(1).

Wilson, John D., and David Wildasin (forthcoming). "Capital Tax Competition: Bane or Boon?" *Journal of Public Economics*.

11 How Would You Like to Reform Your Pension System? The Opinions of German and Italian Citizens

Most economists would subscribe to the view that the public pay-as-you-go (PAYG) pension systems in many European countries are unsustainable and in need of reform. Yet, such reforms are politically very difficult. A recent line of research has tried to understand the nature of these difficulties by analyzing the citizens' opinions on different aspects of the welfare state and its redistributive programs (Boeri and Tabellini 1999; Bowman 1999; Devroye 2001; Boeri, Börsch-Supan, and Tabellini 2001). Alesina, Glaeser, and Sacerdote (2001) touch on related issues in their comparison of European and U.S. welfare states. In this paper, we focus specifically on the German and Italian public pension systems and report the results of a survey conducted in these countries in the spring of 2000 and the fall of 2001.

Germany and Italy are particularly interesting countries in this respect because their PAYG pension systems are very generous, but also they are very expensive and, therefore, especially threatened by population aging and in need of reform. In addition, Germany carried out a pension reform in 2001, in between two waves of our survey. Thus, we also have a "natural experiment" to draw on, and we can combine cross-national differences with changes between the two waves.

In both countries, the public pension system is the single largest item in the social budget. In 2000, public pension expenditures amounted to 14.2 percent of GDP in Italy and 11.8 percent of GDP in Germany. These are the two largest pension budgets in the OECD, much larger than U.S. Social Security (4.4 percent of GDP) or Japan (7.9 percent of GDP).[1] The main reasons for these large budgets are an early average retirement age, which is 60.3 years in Germany and even earlier in Italy with 58.8 years, and a high effective replacement rate, which is 66.8 percent in Germany and 86.3 percent in Italy.[2] About 85 percent of the

[1] OECD (2001).
[2] OECD (2001). Tables 5.1 and 2.1, respectively.

average retiree's income is provided through the public pension systems, with only 15 percent from other sources such as occupational pensions or private savings.

Although the generosity of the German and the Italian public pension systems is considered a great social achievement, which provides not only income security for the elderly but also societal stability, population aging is threatening the very core of these pension systems. All industrialized countries are aging, but Germany and Italy, together with Japan, will experience a particular dramatic change in the age structure of the population. The severity of the demographic transition in these two countries has two causes: a quicker increase in life expectancy as elsewhere, partly because of a relatively low level still in the 1970s, and a more incisive baby boom/baby bust transition (e.g., relative to the United States) to a very low fertility rate of between 1.2 and 1.3 children per women. Consequently, the ratio of elderly to working-age persons – the old-age dependency ratio – will increase steeply. According to the latest OECD projections, the share of elderly (aged 65 and above) will exceed a quarter of the population in 2030, and the old-age dependency ratio will almost double from 24.0 percent in 2000 to 43.3 percent in 2030 in Germany, and from 26.9 to 49.1 percent in Italy.[3]

The increase in the dependency ratio has immediate consequences for a PAYG social insurance system because fewer workers have to finance the benefits of more recipients. The threat of insolvency led to several pension reforms. In Germany in 1992, the indexation of pensions to gross income was abolished and substituted by indexation to net wages. Moreover, early retirement was discouraged by introducing a 3.6 percent penalty for each year of retirement entry before age 65. In 2001, Germany bade farewell to the pure PAYG system and introduced a multipillar pension system with a small and voluntary – but, in the eyes of many Germans, revolutionary funded – pillar.[4] In Italy in 1992, the indexation of pensions to real wages was abolished by indexing benefits to prices, and the reference period for calculating pensionable earning was lengthened. In 1995, a reform changed altogether benefit formulae and eligibility conditions for workers with fewer than 18 years of contributions, by introducing a "virtually" funded pension regime under which pensions are still financed under a PAYG scheme, but each worker holds a claim based on his or her accrued contributions to the system. Finally, in 1997, asymmetries in the treatment of civil servants versus private employees were significantly reduced.[5]

Although all these reforms did indeed improve the solvency of the still largely PAYG public pension systems in Germany and Italy, projections of the unfunded pension liability in 2030 and later still look threatening.[6]

---

[3] OECD (2001). The OECD dependency ratio relates persons age 65 and older to persons between ages 15 and 64.

[4] See Börsch-Supan and Schnabel (2002) for a survey of the German pension system and recent reforms.

[5] See Brugiavini and Fornero (2000) for a survey of the Italian pension system and recent reforms.

[6] OECD (2000).

Why are pension reforms so politically difficult despite the almost palatable threats? Despite the rapid proliferation of a recent literature on political economics, the answer to this question is still largely unknown. There is now a solid and detailed understanding that politics can affect policy decisions in a variety of ways, leading to inefficient outcomes and a bias toward the status quo – Persson and Tabellini (2000), Drazen (2000), and Roland (2000) survey this recent literature. But, most existing contributions are theoretical and, hence, there is not always a good sense of which of the many theoretical models and insights best applies to the current European situation. Moreover, this existing literature is fairly abstract and thus devoid of detailed institutional content and of sharp implications for politically viable but concrete reforms. As a result, the more applied policy debate on these controversial issues is often grounded on a detailed knowledge of the economic pros and cons of alternative reforms, but it is not guided by a sophisticated analysis of the political constraints and of the political incentives of the key decision makers. Policy advice is still often offered as if governments were benevolent social planners who only need to know what is in the best interest of society.

To make progress in answering these questions, we directly investigate the opinions of European citizens on the welfare state. We drafted our own questionnaire because we could not rely on publicly available opinion polls. The first wave took place in the spring of 2000 and drew a representative sample of the entire population in the four biggest countries of Continental Europe: France, Germany, Italy, and Spain. The results are described in Boeri, Börsch-Supan, and Tabellini (2001). We repeated the exercise in Germany and Italy in the fall of 2001. Our questionnaire was designed to shed light on the following issues: Are citizens aware of the unsustainability of the pension system and informed of its costs? Are reforms opposed by a majority or by a powerful minority? Which reform options seem politically more feasible and why? Which groups of citizens are more likely to favor reforms? Do citizens' opinions reflect their economic self-interest, as presumed by the literature on political economics?

Our main results can be summarized as follows: citizens are aware of unsustainability but lack information about the cost of the PAYG system. The status quo is a majoritarian outcome along many dimensions: most reform proposals lack a majority and reformers rarely support more than one reform option. Later retirement is the easier reform in Italy (where effective retirement age is lower), whereas lower pensions are more popular in Germany where the effective replacement rate is higher. Preferences over policy options seem to reflect both economic self-interest and one's normative view about the role of the state. Opposition to any reform is high even among those aware of unsustainability. This could be procrastination or selfishness (shifting the burden onto future generations); some answers suggest that the latter could play an important role.

The paper is structured as follows. Section 11.1 introduces our survey. Section 11.2 describes how informed the citizens in Germany and Italy are. Section 11.3 presents the opinions of these citizens on various reform options.

Section 11.4 analyzes the opposition to reform. Section 11.5 adds a case study of the German pension reform in 2001. Section 11.6 concludes.

11.1 The Survey

We designed identical questionnaires for all countries, both in Wave 1, which we conducted in France, Germany, Italy, and Spain in February/March 2000, and in Wave 2, which we conducted in Germany and Italy in September/October 2001. In this paper, we focus on Wave 2 and the differences between the two waves. In addition to the standard set of socioeconomic background variables such as age, education, and income, the questionnaire included questions that elicited the information and the preferences about the current pension systems and potential reform options.

We are not the first in gathering public sentiments toward the welfare state in Europe and in the United States.[7] There were several reasons to conduct an own survey rather than to rely on existing surveys. First, compared to existing surveys, we do not ask open questions ("Do you want more benefits?"), but we posed specific tradeoffs among specific policy options ("Are you willing to pay x percent higher contributions in order to obtain y percent higher benefits?"). These types of questions are in the tradition of "contingent valuation," and we use the "stated preference" questionnaire techniques described in Louviere, Hensher, and Swait (2000). We combine this technique with a focus on two specific aspects of the welfare state: namely, unemployment protection and pensions. Second, we seek to relate these rather specific answers to general attitudes toward the welfare state. Third, we tried to design survey instruments as similar as possible for the countries involved in order to exploit the cross-national institutional and historical differences that we have highlighted in the previous section and to identify how and why answers to our questions diverge across countries. Finally, we want to relate policy preferences to individual characteristics of the respondents, and this is generally not possible with other publicly available surveys.

The questionnaire is divided into four parts. Part One collects information on the individual respondent, such as age, family situation, employment status, sector of occupation, and so on. These questions were part of an omnibus survey. We augmented this general background information by information on general political opinions and whether the workers are affiliated with a trade union. These latter and more sensitive questions were asked at the end of the interview.

In Part Two, we assess how informed the respondents are about the costs and sustainability of the public pension system, and whether they would like to opt out of it (eventually at some cost). The questions are designed to obtain information about the respondents' preferences on these programs: we try to elicit their

---

[7] A survey of existing studies can be found in Boeri, Börsch-Supan, and Tabellini (2001).

personal demand for public and private old-age provision. In Part Three, we solicited the respondents' opinions on possible directions of pension reforms. Finally, in Part Four, we tried to assess the respondents' political opinion on the desirability of reforms in general, not just for their own personal situations.

The interviews were carried out by the means of Computer Assisted Telephone Interviews (CATI). Coordination among the agencies carrying out the survey (Demoskopea in Italy and Infas in Germany) was provided by the Fondazione Rodolfo Debenedetti. The survey universe is the population aged 16 to 80 living in households with telephone connections. In each country, we sampled 2,500 households. In Germany, 1,500 households lived in the West and 1,000 households in the East. We applied a random-sample design and took great care to minimize nonresponse.

Economists are used to revealed preference data and many mistrust data based on stated preferences. We think that this mistrust is unfounded, for several reasons. First, our results largely confirm similar findings of earlier surveys, at least in those questions where there is overlap (see, in particular the Eurobarometer,[8] the International Social Survey Programme [ISSP] Project,[9] and Boeri and Tabellini [1999]. Second, we checked the answers for internal consistency – for example, by ascertaining that a respondent did not say "no" to an offer if he had already accepted a less generous version of it, and the results were very satisfactory. Third, we regressed stated choices on socioeconomic characteristics, looking for the correlation patterns that we expected from theoretical priors or from revealed preference data. Inconsistencies were rare and the agreement with the expected correlation patterns was strong.

A common difficulty faced when asking about opinions is that answers to such questions are particularly prone to framing biases. For this reason, we tried to avoid suggestive formulations. Where we wanted to ascertain the individual's answer on what is good for her or him, not some answer on what she or he thinks is good for society at large, we took great care in describing the applicable situation for the respondent and the corresponding offers in detail. Finally, we tried to avoid hypothetical-situation bias by anchoring the answers around realistic country-specific numbers – for example, pension benefit levels – and by varying potential answers by socioeconomic situation – for example, between employed and unemployed.

11.2 Are Citizens Informed?

The first thing we wanted to find out is how informed individuals are about the cost of public pensions, about their sustainability, and the likelihood of future

[8] See Ferrara (1993).
[9] See Toš, Mohler, and Malnar (2000) for a selection of studies based on the ISSP, together with a set of methodological papers. Closely related papers based on the ISSP include Edlund (2000), Corneo and Grüner (2000), and Alesina and La Ferrara (2000).

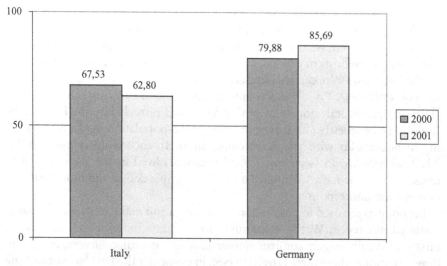

Figure 11.1. Awareness of a Pension Crisis
Note: Percentage answering yes to the question: "Do you agree with the statement that there will be a pension crisis within the next 10–15 years?"

reforms. As discussed in the introduction to this paper, the costs of public pensions in Germany and Italy have become extremely high and, at current legislation, are projected to rise even further. How aware are individuals of these costs and future trends?

Figure 11.1 shows that there is widespread awareness of the unsustainability of the pension system. A large fraction of the two populations (85 percent in Germany and 63 percent in Italy) agree with the statement that "the pension system will face a crisis in the next 10–15 years." This crisis perception is strong despite the many pension reforms that have taken place in recent years. Italy has experienced three reforms in the last decade (the so-called Dini, Amato, and Prodi reforms) and the German parliament has just approved a transition to a multipillar pension system (the so-called Riester reform). In fact, only a very small fraction of the citizens agree with the statement that "the recent reforms have stabilized the pension system," whereas 43 percent of the respondents think that the reforms were ineffective; see Figure 11.2. Unsurprisingly, a majority of citizens in both Germany (81 percent) and Italy (58 percent) believe that "in the course of the next ten years there will be another pension reform soon which reduces significantly the benefits of public pensions"; see Figure 11.3. Although these results show quite clearly that the respondents are aware of the crisis of their pension systems and of the need to reform them, respondents seem to ignore or underestimate the cost of the public pension system. Only a minority understands how a PAYG system operates: 40.5 percent of the citizens know that their contributions are used "to pay the pensions of

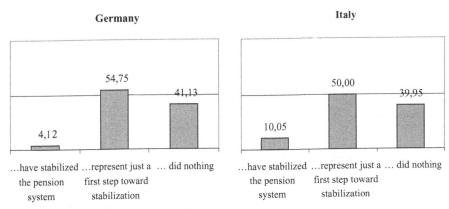

Figure 11.2. Effectiveness of recent reforms
Note: Percentage agreeing with the above statements.

current pensioners only," and the other 59.5 percent think that at least some of their contributions go into a fund; see the upper left corner of Table 11.1.

Even worse is the knowledge about the actual costs of the system. We asked two questions, to employees only, in all four countries: one on the contribution rate and another on the balance of the PAYG system. We first asked whether respondents know how much employers' and employees' contribute into the public pension system. We listed several brackets of possible answers, which were completely read to the respondents before they made their choice, and we specifically stressed both

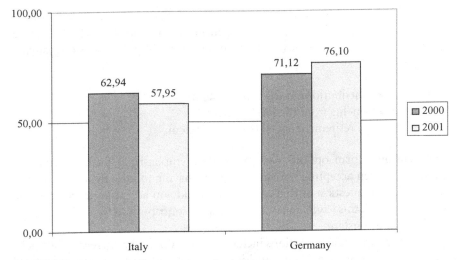

Figure 11.3. Expectation of a renewed pension reform
Note: Percentage answering yes to the question: "Do you agree with the statement that there will be another pension reform soon that reduces significantly the benefits of public pensions?"

Table 11.1. *Information and perception of pension crisis (percentages)*

	Understood PAYG system		Knew PAYG contribution rate	
	Yes	No	Yes	No
All respondents	40.5	59.5	18.3	81.7
Percent with perception of pension crisis	84.1	80.7	85.3	79.2

employer and employee contributions. The brackets were large and located to fit each country's correct value: 15–30 percent of gross earnings in Germany, and 25–40 percent in Italy. Nonetheless, less than 20 percent of employees who pay contributions know the overall contribution rate; see the upper right corner of Table 11.1. Almost all who did not know underestimated the contribution rate.

Information about the pension system and crisis awareness is correlated. As the lower row of Table 11.1 shows, the perception of a pension crisis is stronger among those who are informed about how the pension system works (84.1 and 85.3 percent have crisis perception) than those who are ill-informed (80.7 and 79.2 percent have crisis perception). Regression analysis shows that the more informed individuals are middle-aged, males, richer, and more educated. Workers with a permanent contract are more informed, union members less informed. Individuals to the right of the political spectrum answered more often incorrectly.

11.3 Which Reform Options Are More Popular?

The core of our survey concerned the popularity of pension reform. We confronted currently working individuals with six pension reform options. The first three reform options would change the main parameters of the public pension system – namely:

- increase contributions to the PAYG system
- decrease benefits from the PAYG system
- increase the retirement age of the PAYG system

The pension reform options were juxtaposed emphasizing the intertemporal tradeoff between accepting reform now versus having to raise the contributions later. A typical question of this type was, "Would you accept an increase in the retirement age if this would mean that the future contributions to public pensions could remain constant?"

The other three reform options included opting out of the current public pension system; hence, an explicit transition to a multipillar system. We formulated these options as to mean that they and their employer would only pay half the contributions in the future, but they also would receive only half of the pension

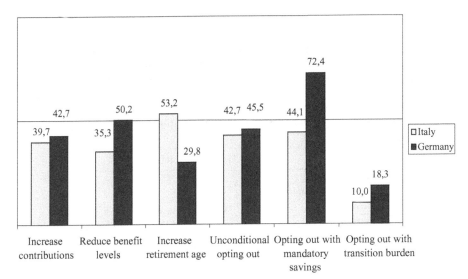

Figure 11.4. Popularity of six pension reform proposals
Note: Percentage agreeing with reform option.

rights once they opt out. Past contributions would be valued at their old benefit levels. We asked about three variants:

- an *unconditional opting-out* proposal, in which employees could choose to pay 50 percent less contributions in exchange for 50 percent less benefits in the future
- the same *opting-out* proposal *conditional* on putting the saved contributions in a retirement savings account
- an asymmetric *opting-out* proposal *with a transition burden*, in which employees would receive only 50 percent of benefits in the future, but have to pay 50 percent contributions plus a transition burden

Table 11.2 shows the exact formulation of these opting-out proposals and shows that item non-response is fairly low, indicating that most households understood the questions. Realistic pension reform is not a popular business. This is shown in Figure 11.4. Italians and Germans have rather different preferences over the parametric reform options. An increase in retirement age finds a majority in Italy, where the effective retirement age is lower, but it is the least attractive change for German workers. In turn, a reduction in the benefit level of the public pensions finds a slim majority in Germany, where the effective replacement level is higher, but it is the most disliked option among Italian workers. The differences between Germany and Italy are, therefore, in line with where a reform may hurt least. No opting-out variant finds a majority in Italy. Opting-out is very popular in Germany, but only if it requires mandatory savings and does not involve a transition burden. The finding that individuals are much more willing to opt out if

Table 11.2. *Opting out, unconditional and conditional proposals*

Unconditional opt-out question: *"Suppose that you were offered the following 'less contribution-less pension' deal. Namely, you were offered to reduce your contributions to <national public pension system> by one half (e.g., rather than paying 30 percent, you pay 15 percent <adjusted by country>), and receive this amount in your pay slip. When you retire, you will get a lower pension as if you had worked at 50 percent of your salary from tomorrow onwards. Would you accept such a deal?"*

	France	Germany	Italy	Spain
Don't know/no answer	6.5%	4.3%	6.6%	7.5%
% of those who answered:				
Yes (Spring 2000)	24.4%	47.2%	46.9%	18.9%
Yes (Fall 2001)		45.5%	42.7%	

Use of money question: *"What would you do with the money? (a) save all for old-age provision, (b) spend all, (c) spend the smaller part, save the larger part for old-age provision, (d) spend the larger part, save the smaller part for old-age provision"*

(Spring 2000)	France	Germany	Italy	Spain
Save all	64.3%	66.8%	64.9%	30.1%
Spend all	6.1%	1.4%	1.8%	18.6%
Save most	22.8%	28.0%	25.7%	30.7%
Spend most	6.9%	3.8%	7.5%	20.5%

Conditional opt-out question: *"Consider a slightly different proposal: The compulsory contributions rather than being put in your pay slip would be put in an investment fund of your choice. You would be free to cash in from that fund only upon retirement. Would you accept such a deal?"*

	France	Germany	Italy	Spain
Don't know/no answer	11.8%	4.3%	9.7%	13.2%
% of those who answered:				
Yes (Spring 2000)	49.7%	70.9%	67.0%	63.1%
Yes (Fall 2001)		72.4%	44.1%	

constrained to save the contributions rebated is surprising, in particular, because most Germans and Italians would anyway invest most of the rebated contributions into instruments for old-age provision (see Table 11.2). It could reflect time inconsistent (social or individual) preferences. We will come back to this issue in the following section.

Table 11.2 also shows that opting out did lose some of its popularity between the surveys in the spring of 2000 and the fall of 2001, possibly because of the poor performance of the stock market. The decrease, however, is rather small in the unconditional opting-out proposal, and the change is of opposite direction in the conditional variant.

Table 11.3. *Multiple reform options: Approval and opposition (percentages)*

Reforms that:	Increase sustainability[1]		Shrink size[2]	
Number of reform options:	Approved	Opposed	Approved	Opposed
0	23.7	2.4	37.1	5.1
1	36.8	15.5	41.8	26.6
2	27.6	30.6	18.7	38.8
3	11.0	32.3	2.5	29.7
4	1.0	19.2	–	–
Total	100	100	100	100

[1] Lower benefits, later retirement, opting out with transition burden.
[2] Lower benefits, later retirement, opting out with transition burden plus higher contributions.

11.4 The Structure of Opposition to Pension Reform

The mixed reaction to the various pension-reform proposals could reflect a general disagreement in the population of the most preferred option. We, therefore, analyzed how many reform options are approved or opposed by the same individual. Do the same individuals approve/oppose all reforms, or is there also disagreement over how to reform?

We considered four pension-reform options that realistically address the unsustainability of current pension policy:[10]

- opting out with transition burden
- higher retirement age
- lower benefit level
- higher contributions

and counted the number of approvals and disapprovals by each respondent. Results are depicted in the first two columns of Table 11.3. The responses are pooled over the two countries.[11] Many respondents approve few and oppose many reforms: 24 percent of the respondents do not approve any reforms at all, and more than 50 percent says no to three reforms or more. Only 12 percent agree to three or more of the four realistic options, and less than 18 percent oppose only one or no reform option. This makes it more difficult to reform: not only is there strong opposition on whether to reform but also a division among those in favor on how to reform.

[10] Among the opting-out proposals, only the one with transition burden really addresses the unsustainability of current policy.
[11] The pattern of how many (as opposed to which) reforms were approved or opposed is very similar in the two countries.

Table 11.4. *Transition to private old-age provision*

(i) Fairness of reform: "The recent pension reforms put more emphasis on own provision for retirement and less on the state. Do you think this is fair?"
(ii) Advantage of reform: "Do you think that private pension plans are giving a better deal than the public pension system; i.e., provide a higher pension benefit per Euro contribution paid?"

| | (i) More own provision fair | | (ii) Private pensions better deal | |
	Yes	No	Yes	No
Germany	35.9	64.1	69.5	30.5
Italy	44.9	55.1	55.4	44.6

Note: Percentages.

The four reform options have very different implications for the extent of inter-generational redistribution. But opposition to reform is even higher if we neglect the option of higher contributions, restricting attention to the three reforms that reduce the size of the PAYG system: lower benefits, later retirement, and opting out with transition burden. This is shown in the last two columns of Table 11.3. Less than one in five approve more than one reform option, and more than one in three approve none of them.

The evaluation of these reform options reflects one's opinion on the role of the state in caring for the elderly. We asked (i) whether it was fair to induce workers to put more emphasis on own provisions for retirement, and (ii) whether private pension systems were deemed as more advantageous than the PAYG system. Table 11.4 shows some that, on the one hand, the respondents did not think that shifting the burden of financing old age from the state to oneself is fair, more so in Germany than in Italy. On the other hand, the respondents in both countries thought that private provision for old age is a better deal than public pensions. This apparent discrepancy is not necessarily a kind of cognitive dissonance; it also may reflect awareness of the transition burden that is imposed when one generation has to invest for their own savings and at the same time maintain the PAYG transfers to the old.

Those who answered positively to the two questions in Table 11.4 also were much more likely to favor reforms shrinking the PAYG. For instance, 85 percent of those who approve more than one of the three reforms shrinking the size of the PAYG system also respond positively to either question (i) or (ii).

Individual features such as age, income, and education play an important role in shaping both the general views on the role of the state and the evaluation of these reform options. Table 11.5 reports the results of two regressions. The ordered probit regression on the left relates the number of reform options to which the respondent was opposed to a set of socioeconomic characteristics and the perception of crisis. The probit regression on the right of Table 11.5 relates an indicator variable on the same set of explanatory variables. This indicator

Table 11.5. *Opposition to reform and individual characteristics*

Variable	Ordered probit		Probit	
	Opposition to 1, 2, 3 Reforms		No shift responsibilities & no private more advantageous	
	Coeff.	St. Error	Coeff.	St. Error
Young	−0.14	0.07	−0.32	0.07
Old	**0.23**	0.10	**0.24**	0.06
Male	0.01	0.06	−0.24	0.05
Comp. Education	**0.17**	0.08	0.09	0.06
Univ. Degree	−0.16	0.08	−0.02	0.07
Union	−0.01	0.07	0.12	0.06
Left	0.007	0.08	**0.20**	0.07
Right	−0.21	0.11	0.03	0.09
Rich	−0.02	0.07	−0.18	0.07
Poor	0.04	0.09	**0.21**	0.06
Unskilled	**0.34**	0.12	0.11	0.08
Crisis	−0.08	0.09	−0.38	0.06
Private Ret.	−0.22	0.07		
Poor Region	**0.16**	0.07	**0.14**	0.05
Italy	−0.21	0.08	**0.14**	0.07
	N. obs.	1,275	N. obs.	3,049
	Pseudo R2	0.0213	Pseudo R2	0.0619

Note: The dependent variable of the ordered probit model is whether there is opposition to none, one, two, three, or all of the following reform proposals: (1) opting out with transition burden, (2) higher retirement age, (3) lower benefit level, and (4) higher contributions. The dependent variable of the binary probit model is whether respondents both declined to put more emphasis on own provision for retirement and thought that private pensions are less advantageous than public pensions.

The explanatory variables are dummy variables taking a value of 1 if the individual possesses that attribute, 0 otherwise. *"Young"* (*"old"*) means less than 35 (more than 54) years of age. *"Private Ret."* means that the individual believes that the private system is more advantageous than the PAYG system. *"Crisis"* means that the individual expects an imminent crisis in the PAYG system.

variable takes the value of one if the respondent chose "no" to both questions in Table 11.4. These are those respondents who thought that shifting the burden of financing old age from the state to oneself is unfair, and that private provision for old age is a worse deal than public pensions. Boldface fonts indicate significance at the 10 percent confidence level. The younger, more educated, richer males tend to say yes to either (i) or (ii) – Columns 3 and 4 in Table 11.5 – and to approve more reforms shrinking the size of PAYG – Columns 1 and 2 in Table 11.5. Union members, residents of poor regions (the Italian South and East Germany) and those with a left-wing ideology tend to say no to both (i) and (ii) and oppose more reforms.[5]

In a previous version (available upon request), we also estimated probit regressions of specific reform alternatives against the respondents' characteristics. Two sets of variables appear significant in most regressions: age and education (or skill level). Younger workers, and more educated or more skilled workers, are less likely to oppose any specific reform. Individual income seems to matter only in the choice of benefits versus retirement age, with richer individuals more willing to accept lower benefits. Having a left-wing ideology or being a member of a union only plays a limited role. Opting out is more popular among those, who think a crisis in the PAYG is imminent, who expect higher returns from private pensions, and who are under a defined-contribution system. Note that the new PAYG regime in Italy only applies to younger generations; older workers are still under a defined-benefit PAYG system.

Altogether, the regression results in Table 11.5 suggest that preferences reflect the economic interests of individuals, as presumed by the theoretical literature on political economics. There is also a subtle interaction between economic self-interest and one's general views of the role of the state. Economic self-interest is correlated with the view about what is right or wrong. Those who say that it is right for the state to take care of the elderly are also more likely to benefit from it (the older, the less educated, the poorer) and vice versa.

Aspects of these general views of the role of the state are captured in Table 11.6. Individuals were asked whether they wish further increases in the size of the welfare state – that is, an "increase of pensions and transfers to households" obtained by "raising taxes and compulsory contributions" – reduce or maintain the size of the welfare state. Only a minority of respondents wants to increase the welfare state. In Germany, the status quo is a majoritan outcome. Between 2000 and 2001, the German respondents shifted their views somewhat toward reducing the welfare state; in Italy, we observe the opposite tendency.

We continued to ask the respondents about an intergenerational reallocation of transfers – that is, "Should the state allocate less/equal/more resources to pensions and more/equal/less to unemployed or young job seekers?" Again, the Germans like their status quo, while the Italians rather reallocate transfers to the younger generation. The answers to this question are not strictly comparable across waves because in the first wave, we asked this question only to those respondents who wanted to maintain the size of the welfare state, whereas we asked the reallocation question to all respondents in the second wave. As we have seen in Figures 11.1 through 11.3, the respondents are aware of the unsustainability of the public pension systems in Germany and Italy. Why don't they want to do something about it? The questions in Table 11.6 can shed additional light on this issue. Table 11.7 conditions the answers to these questions on being employed and having a perception of crisis, and pools the answers over the two countries. Among those workers who also expect an imminent crisis of the PAYG, there is overwhelming opposition to further increases in the welfare state (80 percent oppose further increases) – see the first row of the left side of Table 11.7. Given that these same individuals believe that

Table 11.6. *Views on the welfare state*

(i) Size of welfare state: "Should the state (+) increase taxes and compulsory contributions, cutting pensions and/or transfers to households, (0) maintain taxes and compulsory contributions at current levels, or (−) reduce pensions and/or transfers to households, by raising taxes and/or compulsory contributions?"
(ii) Intergenerational redistribution: "Should the state (+) allocate more resources to pensions and less to unemployed or young jobseekers, (0) keep the current situation (−), or allocate less resources to pensions and more to unemployed and young jobseekers?"

| | (i) Increase size of welfare state | | | (ii) Redistribute to pensioners | | |
	(+)	(0)	(−)	(+)	(0)	(−)
Germany (Spring 2000)	14.0	59.1	26.9	16.6	61.8	21.6
Italy (Spring 2000)	17.4	39.7	42.8	18.5	35.2	46.2
Germany (Fall 2001)	12.8	51.3	35.9	26.5	50.7	23.4
Italy (Fall 2001)	23.4	46.9	29.7	33.5	28.3	38.3

Note: Percentages. Answers to (ii) are not strictly comparable across waves; see text.

pension promises cannot be met without increasing taxes and contributions, they should consistently support reforms reducing benefits, increasing retirement age, and partly privatizing social security. They do not, however. As shown in the last two columns of the left side of Table 11.7, the approval rate of these three reforms is the same irrespective of whether one opposes further expansions of the welfare state. There are two possible interpretations of this finding: Procrastination (time inconsistent preferences) or intergenerational selfishness (current workers really want to gain at the expenses of future generations). The question on the reallocation of transfers – see the right side of Table 11.7 – helps us to discriminate between these two potential explanations. The answers indicate that selfishness plays an important role. As shown in the upper right quarter of Table 11.7, only one out of five respondents who are aware of the crisis are also altruistic with respect to intergenerational redistribution. And, indeed, there are more reformers among

Table 11.7. *Procrastination or intergenerational selfishness?*

| | Employees aware of crisis and wishing to ... | | | |
| | ... increase the welfare state | | ... redistribute to young | |
	Yes	No	Yes	No
Percent of respondents	20.3	79.7	20.2	79.8
Yes to no reform*	38.0	37.1	17.8	23.2
Yes to all 3 reforms*	3.0	2.8	2.5	0.8

* Reform options include: opting out with transition burden, less pension, increase in retirement age.

those who are aware of the crisis and care about young generations (Columns 3 and 4 of the right side of Table 11.7). Although we cannot rule out that procrastination is also present to some extent, intergenerational selfishness certainly plays a major role in the opposition against pension reform.

11.5 A Case Study of the German Pension Reform in 2001

The recent pension reform in Germany sheds more light on the nature of the opposition described herein. To appreciate the nature of this reform, which is called "Riester reform" and was approved by parliament in January 2001, just in between the two waves of our survey, it is helpful to note that the last "major" pension reform in Germany was 12 years ago and was purely parametric. The main changes in the 1992 reform were to anchor benefits to net rather than to gross wages. This implicitly has reduced benefits because taxes and social security contributions have increased, reducing net relative to gross wages. Although this mechanism is quite helpful when population aging will speed up, other countries have shifted to inflation indexing in the meantime. The other important change in the 1992 reform was the introduction of adjustments to benefits in some (not all) cases of early retirement and a change in the "normal" retirement age for women. They will be fully effective in 2004 and will reduce the incentives to retire early; however, they are still not actuarially fair even at a zero discount rate.

The 2001 reform is intended to change the monolithic German system of old-age provision to a genuine multipillar system. Benefits will gradually be reduced by about 10 percent, lowering the replacement rate with respect to the average net earnings from 72 percent in 1997 to 64 percent in 2030. The effective benefit cuts are even larger because the credit of earnings points for education and training will be greatly restricted. By contrast, a redefinition of the "official" replacement rate minimizes the perception of these cuts because the so-defined new replacement rate will be 67 percent with respect to a smaller net-earnings base. The resulting "pension gap" of slightly less than 20 percent of the current retirement income is supposed to be filled with occupational and individual pensions. This new pillar is not mandatory, but the required private savings will be subsidized or tax privileged. The 2001 reform does not change the "normal" retirement age or the adjustments factors with respect to early retirement age that were established in 1992, and still provide large incentives to retire early.

Because no further reform took place in Italy during this time, our two surveys permit a "difference-in-difference" approach for the questions posed in this paper. Of course, other events took place in both countries, diluting the pure experimental character. Moreover, many of the impacts will be medium or even long term and are not visible in our data yet.

As we have seen in Figure 11.1, the Riester Reform obviously fostered the awareness that there will be a pension crisis in the near future. The percentage of German respondents answering yes to the question: "Do you agree with the statement that there will be a pension crisis within the next 10–15 years?" rose from 79.9 to 85.7 percent, whereas declined in Italy from 67.5 to 62.8 percent. Moreover, the Riester reform increased the awareness that dramatic benefit reductions could be unavoidable (from 71.1 to 76.1 percent), whereas in Italy this perception decreased from 62.9 to 58.0 percent; see Figure 11.3. This is an interesting result: The Riester reform obviously succeeded in conveying the message that there is an end to pension generosity.

The Riester reform did reduce the status quo bias. In Germany, only 51.3 percent rather than 59.1 percent before the reform want to leave taxes and benefits unchanged, whereas 35.9 percent rather than 26.9 percent want less taxes and less benefits; see Table 11.6. This did not happen in Italy – actually, the share of respondents favoring the status quo remained unchanged, while there are now more people in favor of a larger welfare state than last year. At the same time and unlike in Italy, 50.7 percent of German respondents (still a majority but less than the 61.8 percent in the spring of 2000) want the generational balance between pension recipients versus young and unemployed unchanged – but almost all of that change went into an increase in favor of pensions and against unemployment (up from 16.6 to 26.5 percent; see Table 11.6). In this sense, the Riester reform seems to have backfired.

Further contributing to this almost ironic situation are the findings of Figure 11.2. Although the Germans apparently want to increase pensions at the expense of the younger generation, they do not think that the Riester reform went far enough; 41.1 percent of the respondents think the reform did nothing at all, and 54.8 percent judge it as just a first step toward stabilization. One explanation is again selfishness. Although the respondents know that an incisive reform is necessary, they do not want to pay for it.

Indeed, the responses exhibit clearly logical and economic rationality. Table 11.8 correlates the "fairness" of the Riester reform with the general views on the welfare state. Those who want to increase the welfare state are particularly convinced about the unfairness of the Riester reform (72.9 percent), whereas among those who want to shrink the welfare state, almost 40 percent characterize the Riester reform as a fair deal. A similar pattern is visible with regard to intergenerational reallocation of transfers. Those who want to reallocate transfers to the young are more in favor of the Riester reform, whereas the respondents who want to strengthen transfers to the elderly find it unfair. In addition to the internal logic visible in Table 11.8, economic rationality of the responses is exhibited in Table 11.9. More of those respondents who think that private retirement accounts are a better deal than public pensions have opened new retirement savings accounts or increased the investment into existing accounts. All these results strengthen the impression that selfishness is an important explanation for the opposition to pension reform. Although these results may be depressing for those who think that pension reform is necessary to stabilize the PAYG systems and to maintain

Table 11.8. *Riester reform and views on the welfare state*

(i) Fairness of reform: *"The recent pension reforms put more emphasis on own provision for retirement, and less on the state. Do you think this is fair?"*	

(ii) Size of welfare state: *"Should the state (+) increase taxes and compulsory contributions, cutting pensions and/or transfers to households, (0) maintain taxes and compulsory contributions at current levels, or (−) reduce pensions and/or transfers to households, by raising taxes and/or compulsory contributions?"*

(iii) Intergenerational redistribution: *"Should the state (+) allocate more resources to pensions and less to unemployed or young jobseekers, (0) keep the current situation (−), or allocate less resources to pensions and more to unemployed and young jobseekers?"*

(i)	(ii) Increase size of welfare state			(iii) Redistribute to pensioners		
	(+)	(0)	(−)	(+)	(0)	(−)
Reform is fair	27.1	36.2	39.0	30.9	36.5	39.6
Reform is unfair	72.9	63.9	61.0	69.1	63.5	60.4

Note: Percentages.

economic growth, there is some hope for them. Table 11.10 shows that information about the pension systems' state help to foster a transition to more own provision for old age. Table 11.10 distinguishes the somewhat vague awareness of crisis from the more precise information about the systems' cost. Fewer of those who are informed do nothing, and in particular those respondents, who are well informed about the contribution rate, save more for their own old-age provision.

Table 11.9. *Reaction to reform*

(i) Reaction to reform: *"As a reaction to the pension reform, did you put money in a retirement account?"*

(ii) Advantage of reform: *"Do you think that private pension plans are giving a better deal than the public pension system, i.e., provide a higher pension benefit per Euro contribution paid?"*

(i)	(ii) Private pensions better deal		
	Yes	No	All
Started new retirement savings account now	9.8	6.4	9.1
Increased amount into existing retirement savings account	15.6	13.5	15.1
Unchanged amount into existing retirement savings account	47.4	31.8	43.9
Did nothing	27.2	48.3	32.0

Note: Percentages.

Table 11.10. *Information and reaction to reform*

(i) Reaction to reform: "As a reaction to the pension reform, did you put money in a retirement account?"
(ii) Awareness of crisis: "Do you think that there will be a pension crisis within the next 10–15 years?"
(iii) Informed about contribution rate: "Which percentage of your salary are you and your employer paying together into the public pension scheme?"

(i)	(ii) Aware of crisis		(iii) Informed about contributions	
	No	Yes	No	Yes
Started new account	3.3	9.6	7.9	12.2
Increased amount	27.0	13.6	13.7	19.7
Unchanged amount	27.9	45.6	44.4	40.8
Did nothing	41.6	31.3	34.0	27.4

Note: Percentages.

11.6 Conclusion

Governments wishing to carry out reforms will have to work hard to highlight the unfairness of the status quo for future generations and to explain the efficiency benefits of partial privatization of social security. The Riester reform seems rather unsuccessful on both accounts: it made people aware of what they might lose but not aware of the potential gains. As perceptions of what is right and wrong appear to be strongly correlated with self-interest, there can be synergies in highlighting individual advantages involved by various reform options and the redistributions they operate. Clearly, better information about and more transparency of our nations' pension systems is a precondition for successful pension reform.

REFERENCES

Alesina, A., E. Glaeser, and B. Sacerdote. 2001. "Why Doesn't the U.S. Have a European Style Welfare State?" Mimeo, Harvard University.
Alesina, A., and M. Ferrara. 2000. "Participation in Heterogeneous Communities." *The Quarterly Journal of Economics*:847–904.
Boeri, T., and G. Tabellini. 1999. "Un Problema di rappresentanze più che di maggioranze," in Boeri, T., and Brugiavini, A. (a cura di) *Il muro delle pensioni*, Il Sole 24Ore, Milano.
Boeri, T., A. Börsch-Supan, and G. Tabellini. 2001. "Would You Like to Shrink the Welfare State? The Opinions of European Citizens." *Economic Policy*, Spring 2001.
Boeri, T., A. Börsch-Supan, and G. Tabellini. 2001. "Would You Like to Reform Your Pension System? The Opinions of European Citizens." *American Economic Review*, May.
Börsch-Supan, A., and R. Schnabel. 1999. "Social Security and Declining Labor Force Participation in Germany." *American Economic Review* 88(2):173–8.
Börsch-Supan, A., and R. Schnabel. 2002. "Incentive Effects of Social Security in Germany," in J. Gruber and D. A. Wise (eds.), *International Social Security Comparisons*. Chicago: University of Chicago Press.

Bowman, K. 1999. "Social Security: A Report on Current Polls." American Enterprise Institute Occasional Papers.

Brugiavini, A., and E. Fornero. 2000. "Pension Provision in Italy," in R. Disney and P. Johnson (eds.), *Pension Systems and Retirement Incomes across OECD Countries*, forthcoming from Edward Elgar Press.

Conesa, J. C., and D. Krueger. 1999. "Social Security Reform with Heterogeneous Agents." *Economic Dynamics*, 2 (Nr. 4).

Corneo, G., and H. P. Grüner. 2000. "Social Limit to Redistribution." Forthcoming from *American Economic Review*.

Devroye, D. 2001. "Who Wants to Privatize Social Security? Understanding the Income Gap in Public Opinion." Mimeo, Harvard University.

Drazen, A. 2000. *Political Economy in Macroeconomics*. Princeton University Press.

Edlund, J. 2000. "Attitudes to Income Redistribution and Taxation in Social Democratic and Liberal Welfare States: A Comparison Between Sweden, Great Britain, and the United States," in N. Toš, P. Ph. Mohler, and B. Malnar (eds.). *Modern Society and Values*. Ljubljana, Mannheim: FSS University of Ljubljana and ZUMA.

Ferrera, M. 1993. *EC Citizens and Social Protection: Main Results from a Eurobarometer Survey*. European Commission.

Heijden, E. van der. 1996. *Altruism, Fairness and Public Pensions: An Investigation of Survey and Experimental Data*. Tilburg University: CentER Dissertation 15.

Louviere, J., D. Hensher, and J. Swait. 2000. *Stated Choice Methods: Analysis and Application*. Cambridge: Cambridge University Press.

OECD. 2000. *Reforms for an Aging Society*. Paris: OECD.

OECD. 2001. *Aging and Income: Financial Resources and Retirement in nine OECD Countries*. Paris: OECD.

Persson, T., and G. Tabellini. 2000. *Political Economics – Explaining Economic Policy*. Cambridge, MA: MIT Press.

Roland, G. 2000. *Transition and Economics: Politics, Markets, and Firms*. Cambridge, MA: MIT Press.

Toš, N., P. Ph. Mohler, and B. Malnar, eds. 2000. *Modern Society and Values*. FSS University of Ljubljana and ZUMA: Ljubljana, Slovenia; Mannheim, Germany.

Index